VIOLET

*The Story of the Irrepressible Violet Hunt
and Her Circle of Lovers and Friends—
Ford Madox Ford, H. G. Wells,
Somerset Maugham, and Henry James*

BARBARA BELFORD

SIMON AND SCHUSTER

New York • London • Toronto • Sydney • Tokyo • Singapore

SIMON AND SCHUSTER
Simon & Schuster Building
Rockefeller Center
1230 Avenue of the Americas
New York, New York 10020

Designed by Edith Fowler
Manufactured in the United States of America

10   9   8   7   6   5   4   3   2   1

Library of Congress Cataloging in Publication Data

Belford, Barbara.
    Violet : the story of the irrepressible Violet Hunt
and her circle of lovers and friends—Ford Madox Ford,
H. G. Wells, Somerset Maugham, and Henry James
/ Barbara Belford.
       p.   cm.
    Includes bibliographical references and index.
    1. Hunt, Violet, 1866–1942—Biography.   2.
Hunt, Violet, 1866–1942—Relations with men.   3.
Hunt, Violet, 1866–1942—Friends and associ-
ates.   4. Novelists, English—20th century—Biog-
raphy.   5. London (England)—Intellectual life—
20th century.   I. Title.
PR6015.U55Z59   1990
823'.912—dc20
[B]   90-37818
                                                       CIP

ISBN 0-671-64351-7

Contents

To Alf and Berthe Wallis

Preface

This is the story of a woman who wanted to be remembered, who wanted to be written about, a woman who refused to obscure the unflattering aspects of her life. Violet Hunt lived with the biographer in mind, typing her diaries from handwritten notebooks and typing much of her correspondence to and from literary figures. Situated at the intersection of two centuries and two moral worlds, half Victorian and half modern, her life stands out amid the monotony of a decorous age.

Quirky and complex, but always fascinating, Violet was a triumphant flirt: she could, as they said, open an oyster with a wink. Men remembered her sensual, petulant mouth, her burning brown eyes; most women recoiled from her sharp, viperish tongue, her willingness to sacrifice friendship for the sake of an epigram (though Rebecca West said Violet was only "like a bird chirping"). Long before the term "new woman" gained popularity in the late nineteenth century, Violet had sexually and professionally emancipated herself, pursuing pleasure relentlessly and recklessly.

A journalist, critic and novelist, she did some of her best writing in her diaries, where she loosened the ligaments, as Virginia Woolf described the process. Violet started keeping a record of her life when she was fourteen and never stopped until 1939, three years before her death at the age of seventy-nine. In a cramped, left-handed script, she wrote about her famous lovers—W. Somerset Maugham, H. G. Wells and (for a decade) Ford Madox Ford; and her famous friends—Oscar Wilde, Henry James, Joseph Conrad, D. H. Lawrence, Rebecca West, Radclyffe Hall, Ezra Pound.

Surrounding herself with the writers, dandies, eccentrics, prophets and impresarios of art who mattered, she provided an unvarnished view of what it was like to grow up in the Victorian middle class: to desire sexual freedom, but to need respectability; to yearn for the wayward journalistic world of Fleet Street, but to settle instead for turning passionate feelings into novels.

Violet used her diary as an apologia, a record of fact, a projection of fantasies, as a sounding board that vibrated with optimism or unhappiness, as a mirror in which she made strange faces when no one was looking. She recorded rainy days with all their luxuries and sunny days with all their liabilities, always reflecting on the sorrows of her life, but unlike most women diarists she never dreaded public disclosure of her intimate thoughts. While others secreted their intimate words, she typed them out, seeking publication and immortality. As Oscar Wilde once said of diaries: people like to read something sensational on the train.

Following Violet's death in 1942, her papers were buffeted by fate, some turning up at Cornell University in the mid-1960s to enrich *The Saddest Story,* Arthur Mizener's biography of Ford Madox Ford, some a few years later at Pennsylvania State University (in particular the 1917 diary). There existed early diaries or appointment books from 1882 through 1890 (excepting 1885–86). For the twentieth century, there were complete diaries for 1907 and 1917, but only sketchy entries for 1903–4 and 1908–9. All of these diaries were typed; the only original handwritten book was for 1917. Yet to be found were diaries for the crucial years with her lover Oswald Crawfurd (1891–1900) and the Ford years (1910–19), excluding 1917.

Still, sufficient material existed for authors to cast Violet as a minor but bewitching character in biographies of Wilde, Ford, Maugham, Wells, James, Pound and Lawrence. I first encountered Violet in Ted Morgan's biography of Somerset Maugham, where Morgan referred to her as "Violent Hunt," reprinting a typographical error from her obituary in *The Times* of London, which more than one writer has unfortunately taken verbatim.

At first it was difficult for me to view the whole woman, because an entire decade of her life beginning in 1891, when she was twenty-

nine, was vague and sketchily documented. There were letters but
no diaries from this period. No matter, I was committed to uncover
this unwritten life and finally spent five years living with Violet and
her capricious friends. Two years into the research, I was in London
and through a fortuitous set of circumstances found some of the
missing diaries, which had been gathering dust for twenty years in
an antiquarian bookseller's warehouse. With this discovery, I was
doubly blessed, for I met Alf and Berthe Wallis, who became indispensable mentors and guides through Violet's life and times.
They also told me the story of the Violet Hunt papers.

When Gerald Henderson, librarian of St. Paul's Cathedral and
Violet's literary executor, received her bequest, he virtually ignored
it. He never wrote her biography, he never catalogued her papers;
but he did willingly collect a few hundred pounds here and there
for permissions to reprint her copyrighted work. After his death in
1962, the bulk of this material was given to Newnham College at
Cambridge University, where it briefly resided before being purchased by Cornell University in 1966.

Because Henderson had no heir, his executors sold off his
possessions to a furniture dealer, who, on closer inspection of his
acquisition, found a cache of Pre-Raphaelite papers, including Violet's diaries and letters, and some papers of Ford Madox Ford.
These were sold to a book dealer, who asked the Wallises to store
them; following the dealer's death in 1972, the Wallises purchased
the papers but, busy with their own bookshop, did not catalogue
the material until 1986.

That fall and winter I sat in the Wallises' sun-filled study,
overlooking the garden of their Surrey home, and read in the diaries
of 1891 through 1900 the painful chronicle of Violet's affair with
the diplomat-publisher Oswald Crawfurd, a journey from trust
through betrayal and disillusionment. I soon began to understand
how Violet came to be a Victorian vixen and an Edwardian Egeria,
how the wellspring of her bitterness toward men grew and how
her torment of Ford inspired his best work and stimulated her
novels.

Never did I falter in my admiration for her resilience. To me,
she was the enviable strong-minded, emancipated woman, glam-
orous in her time and far ahead of it with her sexual risk-taking.
She was someone to whom I would have enjoyed telling my secrets,

knowing all too well I would hear my words repeated the following day by someone else.

Like most writers, Violet had her own version of the truth and, once formulated, whether in her diaries, her memoirs or her autobiographical novels, that version became the reality. During her tempestuous rows with Crawfurd, she recorded both sides of an argument. Are Crawfurd's words really his? Or her fantasies? She was given to hyperbole, but would she lie to her diary? I think not. Indeed, she never revised her account of events when she sat down years later to type out her life.

The Wallis collection contains handwritten diaries (except 1892) for 1890–1900, and 1935–39, and transcripts for 1890–93, and 1895. A line-by-line comparison shows that Violet did embellish some incidents (adding notes on people and clothes), and probably steeped some scenes in melodrama, but never did she alter the facts as first reported.

Why should Violet clean up her life? She was proud of what others called sins. When Marc-André Raffalovitch, a member of Oscar Wilde's circle, said her epitaph should read "A woman made for irregular situations," Violet eagerly embraced the mot as a tribute. That such situations did not bring her happiness she realized years later, noting that modern women were quite different from her own version of the new woman. "Does post-war woman realise the differentiation of the standard of manners that had obtained since 1918?" she asked. "In pre-war days Hamlet's brutal suggestion to the debutante Ophelia was perfectly practical politics—'Be thou chaste as ice and cold as snow, thou shalt not 'scape calumny,' or accept male escort in any circumstances whatever. One could not go out in the dark, one could not go out in the rain even, because one's dress was so long that it took any amount of holding up lest it got 'messed' about the hem. One had to take, in fact, all the care in the world to prevent one's flopping, feminine, vulnerable character from getting smirched or, at least, needing a new 'bind.' Marriage?"

This was Violet's way of saying that she was indeed an uncommon woman. Although Victorian women had affairs, they were usually married; Violet was not. Although women wrote short stories and novels, they usually did so to appear stylish; Violet did it for a living. Although some women casually boasted of being immortalized on canvas or in fiction, Violet outdistanced them, appearing in paintings by artists as diverse as Edward Coley Burne-Jones and Walter Sickert. Her personality and nasty wit informed many fictional women, but none so daunting as Ford Madox Ford's Sylvia Tietjens, whom Graham Greene called "the most possessed evil character in the modern novel." In playing muse to Ford, Violet succeeded in unlocking the emotions of this neurotic pseudo-gentleman; she taught him about malice and jealousy, and he translated her into the elegant witch-bitch of _Parade's End_.

But who _was_ Violet Hunt? This question was persistently asked of me through my years of research and writing. Seldom could I give a facile answer. I could not say that she was a preeminent Victorian writer who influenced the development of the modern novel. I could say, though, that she was an Edwardian literary figure who knew, or loved, everyone worth knowing in the arts. And always I said that she had an incandescent presence, wanting to be extravagant, wanting to shock the world, but needing love, needing to be recognized as someone of value.

Through her diaries she produced a clamor of voices that will now be heard. The most important is her own: the voice of the new woman who horrified the Mrs. Grundys; the voice of the self-indulgent and obsessive Yorkshire lass; the voice of a victim of Victorian morality. Violet could be vicious, and she could be soft as velvet. And she would be pleased, I am sure, to find her various voices fused and reborn in this biography.

PART ONE

1862-1889

I

Preachers and Painters

VIOLET HUNT was an odd mixture of ancestral voices: erudite clergymen and antiquarians from Durham and meticulous craftsmen and artists from Liverpool. But it was her maternal Northumberland roots that she cherished most: there the people were tough and resilient—tenacious like herself. To her, the North of England was a state of mind, and she never forgot it, frequently returning there in her novels. The nineteenth-century cities of commerce and manufacturing, of textiles and coal and iron, were bleak places covered with grime, but Durham, the city where Violet was born in 1862, was different from Liverpool, Sheffield, Bradford and Newcastle upon Tyne; it had an intellectual community—and a medieval cathedral.

The history of Durham began with Cuthbert, a saintly shepherd boy who became Bishop of Lindisfarne, died in 687, and eleven centuries later influenced the career of Violet's grandfather. According to legend, St. Cuthbert's body was perfectly preserved, and his coffin was carried by his followers when they fled south after two centuries to escape the Danish raids. Moving again a hundred years later in 995, they rested awhile in Dunholm, the "hill island," the ancient name for Durham. But when it was time to move on, the bearers could not lift the coffin, a sign that St. Cuthbert wanted to remain where he was.

In 1017 a stone cathedral was constructed to contain the shrine. Five years later the remains of the Venerable Bede were brought

17

there from the nearby monastery at Jarrow. In 1093 the Normans started the cathedral that still stands in Durham, with the last major addition, the 218-foot central tower, completed in the late fifteenth century. A castle and a Benedictine abbey were built adjacent to the cathedral, and Durham became the ecclesiastical and intellectual center of the North. Pilgrims flocked there until the Act of Supremacy, in 1536, when Henry VIII stripped the cathedral of its relics, which purportedly included a rib of the Virgin Mary and a piece of the Nativity manger.

Over the centuries, visitors compared Durham's fortresslike complex, crowning the rocky peninsula enclosed by the River Wear, to Edinburgh, Jerusalem, Avignon and Prague. "I have no more noble city in all my realm," said King Henry VI during a visit in 1448. John Ruskin called the view as seen from the passenger train one of the seven wonders of the world, and J. B. Priestley noted the "Macbeth-like look of the city." In 1798 Thomas Girtin painted the Norman cathedral bathed in a white light, piercing the clouds; in 1835 J. M. W. Turner wrapped the cathedral in yellow mist; and in the 1860s Alfred William Hunt, Violet's father, shrouded it in coal smoke.

By 1791, when Violet's maternal grandfather, James Raine, was born in Ovington, a small village not far from Durham, the city had acquired a patina of elegance with its Georgian buildings and extensive gardens. In the season, a resident might go to the horse races, attend the theater in Saddler Street and dance or play cards in the Assembly Rooms. James Raine's ancestors were farmers, property owners, wealthy merchants, mayors—in Raine's words, "persons of sound sense and integrity of which any pedigree might be proud."

The bright and precocious young Raine moved to Durham in 1812 at the age of twenty-one to be second master at Durham School, where he taught for fifteen years. During his tenure there he was ordained and in 1816 was appointed librarian to the dean and chapter, a church position that he held until his death. Early in his career he met the historian Robert Surtees, who became a mentor and close friend, encouraging Raine's antiquarian interests. Obsessive about historical detail, Surtees prowled the city to collect material for his four-volume *History of Durham*. His coachman once told Raine: "It was weary work; for master always stopped the gig; we never could get past an auld beelding."

Raine assisted Surtees and John Hodgson, an historian of Northumberland, in their research, and when Surtees died in 1834, Raine promoted the idea of founding the Surtees Society to publish manuscripts on the social and religious issues of northwest England. Raine edited seventeen of these volumes for the society, which became a prototype for future academic publishing groups.

In 1828, twelve years after he became librarian, Raine published his own first work. It followed his unsealing of St. Cuthbert's tomb in 1827 and his discovery of the decayed remains. The tomb had previously been opened in 698, 1022, 1104 and 1539, and each time churchmen confirmed that the saint's body had not deteriorated. This reputed miracle, Raine wrote, was "invented for interested purposes in a superstitious age," and kept alive for more than a thousand years by clerical conspiracies. The monograph established Raine's position as an antiquary, and he next wrote the first part of the _History of North Durham_, a companion piece to Robert Surtees' _History of Durham_.

Raine was, as his obituary in the _Durham County Advertiser_ noted, "no mere antiquarian. He could reason, and draw inferences and conclusions from the dusty record and the half-illegible roll or charter, and winnow out the precious grain from the useless chaff with the acumen and perspicacity of a scholar." There was a twinkle in Raine's eye and a stern set to his jaw, judging from one surviving portrait. A man of wit and humor, ready to offer a sharp "reproof to vulgar assumption, presumptuous ignorance, or irremediable conceit," he studied bees and native birds, and even by today's standards his writing is surprisingly lively.

By the time he was thirty-seven, Raine had settled into the intellectual life of Durham, and on January 28, 1828, he married Margaret Peacock, the oldest daughter of the Rev. Thomas Peacock, who was a curate and headmaster of a school in nearby Denton. Margaret Peacock's brother George, who would later figure in some of Violet Hunt's novels, was the youngest of five sons and a bit of a child prodigy. An inspired teacher and lecturer at Trinity College, Cambridge, he was particularly revered for his interest in students' personal problems, an attitude not yet cultivated at universities. He reformed and changed the focus of Cambridge mathematics to include more analytical studies, spearheaded the building of a new observatory and supported library expansion. When appointed Dean of Ely Cathedral, he restored the church, improved the city's drainage system and championed education for the poor.

Violet's mother, Margaret, was born on October 14, 1831, the second of three daughters of James Raine and Margaret Peacock. (The oldest, Annie, would edit the writer Fanny Burney's diaries; James, the only son, would become rector of All Saints Pavement Church, York.) Three years after Margaret's birth the family moved into Crook Hall, a medieval manor dating from the thirteenth century; the house had (and still has) a ghost, called the White Lady, who lived in the kitchen. The ghost was "a feature of our childhood," Violet said, proudly adding, "It is not everybody who has lived in a house of Edward the Second's time." From Crook Hall there is a fine view downriver, perfect for watching the Durham regatta, the oldest in England. The ever considerate James Raine hung a flag out the window when he was absent so that friends would not make unnecessary trips upriver.

John Ruskin, Sir Walter Scott, William Wordsworth and his sister Dorothy were among the notables who visited Crook Hall. Margaret Raine later recorded a charming anecdote about a walk Wordsworth took with her father and sister. "They talked about Milton's poems, especially 'Lycidas,' and Wordsworth quoted the line, 'We drove afield and both together heard, what time the gadfly winds its evening home. Together both, ere the high lawns appeared under the opening eyelids of the dawn,' as one which he very admired. Seeing my sister listening with great attention, he said, 'Now little girl, can you tell me the next line,' which she at once did. He was so surprised and pleased that he stooped down and kissed her, and then said, 'When you grow up always remember that an old poet kissed you for knowing that line.'"

Margaret Raine was tutored at home, read widely in her father's library and studied art with William Bell Scott, master of the Government School of Design in Newcastle. Her family expected her to wed Canon William Greenwell, member of an old Durham family, and eleven years her senior. Among Greenwell's passions were archaeology (his collection of prehistoric bronze implements is in the British Museum) and fishing (his name was given to salmon and trout flies).

Violet's diaries confirm that Greenwell was an important romantic liaison and a pleasant memory for her mother: "I began . . . a charcoal head of Mamma—and got her to talk of her love affair with G.W.G. It gave her a sweet dreamy expression." But when Margaret turned twenty-five, she met Alfred Hunt and broke off her engagement. James Raine, not surprisingly, was unhappy with his daughter's affection for an academic yearning to be an artist, and he died before Margaret, as Violet later wrote, had "consummated the sacrifice of a clerical virgin to the monster of pre-Raphaelitism."

Margaret was twenty-seven when her father died at Crook Hall in 1858 at the age of sixty-seven. On the day of the funeral all the major shops closed, and their owners joined city, university and church dignitaries in the procession to the cathedral, where services were held. Shortly thereafter the family moved from Crook Hall to a narrow Georgian house at 29 Old Elvet, a wide, busy street where crowds gathered for the horse fair. From their drawing-room window the Raines had a view of the public hangings at the jail across the street.

Compared to the Raines and the Peacocks, Alfred Hunt's antecedents were ordinary, almost humble. The kindly, self-effacing thirty-one-year-old Oxford classics teacher who spirited Margaret away from the canons and deans and preachers of her Durham youth was born in Liverpool on November 15, 1830. He was the seventh child, and the only son to survive infancy, of the painter Andrew Hunt and Sarah Sanderson. Alfred's paternal grandfather had earned a living painting clock faces. A friend of the distinguished landscape artist David Cox, Andrew Hunt had learned to draw from the engraver Samuel Lines and eked out a living as a landscape painter, augmenting his fees by teaching art. His wife, who came from an old Scottish family, worked in a shop to supplement their meager income.

Alfred and his sister Maria, who herself became a well-known painter of fruit and flowers, often accompanied their father on sketching tours to Wales and Ireland. When he was eight, Alfred painted his first spun-sugar clouds in homage to Turner, an artist whose poetic subtleties his father had praised long before Ruskin became his champion. Although Alfred's artistic talents were encouraged, his parents wanted a more secure career for their only son, perhaps in the church. Always a delicate child, with sensitive, myopic eyes, he compiled a brilliant record at the Liverpool Collegiate School and won a coveted Oxford scholarship to Corpus Christi College in 1848.

Alfred enjoyed college but was anxious about his abilities. "Oxford is a splendid place for taking the conceit out of one," he wrote to Maria in 1850. Letters home, often illustrated with pen-and-ink drawings of the college, prepared his parents for the worst. During his second year he warned, "I hope Mama does not encourage any high anticipations about my turn out. A third class is as much as I hope for, and I do not think I shall descend to get the Newdigate." Despite such pessimism, he won this legendary competition for the best original poem on a classical subject, "Nineveh," the ancient Assyrian city.

Winning the Newdigate raised him "from obscurity to the highest honor," he wrote Maria, adding, "I would give anything to escape from the recitation. If I can get over the first four lines without fainting!!" Hunt was exaggerating his stage fright, for he had earned a reputation at Oxford as a public speaker with an interest in politics. On July 3, 1851, in accordance with tradition, Alfred Hunt walked in procession with the vice-chancellor, heads of colleges and other dignitaries to the Sheldonian Theatre, where he recited "Nineveh": "It is the hour, when thousand gorgeous hues / Rose-flushed and golden all the west suffuse; / It is the hour, when o'er the desert air / Peals the soft chant which calls to evening prayer . . ."

In 1852, when Hunt was graduated with a second in classics, his reputation as an artist was growing. Even before going up to Oxford, he had exhibited at the Old Water-Colour Society (now the Royal), the highest honor available for a watercolorist, and at the Liverpool Academy and the Portland Gallery. By the age of twenty, he was deft enough to join his father as a member of the Liverpool Academy. In 1854 his first oil, *Wastdale Head from Styhead Pass, Cumberland*, was hung at the Royal Academy; two years later *Stream from Llyn Idwal, Carnarvonshire* was hung there "on the line" (at eye level, a sign that the hanging committee approved) and praised by Ruskin. At Oxford, he was encouraged by James Wyatt, a prominent print-seller, who sold his landscapes (often for shillings rather than pounds) and gave him a commission to paint in Wales.

Another Oxford student, Edward Jones (who later changed his name to Burne-Jones), frequented Wyatt's shop, where he once saw Hunt. "It would have been too great an honour to speak to him," recalled Burne-Jones, a Pre-Raphaelite painter who would later become a friend of the Hunts. Like other accolades accorded Alfred Hunt, his university and artistic achievements surprised him, for he lacked the self-esteem and confidence that men of talent need to promote themselves and their ideas. He was moody and easily depressed. "The first moment of defeat is something which no one can imagine unless he has felt it," he wrote his father.

By 1856, when he met Margaret—perhaps through her art teacher, William Bell Scott—his reputation as a painter was solid, if not spectacular. Needing the time and money to further his reputation, he decided to remain a fellow of Corpus Christi for five more years. He managed to be excused from taking orders, a requirement for fellows, along with the vow of celibacy. The latter would have been difficult to maintain, for Hunt already had had at least two romances, first with a cousin and then with Edith Macdonald, youngest of the famous Macdonald sisters. (Alice and Louisa became the mothers of Rudyard Kipling and Prime Minister Stanley Baldwin, respectively; Georgiana married Burne-Jones; and Agnes wed another Pre-Raphaelite painter, Edward Poynter. Edith herself never married.)

Stately, with a tiny, corseted waist, Margaret looked like a stern Sunday school teacher, her brown hair pulled off her face, emphasizing the large Raine nose. Her patience and dignity masked a forceful personality; what she lacked in beauty she made up in verve, overcompensating with a wicked tongue, or, as Violet put it, when "one is born and made passionate and impulsive—there is an end of tact."

After living with her widowed mother for a year, Margaret wanted to marry, but Alfred with his "insane dread of poverty" was reluctant to set a date. Their courtship was largely by correspondence (she lovingly arranged the letters by date, with the first line written on the envelope). A year younger and only slightly taller than his wife-to-be, with dark brown hair, a beard and deepset melancholy eyes, Alfred looked more professorial than artistic. He had frequent mood swings, a black cloud usually following him around. "If I can ensure myself against grumbling & depression of spirit, I would get married almost directly," he wrote his fiancée in

1859. When Margaret pressed him to set a date, he hedged, "I won't get married in cold weather or rather I'll take the cold weather as the time for thinking about getting married—and I know which way I will incline—Poverty in summer seems comparatively endurable."

There were real financial pressures. Hunt had to sell enough pictures to pay for sketching trips to produce even more pictures to submit to the Royal Academy. Founded in 1768, the Academy did not simply mount exhibitions—it determined the art of Great Britain. At this time it was crammed into the eastern half of the building in Trafalgar Square that is now the National Gallery. There was always a shortage of wall space, especially during summer exhibitions. The proportion of rejections to acceptances made life precarious for artists, for it was at such exhibitions, and hardly anywhere else, that they could hope to sell their paintings or maybe obtain a commission.

The Royal Academy had great power, as Violet later noted: "To be an R.A. in those days was to have received a Royal Charter to the effect that one was *rangé*, settled, a householder, with papers, favourably known to the police—that sort of thing! And it was that sort of thing that appealed to my quiet, God fearing, non-notoriety seeking father—small blame to him. He did not wish to figure as an iconoclast, to be noted as one of the young generation that is always thundering at the doors. His ambition was to be able to paint on tranquilly, doing good work with some assurance of a regular livelihood. To this end the membership of the Academy would have very much conduced. It would have meant for him the yearly and inalienable right to exhibit so many pictures in a good place on the line . . ."

Thus far Alfred Hunt's work had been well received. In the Academy notes of 1856 Ruskin praised *Stream from Llyn Idwal*, calling it "the best landscape I have seen in the exhibition for many a day—uniting most subtle finish and watchfulness of nature with real and rare power of composition." Such lavish praise continued the following year on two more of Hunt's landscapes, which were exhibited prominently. Ruskin, however, objected to the fact that a third painting—to him the most important—was "hung out of sight."

Not surprisingly, members of the Royal Academy took the

best space for themselves, and Ruskin's blatant criticism of elite privilege was not well received. As the most powerful and original thinker of nineteenth-century Britain, Ruskin was teacher, reformer, author and critic. His career spanned the century and was inextricably entwined with the fortunes of the Pre-Raphaelites. Ruskin wanted to boost Hunt's career for he thought him the most promising landscape painter exhibiting. The two men had much in common. Both had doting mothers and had rejected the church in favor of art. Both were Newdigate winners (Ruskin had captured the poetry prize on his third attempt, in 1840, with an Indian subject, "Salsetta and Elephanta"), and both idolized Turner, believing landscape painting to be the superior genre. Ruskin's income, however, provided by his father's prosperous sherry-importing business, allowed him a life of intellectual leisure and travel that would be denied Hunt until later in life, and then made possible only through the generosity of patrons.

The fact that the great English landscape period had peaked— Bonington had died in 1828, Constable in 1837, Turner in 1851 and Cox in 1859—mattered little to Ruskin, who championed painters like Hunt and disparagingly called the work of contemporary artists "cattle pieces" or "fruit pieces." When Turner died, there were only three landscape painters in the Academy, and no more were elected until Vicat Cole in 1869, a situation that hindered acceptance for someone like Hunt, who did his best work in watercolor, not in oil, the Academy's preferred medium.

In times of disappointment, though, Ruskin was most supportive, commiserating with Hunt after one of his landscapes had been rejected by the Academy. Ruskin advised his friend to paint smaller pictures (they sold better) and to copy the master, Turner. Violet always maintained that Ruskin's challenge of 1857 on behalf of her father turned the members against him, but Hunt never accepted this as a primary reason for their refusal to put "R.A." after his name; to him, the Academy's continual rejection of his work indicated lack of talent, not an inability to play politics.

Realizing that membership in the Academy might take years, Alfred and Margaret decided not to wait to marry. By Alfred's calculations, they would require £500 annually to live in London, an amount that included servants. Margaret's inheritance provided only £300. Hunt worked so slowly that making money from art was difficult. By painting in the studio, he could have produced many more paintings, but he preferred, like his idol Turner, to work directly from nature. He had an obsessive, quasi-scientific interest in rocks, pebbles and lichenous stones, which he stippled into landscapes with meticulous detail. It was an exhausting effort, considering his weak eyes—and a time-consuming one.

By January 1861, however, he had lowered his financial expectations, convincing himself that by living in Durham they could manage on £90 a year, with £100 in reserve. Margaret responded sympathetically, "I am willing to marry you or to wait as long as you like but I prefer to have some idea which it is to be?" Eleven months later, on November 16, they wed in St. Oswald's Church, in the shadow of Durham Cathedral.

Margaret and Alfred were a good match. She wanted to expand her life beyond the limits of rectory and library. He wanted the solicitous care he had grown to expect from five sisters and a devoted mother, a strong woman to "hammer him into something better." She offered exactly what he needed: courage and devotion. Through thirty-five years of married life each fulfilled the other's expectations—he painting, and she writing and gathering the famous into her drawing room, and raising their three disparate daughters.

2

Pre-Raphaelite Childhood

Isabel Violet Hunt was born on September 28, 1862, at 29 Old Elvet in Durham. Her godfather was Canon William Greenwell, her mother's spurned suitor. It was a doubly odd choice because Greenwell had recently rejected Alfred Hunt's paintings, refusing to buy "the appreciation of an inferior mind." Greenwell had succeeded Violet's grandfather as librarian for the dean and chapter and manuscript editor for the Surtees Society, and was becoming a crotchety, moralistic bachelor.

The year of Violet's birth was one of unrest in Europe and America. The United States was in the midst of the Civil War (the Durham newspaper described Lincoln as "a very good story-teller, but a very bad statesman"); Italian patriot Giuseppe Garibaldi's attempts to take Rome were foiled; there was a revolution in Athens; the French annexed Indochina; and Otto von Bismarck became Premier of Prussia.

It was a year of stagnation in Britain. The war in the United States created a cotton shortage in the North of England, forcing textile factories to close. Unemployment and crop failures led to widespread hunger. Queen Victoria was a recluse following the death of her beloved Albert the previous December, when the country was plunged into a paroxysm of mourning never seen before or since; it would be five years before the Queen again interested herself in the leadership of the nation.

People were reading Victor Hugo's *Les Misérables* in English,

Thomas Carlyle's mammoth life of Frederick the Great and the novels of Wilkie Collins, George Eliot and Anthony Trollope. The xenophobic French announced that the Louvre would have a gallery devoted to English painting. A London exhibition of Japanese silks inspired new trends in fashion and design, and an eighteen-year-old clerk, Arthur Liberty, was selling Oriental fabrics on Regent Street; thirteen years later he would open Liberty's.

As a small child Violet was surrounded by her mother's relatives, living for a while at Elvet Hill, a rambling estate on the outskirts of Durham owned by Margaret's cousin Mary Peacock and her husband, John Fogg-Elliot. He was the local justice of the peace, and active in many civic organizations ranging from the local penitentiary to the mechanics' institute. Spacious and comfortable, Elvet Hill became a gathering place for Durham's intelligentsia, where historians and antiquarians conversed seriously on the past and wittily on the literary and political gossip of the moment.

Although Alfred Hunt longed to be at the center of things in London, he assiduously honed his artistic talents in Durham during his first five years of married life, painting views of the cathedral, sending paintings to the Academy and keeping up with the Pre-Raphaelite Brotherhood, some of whom disdained the Academy. The rebel Dante Gabriel Rossetti ignored it; if he were ever elected, he would put the matter in the hands of his solicitor, he said. Rossetti's brother, William, admired Hunt's watercolors and felt that Hunt's need for recognition was superfluous to his integrity as an artist, but Alfred's insecurity made him ever needful of the Academy's approval.

The Pre-Raphaelite Brotherhood, the most avant-garde artistic and literary group of its time, was founded in 1848 by seven painters, including Rossetti, John Everett Millais and William Holman Hunt (no relation to Alfred). The PRB, as they called themselves, never had a clear artistic purpose, although the name indicated a desire to recapture the spirit of the age preceding Raphael and his followers. Brash young men just entering their twenties, the Pre-Raphaelites rebelled against their academic training and what they regarded as the dreary genre pictures that had dominated art since Raphael.

Their philosophy, which evolved during long evenings of wine, food and debate, maintained that acceptable subjects for painting were myth, medieval fantasies, Christian legends and contemporary morality scenes. Holman Hunt's *The Awakening Conscience*, Mary Magdalene in modern dress, was a paradigm, but the artists interpreted these categories freely; they were thoroughly individual, and the work of one was never mistaken for that of another. Rossetti, in particular, transformed his models into statuesque goddesses clad in flowing gowns, with luxuriant tresses, frequently red, and mesmerizing, somnambulistic expressions bordering on sexual ecstasy, as in his *Beata Beatrix* and *Astarte Syriaca*.

For the most part the Pre-Raphaelites depicted themes of love and romance (but never complete happiness). They used glowing primary colors of a translucent quality, achieved by painting onto a prepared ground of white while still wet. Violet saw herself as a daughter of Pre-Raphaelitism: she copied her gowns from Burne-Jones's paintings, and sympathized with Rossetti's wife, the painter Elizabeth Eleanor (Lizzie) Siddal, who committed suicide the year Violet was born. Alfred Hunt admired these artists, whom he met through his friends John Ruskin and Holman Hunt. But although his landscapes exhibited the minute attention to detail associated with the movement, he was never a true Pre-Raphaelite.

By 1854 the artists had abandoned the brotherhood, going their individual ways, but Pre-Raphaelitism was by no means dead; its technical innovations and influence were felt well into the 1890s, particularly in the art of Aubrey Beardsley of *The Yellow Book* fame. The PRB was also the foundation for the Aesthetic Movement as personified by Oscar Wilde and, more important, it invigorated English painting through its homage to the masters of the Quattrocento, its rejection of the Royal Academy and its sometimes unsettling topics.

By the time Violet's sister Venetia Margaret was born on August 4, 1864, the Hunts had moved to 21 Old Elvet, a townhouse near Violet's birthplace. Venice, as Venetia was usually called, was named after *The Stones of Venice*, by John Ruskin, who became her godfather. Asked to take on the responsibility of the child's religious training, the freethinking critic accepted on the condition that there be no rituals at the baptismal font. He pledged that he would teach "the child what any one who looks to the light of heaven and the laws of Earth, may know of the truth of God." (He did no better by his goddaughter than Canon Greenwell would by Violet, eventually reneging on his pledge to leave Venice £200 in his will.)

The birth of the Hunts' third daughter, Sylvia Kingsley, on September 8, 1865, followed so quickly after Venice's that Margaret Hunt was unable to breastfeed, which Violet believed contributed to her mother's neglect of her youngest daughter. The baby was named after Holman Hunt's 1851 painting *Valentine Rescuing Sylvia from Proteus*. Ruskin later suggested changing the spelling to the more poetic "Silvia." Her godfather was Canon William Kingsley, a relative, and master in the science and art department at Oxford.

Like her sisters, Silvia was not overburdened with maternal love, if the impression given in *Their Lives*, Violet's first autobiographical novel, is to be believed. Alfred Hunt came first with Margaret, and when she was not helping her husband sell his pictures, she was busy building her own reputation as a novelist. A shrewd businesswoman, Margaret priced her husband's paintings in guineas—a pound and a shilling—but timid Alfred forgot and sold them in pounds. "My children's bread is buttered with a palette knife and I buy their boots with a splash of dirty water," she said.

Despite Margaret's help, Alfred's career did not flourish. None of his paintings was exhibited at Burlington House, home of the Royal Academy from 1863 to 1870. The Academy was not interested in landscapes, and its president from 1866 to 1878, Sir Francis Grant, an aristocratic portrait painter who enjoyed carousing and riding, was uninformed about art. Once offered a Sanzio (Raphael's last name) for an Old Masters exhibition, Grant refused it, saying, "Well gentlemen . . . we want the pictures of great masters, you know; as for Sanzio, I never heard of him."

Ruskin attempted to cheer Margaret, advising, "None of us can do great things nowadays— The days don't deserve it. We must do little things—and live—and be happy. [Alfred] sells his pictures—& people like them— He makes them honestly as good as he can—and should ask no more of Fate nor of himself." In Hunt's lifetime only thirty-seven of his paintings were hung at Burlington House. His talent was as a watercolorist. In 1862, the year of Violet's birth, he was named—to his muted pleasure—an associate of the Old Water-Colour Society, where he would exhibit 334 watercolors and, in 1888, rise to deputy president.

By 1866, when Violet was four, the Hunts had saved enough

money to risk the move to London. For £120 a year, they rented a house high up on Campden Hill in Kensington with a distant view of Windsor Castle. One Tor Villas (later 10 Tor Gardens) was a three-story gray stucco house with fourteen rooms, including a square studio tower on the top floor. Designed by the Royal Academician James Clarke Hook in 1851, the house had previously been occupied by Holman Hunt. The light was clear on Campden Hill, where Violet and her parents would live out their lives; the air was pure and the surrounding homes substantial enough to attract neighbors of means and influence. Determined to compete socially, Margaret made Tor Villa, as the family called it, a Victorian showcase: there were jewel-colored velvet draperies, Morris wallpapers, yards of fringe and corpulent upholstered furniture. Alfred's paintings were everywhere.

Thursdays were "at home" afternoons when friends stopped by to see Margaret Hunt and meet her charming daughters. Most middle-class Victorian men were distant from their families, but Alfred Hunt was more so than most. "It was mamma's business to amuse the children, nurse them, scold them, do everything for them," Violet wrote in *Their Lives*. "Papa only loved them, and must not be disturbed." Alfred put in a brief appearance on Thursdays only if Margaret made a fuss. He preferred the lively talk of dinner parties, where guests tended toward the literary and he was the genial host who carved the beef while servants passed platters of boiled potatoes and mashed turnips, poured a rich claret and prepared a fresh-cut pineapple for dessert. Margaret's tart tongue was both feared and enjoyed. She "went her way like a pleasant Juggernaut, a privileged libertine of the tongue, which was the salt of dinner tables, as it was the source of her husband's sleepless nights," said Violet.

Living well, or appearing to live well, was raised to an art by Margaret. She never stinted on food or wine. A mix of inherited furniture and secondhand items bought in the North gave Tor Villa the look of genteel affluence. There were, at various times, French, German and Italian governesses to instruct the girls, a cook, a parlormaid and a part-time seamstress—enough servants for entertaining well. But there never was the money to buy a country house or to embrace the leisurely life of the aristocracy; instead, the family spent their holidays with relatives in the North or in rented rooms in seaside resorts on the Yorkshire coast. Margaret's growing income as a writer, however, soon paid for frequent trips to Paris.

The Hunt daughters were taught frugality: their mother's dresses were remade and passed down from Violet to Silvia; walking rather than paying a two-penny bus fare or taking a four-wheeler rather than an expensive hansom were the house rules. Fires were not lit until the evening, and then only in the sitting room, where the family read, often to one another, in the dim amber glow of gaslight. Unlike the fashion in other Victorian households, the children were not hidden in the nursery, but seen, heard and encouraged to make themselves useful. When the coal man delivered his sacks, the girls counted them while he waited—a sure deterrent to any shortchanging.

As the Hunts' social circle expanded, Margaret made friends in the literary world who helped her to publish essays and criticism in *The Spectator* and *Gentleman's Annual*. Alfred had arrived in London well connected in the art world: his father had been an intimate of the landscape artist David Cox, and Hunt was already friendly with Ruskin, Madox Brown and Holman Hunt. He needed no introductions, only acceptance by the Academy. The annual gloom over Alfred's failure to be elected permeated the Hunt household. Like a terminal disease, his rejections were not discussed in front of the children. Violet usually learned of the negative vote from the servants' gossip.

Hunt suffered privately; his family often heard him sighing and sadly humming "Bonnie Dundee" to himself. Observing her mother's anger and her father's withdrawal, Violet proclaimed the Academy's hanging committee "the Supreme Court of the land." Stacked in a corner of Alfred's studio were the rejected canvases. They were marked in white chalk with a large "D" for "Doubtful," which meant the painting had been considered but there had not been room; some other artist's picture, marked "A" for "Accepted," was now hanging on the red, damask-covered walls of Burlington House.

When Margaret Hunt decided to become a novelist, she wrote about what was on her mind—artists and the Royal Academy—publishing her early novels under the pseudonym Averil Beaumont. In those days writers produced three-deckers, three volumes ground out one volume (usually three hundred pages) at a time and circulated through lending libraries. Margaret's first was _Magdalen Wynyard, or the Provocations of a Pre-Raphaelite_, published in 1873, which was followed by _Thornicroft's Model_, her most popular and enduring work. The novel features a Rossetti-type painter (Stephen Thornicroft) who searches for a perfect model; there are also references to the Academy's unfriendly treatment of landscape artists. (The prose style was of the era. A typical passage: " 'Oh, my stars and garters, wife, but this is a bad job,' said Mr. Mac Scumble, Times in hand, to his wife, as she peeped in at the door of his room after a protracted course of shopping.")

Margaret entered into two kinds of book contracts: royalties and profit sharing. Her contract with Sampson Low, Marston, Low & Searle for _Under Seal of Confession_, published in 1874, called for profits to be divided equally between author and publisher. Chatto & Windus, in an agreement for _The Leaden Casket_, to be serialized in _Belgravia_ magazine in 1880 and then published in three volumes, paid her a £200 advance against royalties in monthly installments of £16/13s/4p. A first printing of 1,000 copies was usual. Because Margaret averaged a novel a year until 1886, her income made possible new dresses for Violet, which were passed down to her sisters, and sketching tours abroad for Alfred.

Violet, "the listening pitcher of a schoolgirl," grew up "witty" and "clever," Victorian euphemisms for a girl who was intelligent. Long before her formal "coming out" at eighteen, she was often escorted into dinner at Tor Villa on the arm of a famous author or artist. Encouraged to flirt by her mother, she practiced on the eminent Victorians, including Ruskin, Burne-Jones, Millais, Rossetti, Theo Marzials and Robert Browning. She was a precocious four-year-old when Browning first visited Tor Villa following an exhibition at the Old Water-Colour Society of Alfred's large landscape _Childe Roland to the Dark Tower Came_, inspired by Browning's poem of the same name.

The poet became Margaret's first social conquest. Browning refused all dinner invitations, preferring, as he told Margaret, to take tea "to get much good out of my intercourse with you, and that good scarcely ever comes to me in the shape of a dinner. I never choose that way of seeing friends when I can command a better, and the best will be those daylight visits to you which you must suffer to be neither few nor far between." A lasting friendship grew. Browning told Margaret stories about Shelley, Lamb and Wordsworth, reluctantly recounted memories of his late wife, Elizabeth Barrett, and complained bitterly about unscrupulous publishers. Margaret dedicated *Thornicroft's Model* to Browning and appealed to his vanity when she began *Barrington's Fate*, published in 1883, with a character "lying on a sofa reading Browning's *Dramatis Personae* in perfect contentment of body and mind."

Margaret also gathered around her a group of devoted admirers. One was the poet and popular-song writer Theophilus (Theo) Julius Henry Marzials, who wrote her tritely passionate poems. "In June when the yellow moon grew yellow" was one example. He ingratiated himself into the family by paying special attention to the three daughters. Arriving with boxes of chocolate with "bees on them," Marzials spent the afternoon eating them as he taught the girls his song "Twickenham Ferry." "I was in love with him," Violet recalled years later of this schoolgirl crush. "I had just been to France and I had a brown hat with a white—now yellowish—feather. The tip got dirty and he always accused me of stirring the glue pot with it!"

Another who captured the affections of both mother and daughter was Andrew Lang, a man of universal abilities who was at once a journalist, essayist, novelist, biographer, poet, Scottish historian, classicist, anthropologist, folklorist and dabbler in abnormal psychology. Considered the greatest bookman of his age, Lang collected myths and fairy tales and wrote the introduction to Margaret Hunt's 1884 translation of *Grimm's Household Tales*, on which later editions, called *Grimm's Fairy Tales*, were based. Violet and Silvia helped Lang adapt his tales from the Norse for the *Blue Fairy Book* (1889) and the *Red Fairy Book* (1890), which were used by schools throughout England and became the most popular collections of tales in English.

Lang was married, but childless and lonely. Violet found him intriguing: "I was drawn, unaccountable, by the liquid brown eyes of this tall gipsy-man" who could be serious about "blue china, old books, and fishing flies of sorts," she later wrote. "To me, a romantic, he presented the effect of a man with a slightly broken heart skating all his life on the thin ice of the humourous. . . . He was bewilderingly charming, indeed, but, as a lover he would have been

dull. No flirt could have made the slightest headway with him."
Still, she "loved him—a little."

When Violet was seven, Sidney Courtauld, a patron of the arts
whose family fortune came from textiles, invited Alfred and Margaret to cruise the Mediterranean for six months on his private
yacht. Ruskin, then fifty, offered to care for Violet, Venice and
Silvia for the duration of the cruise. He warned Margaret, though,
that he wanted no runny noses or sprained ankles: "I will not
undertake however to see the children if they should have any _illness_
at present—I am not fit for that kind of work—and you must
provide for it otherwise." Fond though he was of young girls,
Ruskin was frightened of the responsibility. All had to be orderly.

The Mediterranean cruise gave Alfred an opportunity to sketch
in Constantinople and the Holy Land. Margaret studied the folklore
of Corsican funeral rites. When the yacht docked at the port of
Ajaccio in Corsica, the group journeyed inland to the mountain
village of Gatte di Vivario, where, according to Edward Lear's
Journal of a Landscape Painter in Corsica, which Margaret had recently reviewed, two exquisite sisters and their widowed mother
lived in squalor.

Sent to French finishing schools, Reine and Catherine Dausoigne were indeed "beauty blooming unknown—in a dung heap,"
awaiting discovery by the romantic and ambitious Margaret Hunt.
"They had been taught to read, to sing, to embroider, given ideas
about their station, and sent home to be of use to their mother,"
Violet later recalled. "My mother, always on the lookout for sentimental philanthropy, elicited this story and realised the cloud of
boredom that was settling on their young lives."

Ostensibly transported to England to be governesses for the
Hunt children, the Dausoigne sisters were furtively procured by
Margaret to startle Pre-Raphaelite London and allow them to find
wealthy husbands. Their duties were minimal. Violet described
them as "lazy, hot-tempered and greedy . . . just beautiful savages."
Involved with a living fairy tale, Margaret fantasized that Catherine
would wed bachelor Courtauld or the divorced Ruskin, and Reine,
the widowed Holman Hunt.

Trotted around to Pre-Raphaelite parties, the sisters were feted
and painted, but no one wanted them as wives. Courtauld lost

interest, Holman Hunt married his deceased wife's sister and Ruskin found them too old. "I do not like grand faces in women at all," Ruskin wrote Margaret, referring to the sisters, "but infinitely delicate & soft ones—for instance Violet and Venice as I can fancy them at eighteen— And the older I grow—the younger I like faces to be—so foolish am I. I don't think I can possibly care for anybody more than eighteen—unless I've known them before."

Ruskin wanted life on his own terms, and was irritatingly self-absorbed in work and emotionally immature in relationships, particularly those with women. He sought as lovers women who would play Galatea to his Pygmalion. He liked his Galateas young, and as he grew older he liked them even younger. His first love, Adèle Domecq, and his wife, Euphemia (Effie) Gray, were twelve when he was first attracted to them. His unconsummated six-year union with Effie (whom he married at nineteen) ended in an annulment for reasons of "incurable impotency."*

Shortly thereafter Rose La Touche, then ten years old, stirred Ruskin's confused sexuality, although he waited until 1866, when she was eighteen and he was forty-seven, to propose formally. He was rebuffed by the girl's parents not only because of the age difference and his disastrous marriage but also because they distrusted his determined agnosticism. By Victorian standards, however, Ruskin's desires were not that perverted; the age of consent was twelve until 1885, when Parliament raised it to sixteen.

Ruskin's need for youth soon added intrigue to Violet's routine life. In the summer of 1873, Rose La Touche, whom he still hoped to marry, was ill and again had rejected him. He turned for solace to his godchild Venice, then nine years old, inviting her for a prolonged visit at Brantwood, his new home at Coniston in the Lake

---

*Ruskin's recent biographer John Dixon Hunt suggests that Ruskin was more upset with the fact that Effie was menstruating on their wedding night than with the "notorious first sight of pubic hair"; in any event he made it clear that her body disgusted him. Effie later wed Millais, with whom she had fallen in love during a summer the Ruskins spent at Glenfinlas in Scotland, and they had eight children. Despite the scandal, Ruskin went about his life as if nothing had happened, even though his assumed humiliation rivaled the Crimean War as the main topic of conversation in London in 1855. Years later, when Millais visited Tor Villa, Violet brought out her autograph book: "He looked through it. I quaked, I remembered the 'John Ruskin.' He came to it. He said, 'That's a very good man!' I beamed with relief."

District. Always eager to please Ruskin and draw him more securely into the family web, Margaret was thrilled. "It will be a very good thing for her to be under your influence & I think she will make you happier," she wrote. "Don't think me a silly mother when I say she is one of the sweetest little things in the world. She is almost a woman in her power of giving love and sympathy, and yet a childish child. She gets pleasure out of everything. . . . I wish my little Venice may kiss away some of your sad moments."

As events unfortunately showed, this gushing tribute misrepresented Venice entirely. In offering Ruskin her young daughter as companion and "housekeeper," someone capable of diverting a middle-aged man's sorrow, Margaret clearly put her husband's career (and her own) before the welfare of a young child. How could Venice, or any of Ruskin's child-women for that matter, be "the center of order, the balm of distress, and the mirror of beauty" that he desired? Moreover, Venice was a twin of Ruskin—selfish and stubborn. The experiment was doomed from inception.

Plans called for Margaret, Alfred and Venice to stay with Ruskin at Brantwood in June; after that Alfred would find a sketching site with lodgings nearby and Margaret would collect Violet, Silvia and the Corsican governesses from London and join him. Venice would be alone with Ruskin, with the rest of the family across the lake. Ruskin looked forward to watching Venice "grow as a flower does."

To a small child, Ruskin was a ferocious figure. He had a scar on his lower lip where a dog had bitten him as a child and a "cruelty" around the mouth that made Violet think of him as "the kind wolf." "He was *cruel*, foolishly cruel, and kind, extraordinarily, wisely, kind," she recalled. "We children, however, had no experience of his cruelty." In truth he didn't understand children, as Violet accurately noted: "Ruskin loved children, but I think that the abnormal in them was what chiefly appealed to him, while the absolutely natural child puzzled him." In his efforts to share their spontaneity, to enter into their special world, he was clumsy. His own childhood had been an emotional disaster even by nineteenth-century standards: an only child, he was frequently whipped; he had no friends, and his toys were a bunch of keys.

When Ruskin (who advocated total obedience to fathers, mothers and tutors) and Venice did not take to each other, he wrote

Margaret, after less than three weeks, that it was "*temperament* which puzzles me so, in Venice. She and I are both equally irritable about *little* things—which does not do at all." He further complained that while collecting holly Venice chose only the unprickly branches, leaving the thorny ones for his valet's daughter. Venice was living up to Violet's description of her as "a cat that schemes to get the fish without wetting its paws." The following day Ruskin was sufficiently vexed to write Alfred and ask him to take his daughter away. "There is much in the child which I cannot understand," he wrote, "—*something* which displeases me, and which yet is so subtle and so difficult to explain that which I have felt it my duty to tell her mother the impression made on me . . ."

Ruskin subsequently warned that Venice, whose name he shortened to "Ice," is "not a child who can be safely left to herself, or who will grow up into the best she is capable of, as the larks and linnets do. And most assuredly, I am the last person who should attempt to form or teach children—being naturally careless of play, and slow, now to love." Although Ruskin took responsibility for his shortcomings, he made it clear that Venice needed watching, and was prescient about her growth. The discontented girl became a manipulative, greedy woman who plagued Violet for half a century.

Violet was always miffed that she wasn't Ruskin's godchild. She noted in *Their Lives*: "A great man went a very long way with Christina [Violet's alter ego]. She deeply resented Virgilia's [Venice's] prior claim on her own godfather. . . . She could not quite forgive her mother for not having realised that Christina was the baby who would have best appreciated the honour in later years."

Happily, the summer did not end on an embattled note; there were frequent visits across the lake to Brantwood, where eleven-year-old Violet now intrigued Ruskin. "Very curious to study," he wrote in his diary, suggesting that her precocity was sexual as well as intellectual. At this age she wore her dark hair long, demurely tied back with velvet ribbons; she looks sedate and shy in photographs, though her behavior was quite the opposite. Whenever Ruskin was present, Violet actively competed with her sister for the attention of "the prophet" or "the Professor" as she called him, using such attention-getting ploys as telling him she was "disreputable baggage" and Venice was the "flower of the flock."

Most effective was her knowledge of Sir Walter Scott, a favorite author of Ruskin's. "The cult of Scott was the bond between myself and [Ruskin] and an inexhaustible subject of conversation," wrote Violet. Ruskin admired Scott's novels about "nice people": _Guy Mannering_, _Rob Roy_, _Waverley_, _Old Mortality_, _The Abbot_ and _The Monastery_. At summer's end, by default or desire, Violet had won Ruskin's attention and admiration.

Considering herself a flawless, though permissive, mother, Margaret was distressed with Ruskin's criticism suggesting that Venice's problems stemmed from too much independence and parental indulgence. "If good fathers and mothers always had as good children the world would soon be angelic. It is not so; very curiously often otherwise," Ruskin wrote. "A single phrase which you used yesterday explained much to me. 'I have not the heart, to do so and so' you said. In reality, you have not heart _enough_ to do it—yet."

Ruskin's admonition rang true; Margaret did compromise with her children in order to keep a tranquil home so that Alfred could paint undisturbed, but she would not change to please Ruskin nor would she endorse his rigid rules when she consciously valued independence, originality and spontaneity in herself, her children and her friends.

Three years later when an insane Rose La Touche died at the age of twenty-seven, Ruskin sank into prolonged melancholia. On hearing the news, thirteen-year-old Violet impetuously told her mother she would marry him. Margaret, who should have had more dignity than to grovel, and more love for her daughter, promptly wrote Ruskin of the offer. She stipulated, however, that he wait until Violet was sixteen, echoing the three-year waiting period imposed by Rose. Ruskin's reply hints at some interest in the proposal: "I really think Violets must be nicer than roses after all— Another three years to wait—though! What a weary life I have of it . . . I do so long for any place where I could rest and have—Violet, or the like—to manage everything for me—and nurse me—and no one hear of me more."

Fortunately, Violet never had to fulfill her promise. She would choose many inappropriate men, but none so unavailable as the bearded prophet she wooed away from her younger sister. Perhaps the preference for older men who would fuss over her more than her self-absorbed father can be traced back to that Brantwood summer when she made Ruskin her first conquest.

3

Adolescent Dreams

Violet read Sir Walter Scott to please Ruskin, fairy tales to please Mamma and popular French novels to please herself. Her taste in literature ranged far beyond that of the typical middle-class Victorian teenager, or as she put it, "Life is so dull unless *on se permet des petites distractions.*" Every evening in her cold, drafty garret bedroom she read by gaslight, often until dawn, or dreamily stared out the window, glimpsing the fireworks at Cremorne Gardens, a famous amusement park on the banks of the Thames.

Writing and sketching were encouraged in the Hunt household. Violet's youthful stories had tantalizing titles: "Miss Bertram's Mistake, or Not to Be Trusted" by the author of "Grace Sylvester," "The Wanderer's Child," "Mabel's Playmates," "The Snow Maiden," "Adrift in a Boat" and "Cecile's Fault."

Until age eleven Violet's education was left to foreign governesses and to her own inclination for eclectic reading; she then enrolled at Notting Hill and Ealing High School in Norland Square, Kensington, one of the first girls' public (fee-paying) day schools in London. Shut in by tall houses, the school playground later reminded Violet of a prison yard like the one in Oscar Wilde's *Ballad of Reading Gaol.*

She found school "not unamusing," observing that the process of education changed daily as the teachers learned their skills. Describing herself as "wheedling and daring," she did pretty much what she wanted, took "easy firsts" in composition and history, and attracted the attention of the headmistress, who found her a "good, quick, clever pupil, whose behavior was correct on the whole." At the age of thirteen, Violet had poetry published in _Century_ magazine.

Her classmates included Margaret Burne-Jones, daughter of the painter, and the two daughters of the poet and artist William Morris, Jane and Mary. Violet said Mary was "the most beautiful girl I have ever seen." At seventeen, she had an adolescent crush on an older student, a not uncommon Victorian occurrence. Rose Cumberbatch was "pretty, very distracting . . . (she is) my passion and holds my love letters." In one note Violet wrote, "I feel as if last term was all a dream, that I shall perhaps never see or hear from you again, and it is such a horrible feeling! . . . I suppose you are coming out & will get married etc. (Don't)."

Victorian schoolgirls were also infatuated with Henry Irving, the charismatic Shakespearean actor-manager, and the first thespian to be knighted and to have a statue in Trafalgar Square. Violet loved the stage and had more than a passing thought about becoming another Ellen Terry, Irving's leading lady at the Lyceum. By the time she was twenty, though, she told her diary: "I would like to act, people say I could act, but I don't think I shall act."

A true fan, Violet pasted Irving's pictures inside the top of her desk, collected newspaper clippings, learned all his roles by heart and boldly walked into pubs asking for "the flaming posters in three fierce colors" of her idol displayed in the window. (Far from pinup perfect, Irving had skinny legs, an awkward walk and a voice that George Bernard Shaw called "a highly cultivated neigh.")

Violet began keeping a diary as early as 1876, when she was fourteen. That volume contains a detailed account of a month-long yacht cruise along the coast of France with her parents and one of Alfred's patrons. Violet was happy to miss school, and noted all the sights, the weather and the time she went to bed. No intimate thoughts or feelings presage her future diaries, but the entries reflect a growing sophistication. She liked Cherbourg but disliked Guernsey for being "so English." Le Havre was "nasty, ugly, new-housed

& Brighton-like." When the yacht anchored in Dieppe, the party climbed to the castle, where Alfred and Mr. Payne, the host, and Violet collected cowslips.*

At ease with adults and seldom shy, Violet accompanied her mother on social visits when she was seventeen and the following year was presented to society at a private party. After she was graduated from high school she took classes at Kensington Art School, where she spent three languid years honing her artistic talents. She received a certificate for model drawing on August 11, 1879. "*I could* draw but wouldn't," she later said. Surviving charcoal or red-chalk sketches of family members indicate technical skill but little attention to detail as practiced by Alfred Hunt. (Some of her work from this period was displayed years later, in 1931, at an exhibition of author-artists at the Foyle Art Gallery. *The Observer's* critic noted: "The carefully shaded portraits by Miss Violet Hunt show unmistakably her affiliation to the Pre-Raphaelite brotherhood.")

Nourished by her mother as a dreamy romantic, Violet now demonstrated inherited maternal traits: a sharp, witty tongue, literary aspirations and the magnetism to attract influential people. Dressed in Pre-Raphaelite peacock-blue serge, the young Violet demurely poured tea at the home of Alexandra Sutherland Orr, the sister of Lord Frederic Leighton, president of the Royal Academy. "She was gracefully shy; enchantingly bold, all things to all men— and women, for at this stage of her development she took the trouble to please members of her own sex," Violet later wrote of herself at this age. She longed to be taken by her parents to Leighton's famed musical evenings held on the eve of "sending-in day" for the Royal Academy summer exhibition. At his Holland Park Road home, Leighton had created an Arab Hall with dazzling antique tiles of varied hues of blue. It was a fantasy place that infused Violet's dreams.

---

*In addition to patrons like Payne and Courtauld, there were collectors regularly purchasing Alfred Hunt's paintings. He also profited from the opening of the Grosvenor Gallery in 1877, a milestone in the art world that broke the hegemony held by the Royal Academy for more than a hundred years. The Grosvenor exhibited contemporary French paintings and the avant-garde in British art, as embodied by Whistler. The gallery had a separate room where watercolors were appreciatively hung. Alfred Hunt had his own show there in the winter of 1878.

□

One day in 1879, at the home of her mother's former art tutor, William Bell Scott, Violet met Oscar Fingal O'Flahertie Wills Wilde, the lanky Irish poet, down from Magdalen College, Oxford. Wilde was flush with success from having captured the Newdigate Prize for his poem "Ravenna." For two hours Violet monopolized Wilde and fell "a little in love to boot." They sat on a window seat where "there was hardly room for the slip of a girl that I was and the lusty big fellow with the wide, white face, the shapely red mouth and the long lock of straight peasant-like black hair that fell across his fine forehead."

This encounter captivated Violet's imagination, and she never tired of talking about Wilde's marriage proposal, eventually writing several versions of "My Oscar (a Germ of a Book)." In one she regretfully noted that "all the proposal that got through to me was a single white Eucharist lily [one symbol of the aesthetic movement] without a stalk, reposing on cotton wool in a box, ridiculed by my younger sisters."

In her memoirs she wrote that she "as nearly as possible escaped the honour of being Mrs. Wilde," and told her diary: "I believe that Oscar was really in love with me—for the moment and perhaps more than a moment for Alice Corkran told me quite seriously that he had said to her quite seriously, 'Now, shall I go to Mr. Hunt and ask him to give me little Violet?' and Mamma . . . was continually drawing parallels between Oscar and my other lover Bryan Hook [son of Tor Villa's landlord]."

There is no evidence that Oscar Wilde ever asked for Violet's hand as she always claimed, although he did write Margaret in 1880 that he thought her daughter "the sweetest Violet in England." When Violet turned the episode into fiction in *Their Lives*, Philip Wynyard (Wilde) wants to marry Christina (Violet) but hesitates because her parents have no money. Finally the father settles the problem by announcing that he "would never give [his] daughter to him." In retrospect, Violet made Wynyard physically repulsive: "His full pouting pale lips reminded her of those of the debased Roman Emperors whose busts stand in one of the corridors of the British Museum. His habit of drawing in his breath in a susurrant, self-satisfied manner at the end of a would-be poignant sentence, disgusted her."

It was hardly surprising that Wilde gave more than passing attention to Violet. She was then a great beauty, with deepset smoldering brown eyes under heavy-hooded lids. Five feet five and slender (110 pounds), she was exceedingly vain about her appearance and hated her large Raine-family nose. Fine-textured auburn hair, worn in a bouffant on top of the head in the fashion of the day, dramatized her pale, magnolia skin. She had a velvety voice, which made her vicious barbs all the more startling.

"Out of Botticelli by Burne-Jones," commented actress Ellen Terry on meeting Violet. When a friend of her mother's predicted that she would be "a beautiful woman," Violet demanded: "What about now?" The novelist Mrs. Humphry Ward said Violet had the " 'naiveté' of a schoolgirl of fifteen and the 'savoir vivre' of a woman of fifty." It was Violet's extravagant personality more than her physical beauty that would intrigue and entrap men. Always a rebel, she never adapted as did other Victorian women to men's expectations. Instead, she demanded they bend to her desires.

When Violet met Wilde, it was a successful audition of her youthful charm. She wore a "terra cotta plain gown" with her mother's "black fichu" around the neck—the last of the hand-me-downs, for she insisted on a new dress and it was ordered the next day. Violet and the young Oxonian sat on the window seat talking of Rossetti and Swinburne; Violet told stories about her mother.

"Do you know, I am almost beginning to be afraid of your mother?" Wilde said. "I shall not dare to ask her to let me call." Then, changing the subject, he told exuberant anecdotes about Sarah Bernhardt in his best voice ("he always talked less in italics than in Capitals," said Violet). "Beautiful women like you hold the fortunes of the world in your hands to make or mar," he beguilingly told her. "We will rule the world—you and I—you with your looks and I with my wits. But you will write too, surely, you who have inherited the literary art from your dear mother." Oscar was flattering. Oscar was stimulating. Oscar created Violet's image of herself as the seductive woman.

Though Wilde probably did not have marriage on his mind, he was nonetheless smitten. His letters to Margaret were certainly intended for Violet, to whom it would have been improper for a young man to write. "I hope that you have not forgotten your promise to have tea with me tomorrow," he wrote, "and that your

Violet—the sweetest Violet in England I think her, though you must not tell her so—will come too. I can hardly hope Mr. Hunt will come though I am very anxious to introduce him to my mother . . ."

In May 1880, when Wilde accepted an invitation to call on the Hunts, he told Margaret, "I always enjoy my evenings with you so much: but you really must not write me such charming letters or I shall be coming a great deal too often. I count it a very great privilege indeed to know anyone whose art I have always loved and admired so much as Mr. Hunt's (though he *has* this terrible passion for barricades and revolutions!) and it is very nice of you to think of me as a friend—indeed I should like to be one."

Wilde continued to correspond with Margaret and called at Tor Villa almost every Sunday, lending Violet an "unenviable notoriety," she said. Mother and daughter were invited to gatherings at Thames House at 13 Salisbury Street off the Strand and later to Keats House at 1 Tite Street in Chelsea, where Wilde and his artist friend Frank Miles moved in 1880. The center of new artistic ideas, Chelsea had already claimed Swinburne, Morris, Rossetti, Whistler and Burne-Jones.

Wilde told Margaret that Tite Street was more convenient to Tor Villa and he hoped that they would often have "dishes of tea" at one another's house. In one letter he included his poem "Ave Imperatrix" for Violet to read. "I hope she will see some beauty in it, and that your wonderful husband's wonderful radicalism will be appeased by my first attempt at political prophecy. If she will send me a little line to say what she thinks of it, it will give me such pleasure."

In November Wilde invited the Hunts to share his box at the Court Theatre to see the fiery Polish actress Helen Modjeska in *Marie Stuart*. "It is a large box and will hold you all," he wrote Margaret, "including I hope Mr. Hunt whose republican sympathies will vanish before the misery of that lovely treacherous Queen of Scots," a reference to Alfred's support of home rule for Ireland, which Wilde, an Irishman, did little if nothing to promote. Indeed, Wilde left politics to his spirited mother, Jane Wilde, who dubbed herself "Speranza" and was an outspoken nationalist. In her salon in Dublin and later in London, she startled guests by wearing outlandish costumes, bizarre headdresses and clunky jewelry.

When Violet looked back on the Wilde years, she recalled a Sunday evening at home with him talking about maps of the ancients: "Oh, Miss Violet," he exclaimed, drawing his breath through his teeth in a sibilant whisper of intense appreciation, "think of a map drawn of a whole continent, and beside the names of an insignificant city or two a blank and *Hic sun leones!* Miss Violet, let you and me go there."

"And get eaten by lions? said I."

The swaggering Wilde so overpowered Tor Villa that even Alfred emerged from the cocoon of his studio to sit by the fire and listen to the poet's mezzo-voiced epigrams. An intuitive self-promoter, Wilde at twenty-five had done little of note except successfully invent himself as the apostle of aestheticism, a movement grounded in the fear that industrialization was obliterating "Beauty and Art." Violet and other fashionable ladies were seen at balls and private views (invitation-only art exhibits) carrying the movement's symbol: the lily and the sunflower.

"Peacock feathers and sunflowers glittered in every room," wrote Max Beerbohm, "men and women, fired by the fervid words of the young Oscar, threw their mahogany into the streets. . . . Into whatever ballroom you went, you would surely find, among the women in tiaras and the fops and the distinguished foreigners, half a score of comely ragamuffins in velveteen, murmuring sonnets, posturing, waving their hands. 'Nincompoopiana,' the craze was called at first, and later 'Aestheticism.' "

Cartoons in *Punch* by George du Maurier ridiculed Wilde for his posturing and the way he murmured aesthetic appreciation with words like "consummate" and "sublime." Wilde once asked André Gide, "Would you like to know the great drama of my life? It's that I've put my genius into my life; I've put only my talent into my works." A large part of this genius was spent in meeting and charming the right people, among them the Hunts' friend John Ruskin. Wilde accompanied Ruskin to the famed production of *The Merchant of Venice* featuring Henry Irving as Shylock and Ellen Terry as Portia, and afterward to a ball given by Ruskin's former wife Effie Gray and John Millais to celebrate the marriage of their daughter.

In April 1881 Gilbert and Sullivan's *Patience* appeared on the London stage, satirizing Wilde's lofty philosophy. Although Bunthorne, the "Fleshy Poet," bore some resemblance to Rossetti and Swinburne, the public immediately identified the character as Wilde. When the operetta opened the next year in New York, the producer decided that a lecture tour would generate publicity, and Wilde spent many months traveling across America, generally applauded for his views and always noticed for his flamboyant costumes.

Violet kept up with his travels. Wilde was quoted to have remarked during his ocean voyage, "I am not exactly pleased with the Atlantic. It is not so majestic as I expected. The sea seems tame to me. The roaring ocean does not roar." "Mr. Wilde Disappointed with the Atlantic," read the headline in one British newspaper pasted in Violet's scrapbook.

She visited Wilde's mother for news. "Lady Wilde sits there in an old white ball dress, in which she must have graced the Soirees of Dublin a great many years ago," Violet observed, "and talks about Oscar, his success in America, the 'costume Oscar' [knee breeches with silk stockings] which he has originated, and which all the young men of fashion are wearing." In America, in hundreds of cities and towns, Wilde lectured on "the beautiful," with numerous household hints, foreshadowing the "how-to" books.

While she awaited his return, Violet spent a busy twenty-first year, as befitted a young lady ready, if not overripe, for marriage. She visited Paris in the spring, studied German with her mother, attended meetings of the Browning Society and a dress rehearsal of W. S. Gilbert's play _Broken Hearts_. She described Gilbert as "redhaired, with a rather disagreeable mouth & chin."

She first met Henry James, who would become a crucial friend, looking "not prepossessing, short, stout, square, with cropped hair & disagreeable (or perhaps intellectual) twist in his lip." She spent time with her father at the studio of Millais, who was in his childpainting phase, which Violet abhorred. "I am so tired of Millais' children," she wrote in her diary, unimpressed by the Victorian cult of children which expressed itself on varying levels: from Ruskin's repressed yearnings to London's child prostitution to Lewis Carroll's _Alice in Wonderland_.

Languishing in Tor Villa's lilac-scented garden, she read Christopher Marlowe's plays, and Chaucer and Hazlitt aloud to her younger sister Silvia at bedtime. There were garden parties, dances ("every single partner I had was an artist") and tennis matches ("the elevated language they used about it [tennis], one would think it was a fine art"). Her diary for 1882 drops fashionable names—du Maurier, Browning, Huxley, Burne-Jones, Whistler—and one not so well known: the artist George Henry Boughton, a Campden Hill neighbor. As an artist's daughter, it was acceptable to be an artist's model, so Violet sat for Burne-Jones and his son, Philip, but found the younger artist unattractive. "[He] obliges me to take an interest in him, which his own manner and appearance do not warrant," she wrote.

In August 1882 the Hunts vacationed in the village of Warkworth in Northumberland. Alfred sketched, while his wife spent mornings writing in her bedroom. Assuming that Violet would marry Byron Hook that winter, the cook taught her to make gingersnaps and tea cakes. But Violet had no intention of marrying and escaped into the life of George Sand, deciding that she preferred biographies to everything else. "There is something so fascinating & real in beginning at the beginning of a man's life," she wrote, "& going through with it, through all, till death. It makes one feel like knowing them."

On holiday or at home, Margaret worked on her translation of Grimm's tales, assisted by Andrew Lang, whom Violet found "bewilderingly charming." When she returned books to Lang's home, his wife often shooed them out for a walk in Kensington Gardens. The first to take an interest in Violet's writing, other than her mother, Lang helped shape her poetry ("stamping out sentiment; anything bittersweet") and had the results published in *Longman's Magazine*; she was thrilled when he surreptitiously passed her fees—two gold sovereigns—over the "tea table at Lady Macmillan's."

Lang's connections put Violet in good company. In July 1883 *Longman's* published her romantic poem "The Death of the Shameful Knight" in the same issue with Bret Harte, Thomas Hardy and Robert Louis Stevenson. But her poetry was too romantic, too melancholy for Lang, who told her to concentrate on sketching and paid her to draw his wife. One poem of Violet's he did like was about a couple who stay in London rather than go on holiday: "Here in the Park on the scanty grass / The dun sheep nibbling here and there / Round the leaden Pond, like a dull grey glass / I had rather be here than anywhere."

When Dante Gabriel Rossetti died in 1882, Lang and Violet walked from Kensington to 16 Cheyne Walk in Chelsea, Rossetti's last home, where his furnishings were to be sold at public auction. They explored the "dreary studio" and looked at the paintings by Rossetti's late wife, Lizzie Siddal, in particular _The Ladies' Lament_. Months later Violet complained to her diary that Lizzie was "most ill-tempered & jealous & he [Rossetti] gave her cause. Her death is always glided over in the lines of Rossetti, but his most intimate friends know well that she intentionally poisoned herself, putting a piece of paper on her breast, telling them all so." Violet had overheard this apocryphal story (at that time) about Lizzie's death, and it eventually germinated into her final book, _The Wife of Rossetti_ (1932), in which she unleashed all her pent-up anger against men who love and abandon women.

Even though the Academy ignored Alfred Hunt, he could celebrate his appointment in 1882 as an honorary fellow of Corpus Christi, a title also held by Ruskin, then Slade Professor of Fine Art at Oxford. For a brief time it seemed that Hunt might succeed to this position, replacing Ruskin, who was recuperating abroad from recurrent manic episodes; but Ruskin decided to return for a third term. He never fully recovered his health, and when Violet saw him at a private view the next year he had grown a mustache and beard and looked older than his sixty-three years. "Do you know me?" she asked him. " 'No—no—unless'—a radiant smile— 'unless you're Violet?' He is quite mad," she accurately concluded.

Meanwhile Margaret was working furiously and had two three-deckers—_Barrington's Fate_ and _Self-Condemned_—ready for publication in 1883. And there was further pride in the household when the Old Water-Colour Society, of which Alfred was a member, became the Royal Society of Painters in Water-Colours and members received a diploma from Queen Victoria. _The Times_ noted: "It is as if it were announced on authority that the country invites the Society and its chiefs to share with the elder and larger fellowship at Burlington House the trusteeship of British art." Violet ecstatically recorded: "Papa got his diploma. It is an imposing arrangement on cardboard, half-imperial size, the Queen has signed in a very sweet hand, but in the wrong place, not that it matters. It is, word for word, like the Academy Diploma."

On his return from America the now-celebrated Wilde paid a

call at Tor Villa, and Violet, observing him from the first-floor landing preening his locks "à la Nero" in the hall mirror, pronounced him changed: "His hair was curled, and *anointed,* making him look more like a prosperous Jew than the 'young Greek conqueror.' . . . And he was not nearly so nice," just another ambitious young man with "courteous manners and splendid sins."

Any nascent romance had cooled. Nonetheless, Violet remained loyal to her knight even after his notorious trials for sodomy and subsequent two-year imprisonment, when he was, in his own words, "the pariah dog of the nineteenth century." No matter Wilde's sins, he was Violet's sole ethereal love, pure and above reproach, the last of her unconsummated adolescent dreams.

4

Irregular Situations

WHEN SHE WAS seventeen, John Ruskin cautioned Violet to find "a human creature—old or young— whom you may reverence—please—and love—in constant and prudent ways." That she disregarded his prim counsel was not surprising; that she initiated an affair with the married George Boughton, who was fifty-one to her twenty-two, only three years younger than her father, was startling.

Boughton is known from his fictional alter ego in Violet's *Their Lives*, Emerson Vlaye: tall, slim, well dressed, with a "queer sunbrowned face, lined and leathery," a "twisted humorous smile" and charming manners—"the best raconteur in London," and a perfect "subject for amorous experiment." On both sides it was an intense relationship, beginning one day when Boughton kissed her wildly and she threw her arms around him.

At this time George Boughton was a successful painter, a man in control of his life and career. Photographs show a serene, confident man of average height, with a receding hairline, arrogant eyes and bushy mustache. Loving Violet may well have been the only risk he ever took in a safe and stolid life. He had nothing in common with Rossetti or the other Pre-Raphaelites, who endured the scorn of a philistine public; he did not seek solace with his models (there is no evidence that Boughton was unfaithful before or after his affair with Violet); and belonging to no school or movement, he socialized comfortably with artists of opposing views and temperaments such as Frederic Leighton and James Whistler.

Witty and charming, Boughton claimed a background that mingled tragedy, adventure and instant recognition. He maintained that as a baby he had been stolen for an hour by gypsies and that afterward his mother never believed he was her child. Born in 1833 in a village near Norwich, where his father was a farmer, he was brought a year later to Albany, New York, and orphaned a few years after that. A childhood fall kept him in bed for many months, and his older brother amused him by drawing pictures. Soon young George himself was sketching, impressing his physician, who took him to Albany galleries after his recovery.

Success was quick and easily earned. Boughton won a prize the first time he entered a local competition and immediately sold the painting in New York for fifty dollars. In 1862, after traveling in England and studying in Paris, the twenty-nine-year-old artist settled in London and had no difficulty exhibiting at the Royal Academy, where his paintings were hung annually, with eighty-seven exhibited during his career.

He once boasted that he never had a painting refused. In 1879 he was made an associate and, in 1896, a member of the Royal Academy. Boughton painted women who looked like chocolate-box decorations: ethereal maidens—demurely placed in frothy, pastel-colored settings—whose purity was beyond reproach. To hang such ingenuous art in the drawing room was fashionable.

In 1904, the year before his death, *Art Journal* devoted its Christmas issue to an appraisal of Boughton's work, noting: "There is a large public which is quite prepared to appreciate pictures that present a pretty idea in the right way, and this public he has done his best to satisfy." It was clear that Boughton never attempted anything new or radical. "He came into the English art world," the article continued, "at a moment when an artist of his temperament was wanted."

Although primarily a figure painter, Boughton was considered a superior landscape artist, expert in the "realisation of the solemn beauty of a winter twilight or the brilliancy of a clear, frosty sky." In addition to painting, he illustrated *Rip Van Winkle*, *The Legend of Sleepy Hollow* and *The Courtship of Miles Standish* and wrote short stories for *Harper's* and *Pall Mall Magazine*. Writing, said Boughton, took more out of him than "the severest painting."

Although conventional, Boughton stood apart from the more

radical artists Violet had attracted at private views. From the moment her school chum Flossie Boughton, the artist's niece, introduced her, Violet was infatuated. The Boughtons and Flossie lived at West House, 118 Campden Hill Road, a three-minute walk from Tor Villa toward Notting Hill Gate. Designed in 1878 by Richard Norman Shaw, the architect of Scotland Yard, this distinctive home (whose exterior today is largely unchanged) featured a fanciful slate-and-red-brick exterior, greatly admired at the time.

The drawing room was designed for the staging of private theatricals, which Violet attended, covetously noting the fashions: "Lady Lindsay defied the proprieties in dress in a gorgeous flowered brocade mantle, almost white—Mrs. Boughton scarcely less gorgeous. . . . May Morris' dress was simply a literal reproduction of some old mediaeval picture."

Boughton's first-floor studio had a skylight, a balustraded mahogany gallery at the south end and an outside balcony on the north. A contemporary engraving shows the spacious studio as a most agreeable place to work. It was cozy and cluttered, with all manner of chairs, a velvet-fringed chaise, china cabinets topped with bric-a-brac, an enamel stove, Oriental lamps and rugs, hanging plants and, on easels and walls, Boughton's sentimental portraits of picturesque peasant life in Brittany, Holland and New England. Violet said it reminded her of the "inside of a church."

In 1883, when Boughton returned from Holland, he entertained Violet and Flossie with some Dutch words ("very hideous they sounded") and then asked Violet to sit and talk to him ("so I did, & enjoyed it very much"). Violet arranged to be invited regularly to West House. She schemed to run into Boughton accidentally along Campden Hill Road, and attended the same dances, where his name was frequently scrawled across the dotted lines of her always-filled dance cards.

Besotted with an older man, she ignored her landlord's son, Bryan Hook, and other suitable red-cheeked Oxbridge boys, whom she pronounced shallow and boring. No matter how attractive, the young and available never survived Violet's scrutiny: a nose too small, eyes so dull, a raspy voice, hairy chin or clothes badly tailored. Single men were unappealing. "I did snub eligibles," she said, "on principle and used to aver that I preferred married men because no one could imagine that I wanted to catch them!"

In the morning Boughton and Violet would meet in a secluded alley midway between West House and Tor Villa, later venturing to Kensington Gardens and ultimately to borrowed rooms and cottages. In the afternoon Violet would take tea with Flossie, who eventually sensed the sexual undercurrents between her uncle and schoolmate and withdrew her friendship, and with it invitations to West House. Undaunted, Violet secured her father's permission to sit for Boughton, and was soon admitted to his studio as a model. Once she dropped her dress to the waist, noting that Boughton had taught her "the sacredness of the female form." (H. G. Wells later observed that Violet's body "still lives prettily in one or two of Boughton's paintings.")

One spring day during one of their many walks, Boughton gave Violet "a sort of serious little lecture on necessary Mrs. Grundyisms," indicating that her conversation was peppered with escapes from prudery. In November 1884, when Violet returned some borrowed books (another excuse) to West House, she found Boughton painting a young woman "in autumn colours, holding a dead rose." Following the model's departure, Violet posed in her place. "We amused ourselves very much, & then we walked down to Kensington," she wrote.

The Boughtons were childless, and Flossie, gossip said, was the illegitimate child of the illegitimate son of "Cora Pearl," the best-known courtesan of the Second Empire, and of Kate Boughton's sister Henrietta. Gossip soon circulated about Violet, although she was careful not to let the landlord at the Windsor Castle pub observe her comings and goings across the street at West House. Surprisingly, Kate Boughton allowed Violet to model for her husband for nearly three years, until the fall of 1886, when she told him to stop; Boughton gratefully obeyed and bolted for a sketching tour of Scotland.

Writing cautiously, he told Violet, "Your letter was a delight to me in many ways, in all ways except for the restless tone of it. Look at Gods lovely handiwork & try to let it inspire your heart." He hinted at future meetings, "which I long to do by the way." Violet's diaries record frequent meetings during February 1887; in early August he "came to say goodbye, as I knew since. I cried and he almost did." Their furtive trysts tapered off, but not the attraction they felt for each other.

☐

Remorse, particularly in matters of sexual intrigue, was not in Violet's vocabulary. At first she blamed her mother for allowing her "to wander about the streets alone, or be sent into people's houses, and worse, artist's studios with notes, to wait for an answer like a maid-servant!" Ruskin was right when he chided Margaret for her lack of discipline. By Victorian standards, though, Boughton was the villain, for he had ruined the daughter of a respectable family. Fearing a divorce scandal, Margaret sent Violet to Paris to mend her broken heart, kept the sordid details from Alfred and had the good sense not to castigate her daughter.

Returning from Paris more romantically inclined than ever, Violet stalked Boughton around town, flirting with him whenever they met. He responded from time to time, unable to resist her provocative behavior. A brave young suitor, Henry Howard, proposed and was rejected: "Poor Boy how he cried," she triumphantly noted. To the utterly charming, selfish and capricious Violet, life was a game of hide-and-seek, a masked ball, an endless flirtation. "The loveliest thing in all the world," she said, "is to carry on a secret love intrigue, not necessarily a wicked one, to meet and glance across ballroom floors at each other."

That summer of 1887 the family vacationed in Whitby, on the north Yorkshire coast, a medieval fishing village that grew into a Victorian resort. Then, as now, Whitby was a misty-mystical place, with a Royal Crescent built to rival that of Bath. The Hunts had visited there since 1876 and often took rooms with a view of the bleached skeleton of the thirteenth-century abbey and the twelfth-century church of St. Mary's.

Whitby was a place of history and legend. Captain James Cook left its port for his three voyages that changed the Pacific from imprecise myth to the map known today. In 1885, a captainless Russian schooner ran aground in the harbor, an event that made Whitby known to millions of readers of *Dracula*, after its publication in 1897. Bram Stoker, author of the famed vampire legend, was but one of many artists, actors and writers who summered in Whitby and adjacent Robin Hood's Bay. The town's famed visitors ranged from Caedmon, England's first recorded Christian poet, to C. L. Dodgson, the future Lewis Carroll, who had his first essays published in the *Whitby Gazette* and wrote parts of *Alice in Wonderland* on the beach.

Inspired by the rugged coastal landscape, Alfred Hunt painted some thirty-three watercolors of the area at various times. He was particularly fond of the abbey, founded by St. Hilda in 657, which he painted from various angles and in different moods: at low tide and high tide, in morning and afternoon, in twilight and moonlight. *Whitby Morning* and *Whitby Evening*, Violet recalled, "sent us all to school, and provided us with summer holidays as well."

Lovesick and brooding, Violet spent unprecedented time with her father on his sketching tours. She was amazed at Alfred's dexterity as his "long nervous bird-like fingers" moved a brush "within the merest fraction of an inch in any given direction to place a dab of colour here or there with the force of a hammer or the lightness of the swish of a bird's wing." Hunt was a perfectionist, easily dissatisfied with his work, fussing over details, overpainting, often destroying canvases that displeased him—to the horror of his wife, who deemed anything he painted a marketable commodity.

Often the landscape he coveted was a two- or three-mile walk from their lodgings. If he could not find a nearby cottage to store a five-foot canvas for an oil, then he wheeled it back and forth in a barrow; for a watercolor he carried the supplies on his back. Soda water and bread were his only food, but his concentration was so intense that he forgot to eat. It was a harsh regimen: two long walks daily, one to a morning subject, another to an evening subject. Invariably the morning sketch would be put aside for a new version at midday, and the afternoon subject postponed while he drew a sunset scene. Painting itself was painful. "The attitude of out-of-door water-colour painting [without an easel]," Violet wrote, "is cramping; the drawing laid across the knee entails the stooping back. There is something as bad as writer's cramp, a disease that one might call landscape painter's chest."

Following the dictates of Turner, Alfred painted outdoors in all kinds of weather. That summer, whenever a North Sea gale blew up he quickly packed his gear and was off to the windswept cliff. He would sketch until his hands became too numb from cold to work, forcing him home to the fire and his adoring family. Once Violet sat with him, among the anemones and rock limpets on Whitby Scaur, keeping her eye on the incoming tide, ready to warn him when to evacuate his position. In calmer weather, he sat on the roof of the Whitby railroad station, where he had a clear view to the harbor. Obsessed with creating the perfect landscape, Alfred Hunt found it difficult to relax. (When Violet took him to see *A*

Midsummer Night's Dream in 1889, it was his first time at the theater in twenty-five years. "He enjoyed it as a child," she said.)

Whitby had ample diversions for a girl with a broken heart. Violet took roles in the amateur theatricals performed at the Saloon, danced late into the night at the Spa, Whitby's social center, laughed at the visiting American circus and politely applauded the awkward talents of regional acting companies. The summer group of young people were christened "the Vi-Queens of Whitby" (a play on "Vikings") by George du Maurier, whose daughter, Sylvia, was a friend of Violet's.

She began a flirtation with a young Etonian, Eustace Strickland, eight years her junior. "He fell in love with me," Violet said, "and out of pure desolation, I tried to console myself." The Stricklands, who traced their lineage back to 1555, lived elegantly in Abbey House on East Cliff in the summer and the rest of the year divided their time among four country houses. The eighth baronet, Sir Charles William Strickland, had one son by his first wife and three sons by his second. Violet's redheaded conquest, sixteen that summer, was the youngest, with a slim chance of inheriting the family's 21,000 acres (the first son happened to outlive his half-brothers).

Mutual sadness brought them together. Violet missed Boughton. Euty missed his beloved mother, who had died recently, leaving him to the mercy of two stern spinster aunts, who had decided that he—the quintessential country gentleman—must enter the church. Euty loved hunting and riding, proclaiming London "a brutal place! no woods! no nothing! except theatres & pickpockets!!" As his niece put it, "It must have been _much_ more amusing to visit Violet Hunt than to stay at home."

The flirtation may have been a lark on Violet's part, a topsy-turvy version of the Boughton affair, but the adolescent Euty was dead serious. Whether there was an intimacy beyond tender kisses is uncertain. One has to read between the lines of the fifty-three letters Euty wrote to Violet from Eton and Yorkshire between September 1887 and June 1888. At best, the relationship remains ambiguous, a tangle of Victorian verbiage, of references to kisses on the riverbank and of innuendos: "your hair is always tidy, except when you have been with me for a little time. . . . Does Mrs. D know we were very intimate at Whitby?"

Also ambiguous is whether Euty was an innocent lad seduced by an older woman or whether twenty-four-year-old Violet was his second romance. His letters reveal that the thirty-two-year-old matron of his old school, Rose Peach, wrote him love letters, though he admitted to Violet only a "sisterly" affection for her.

There survives only one undated note from Violet to Euty, written on the back of a share application for the Folkestone Pier and Lift Company, probably during one of her visits to Eton: "Are you very ill? Oh I'm so awfully sorry—I knew you were going to be. Shall I come up now & say goodbye to you? for a moment or could you come down & speak to me— Have no paper in my room. Your loving, Violet." Euty responds on the same piece of paper, perhaps slipping it under the door: "No I am not very bad only headache & toothache but I am in bed—I am awfully sorry I can't come up to see you."

Euty was young. Euty was attentive. Euty was adoring: he worshipped Violet from the moment he saw her at a Whitby party that summer in her "dear striped dress," posed against a drawing-room window, looking out toward the lawn. They chatted and then sneaked away from the party to take a boat out on the River Esk, where they kissed. Over and over again in his letters, Euty describes the magic of those kisses. At other times his moods ranged from elation ("How funny it seems that you should care for a *boy*!!!") to jealousy ("one thing darling which I don't at all like & that is your having loved that man [Boughton]. I *can't* forget it").

Usually accompanied by her mother, Violet visited Euty at Eton during the fall and winter terms; Windsor was close by, and Alfred was working there on a study of the castle. In December she remained for six days, staying with friends. She and Euty chatted in his room, walked around Windsor, sketched by the Thames and sipped tea in shops away from the student herd. But Violet's departures always increased Euty's insecurity, and he worried about keeping her interested in "only a boy." Unable to concentrate, he fell behind in his studies and in desperation cheated on a Greek exam.

They performed all the rituals of young love. Violet made several sketches of him and kept his framed photograph in her bedroom. He sent her a pencil case for her twenty-fifth birthday. She sent him a sketch of Robin Hood's Bay and a lock of her auburn hair. He kissed her photos before going to bed. She gave him violets and poked around in his room, discovering—and reading—the letters from Rose Peach. She even teased Euty about marrying her when he reached eighteen. "No dear I should not like to run away with you for I should have nothing to keep you on darling!" he replied, adding, "I don't think darling that if your people were positively to forbid you to marry me that you would run away with me—would you?"

By February 1888 Euty's ardor had cooled. His father disapproved of Violet's visits, and the Cambridge entrance exams were approaching. He wrote fewer letters and begged off from meetings or made them insultingly brief ("Yes, come down on Tuesday, I can get away from a quarter to 3 till a quarter past five"). By May he wanted to end everything and forget it had ever happened ("I am _very_ sorry for one thing that I ever met you, & I heartily wish I could begin last summer again, for then I should not have gone beyond _very friendly_ terms with you, for I am heartily ashamed of the way I did act . . . I _do_ wish I loved you as much as you love me!! Why don't I? Curse me!").

Violet accepted his decision without feeling rejected; she could appreciate youthful problems. Three years later while visiting Cambridge—where she was shocked to see students at Newnham, the women's college, dancing together ("How dreary!")—she ran into Euty, an undergraduate at Trinity College. He surprised her with "a rather apathetic expression of renunciation in his face," a state, she surmised, caused by not being "allowed to participate of the ordinary joys of young manhood."

Still, the meeting brought back memories. "I am very fond of him, but there is something very bitter to hear in his attitude to me—so kind & loyal but not _épris_ [in love] any more—a mere boy! Why should I care? but it was so charming for me to be loved by him. . . . What a fool I was but _il faut vivre et aimer, n'importe qui_ [one must live and love—no matter who]. When they met the next year, Violet was less charitable: "Euty is developing a heavy jaw and seems a bit of a fool. How I did love him, once! He gave me a chaste brotherly kiss at parting by the umbrella stand and the plant in the hall or rather I gave him one . . . it was for the sake of old times; it was no earthly satisfaction to me."*

*After being graduated from Cambridge, Euty lived the country squire's life until 1898, when he was sent to Cairo for his health. He died there of blood poisoning at the age of twenty-seven. He never married and appears in _Their Hearts_ as Freddy Riven, her "small conquest," who was "tall, with a figure that even in clothes of a country tailor's confection" looked good.

□

When Violet's affair with Boughton ended, her sisters Venice, twenty-two, and Silvia, twenty-one, were waiting to marry. They worried that Violet would not follow tradition and, as the eldest, marry first. That Violet's complex life was inhibiting her sisters mattered not one whit to her; the sisterly relationships had always been competitive, combative, with tensions extending far beyond the usual sibling rivalries or adolescent jealousies. Violet and Venice were willful, stubborn, selfish. Silvia was quiet, patient, immature. Considered the ugly duckling, Silvia was ignored, while Violet tried to curb every "progressive instinct, every movement of natural growth" in Venice.

When Violet snidely told Ruskin that Venice was the "flower of the flock," she spoke the truth. Venice was the prototypical middle-class Victorian daughter; she cultivated friends who had country houses, was a good horsewoman, flirted only with umarried upper-class suitors and would marry above her social and economic station. Her husband, William Arthur Smith Benson, ten years her senior, was a follower of William Morris, whose esteemed decorating firm, Morris and Company, rejuvenated Victorian taste by promoting flowered chintzes and wallpapers.

Violet was horrified at having a brother-in-law "in trade," but Benson was far more than the small shopkeeper he appeared to be. He began by teaching metalworking, pottery and weaving at his workshop in Chiswick, where Venice met him as a student in one of his classes. Born in London and educated at Winchester and New College, Oxford, where he studied to be an engineer and met William Morris, he was the oldest in a large and talented family of four sons and three daughters. Frank, a Shakespearean actor-manager, would be knighted, and Godfrey, a Liberal politician and man of letters, became the first Baron Charnwood.

By the time of his retirement in 1920, Benson was a respected and successful designer, whose innovative lamps, combining copper and brass, made him a leader in the arts and crafts movement that began in Britain in the 1860s. He sold Art Nouveau pieces in Paris, and his experiments with reflectors led to lamps that produced more light than shadow. Described by contemporaries as reticent but possessing an "extraordinary gift of omniscience," Benson was the kind of man who could discourse on almost any subject, drawing on "an unusual fund of accurate information."

Marrying Benson was a social triumph for Venice and a social disgrace for Violet, who by rights should have married first; she was further humiliated when wedding gifts arrived addressed to her. In an uncharacteristic gesture of generosity, Venice allowed Violet to keep one gift: a gray Persian kitten, the first of many generations of cats that Violet would breed, then give away or keep as companions.

Violet chaperoned the engaged couple, pretending to be happy about the approaching wedding, which had the Hunt household in a dither of preparations. Alfred Hunt was shown off to the Bensons and their friends as the talented landscape painter; Uncle George Peacock, Dean of Ely, was brought to London to represent the prestigious Raine family. Venice's wedding concludes *Their Lives*, and Violet gives a ghastly description of the bride as "pulpy, calm, white, like a large pale slug, that has crept out on the garden walk after rain." The wedding reception was a nightmare for Violet: George Boughton was there with his wife and niece Flossie.

A year after the wedding, Benson opened a shop for his distinctive designs at 82 Bond Street, at the then unfashionable end of Oxford Street. The couple moved into a ground-floor flat at 29 Montague Square, off Baker Street, where Benson created a miniature Pompeiian courtyard in the back garden. Having lunch there, Violet said, was "a useful discipline," for Venice's world must be pleasant, "nobody may be ill or depressed in it!"

As a Morris follower, Benson was interested in handwork but soon became fascinated with the capabilities of mechanical production. He borrowed from his father and also from Margaret Hunt to help build a factory in Hammersmith. "Visitors to the works who knew him as a rather dreary artist," noted *The Times*, "were amazed and almost aghast to find themselves in what appeared to be an engineering workshop full of large machines . . . and a lacquering department which had benefitted so much from his inventive genius that constant efforts were made by trade rivals to penetrate its secrets." Benson was a worthy mate for the ambitious Venice.

The Bensons led a self-absorbed and childless life. Until the early 1900s when the relationship between the three sisters turned bitter, Violet took full advantage of the family connections. Through Frank Benson (with whom she flirted) and Godfrey Benson (who courted her), she met the theater elite and attended parliamentary and academic parties. But Godfrey, a future baron and author of acclaimed biographies of Abraham Lincoln and Theodore Roosevelt, was too austere and boring for Violet.

In April 1888 Boughton, after much badgering by Violet, agreed to meet her. The following month, when he came *"si heureux!"* to her studio, she felt their reconciliation "was complete." The flirtation started anew. At a West House party, where the Hunts were invited to keep up appearances, Boughton gave her a sign (a hand to his head) that he *"remembered yesterday* and did not disown me." But Boughton never committed himself to more than teasing encounters.

Following a trip to France, Violet was invited to Albert Fleming's country home in Scotland, a welcome diversion as her twenty-sixth birthday approached. Fleming, a lawyer and admirer of Ruskin's, had recently involved Margaret in an intrigue to stop Joan and Arthur Severn, Ruskin's niece and her husband, from institutionalizing the ailing old man and taking his property and money. Fleming may have invited Violet as a way to repay Margaret for her support, but it was matchmaking he had in mind. The only other houseguest was Fleming's protégé Harold C. Dowdall, a twenty-one-year-old Oxford undergraduate.

Arriving on September 7, Violet received a proposal on the ninth, as Dowdall drove her to church in the dog cart. "I thought he was insulting me, and I had to drive home, he was so careless and overcome. I begged him not to tell A.F. [Albert Fleming], but he did," she wrote. Melodrama followed upon melodrama. Fleming encouraged the match, offering to give the couple £250 a year if the Hunts matched the amount and agreed to postpone the wedding until Dowdall was twenty-three.

"I yielded, I was so plagued," wrote Violet, but then she turned ornery, and the engagement lasted only two days. "D[owdall] offended me with over zeal in some matter. I was angry, he took to his bed. At 9 o'clock A.F., who cannot help forcing the note, made me grant him an interview in his room, and D. gave me up, but I did not understand till after. A.F. took me aside, *wept* and upbraided me for a flirt—well I did flirt yesterday, but I cured D. of his infatuation, so A.F. owned that he loved me. What a kettle of fish." And that was the finale to Violet's second proposal.

Violet returned to a terrified London. While she was in France, the first of the Jack the Ripper killings had occurred on August 29 in Whitechapel. These macabre murders—unsolved to this day— brought the plight of the East End slum dwellers into the drawing rooms of the middle class. Although they were far removed from poverty-stricken areas of London, the Hunts and others were in a panic. The fear of sexually motivated crime, which pervaded London's middle class, was now spoken aloud—for it had happened not in Kensington or Knightsbridge but in the shameful depths of Whitechapel. By October 24, when Venice arrived at Tor Villa to play whist with her mother, three more prostitutes had been found slashed and eviscerated. That night Margaret escorted Venice home, "armed with a poker, for fear of 'Jack the Ripper'!" On November 9, when Silvia and Violet paid some evening calls, their "whole walk [was] coloured gloomily by the news of another Whitechapel murder."

Later in November Violet visited relatives of her mother's in Oxford. She had been to Cambridge, but this may have been her first glimpse of this university town, for she recorded: "Like Oscar Wilde, who was disappointed with the Atlantic, I am, rather, with Oxford. I thought the 'High' [Street] would be more like a mediaeval town, more 'trimmed.' " She met her infatuated undergraduate Dowdall, "looking very gorgeous," who came to tea at her aunt's and, to her surprise, treated her kindly. He saw her home and "renewed his suit more or less. He is mad." A few days later she told her diary that "H.D. came & made love to me, but I despise him, for despising *me!*"

Unlike her sisters, Silvia had no special beau and settled in 1889 for longtime friend John Walton Fogg-Elliot, a relative by marriage. (His father's deceased first wife was her maternal grandmother's sister.) Through the years the Hunts had visited the family at Elvet Hill, which John Walton, as the eldest, would inherit. He also built Bedburn Hall at Witton-le-Wear, south of Durham. Margaret Hunt gave him a small loan for the new house, which was designed by Willie Benson, Venice's husband. Initially, at least,

Margaret was generous to both sons-in-law, much to Violet's annoyance.

Violet loved Elvet Hill. There was "no asceticism, no rules, no coals to count, no mattresses to pick, logs of jam and new bread . . . gardens and paddocks, carriages, pony-carts, croquet, blackberrying expeditions, an uncared for library with heaps of old and queer books." She was particularly fascinated by the billiard room; its walls were covered with oars and cricket bats, and there were cases "with coloured plaster casts of great fish, and pictures of famous horses."

John Walton, said Violet, was "delicate, he did not tan easily, and his crystal-clear redness, and blue eyes gave him the waxen charm of a camellia, or a piece of china, especially when he was overtired." A portrait from 1906 shows a severe gentleman with dark, sinister eyes and a full black mustache. Like Euty, he wanted a carefree life as a country squire: at Jesus College, Cambridge, he ignored academics in favor of rugby and rowing. The only position he ever held was his late father's largely honorary post of justice of the peace.

Silvia was not his first choice; he loved Venice and believed mistakenly that she was interested in him. He was depressed after her marriage, and by 1889, when he was twenty-two and needed a wife to look after things, Silvia was twenty-four and desperate to escape Tor Villa. Flattered by any attention, Silvia agreed to wed and move to Durham, where she soon discovered her husband to be a boor and an indiscreet philanderer. For the wedding on November 21, Violet wore a lilac bridesmaid dress; Euty and Godfrey. Benson were groomsmen. Silvia looked lovely, although weeping "silently under her veil."

Now Violet was alone with her parents, the servants and frequent litters of cats. But she had taken her first steps toward a career in journalism, writing bits and pieces for magazines published by friends, and was warned by her father not to exploit her social position for news. As the decade drew to a close, she could boast of some success. Using the *nom de plume* Violet Herris, she published a short story, "A Thief in the Night," in *Belgravia*, receiving 30 shillings—"not bad for one's first story," she noted.

Although George Boughton was still on her mind, Violet did not ignore other suitors. She had a new admirer: avuncular Dr.

Henry Patrick Cholmeley, a twenty-eight-year-old Oxford man with a commendable collection of rare books; he had recently set up a medical practice in Kensington. Following their first meeting, when Violet consulted him about her indigestion, Cholmeley became a Tor Villa regular and a faithful—but unsuccessful—suitor.

Also pursuing Violet was an older married man, Walter Harris Pollock, who as editor of the *Saturday Review* had helped Margaret's career. A versatile scholar who wrote on fencing, Jane Austen and the French theater, Pollock was also a seasoned flirt. Though Violet resented his "eternal smirk," she did respond to his advances (but "not dangerously. I did not care for him, only I liked the excitement of flirting"). Margaret observed this new intrigue and warned Violet about Pollock becoming another Boughton.

During the season of 1889, at many parties and balls, Violet collected visual impressions of her favorite authors: Henry James was "fat & pleasant & growing old . . . taking his chair with him, like a snail in his shell, from lady to lady. . . . He doesn't look like marrying Sylvia du Maurier. He is afraid of a love scene in real life as he is in his stories." Thomas Hardy was "mean featured and unnoticeable in many ways & Elizabethan in type, with fine deep blue eyes, and reddish hair. His wife takes the words out of his mouth all the time! She is a lady much 'superior' to him . . . the daughter of a consumptive parson, and he the son of a stone mason."

Her journalism assignments kept her away from home at all hours, and she joined a bohemian group headed by Marc-André Raffalovich (Raff), a homosexual poet from a wealthy family of Russian-Jewish bankers living in Paris. They were introduced by Oscar Wilde at one of the lavish dinners Raff gave at the Café Royal. A onetime friend, Raff would turn against Wilde, particularly in his account of male homosexuality, *Uranisme et Unisexualité*. The book, published in France in 1896, contained the first full account of Wilde's trials to appear in any language.

Violet claimed that Raff, whom she called her "little Russian masher," had proposed marriage to her; he called her "a woman made for irregular situations." Violet observed that Raff was "extremely ugly, knows it, & has a confiding, ingenuous, apologetic manner, which is pretty." (It was said that Raff was so ugly his mother sent him to London to avoid looking at him.) In *Their Lives* he is Boris Ivanoff, who is looking for a marriage of convenience:

"He had not wanted to marry at all. But Christina was the only girl who had been even flightily kind to him, and his father had rather liked the idea of a simple English daughter-in-law." Saddened at her reproof, Boris tells his sister that his wife could have worked out "her own particular perdition under the shelter of my name. It was all I could give her. As it is I fear she will never marry. She'll run about the world, misusing her eyes and in the end do something rather great." Perhaps Violet should have accepted a life of freedom under the protection of an immensely rich husband; it was an arrangement for which she was well suited.

Though nonchalant about her slightly scandalous life, Violet often wondered why she had not married. She compared herself to Venice: "Why am I cleverer than she is—& yet I have made nothing of all my opportunities, so far? I don't write *much*—I don't draw—I don't *marry*. I feel pretty, but surely—whose fault is it? George's; who stole the best years of my life & threw them back at me 'Othello's occupations gone'—I feel as if I were waiting for something—all other affairs merely interludes—I love my mother but worry her & criticise her—my father *également* & when I get to bed I long to go back & talk lovingly to them & heal the wounds I have perhaps made—but one *knows* that it would only bother or make them worse: what is the good of repairing one emotion with another?"

Her sadness deepened on the death of Robert Browning in 1889. She thought him the perfect man, "an example of the noble age . . . a poet who has known how to control his presumed erratic impulses, and has left not an unkind word to be said of him . . . never forgot a friend, or did any cranky, ill tempered action that I know of . . . a testimony to the sanity of true genius."

Violet was touched by the candlelight service in Westminster Abbey when Browning was buried on December 31 and deplored the fact that to others the funeral was only a show. Her father and mother cried when the hymn "O God Our Help" was sung. At twenty-seven, with tears staining her face, she longed for a kindly man like Robert Browning.

PART TWO

1890-1907

5

The Rake's Progress

IN THE WINTER of 1890 an influenza epidemic kept fashionable London in bed. Theaters echoed with empty seats, "at homes" were canceled, and fruit merchants ran out of oranges, sold to fend off symptoms. Violet felt fine. She laced her corset as tightly as ever, and never forgot to carry a fan in case she felt faint. At sparsely attended parties, the "little dramas were painfully naked to the eye," she wrote. Guests argued about Rudyard Kipling's earthy stories (he "tumbles all his gold dust into one's lap for one to sift," she observed) and whispered about Oscar Wilde's veiled homosexual novel, *The Picture of Dorian Gray*. Irish Home Rule was debated, but Violet dismissed the issue, calling Irishmen "babies" who could never govern themselves.

Though socially active, Violet was aware that time was being filled rather than experienced. All her friends were getting married, and she dreamily imagined that for herself: "I know I shall be so happy as I walk up the aisle that I shant know if I am standing on my head or my heels," but she feared that life was "growing quiet and old-maidenly."

Voices from the past reminded her of happier times. One day while reading *Tristram Shandy* after lunch, she was startled by a knock. It was Euty. He poked his head in the door and asked her to change a ten-shilling note. "Well, I *was* pleased to see him, but how *young* I must have been two years ago, when that nice boy raised all sorts of emotions in me! I am wiser but I am not sure that I enjoy it all so [much] as I did. It is nice to 'be in love with love.' "

Henry Cholmeley, the stuffy physician who passively pursued Violet, fussed over her health, analyzed her face powder and gave her dyed-green carnations, a symbol popularized by Oscar Wilde, which was the distinguishing mark of homosexuals in Paris. In her diary, he remained the "faithful" Cholmeley. Walter Pollock, the flirtatious older married man with his clever conversation and world-weary seductiveness, still pestered her.

The most eligible man circling round was D. S. (Dugald Sutherland) MacColl, a refined Oxonian, three years her junior, and a Newdigate winner like Ruskin, Wilde and her father. He was art critic for *The Spectator* and had a private income enabling him to travel, paint, write, lecture and organize art exhibits, including, in 1900, the first in Britain featuring the French Impressionists. He was molding an influential voice in the art world, and would one day be named director of the Tate Gallery and the Wallace Collection. MacColl was tall and slender, with chiseled, aristocratic features and a manner bespeaking an inner rigidity—not the earthy, exotic type Violet preferred.

One evening MacColl and Cholmeley dined at Tor Villa. Their competition amused Violet as they tried to outwit each other, "neither shining as much as he would have done separately." Violet pronounced them "as jealous as two girls and worse show it, which women are generally too clever to do." Bored with these suitors, she aroused in herself an infatuation with Frank Benson, Venice's brother-in-law, one of the famed actor-managers who followed Henry Irving. Benson's touring companies were nurseries for the English stage, bringing Shakespeare, often for the first time, to the provinces and to America. Benson staged the first Stratford-on-Avon Festival in 1886 and was knighted in 1916.*

Violet spent most evenings in the dress circle, watching the married Benson play Hamlet and weeping during the death scene. That he had never kissed an actress on stage added to his allure.

---

*Following his curtain call at the Drury Lane Theatre on May 2, 1916, Benson, clad in the bloodstained robes of the murdered Julius Caesar, was knighted by King George V as he knelt in the private room behind the royal box. It was the only time the ceremony has ever been performed in a theater. Although rumor had it that a stage sword was used, there is no evidence of this.

She flirted with him because she was "tired & bored & I feel I am wasted—I miss George awfully— Oh, it is dull without a lover." Even as she pledged not to fall in love with Frank Benson, she mused how "a hopeless passion" keeps "one up through life— especially through old maid-dom."

Critically astute, she cared more about the play and the performances than most theatergoers, who came only to gawk at the fashions and the scandalous lovers. The theater was *the* social occasion, and patrons expected to be received there as in their own drawing rooms; even program sellers wore the apron of a parlor-maid. Aristocratic ladies decked themselves out in diamonds, which glittered in the new electrical brightness; in fact, the first public building electrified in London was Richard D'Oyly Carte's Savoy Theatre on the Strand, which had twelve hundred arc lamps.

After the theater Violet met her bohemian friends for a late dinner, sometimes at the Savoy restaurant or the Café Royal. She finally had her own latchkey, letting herself in with the cat and the milk bottles, but she worried that emancipation was leading nowhere: "I wish *I* had something on hand—I want to be made to work," she wrote in her diary, and then escaped into Paul Bourget's vulgar French novel *Le Disciple*.

At a party one Sunday in June 1890, while involved in a heated discussion about Kipling, Violet was introduced to Oswald John Frederick Crawfurd, the British consul in Oporto, Portugal. Violet found him a "very goodlooking dark-haired sort of George—a better nose & a worse mouth . . . very tall & stately . . . priggish & conceited . . . an Italian bandit," whose eyes were "dark brown, with a kind of smothered, almost blue, light in them; the eye-lids had a bulldog droop at the corners." He dyed his hair black (shocking in Victorian times), was fifty-seven and married, with a well-earned reputation as a libertine. Violet was fascinated with his forceful, passionate personality; it was an explosion of feeling, frightening and irresistible.

Born in 1834, only four years after Alfred Hunt, Crawfurd was the only son of Horatia Ann Perry, goddaughter of Lord Horatio Nelson, and John Crawfurd, who became a recognized expert on Indochina, producing, among other works, a two-volume dictionary of the Malay language. His mother, who died when he was twenty-one, was a delicate, repressed creature, bullied by a cold, pedantic husband. In *Their Hearts,* her second autobiographical novel, Violet has the Crawfurd character, at the age of ten, cutting the wedding ring off his mother's finger to protest his father's unkindness to her. His father had started his career as an Edinburgh-educated physician in India, moving on to civil and political posts in Java, Siam, Indochina, Burma and Singapore, where he replaced Sir Stamford Raffles as governor in 1823.

Educated as an English gentleman at Eton and Oxford's Merton College, Crawfurd left university without a degree to follow his father into the foreign service. After completing a junior clerkship, he was posted to Oporto, the center for the export of port wine since the 1700s. He worked his way up to consul and stayed in Portugal for twenty-five years, enjoying the good life provided by the British wine trade.

Initially considered suitable only for the boorish country squire demanding immediate stupefaction, port's sweet taste eventually seduced the aristocracy, who passed it in a crystal decanter at meal's end, by custom always to the left, after the ladies had departed to the drawing room for coffee and gossip. In Oporto, dinners were held at the Factory House, a bastion of Britishness since 1785 and probably one of the most exclusive clubs in the world. (Today its thirty-one members, all Englishmen, meet for lunch every Wednesday to taste the vintage.) As the ranking consular officer, Crawfurd traveled in the highest social circles and charmed his way into the bed of many a bored wife. He later boasted to Violet of illegitimate sons attending Eton.

Crawfurd immediately sensed Violet's lust for excitement, and he asked to call at Tor Villa; within days he was entertaining the Hunts with tales of the recent student riots in Oporto, the high point of his long career. Up until 1890, Crawfurd's diplomatic jousting had been fairly routine. But then the Portuguese occupied British territory in East Africa, and following Lord Salisbury's demand that they withdraw, anti-British riots erupted in Oporto and Lisbon. Crawfurd's house was stoned, and the students demanded his recall as British consul. He stood firm and later was decorated with the Order of St. Michael and St. George for his efforts.

Planning to retire in 1891, Crawfurd had comfortably settled his wife at Queen Anne's Mansions. He had married Margaret Ford, daughter of Richard Ford, who wrote the highly regarded _Handbook to Spain;_ their only child, a son, died in infancy. Invited to their home for tea, Violet observed that his wife was "_passé_ well-dressed, almost too clever . . . very pretty, yet sad and a potential virago." She was also, conveniently so for Crawfurd, a Victorian invalid, with no specific disease, only a chronic frailty and a lingering depression—weaknesses then regarded as attributes of social refinement. She stayed in bed when it suited her and luxuriated at spas, receiving special attention and care, and was not expected to exert herself. As her antithesis, Violet wondered if Crawfurd was kind to her. "He is certainly not _true_ to her in a certain sense. She doesn't like me—but she thinks me clever."

Scarcely a month after Violet met Crawfurd, Margaret Hunt astutely envisioned a replay of Walter Pollock or, worse, George Boughton. Violet assured her mother that she was "tired of unreal passions," but after only four meetings Crawfurd bluntly asked whether she wanted him to fall in love with her. Violet was shocked. "It was all so strange & so sudden & I did not expect it of him," she wrote. "No indeed. I hope you won't," she told him, hinting that she loved another. To protect herself, she doubled her efforts to charm eligible bachelors, such as Joseph Austen Chamberlain, the half-brother of Neville, the future Prime Minister, and a young man who would himself become Chancellor of the Exchequer.

Undaunted, Crawfurd "put dangerous sentiments on paper!" which worried Violet, for "a man that writes recklessly never takes care of the letters he receives—so I shall take care—poor George never wrote one compromising thing on paper." Crawfurd followed up his fervent correspondence with an unscheduled visit to Tor Villa, where he found Violet, by her description, in a strange "half asleep state—already half hypnotised." When he did not apologize for his previous impertinent conversation, she reminded him that she loved another. Instead of being rejected, Crawfurd appeared sympathetic, and she "loved him for it (almost). What shall I do?" she asked herself. "I swing like a pendulum between good & bad instincts— Why would it be so wrong to snatch a little love where it is? I get on best too with an 'homme arrive' who understands me."

Unlike most unmarried Victorian women, Violet did not cultivate female confidants, preferring the company of men, particularly married men to whom she could comfortably talk of delicate matters. Her diary was a private cave which she nightly entered to assuage loneliness, where she confronted her daring impulses, often writing in French. "I must be good for my sake—but my instincts I fear are really bad—I *want* people to love me—but I don't seem to care for young men," she wrote. "I feel a dual consciousness in me—one that makes me behave like a sort of Sarah Bernhardt—lead men on—the other that laughs at me & then criticises from a dramatic point of view—only with George was I absolutely singlehearted—I thought only of him—& see how he repays me!"

And again: "No I am not ashamed of myself at *present*—a woman is a woman—& it is so long since anybody has kissed me— Why is everything to end in marriage?— But I suppose I want it to—I want an anchor, a husband I could adore. But I can not make up my mind to 'decline' in mediocrities. Shall I flirt to the end of my natural existence—ie. 30-or-35—or marry & reform."

The summer exodus to Whitby postponed any fateful decision, but did not curb Crawfurd's provocative correspondence. While reading one of his letters, Violet feigned shock but secretly enjoyed his frankness, which made her feel like a naughty French heroine. "He does not love me—yet!" she wrote. "Then why write such things to a woman who merely attracts him but does not inspire the holy passion, only a base one, as he is at pains to show, without considering how insulting to me! I ought to be *so* angry but somehow I can't be. . . . Once you give a man tacitly the right to speak to you quite openly of everything—and that is what I love to do— on principle—you have not the right to resent plainspokenness, nor do I." She answered his letter, went to bed and read *Femme Impossible*. She barely slept; she recalled the night as "a strange debauched kind of vigil" between her "own bewildered thoughts and the practical indecencies of the book which followed. . . . I am not immoral but somehow I felt so that night."

Returning to Whitby had revived memories of George Boughton and Euty Strickland. She was depressed at first but, once settled into Broad Ings Farm, concentrated on meeting new people like Bram Stoker, Henry Irving's manager, and greeting old friends like George du Maurier, the *Punch* artist who would write *Trilby,* the novel which gave its name to the snap-brimmed hat. Invited to tea by the Hunts, Stoker struck Violet as a "nice healthy stalwart Irish-man as sweetnatured and gentlemanly as it is possible to be." Over a plate of cakes he pronounced his views on actress Ellen Terry (pathos but no passion) and Tennyson (a villainous mouth). During the summer of 1890 Stoker worked on his *Dracula* plot: he already had met Van Helsing's alter ego (Professor Arminius Vambery, a Budapest folklorist) and, seeking further inspiration, found it in the story of an 1885 Whitby shipwreck which became the *Demeter* chartered by Count Dracula to bring fifty wooden boxes filled with dirt to Purfleet, Essex.*

Though Violet sought to shroud herself in solitude, family life intruded. Silvia was pregnant, and Alfred, who was ailing, wanted a grandson, a namesake. Godfrey Benson and D. S. MacColl arrived for a visit, making "a pleasant change from conversations about oneself and one's psychology to discussions about the present French Republic." The presence of the eligible Benson brother prompted Violet to take a closer look, but he did "not know what a woman is, though he is not quite so absolutely unsexed as Frank his brother." She found MacColl clever and poetical, with a fine accent and gestures ("I think a woman could refuse a man with a fine tenor voice *nothing*"), but he irritated her by cutting great chunks off the loaf of bread at dinner. In a matter of weeks both suitors were so annoying that she could not bear to be in the same room with them.

Despite physical complaints, Alfred continued the sketching regimen synonymous with a Whitby summer. Every afternoon his wife pounded up Abbey Hill to lure him home out of the chilling wind. He had fallen in love with a view of the ruined abbey, but had to perch himself near the top of East Cliff to paint it against the sunset, and refused to budge until the tracery of the windows stood out against the vermilion sky. Even when unwell, he preferred

---

*Whitby figures in three chapters, with Stoker utilizing the town's distinctive features: the 199 steep steps leading to St. Mary's Church, the graveyard, the abbey and the unpredictable North Sea weather ("masses of seafog came drifting inland—white, wet clouds, which swept by in a ghostly fashion, so dank and damp and cold that it needed but little effort of imagination to think that the spirits of those lost at sea were touching their living brethren with the clammy hands of death, and many a one shuddered as the wreaths of sea-mist swept by"). Stoker did not return to Whitby; he wrote *Dracula* in the Scottish village of Cruden Bay, below Aberdeen. It was published in 1897.

to sketch from nature, carefully watching the lighting conditions. Gout aggravated his weather-exposed hands, but he objected to creaming them for fear of soiling the canvas.

In mid-September, Silvia arrived in Whitby with her new baby, christened Rosamond. Alfred did not conceal his disappointment that his first grandchild was a girl. "He has so little prospect of any other grandchild," Violet noted sympathetically. "Venice is evidently going to have none and I shall make a mess of it, he feels." There was a lot to tell about the birth. Silvia had locked herself in her bedroom, and her husband broke down the door with an ax; later she mistook the water bottle for the baby and "pounded away at it with feeble blows hoping to kill it . . . saying so." When she couldn't nurse, she told the doctor to "take him [*sic*] away and put him in the Zoo." Violet was repulsed by the ugly "long yellow legged rickety baby," for which she "had no fondness."

Crawfurd's ardent courtship by mail continued. "The history of the last few weeks has been wild from a moral point of view," wrote Violet. "I am leading a sort of double life. O.C. in his letters makes me a scene every day more or less. . . . His last letter but one was a declaration of love. . . . I think he really meant it but I felt bound to answer as if I didn't think he was sincere. . . . There would be something very ridiculous in my being engaged for a second time in an intrigue with a married man! He is aware of the history of George but it does not, apparently, deter him. He is *really* in earnest. I have not done anything to be ashamed of—yet—and I won't. It isn't possible to flirt by *letter,* yet O.C. would have now that I have. He is enraged with me—for my *virtue.* I think I can manage not to make a fool of myself with him. . . . He telegraphed to me today and poor dear Papa never asked any questions!!"

That same evening her heart skipped a beat when she saw Euty at a dance in the Saloon; they kissed affectionately and she left with him, strolling arm in arm up the cliff as they had three summers before. Her abandoned escort, MacColl, remarked grimly, "You've lost your character tonight!" Since Violet never worried about gossip at the worst of times, it hardly mattered; what mattered was that she had not been kissed since breaking off with Euty. Why not take pleasure (particularly known pleasure) when offered? After all, "a woman cannot live altogether without love." When Euty visited her the following morning, however, the romance of moonlight was gone, and she remorsefully pronounced her carrot-top love a "commonplace, tongue-tied young Briton with far too large a development of jaw."

Celebrating her twenty-eighth birthday on September 28, Violet consoled herself that she had "plenty of lovers, of a sort, quite enough to amuse me, but my looks, such as they are, cannot last for ever, and then where am I?" When she thought of her first lover, she wrote longingly that she had "not looked into the eyes of a man I love since George," who "initiated me into the secret of what I *could* feel and has now left me—*inassouvie* [empty]."

When Silvia and her baby traveled home to Bedburn, Violet accompanied them; on their arrival the new father immediately packed up for a hunting trip, leaving the sisters to an awkward (for Violet) domesticity of reading, sewing and visiting the nursery. Crawfurd's love letters reached her there, imploring a return to London; but Violet felt "safer away."

For the first time since her difficult childbirth, Silvia saw the broken door (which her husband had inconsiderately not repaired) and, remembering her fear and pain, fell to the floor, screaming hysterically. Violet's presence was no comfort. Silvia criticized her sister's haughty behavior, berating her one evening for not letting a guest finish his sentences. In her peremptory North Country manner, Violet shot back that the "best blood in England accepted me with this bad habit, why not a little country doctor?"

When Violet had had enough of country boredom, she left for London, bringing back a black kitten for her father. Alfred named him Tommy and took him into his studio, where he grew up, a companion, a silent listener and observer to Hunt's triumphs and failures; in fact, Tommy became closer to Alfred than any of his children.

Once inside Tor Villa, Violet wired Crawfurd, and an unchaperoned meeting was scheduled in the South Kensington Museum, for tea. They greeted each other in the foyer, and without ceremony Crawfurd suggested they become lovers, "living in the bonds of social custom and observance" to spare his wife and her parents. He wanted a surreptitious relationship with no public acknowledgment of Violet as his mistress; he would pay for private dinners and comfortable seduction rooms. In return, she would have an experienced lover. Arguing the situation in her diary, Violet concluded that she desired Crawfurd "out of sheer *ennui*—as well as a great liking for him," but made no move to accept his offer.

As Christmas approached, she made a kettle holder for Cholmeley ("no one shall say that I encourage him!") and a letter case for Crawfurd, which she sent off early, hoping for an immediate thank-you in person. By Christmas Eve there was still no reply. "How I do miss him—at least his letters," she lamented. "I am walking the paths of virtue with a vengeance, and great dullness." Then she met George Boughton at an exhibition; he took her hand, pressing it affectionately and driving out all thoughts of Crawfurd. "No other man's hand clasp can stir me like that of George," she wrote, "and yet I had a wild thought of saying to George, 'I've got another. What shall I do with him?' "

When the bells rang in the new year, 1891, Violet was with MacColl at his parents' home. Everyone sang madrigals, and she wondered "if it will be all as nice as now next year? For I am very happy in the main and the world keeps me amused. How miserable I shall be when as Madame Récamier said the crossing sweepers no longer turn to look at me in the street!" When she returned from the party, there was a noncommittal note from Crawfurd, thanking her for the gift. "I've lost him, I suppose? But if I have it is in a way that is very creditable to us both—exalted virtue on my side—care for my reputation, more or less, on his."

On New Year's Day, as she dressed in a green tea gown for dinner, Crawfurd unexpectedly arrived, bearing a silver box as a gift and the message that he could be neither a friend nor a lover at the moment. Violet was visibly shaken, on the verge of tears, but remained calm.

"Shall you come and see us sometimes?" she inquired politely.

"Not very often."

"Did you want to burn the letter case I sent you?"

"Yes," he replied. "I did, but I felt if I did, it would be burning you."

Rebounding quickly from this enigmatic conversation, which she recorded in her diary, Violet explored London, unchaperoned, with "The Beamer," a British lawyer who lived in Serbia, whom she had met at a party. He scorned British conventions and challenged Violet to an adventure at the right psychological moment. For their first excursion they went to the Aquarium, an amusement park that displayed freaks. "He did not treat me casually or any different," she wrote, "as if I had lost ground by going alone with him. It was an awful thing to do but one must have a lark some-times—and worse, I should dearly like to go [to] the theatre with him as he continually asks me to." A week later she did—to a matinee of _The Dancing Girl,_ and later to see Lillie Langtry in _Cleopatra._ She felt liberated and daring. She was a rebel.

Violet was loitering around London, and her parents were being lenient because they felt Cholmeley was on the verge of proposing. Violet feared the confrontation: "I wish I was still only twenty and could say I should like to 'wait,' but at twenty-eight—what excuse has one?" Cholmeley had spoken to Margaret about his plans to buy a practice in South Kensington, an area Violet hated, but his partner backed out at the last moment. Instead of asking Violet to marry him, he brought his mother to live with him at Onslow Crescent.

"My spirits rose at this apparent postponement of a decision and I was quite civil and very kind to C," she wrote. Margaret, however, was not pleased. Her daughter was unmarried, her husband unhonored and she, who tried so hard, was unappreciated. "I hate being shut up in the house with failures!" she screamed at Violet one day, who accepted the rebuke, commenting that "those are the kind of things she says that make people afraid of her." But Margaret was not just frustrated or angry, she was bitter, and remained so, for her husband and favorite daughter would never live up to her expectations.

Crawfurd's change of mind about initiating an affair may have been influenced by his plans for a career in publishing. For many years he had contributed to Frederic Chapman's _Fortnightly Review,_ which published his articles on the history, customs and sports of Portugal, and he had several novels to his credit, notably _Sylvia Arden,_ published in 1888. Of greater importance, though, was his friendship with Chapman, whose firm, Chapman & Hall, published the works of the Brownings, Trollope and Meredith and owned the copyrights to Dickens' and Carlyle's works. There was also gossip about Crawfurd and the sixty-eight-year-old Chapman's young second wife, Annie Marion Harding, and the paternity of her daughter Reine.

In 1891 Chapman was ailing and had but four years to live.

His son by his first marriage had chosen a military career, and Chapman thought about Crawfurd taking his place. The literary elite, however, saw Crawfurd as a dilettante, and were surprised when Chapman named him editor of the *New Quarterly Magazine*, helped him to launch the illustrated journal *Black and White* and later made him a director and then managing editor of Chapman & Hall.

The Athenaeum's obituary preserved this attitude, describing Crawfurd's attitude to literature as "always that of the cultured amateur rather than that of the professional worker. Books and 'the play' were to him the most amenable diversions of a busy career, and he was never obliged, like many of his contemporaries, to adopt them as his principal means of support. It was not unnatural, therefore, that such work as he did should have possessed the shortcomings, no less than the qualities, of work undertaken mainly as a means of recreation."

This was a biased view. As Violet learned to her dismay, Crawfurd took his work very seriously, putting it before any of his relationships with women. He sincerely cared about the success of *Black and White,* the magazine that launched Violet's career; with it he sought to revive the art of illustration, printing high-quality reproductions of etchings and line drawings (he had photography as competition, particularly the new Kodak hand-held camera).

Black and White would survive for twenty-one years, under various editors. Crawfurd published articles by Hardy, Swinburne, Bret Harte and Robert Louis Stevenson (who received a princely £1,000 for a dull serial on the South Seas that Violet disliked). Every issue had a dialogue, a story told without description or narrative reflection. Violet excelled at this genre. A born chatterbox, she was passionate, impulsive and tactless; she loved gossip and eavesdropping, so writing a dialogue was no different than telling anecdotes about Lady So-and-So at the dinner table.*

At *Black and White*'s publication party on January 28, 1891, Violet arrived with her mother and immediately spied George

_____

*Crawfurd encouraged three Hunt women to write for him, and their talents may be compared in *Dialogues of the Day,* an anthology he edited in 1895. Margaret's contribution was "The Girls He Left Behind Him" (three girls flirting to catch a soldier), Silvia's "Doubly Sold" (women shopping) and Violet's "The End of the Beginning" (wives shed boring husbands to flirt at a Henley houseboat weekend).

Boughton—without his wife—looking like "a wrinkled pippen" in a badly fitting frock coat. The former lovers found a quiet corner for a long talk, but were interrupted when Crawfurd wanted to introduce Boughton to someone. "That is the man!" Crawfurd later said, pointing to Boughton. It was only an educated guess. Violet had hinted at the circumstances of her first affair but never mentioned a name. She lowered her eyes and was silent. Crawfurd leaned over, murmuring softly, "My God, how I love you." At that moment, Boughton glanced across the room. "Words cannot tell how awkward I felt," she said, "standing between those two *illegitimates*." When Violet compared Boughton to Crawfurd, she preferred her former lover. "I'd go anywhere for him, not from esteem or reverence, or admiration, but from downright sense of belonging to him."

As another Royal Academy election approached, Violet plotted to help elect her father, who was becoming more and more befuddled, unable even to remember which guests to escort into dinner. At the same time she hoped to rekindle her romance of five years past. She wrote Boughton to ask for his vote, and the following day met his wife on Campden Hill Road. "Miss Hunt, I gave your note to Georgie," said Kate. "It came when he was out and I opened it." Violet wanted to *"riposter,"* as she told her diary, but could not.

Arriving home, she read Boughton's reply: he had voted for Hunt, but a young Scottish painter named David Murray won. "A little less bluntness and more sympathy would have been kinder but he meant well," Violet wrote, noting that Murray, "who sits at Papa's feet and truly calls him Master admires him and is no mean artist, but young enough to wait."

With the launching of *Black and White,* Crawfurd was quite the man-about-town, looking sinister in a long black coat and astrakhan collar; Violet's friends referred to him as "The Melodramatic Oswald Crawfurd." Still awestruck, Violet accepted his every criticism. Once he demanded that she take off "that frightful" hat, saying that she dressed "very unbecomingly." If Violet was insecure about any one thing, it was her wardrobe. With a clothing allowance of only £25 a year, plus whatever extra shillings she earned from her writing, she was constantly economizing. What was available, she recycled; the lilac ostrich feather from her bridesmaid hat ended up on a black straw, which she wore all winter. Once Cholmeley loaned her a yellow dress of his grandmother's, which Violet said made her look like Polly Peachum in *The Beggar's Opera*. Bravely she survived the evening, but "the dress was too old and dirty to do for the Muirs' smart light rooms."

Not being able to compete with fashionably dressed women, she depended on her intellect and wit to distinguish her, and sublimated her bitterness in diary entries, describing how she looked ("I got myself up all in black and it was a failure. I am too skinny"), and how frightful other women looked in their outrageous French frocks. Too often, though, an unbecoming or inappropriate dress ruined her evening, or no one complimented her when she looked attractive.

Crawfurd's impertinence inexorably drew Violet to him; it was a seductive tool perfected by years of practice. One day she concocted an excuse to visit him at home when his wife and servants were absent ("Mama knows I went and somehow does not see the full enormity of it"). While there she flirted shamelessly and on leaving asked for a kiss. He hesitated, then bent forward, kissing her on the eyes and the mouth, stunning her with the force of his passion. Crawfurd said he had "awakened" her, but Violet demurely insisted she felt nothing.

Then Crawfurd cleverly retreated, ignoring Valentine's Day, which made Violet want him even more. Cholmeley brought flowers, and she feared he was going to propose. The following week Godfrey Benson and D. S. MacColl escorted her to the opening of Ibsen's *Rosmersholm* at the Vaudeville Theatre, which featured a "new woman" character called Rebecca West. Everyone had an opinion about the Scandinavian playwright, whom many thought obscene. Violet conceded that Ibsen was a thinker but "a childish thinker . . . a dramatist of a nationality only just beginning to dare to think for itself." MacColl, in a witty mood, said the Norwegians were merely "a nation of savages in connection with a good circulating library."

One day in late February, Crawfurd invited Violet for tea at a restaurant on Lisle Street, with instructions to meet him outside. Violet wondered what unconventional situation she was getting into ("What was it? An hotel? A private house? Or what Humphry Ward calls a *cabinet particulier?*"). She went, of course, being "so curious of life and so greedy of experience," and grateful to "the man who shows it to me before I perhaps marry Ch. [Cholmeley] and get mewed up in conventionalities."

After conspicuously walking up and down for more than an hour, she returned home to find a telegram postponing the meeting. More sad than angry, she worried, "Shall I ever go now? It may be something dreadful that I have been saved from? Oh I wish I knew what precise degree of badness on his part it implied? Isn't a girl ignorant?" Although she pretended to be, Violet certainly was not ignorant.

The Lisle Street meeting was rescheduled, and Crawfurd promised to be well behaved, wanting only to talk privately. At the restaurant, with its Italianate patio lined with large flowerpots, he silently led her by the hand upstairs and opened the door to a room with red curtains, a large gilt-framed mirror over the sofa and a piano. The fire was lit and a table set for tea, with biscuits and cognac. Kisses and caresses followed, but Violet stubbornly refused intimacy.

After two hours, Crawfurd paid the £2 tariff for what Violet referred to as the "interview." Then he turned on her, exclaiming in French: "Do you know where I am going after having met you and not having made love to you and after your having played with my senses, stirred up the flames of my desire? I am going to listen to _The Messiah_ at the Albert Hall." Violet did not record her retort to this upstaging.

More "interviews" followed in the _chambre rouge;_ each time Violet stopped short of giving herself to him. She was content to use her emotions to achieve an effect, excited at being devious and detached; but once she slept with Crawfurd, the control would pass to him. Boughton had taught her that fact of life. Crawfurd said he was the kind of man who should never marry. Violet did not believe him.

"I knew if I once gave in," said Violet craftily, "I could make him. I pretended I agreed with him—he will never get the chance. She won't die. They never do. Kate [Boughton] didn't." Embarrassing her parents worried her more than sullying her reputation. "I myself am dreadfully ashamed when I reflect on what I am going to do—am I?" she wrote. "Still I do feel as if I could honestly say to Mamma—'I am my own mistress and I must lead my own life.

I love you and I am your loving daughter and so I will take care not to disgrace you.' "

In May, Venice's godmother invited the family to Grasse in the south of France. Violet feigned interest in the trip, but remained in London because she would "only vegetate abroad with them." As soon as her parents were on the boat train, she was off to a private view with Venice, with plans to meet Crawfurd afterward. She dressed for him in an ecru skirt topped with a black net blouse trimmed with sequins. ("It didn't look right but what could I do. I was terrified of Venice seeing under my coat—blest if she cared!") Violet was free to do "all the lovely, wild, mad things we may do and perhaps shall do?"

During their "interviews" on Lisle Street and their lunches in Soho and their walks in Kensington Gardens, Crawfurd made it clear that if they became involved he might not be faithful. Again Violet ignored his words: she would change him. But she did worry about the twenty-eight-year age difference: "Old as he is, he is worth a hundred of *cette jeunesse* that doesn't understand me. I am beginning to consider it *a reasonable* passion if a man of the world, strong, clever, passionate, sets himself, which indeed I fear he has done—to conquer the affections of a girl like me, he can hardly fail and every year of his age is only a link in his armour. My dual consciousness which only the most absolutely passionate love can ever suppress, sees well enough the bathos, the comic, foolish, futile side of it all—it hurts me so when I hear him called an elderly dandy as Old Maxwell did at the Academy Soiree."

In August when her parents went to Durham, she put on her serge suit with the pink-and-white-striped bodice and a sailor hat with two veils, packed her sleeping gown and underwear (in her mother's Gladstone bag) and took a four-wheeler to Charing Cross Station, where Crawfurd greeted her. He escorted her into a first-class compartment, drew the curtains and pulled her down on his knees, telling her, *"Ma Chérie, c'est ta nuit de noces"* (My darling, this is your wedding night).

Arriving at the Falcon Hotel in Gravesend, they checked into separate rooms. It was cold and windy, but they walked in the garden, looking at the boats waiting for the tide, delaying the inevitable. Finally she said suddenly, "in a voice I hardly knew for my own; Look here, I'm going to bed." They made love, and in the morning he kissed her eyes; she turned her blue-stone ring around so it looked like a wedding band for all to see.

On her return to Tor Villa, heady and happy, she "slept like a child" in the bed she was born in, and on awakening desired more perfumed, apricot-colored nights.

6

Victorian Sex Games

Violet and Crawfurd were formidable equals in
fueling desire, particularly at keeping jealousy—that great aphro-
disiac—alive during a seven-year affair that was rooted more in
remorse than love. Violet, the consummate flirt, wanted to deceive
a man just enough to make him want her. Initially she did not share
Crawfurd's philandering philosophy; yielding to his rules created a
tangled psychological skein that put them through hell, making a
fulfilling relationship impossible.

Fights followed reconciliations with such frequency that they
were a necessary stimulus for passion. Both lovers were emotionally
damaged, unable to separate love from possession or passion from
domination. Violet felt she was cold, incapable of selfless love. "I
have a very twisted heart," she told her diary. "It took a kink in
growing somehow, like those boughs one sees that have started
wrong from the very trunk of the tree."

The seduction achieved, Crawfurd demanded the right to live
as before: time for his work, time for his wife and—unknown to
Violet—time for a prior mistress. Crawfurd did not reveal her name,
but Violet soon identified her as Frederic Chapman's wife, Annie.
As for Violet, she had to promise fidelity, no flirting, no exciting
escapades; an exception was made for the docile Cholmeley. Any
breach of conduct had to be confessed immediately. She accepted
these restrictive conditions as long as Crawfurd gave her the greater
part of his time. But what kind of love was this? If Crawfurd loved

two women at the same time, he really loved neither, she reasoned. Yet she still succumbed to a cruel cycle of truth games and male domination. The excitement of passion darkly tinged with fear was irresistible.

Her first unburdening involved, not surprisingly, George Boughton. Unchaperoned, she had attended a party at the home of Mrs. Humphry Ward, author of the popular novel *Robert Elsmere,* and there was Boughton, also alone. In an impulsive moment she asked him to take her home. As soon as the brougham moved down the street she flung her arms around him, "murmuring little moans of love and remorse." Boughton asked her what was wrong.

"Do you love me?" Violet demanded.

"You know I do."

"Take me somewhere."

"How can I? I know of nowhere."

"Don't you?" she asked scornfully. "There *are* places."

"Yes I know . . . kept by private detectives with holes in the walls. *Troux* Judas . . ."

Arriving at Tor Villa, she lured him inside so she could light a cigarette, and sent the maid off to bed, after introducing Boughton as her uncle. Alone in the drawing room, she embraced him, saying again and again, "You still love—you do, you do . . ."

"Yes, yes," he answered. "I've never seen any woman like you. I will marry you the moment I can."

"No matter what—I do?"

Boughton took her teasing seriously, and asked tenderly, "Nothing very bad, is it?"

She was "on the point of letting out everything. For tomorrow I was going to the other in spite of myself . . . George loves me a thousand times more than he does. The other has a mistress: George has nobody."

They separated with a kiss on the doorstep. "I was quiet. I had had my kiss. We parted . . . it was as he might have been going to the next world. Now, am I going to confess it all to OC tomorrow? I ask myself. I have promised to be truthful and I will be. The last words OC said to me were, 'Oh be faithful to me!'

"And I said, 'Yes—I hope so.' But I am *volage* [fickle] . . . not meaning it a bit. What made me say it? . . . Oh poor, poor George!

He is too good to me . . . and the other is too bad—I mean too kind only to be cruel. What am I to do? Not only be on with the new love, but keep the old one on! Only George Sand understood this kind of woman I think. . . . I must decide between them . . . But at any rate I will tell OC and he will want to know if George did make me feel or not? Did he? I love him deeply but—he doesn't interest me anymore. I have grown out of him. The other man's splendid energy and a certain want of caution which George always keeps beside him fascinate me. George would never burn his ships as the other does writing love letters recklessly all over the place— letters I wouldn't like any one to know he wrote me. George is *diablement prudent*—that about detectives and *troux* Judas! Now would George—but this is a mean suspicion—spend two pounds every day or so on an interview with me?"

Her confession demanded theatricals; she would have some fun, even if contrite. She arrived at the Lisle Street room wearing a gloomy expression, and as soon as the door shut behind her, she asked Crawfurd to kiss her, warning him that it might be the last time. She put her head on his shoulder. He accused her of being unfaithful. She told him about Boughton, wept and begged his forgiveness. "Of course I do," he said, "and I love you and I honour you for telling me the truth. It is so unlike a woman to have told me when it would have been so easy not to tell." But later, after thinking things over, he wrote to her that night: "I cannot quite trust you as I did though I do love you more for being frank with me."

If Crawfurd had not seduced Violet, someone like him would have: she needed a man who accepted her past. She had tossed her "weary heart away to the first man who has had the discernment to make [my] past a link, instead of a severance." It was simple enough to confess to Crawfurd her feelings for Boughton, but could she tell an eligible suitor the same things? Although she wished for a lover "young not three times my age—that I could love and with whom I could forget all my miserable past," she despaired of ever finding such a person.

At times she was grateful that Crawfurd had rescued her from the boredom of Cholmeley and MacColl, realizing that "the sensuous part of a woman's nature needs to be fed *as well* as the intellectual one which I have developed at the expense of the first." Still, she never seriously considered giving up her flirtatious ways. "I like champagne and failing that claret, which I drink with a dry mouth because it makes me gay and reckless and with gayness and recklessness I gain my little successes," she wrote, knowing full well that her personality rather than her appearance attracted men. "I am badly dressed and not pretty except for eyes. I don't make the most of what I have even, I make the littlest of everything like the fool I am."

To deceive her parents, she continued to accept invitations, but these events, as bitterly recorded in her diary, were joyless. She should have been happier, but she was angry, feeling uncertain and eccentric. At a wedding she was so bored that she went into the "refreshment room and ate foie gras like a pig, or a chaperon or a wall-flower as I am! I shall go into a nunnery, without a Hamlet having to order me there." She loved dancing, but no longer was she the sought-after partner in the blush of youth. "I have almost resolved to give up dances—or else to marry someone to go in with!"

In disturbing daydreams George Boughton nagged at her heart: she fantasized about them being together in the next world. Less clear were Boughton's feelings. Was he telling Violet what she wanted to hear out of guilt or love? Since she persisted in forcing her attentions on him, he had no choice but to pay her pretty compliments, which Violet interpreted as a reawakening of his love. When she learned that his wife was ill, she envisioned herself marrying him, and wickedly wondered whether he was thinking the same thing.

Crawfurd continued to be a frequent guest at Tor Villa, and Violet worried about her parents discovering their clandestine meetings, even as she rationalized that she was not acting "so wrongly in following what old novels call the 'dictates of passion,' no, I mean the 'dictates of Nature.' I belong to myself, and so long as they [her parents] remain ignorant, I only hurt myself." Margaret must have suspected; she was an astute woman but, concerned with her own life, denied the obvious.

Still, precautions were taken to keep the affair secret. In public they flirted at a distance: Violet tingled all over when she telegraphed knowing glances to her married lover across a crowded room, thinking no one noticed. They left dinners and dances separately, meeting later to share a hansom; Violet hid her face with a fan or a bouquet of flowers, and Crawfurd alighted before the cab turned onto Campden Hill Road. They sent coded messages, referring to work: "Your copy—early sheets" meant a canceled meeting.

By July 1891 Crawfurd was postponing more and more "interviews" at Lisle Street. He did not meet Violet daily nor send frequent letters and telegrams, as agreed. Crawfurd had underestimated the time required to edit a new magazine and was spending many late nights at his Bouverie Street office off Fleet Street. As a freelance writer, Violet knew little of the responsibilities of directing a staff, and she could not understand why Crawfurd's work preempted her needs. On one occasion, as they sat in chairs among the sheep in Kensington Gardens, Crawfurd announced in his world-weary way, "I have been thinking, we are not really in sympathy with each other. I shall see you no more in the little red room but here, out of doors, where I am under restraint."

"You don't love me?" Violet asked peevishly, sparking an argument that ended as usual with Crawfurd apologizing, Violet crying and the two embracing.

"Why can't people," meaning men, be faithful? Violet asked him during an afternoon tryst at a Jermyn Street restaurant.

"Inherent disability, I ought never to have married," he told her. "I am just obliged to other men who marry and so provide me with happy hunting grounds. For it is my theory that a man who can't keep a wife doesn't deserve to have one."

"Oh, stop it."

"I disgust you, isn't that so? But I am not conceited enough to think that do what I would, I could retain *your* affections."

"Not if I really loved you?"

"You loved George."

"Cruel!" Violet yelled at him.

He moved toward her, saying, "Is it the end? The beginning of the end, I mean?"

"No, but the end of the beginning. Let me go home," she said, breaking away from him.

□

Physically, Crawfurd was a powerful man, six feet two inches tall (Violet fit under his arm), with a supple and virile body, despite middle age. He delighted in his honesty, his wit and his masculine right to indulge his appetites unrestrained. But he was moody, temperamental, given to tantrums that bewildered and frightened Violet. Although he prized her risk-taking, her desire to seek out the forbidden corners of life, he still made her feel insecure. She noted that her lover "doesn't even pretend to admire me except perhaps for my eyes, my teeth and my hands and some other points I will not mention. He never considers me nicely dressed—never!"

Others thought differently. Walter Sickert, who, in 1911, would form the Camden Town Group, artists who found inspiration in the music halls and the more grotty scenes of that London suburb, asked Violet to model for him in his Chelsea studio. She had first met Sickert at a tea party given in her honor by Oscar Wilde. Although she sat for many painters, Sickert, Millais and Burne-Jones (her features are seen in his bewildered virgin in *King Cophetua and the Beggar Maid*) are the best-known today.

Violet found Sickert "a very nice, kind, gentle soul with neither malice or bitterness towards man or beast or brother artist!" Sickert's father was a Dane, who settled in England when his son was eight years old; although considered an Englishman, Sickert was Germanic in attitude and the artist who brought the most foreign influence to bear on English art in the twentieth century. (Degas was his mentor.) Flirtatious, cosmopolitan and multilingual, Sickert had much in common with his young model.

Violet enjoyed the vicarious thrill of exhibiting her body, dressed or partially unclothed, of shocking friends who viewed artists' models as either servants or prostitutes. She went unchaperoned and sought no pay, but hoped that Sickert would present her with the finished painting. Posing in one costume, she felt "very raw and nude"; it was the "old lilac silk; the dress with the silk train and the border of violets I made myself out of an old Victorian bodice of Mamma's." Three weeks later she wondered, "Of course he *might* make love to me but I should not mind for I could now put him off quite easily." Violet recorded how Sickert, whom she called an "impressionist," placed model and canvas side by side, stood as far away as possible and, with brush poised, rushed forward, stabbing the canvas with color.

With her mother's coaching and Crawfurd's encouragement, she continued to pursue a writing career. Margaret went to the British Museum to edit Violet's reviews for *Black and White;* Crawfurd critiqued her story "Bride of Death" and urged her to write a novel and be *"one of us*—then you can walk down St. James' Street, hand in hand with the man of your heart and no one can say a word."

Her dialogues and book reviews in *Black and White* brought her to the attention of Marriott Watson, an editor of the *Pall Mall Gazette,* and Clement Shorter, editor of *The Sketch,* who was also a Brontë scholar. Watson wanted her to write book reviews and Shorter wanted her to be editor of *Sylvia's Journal.* Crawfurd objected to both proposals, fearful that new interests and friends would take her away from him, and cautioning that by working in an office she might jeopardize her position in society. She refused Shorter's offer with no regrets, and stalled Watson for a while, but eventually wrote "Wares of Autolycus," a weekly *Gazette* column, for two years.

Fin de siècle London was an exhilarating place for Violet. The city on the Thames was growing up and outward, spurred on by technological change; everything, it seemed, came at once—electric lights, motor cars, trams, telephones, cameras. To her great delight, Crawfurd introduced her to the music hall: originally a working-class entertainment with a sprinkling of gentlemen and ladies slumming, it had, by the end of the century, become virtually classless.

Sitting in a box at the Tivoli on a night in August, Violet wore an immense feather boa wrapped around her chin as a disguise, and fastened the curtains of the box with her hat pin; Crawfurd hid huddled on the floor at her feet, and they drank gin sours out of the same straw. ("He looked rather paternal and I liked that, oddly.") Violet got so carried away with the performance that she wanted Crawfurd to stand up and applaud, until he reminded her of their reputations if they were seen together.

She loved the lights, the noise and glitter, the naughty songs, the sing-alongs, the feeling of good fellowship. "Under these maddening influences I am a different woman or a woman revealed. I cry and laugh; anything but be the practical cynical woman I usually am. All my being flows towards the man who is so close to me that

I feel the heat of his body through our two sets of clothes, whose hand holds me in a warm smooth clasp, nothing feverish about it— a lifegiving hand . . . When he puts it on the nape of my neck I shiver."

Of London's many music halls, the Tivoli was Violet's favorite; it was where she first saw Lottie Collins sing and dance "Ta-ra-ra-boom-de-ay." Lottie received £150 a week for a fifteen-minute act, which resembled a cross between an Indian war dance and the cancan. Wearing a provocative short red dress, white petticoat and a Gainsborough hat, she inspired a popular schoolboy rhyme:

> _Lottie Collins has no drawers,_
> _Will you kindly lend her yours?_
> _She is going far away_
> _To sing Ta-ra-ra-boom-de-ay!_

Violet copied the dance's pirouettes and high kicks, learned how to flop her hair over her face on each beat and eagerly sought an audience among her bohemian Fleet Street friends. At the Islington music hall she listened to Jenny Hill sing "The Boy I Love Is Up in the Gallery," later popularized by Marie Lloyd, queen of the music halls.

When the Hunts left town, Violet and Crawfurd stole away for weekends in snug hotels. They traveled first-class, pulled down the train's window blinds, kissed and cuddled and ate sponge cakes dipped in sherry. She watched him shave, a ritual that made her feel married as she awaited a foamy kiss. He told her wicked stories about his former mistresses involving lesbian and _ménage à trois_ couplings.

In other kinky moments they prowled Hyde Park at night, looking for the ugly prostitutes who shunned the bright lights of Piccadilly. Violet was excited by the prospect of being locked in the park all night. Another time, as they sat on the Embankment near the Floating Fire Brigade, a fireman invited them onto the raft, and they excitedly walked from raft to raft, up to Westminster Bridge.

Despite these romantic adventures and a deepening of their love, Crawfurd continued to see Annie Chapman. Violet envisioned their meetings: "Now he is in Her arms; he is making Her laugh, he is talking clever nonsense to Her, not quite the same love-nonsense he talks to me because he doesn't love her, but enough to make her think he does and be happy." Violet rolled about in her bed, "with hot hands counting the hours till six," when she knew it would be over because he was dining out; she imagined Annie's husband surprising them, and the ridiculous look on her lover's face.

Crawfurd cunningly declared that Annie was not too bright. "You are really too clever," he told Violet. "I am quite afraid of your seeing me out—of my getting to bore you." Violet suggested that Crawfurd meet her first and see Annie afterward, a sequence he refused.

Puzzling over her behavior in her diary, she wrote, "It wasn't malice or spite, I have no hatred of this woman who adores him, who is gentle and who knows that she is not loved." No, she decided, "I don't want to hurt her. I believe I want to hurt him, to drive home to him the enormity he is committing in running us both at once." Violet also wanted to prove that her love was stronger than her bitterness, that she was generous to send her lover into the arms of another—or so she thought.

One day Crawfurd canceled his "interview" with Annie. "Will she cry when you tell?" Violet asked childishly.

"Probably," he said, wincing, "she will make me a little scene."

"Oh, you must go to her in a fit of what Victor Hugo would call sublime generosity," Violet said.

"How sweet you are," Crawfurd replied, "and how morbid! I am to go to her and say 'My dear, I can attend you today because the woman I love whom I adore . . . permits it.' "

Violet resisted demanding that he decide between them; she did not want "to assume the responsibility of (catering) for *all* his love!" But the choice was discussed, and Crawfurd took refuge in loyalty. "I must stick to her. It was *your* fault—you did not care for me, then," he said, brutally adding that she should "get another lover." Too often, though, he gave her false hopes about the future, about marriage.

"Darling, it would be a dreadful thing to do but I would do it," he said one day. "And you'll get tired of me when I am white and old—I'm grey now." Thrilled that he might "make an honest woman" of her, she told him he was a good lover. He replied that she said very improper things "out of simplicity and damned down-rightness and Northcountryness"—an accurate observation, for if Violet's excitement focused on sex, her conversation was honest, never prurient.

They had been lovers for fifteen months when Crawfurd admitted that he led not a double life but a multiple one. The new player was Ellie Ursinus, the daughter of a German banker in Oporto, nominally his ward. According to Crawfurd, Ellie's evil stepmother had had her disinherited but Crawfurd had instigated a deathbed change in the will, which made him responsible for her investments.

In her early twenties and unattractive (Violet said ugly but nice), Ellie loved Crawfurd and was slavish in her devotion to him, acting as a go-between in some of his affairs. She now became a chaperon and traveling companion to Violet, letting her spend the night at her apartment following a tryst with Crawfurd. The two women became chums of a sort, but Crawfurd sat securely on the point of the triangle.

On monthly trips to Brighton, Southampton or other resorts, Ellie and Violet booked three rooms, traveled together and awaited Crawfurd's arrival. On a typical evening, after dining, they lounged on his bed—Violet looking provocative, Ellie looking jealous—and told risqué stories. Ellie was led to believe that Violet was an old friend, but after she caught Crawfurd leaving Violet's bedroom, it is hard to believe she suspected nothing, even with Crawfurd's facile explanation.

It was titillating for Violet to observe, without a glimmer of jealousy, another woman infatuated with her lover. One evening in her room all three sat on the bed "in almost indecent promiscuity," while Violet flirted with Crawfurd, suggesting he kiss her on the lips. He refused. "Has he never kissed you?" Ellie asked ingenuously. Violet lied. She admired her lover's skill at flirting: "I see how beautifully he does it. And I—*pas mal!* It seems to satisfy my dual consciousness—this flirtation for the benefit of Ellie and for her sake—and my own. I do it as well as I can. I put away all that has been between us and work hard as if I had a hopeless passion wondering as those women must do if my *moyens* are going to succeed, and then . . . it is heavenly to dive deep into my consciousness and remember that I have succeeded and that our love is a *fait accompli!*" Quite rejuvenated after such trips, Violet saw the affair rekindled as "a new relationship—quite independently of the old original one."

At other times, the two women acted out motherly roles, clucking over their charge, fussing over his choice of food. Ever the stylish juggler, he took one for a walk alone and then the other. "It is ridiculous," Violet wrote, "but then—somehow—*not*," maintaining that Ellie enjoyed these staged moments of sexual tension. "Poor Ellie is so happy with these little modified joys that I procure for her," Violet noted, sounding like a wistful brothel madam.

Soon Ellie became indispensable, in Violet's mind, to her desire to escalate the affair. With Ellie as camouflage, she did not have to wait for her parents to leave London; Margaret Hunt accepted her daughter's explanation that she was spending the night with Ellie or was meeting her in Brighton, which was often the case.

Aggressively jealous at times, Violet prided herself on accepting Annie Chapman as an annoyance, nothing more. But during one Brighton outing she observed a letter beginning, "My own dearest." Later in her bedroom, after restraining herself during dinner with Ellie, Violet demanded an explanation. To whom was he writing? "Dearest, it is to my wife—I didn't want you to know," the evasive Crawfurd explained. "I always put it. It is only a farce, but as she puts it to me." Violet was skeptical but dropped the subject.

At Tor Villa, she had to listen to a jealous Cholmeley, whom she alternately loathed and tolerated, complain about Crawfurd's age, his dyed hair, his pompous airs. As the good doctor prattled on, Violet thought "that in the end 'weariness may toss me to his breast.' Some day when 'the violent delights' have had their 'violent endings.' If he heard of my vileness, he would pity me, and himself— and leave me."

By December 1891, Crawfurd and Violet had worn out their welcome at Lisle Street; the landlord asked them to leave, and they found rooms in Church Place. Since they always had work to discuss, they could be seen during the day at Dick's coffeehouse or the Niagara, where a steam organ played the wedding march from *Tannhäuser*. Crawfurd said he wanted to do more with his life, to write a novel. "Darling, I don't want to sacrifice you who are my life and my love to a novel," he told her one day, "but it is getting awful—I am depressed and oppressed. I ask myself if our love is one of those that have the principle of life in it? . . . And has one the right to expect to be so passionately loved for so long?"

Violet thought so; in fact, she felt more loved than "a few months ago, and then it seemed to me that he loved me more than any man could love a woman. There are certain signs of deep love . . . it takes a very passionate man like O [Crawfurd was either O or, for some unexplained reason, A] to make a woman like V *feel* at all," an allusion to Violet preferring sexual excitement to sexual intimacy. She once told Crawfurd that her "merit as a female rake is that I never seriously wanted to bring anyone to anything! I'm like a child who gathers an armful of wheat ears—say—and loses some without minding. Those that like to slip away from under my arm may do it—I don't miss them . . ."

Although Violet felt married, she suffered the affronts of a mistress. She fought with her mother, who suspected the truth about Crawfurd. She resented his absence when he took his wife to Woodhall Spa, and the decorum that prevented her from visiting his sickroom because she was unmarried. Still, she told her diary that she felt more complete, and noticed an improvement in her tennis and croquet games. She worked days at the British Museum doing research for her articles and when possible spent evenings with her lover.

In September her parents went to Durham for the birth of their second granddaughter, named Amerye Margaret. Margaret was disappointed that her name was second, and Alfred that again he had been deprived of a namesake. Acting on whim, Violet gave the servants the night off and invited Crawfurd to dine. She showed him Tor Villa's upstairs, ending up in her attic room, where a "plain linen nightgown made of Grandmother's old ones" was laid out on the "big pale brown varnished bed" on which Violet was born.

There were still remnants of the decorations made by Venice and Silvia, and Crawfurd found it the bedroom of a child, not of a woman, and the nightgown a surprising style for a coquette; he felt chastened by the innocence of Violet's "little childish school-girlish arrangements." When he noticed the portrait of George Boughton over the mantelpiece, he asked that it be removed. She refused. And so the "spirit of George reigned over us and imposed himself on us and prevented any love making."

After this romantic failure, she rushed to Durham to see her latest niece, then hurried back to meet Ellie and Crawfurd at Seaford, where they stayed at a lonely hotel on the esplanade, and Violet celebrated her thirtieth birthday. Crawfurd came into her bedroom at seven in the morning to wish her many happy returns, and that afternoon they watched the football match on the green; she wore a red-striped skirt with a cream silk blouse and a girlish sailor hat—a costume that Ellie pronounced undignified for her age. As usual she felt sad on her birthday, particularly one marking a milestone in maturity; she told her lover that the world had "lost its savour." She wanted more. "I have lived with you and want to live with you instead of *lodging* at home."

But Violet was not yet prepared to risk her reputation and place in society by living openly with a married man. As for Crawfurd, no matter what his romancing, he never seriously considered leaving his wife.

7

Errant Daughter

ALFRED HUNT was sixty-three and in deteriorating health; everyone noticed his lack of energy. In years past his sketching tours had started in May and ended when the bonfires were lit on Guy Fawkes Day, the fifth of November. Violet recalled that there was much packing and wrapping of the ready-stretched canvases, umbrellas and easels until "the four-wheeler came round, and its roof received all this baggage, while the preoccupied, spectacled artist embraced his family, and, throwing the name of one of the four great termini to the cabman, jumped into the cab, and departed into the green world that was waiting for him and his brush."

No longer feeling fit enough for such strenuous trips, Hunt sketched outlines outdoors, completing the painting in his studio, with Tommy, his beloved cat, always in attendance. He continued to exhibit at the Old Water-Colour Society, and in the spring of 1893 was invited to be an art juror at the Great Chicago Exhibition that summer. Excited over the prospect of seeing America, Margaret started packing, assuming that Violet would accompany them.

But when her parents sailed on the *Umbria* from Liverpool, the errant daughter remained behind. The Hunts arrived in New York on July 1, visited friends in upstate New York and traveled on to Niagara Falls, where Alfred did numerous sketches. During their two-month absence, Violet and Crawfurd's life turned into a marital routine. "It was like being the wife of a city man, who is out all day and comes home at night tired," she noted. Even so, she was often alone while Crawfurd made calls, and depressed when his work prevented a planned trip to Paris and when he returned to his wife at Queen Anne's Mansions.

Financially, he was supporting two households. When he complained about paying nine guineas a week for their Church Place room, Violet found less expensive lodgings in the Strand, at number 376, near his office. She borrowed a small gas stove, bought a new coffeepot and made wifely dinners like Magyar chicken and Crawfurd's favorite dish—tapioca pudding.

She also started her first novel, *The Maiden's Progress*. Arising early, she sat on the window seat overlooking the Strand, watching the meat deliveries to the restaurants below, and wrote what Andrew Lang said should have been called "The Minx's Progress." Published in 1894, the book was a collection of dialogues, some previously published in *The Sketch* and the *Pall Mall Gazette*. It was well reviewed, perhaps more for Violet's knowing the critics than for any outstanding ability. The *Literary World* praised her wit and observations, calling her "one of the smartest dialogue writers of the day."

When her parents returned to England on the *Etruria,* Violet packed her clothes and rushed home to greet them with an innocent smile. Reflecting on her weeks of "married" life, she admitted that while Crawfurd had made her immensely happy, he had also made her suffer terribly because of his irrational jealousy. Crawfurd's ward Ellie was now spying for him, reporting that Violet had been seen around Fleet Street with Marriott Watson or Clement Shorter or the unsavory journalist Jack Stuart. Violet begged him not to control her movements, not to pick her friends. Why should she stay at home alone without a social life when she was not a wife, but a mistress?

Mostly she feared his moods, exacerbated by work pressures. He grew more and more irascible, once ripping the coat off her back, splitting her dress. "You don't know men," he blurted out during one argument. "You are a weak unenterprising woman like all women. They have no initiative; they ought not to have—it is not their *métier.*" Eventually she acquiesced, accepting his need to dominate. Soon the overworked Crawfurd suffered a nervous breakdown, for which he blamed Violet. She was a virago, he screamed.

To the Victorians, a virago was not a strong-minded, vigorous woman, an Amazon, but a mean-tempered scold, which at times Violet certainly was. But there was something menacing, a barely concealed loathing, in Crawfurd's frequent use of the epithet. In deciding to be a "new woman," in rejecting wifely and motherly conduct, Violet found herself part of a pernicious dualism that viewed woman as either virgin or whore, self-sacrificing and sexless mother or virago-vampire. She never understood why men criticized her bold temperament.

One day while riding in a hansom with Clement Shorter, editor of *The Sketch*, Violet glimpsed Crawfurd and Annie Chapman on the other side of the road. In a rash moment, she dismissed her escort to follow them, and when the cab passed by, looked directly at Crawfurd, who coolly doffed his hat while Annie insolently tilted her chin. It was an awful moment, and Violet realized that she was "only one of his harem—he is a part of many women's lives. What a fool I am. . . . I know he loves me now, only why can he exist without me—for two days." On New Year's Eve, while Crawfurd celebrated with his wife, Violet dined at Tor Villa with D. S. MacColl and the artist Walter Firth; she stuffed her ears with cotton to muffle the sound of the bells.

The year 1894 brought more disenchantment. Crawfurd withdrew emotionally and physically; he refused to make firm engagements or to be manipulated. They had moved their assignations to 220 Temple Chambers, and one evening Violet returned to their rooms after attending a dance on her own. "You know, darling," he reprimanded, "I never do love you quite as much after a dance— you never, somehow, seem quite so much mine." Still trying to be the belle of the ball, Violet refused to grow up; she was thirty-two but wanted to live as if eighteen, and to be made much of—as she used to be. At the end of the year, they moved their meetings— for the last time—to an apartment house (Whitcomb Mansions) on Whitcomb Street, off Shaftesbury Avenue, where they would fight and make up for three years more.

One frosty February evening after a first night at the Comedy Theatre, they separated as usual after the final curtain and took different routes to Whitcomb Street. Violet arrived first, lit the fire and scrutinized her face, which she made to look passionate and sad and pretty: "It is such a woman's weapon." When Crawfurd walked in the door, he accused her of flirting. Violet challenged him to leave her. Crawfurd took her hand and shook his head. "I love you!" he cried. "I put you on a pinnacle." She put her arms around his neck; he kissed her repeatedly, sadly. "He will end by detesting me—and I him," Violet wrote.

To his credit, Crawfurd urged her to continue writing, and he made sure she was published. Now at the helm of *Chapman's Magazine* and Chapman & Hall, the publishers, he serialized Violet's next novel, *A Hard Woman*, which later sold 2,000 copies—not a bad showing; and he made Violet theater critic for *Black and White*, a singular honor for a woman. One of her early reviews was of *Guy Domville*, Henry James's play, which closed after five performances. She thought it the "dreariest of plays, as heavy as a piece of black velvet and as dignified," but sympathized when the author was literally hooted from the stage. "It was like prodding a soft, large animal in the Zoo," she recalled. James covered his face with his handkerchief and "from behind it, appeared to issue chunks and gobbets—the maimed fragment of a clever speech." He retired "sadly and patiently, rather like an elephant who had had a stone put into his trunk instead of a bun."

With the £80 advance for *A Hard Woman*, Violet opened her first bank account, at Barclay's. Her name was now seen in the *London News*, *London Review* and *The Athenaeum*. Money meant nothing to her, she said, but the spending of it as well as the losing of it came naturally. Some losses were avoidable, though, like her bad investment in a gold mine on the advice of Burne-Jones.

As Violet's professional reputation grew, she attracted friends outside of Crawfurd's orbit. One was Grant Richards, a twenty-year-old sub-editor of the *Review of Reviews*, who was destined to be a notable book publisher. She took him to dances, which he termed "an act of extraordinary generosity since I could not dance at all." Richards became a close friend, accurately pointing out that if Violet had not given so "much of her time to the arts of conversation and of hospitality she would have done much greater things than stand to her name." He warmly recalled parties at Tor Villa, sitting in the garden, drinking tea or iced coffee and listening to the latest gossip on artists and writers.

Another new friend was Mrs. Ernest (Ada) Leverson, chris-

tened "The Sphinx" by Oscar Wilde. The daughter of a Jewish wool
merchant, she married a diamond dealer twelve years her senior,
who would gamble away his money and then desert her. When Ada
first met Wilde at a party in 1892, he boasted of a Parisian _apache_
who had followed him around with a knife in one hand, to which
Ada retorted: "I'm sure he had a fork in the other!" There was an
immediate match of wits here, and between his trials Wilde lived
with the Leversons.

When Violet first met Ada, in 1895, she thought her "a good
woman. But I can never talk to her for long, she is one of these
women who cannot keep up a conversation except a love conversation [she was flirting with Crawfurd]." Ada, however, enjoyed
Violet's sardonic wit, and judging from photographs, there was
even a physical resemblance, though Ada's daughter saw Violet
differently, recalling her as "coarse and plain with a skin like
leather . . . she symbolised the New Woman on a bicycle, except
that these were depicted in _Punch_ as pretty."

Violet and Crawfurd thrived on London social life. They were
alike in many ways: both were impulsive and passionate; both
wanted to be the center of attention, and through wit and style
achieved it. He played the elegant diplomat-turned-publisher who
still cared for an ailing wife; she played the up-and-coming writer
who always had wicked gossip on her mind and tongue. When
together, they affected a frivolous platonic aura, anticipating trips
when they could escape London's scrutiny. Ellie usually traveled
with them: convention demanded a chaperon and convention could
be flouted only so far.

In September 1895, however, they slipped away alone to Newhaven. During an argument, Crawfurd locked himself in his room.
When her urgent knocks brought no response, Violet climbed onto
the roof ledge and crawled to his window. He tried to shut the
window on her fingers, yelling, "Go away. Go away." Violet could
be seen from the railroad station, a spectral figure wandering on
the roof in her grandmother's white nightgown. More to avoid
discovery than to placate her, Crawfurd let her in, but was so in-
furiated he could barely speak. Violet wept and begged not to be
left alone all night; but he came to her only in the morning and
ordered breakfast, which they ate in silence. In desperation, she
promised not to bother him; they would meet only at meals, and

she would spend the morning sewing ("the gift of Gods to women").

As the day progressed, the squabble faded and by dinnertime she could approach him without rebuke. "I understand the people who are being bashed crawl at the feet of tormentors," she wrote. "It is a joy to be received again better than to be permanently adored. . . . Night came and all misery joy sorrows and the effect of cruelty all merged in one simple emotion. How humiliating for the woman, so exhausted with misery to be a woman when the moment came!"

Entering her thirty-fourth year, Violet was in high spirits on February 18, 1896, when she planned to meet Crawfurd incognito at a costume ball. Wearing a "domino-gray—accordion pleated" mask, she went unrecognized until he heard her voice and they exchanged "risqué, pretty witty things." Suddenly, who should appear to ask Violet to dance but Harold Dowdall, who had proposed to her nine years before. Crawfurd, his identity concealed, exploded at the intrusion. Violet escaped to Kings Cross Station, where she caught a train to Durham. She returned to London and a stony silence from Crawfurd.

As the rows became more frequent, a heavy sadness suffused their time together. On April 30 they stole away again by themselves to Newhaven, returning to London on May 4—the day after her father's death. Alfred had no specific disease, but his last years were marked by ill health and failing eyesight. In one letter to Margaret he complained that his sight was "a very real cause of much vexation and trouble . . . It must be accepted as a constant drawback to all my labours, and what is worse to my powers of invention and design. I cannot arrange pictures out of mere variegations of colours, but must find boundaries and edges somehow."

That old incubus of poverty surfaced, and he worried about money, even as he resigned himself to the inevitable. "Mind, I think you are very patient with my shortcomings," he wrote his wife. "Whatever comes, I am sure you at any rate have made a noble fight of it, and I do not think I have made a very bad one—but I could wish sometimes that things were different."

At the end of his life, Alfred Hunt's achievements were more notable to others than to himself. True, he had not been admitted to the lofty Royal Academy, and his name had been unfortunately linked to the authorship of an anonymous pamphlet attacking the private lives of Royal Academicians;* but he had exhibited 334 watercolors at the Royal Water-Colour Society (and thirty-seven paintings at the Royal Academy), and by 1888 was deputy-president of the society and central to its activities and success. He had brought in Ruskin as an honorary member in 1873; he circumvented the rule requiring a formal application to elect Holman Hunt while he was in the Holy Land (Ford Madox Brown was never a member because he wanted the same treatment as Holman Hunt and was too proud to apply); and he enticed Burne-Jones to rejoin (he had resigned in 1870 after criticism of _Phyllis and Demophoön_ for showing male genitals).

Despite a jaded view of himself, Alfred Hunt was admired by critics and collectors as a man of talent, influence and integrity. Shortly before his death, Sir John Gilbert, president of the Royal Water-Colour Society, became ill, and Hunt was approached as a possible replacement. Alfred gave the position a great deal of thought, as he did everything; he knew he would be a good leader, but worried that fatigue might limit his public-speaking abilities. He fretted for days about whether to accept, only never to be formally asked, passed over in favor of Sir Hubert von Herkomer. It was the final insult from the art establishment.

He died in bed at Tor Villa with Margaret at his side, following a stroke. His beloved cat, Tommy, who would live six more years, was also in the room. No one knew Violet's whereabouts; her sisters sent messages around town seeking to locate her. Violet's diary entry for May 3 contains only three black parallel lines, but in _Their Hearts_ she tells the story of her father's death and funeral, how she arrived home to the tragic news and how her sisters "wanted to make her feel her wickedness in being away in dalliance with her paramour while her father died. They guessed it was something like

---

*This pamphlet, thrown by hawkers into the carriages of Academy members as they arrived for a private view, is mentioned in prefaces written by Ford Madox Hueffer in 1912 for a reprint of Margaret's second book, _Thornicroft's Model_, and in her posthumously published novel, _The Governess_. There is a hint Margaret might have written the pamphlet, but Violet later denied participation by either parent. Ford always felt the Academicians blamed Hunt for the pamphlet and thus boycotted his pictures.

that which had made her inaccessible to their summons." In the novel, after seeing her father laid out, Christina (Violet) runs up to West House to fetch Emerson Vlaye (George Boughton), who was pressed into painting a death portrait, a macabre, perhaps apocryphal scene, for there is no record of such a picture.

His family buried Alfred Hunt on May 7 in a heather-filled corner of Brookwood Cemetery near Woking in Surrey, where the landscape of pines, oaks and flowering shrubs gave it the appearance of a private estate. He had selected the site himself. Crawfurd attended the church service and walked in the procession to the burial plot. Violet was glad to have him nearby. Propriety prevented his taking her arm, and she was sadly alone while Venice and Silvia leaned on their husbands. Walton, Silvia's husband, remarked that "Mr. Hunt was an angel from Heaven and never ought to have come down to this Earth at all!"*

The death of a beloved parent often heals a foundering relationship, but this was not the case with Violet and Crawfurd. Their affair had been untenable before Alfred's death, and thereafter Crawfurd acted more trapped and pressured, resisting Violet's demands for more time and affection. "My idea of a lover," she told her

---

*The Times of London, on May 7, 1896, printed a tribute from Harry Quilter, editor of the Universal Review, which noted that Hunt's work, while delighting many lovers of nature and art for thirty years, had "met with no public recognition and, I fear, but little private reward. That this has been so is due in chief to the action or rather the inaction of the Royal Academy, which declined to elect him even to the minor honour of associateship, which never purchased one of his pictures, which rarely hung his works save in inferior places. I say, without hesitation, what I have said and written of this artist for 20 years, that he was at once the most learned, the most delicate, and the most subtle of modern English landscape painters; that he was, in addition, possessed of an amount of technical skill and of such keen sense of beauty as are rare even amongst the most accomplished artists; and that, lastly, he was during the latter years of his life almost the only man who carried on worthily and completely the great tradition of English watercolour painting—a tradition of which our nation will one day be more proud than of any other portion of its artistic inheritance. . . . For while the Academy can delay it cannot prevent the recognition of first-rate work; the man dies unhonoured, but the work he has done lives after him." (At a 1985 British Museum exhibit, "British Watercolourists from 1600 to 1860," Hunt's Dalwydellan Castle, painted in 1855, was prominently shown. It is a panoramic landscape with Turneresque clouds, sheep grazing by a mountain stream and, in the foreground, a cross section of purplish-blue rock painstakingly layered with veins of gray and white.)

diary, "is a man whose first care is his mistress—his greatest happiness her company—his greatest obligation her happiness"— hardly a description of Crawfurd.

Their time together took on the lineaments of a nightmare: "How often I have seen him put on his hat & rush for the door & I gone & stood in front of it. It is horrible of me—but I want to keep him so much." Annie Chapman's husband had died the previous year, but Crawfurd was no longer interested in her. He had a new mistress: Mrs. Ralph (Lita) Browne, daughter of Hermann von Flesch Brunningen, an Austrian, and sister of Lady Brabourne. It would be some months, though, before Violet realized she had new competition.

Although Crawfurd still paid for the Whitcomb Street apartment, they seldom were there. He canceled appointments, promised to meet Violet at dances but never arrived, leaving her an anxious wallflower hoping to be escorted onto the floor by anyone, young or old. She haunted his apartment at Queen Anne's Mansions, talked to his neighbors and cried when she saw a light in his window. Depressed, she slept the day away, waiting for the postman to bring a kind word. One day, when they finally met, he called her "the most selfish woman he had ever known," predicting his death unless he stayed at home Saturdays and Sundays, away from her. Violet argued that such a plan would turn her "out of his life." That, of course, was the idea.

One evening she trailed him to a party and saw him talking with Lita Browne. Later at their apartment, she intercepted a love letter from Lita. "What of it," Crawfurd sneered when confronted. "I can't prevent a woman being in love with me. You have surprised a woman's secret!" He vowed he had never kissed Lita and "never meant to." Violet, such a seasoned player at self-deception, seems to have believed him: "or does he say it to save her character to me—but I will try and think the other & now I am happier."

But she was far from happy. She was in a panic and sought advice from all quarters. Silvia told her to end the affair. Edward Heron Allen, a dabbler in astrology and palmistry, who would later become an important friend, said the same. Silvia even wrote Crawfurd. "It is not her affair," he shot back in a scolding note to Violet. On July 10, Violet gave him an ultimatum: "I want to leave you— if you can't see me— It is not making a scene for a woman to ask her love to be with her." Crawfurd disagreed: "Yes it is & you are a virago—always were."

In September Violet spent her thirty-sixth birthday alone, having recently discovered that Crawfurd was in Germany with Lita Browne. She contemplated suicide: "I cannot imagine life without him, on some terms or other. That is what is meant by *giving your* life to a person. You could not if you would take it back—it *has been used*. I know I shall be unhappy, perhaps so unhappy that I shall have to put an end to this life, but He has raised up barriers between my passionate love & him, which I shall beg him not to break down, unless it is for *always*. . . . I don't let myself think of the wild joy it might be to meet him again if things could be as they were once." Later, suicide seemed senseless: "What is the point of dying for a man that is 'indifferent' to you. If he even hated me! Don't they ever hate their victims—only are bored by them."

At this time Violet was working on her fifth novel, *The Human Interest*. After *A Hard Woman,* Chapman & Hall had published *The Way of Marriage* and *Unkist, Unkind!* In these early novels, she experimented with the characterization of weak men and strong women, moving toward the anti-romantic themes that inform her post-1904 novels. In *Unkist,* her first gothic tale, she explores the emotions of sexually frustrated women, a trial for her future *Tales of the Uneasy*.

Crawfurd had suggested the plot of *The Human Interest,* the story of Phoebe Elles, a British Madame Bovary. In one of his few surviving letters, written during a German sojourn with his new mistress, he said he was "disappointed in it—agreeably," and gave her a lengthy and intelligent critique, suggesting various changes to make the husband more brutal and the home life more dreary. "The story will run to 30,000 words," he said, "and I will take it for Chapman's, and also sell it for America for what I can get for it for serial rights, but you must make the alterations at once."

Later Crawfurd admitted to financial problems after leaving Chapman's; he had dismissed his valet and was frantically writing short stories, "mostly rot," for extra pounds. "You need not mention all this," he cautioned Violet, "because it does harm to a man—unless your desire to do harm is greater than your desire not to—when you have the opportunity! Forgive the innuendo, but you know you *do* talk."

When Crawfurd returned to London from the continent in October, he sent Violet a gift from France and a note: "I love you, dear, but am a little afraid of you." But soon his letters had a despotic tone: "You have no right whatever to telegraph me in that way— it is a threatening telegram, and I resent it. You talk to people about me and my affairs in the way I have asked you not to talk. I accuse you not of saying anything, but of breaking your promise." Craw- furd said the stress of their relationship gave him heart palpitations. "Do you really think you have the right to dictate to me the hour at which I am to meet you at dinner," he complained, "and because I won't give way to you, to call me names. When you think you can contain yourself we will, if you like, try to meet again."

When Violet was at her lowest ebb, with life a "hell & agony," an unfriendly gossip whispered to her that Crawfurd had written passionate letters three times a day to May Bateman, an acquaintance of Violet's. And this when he was seeing Violet and Annie Chap- man. Furious, she visited May and demanded to see the letters; May let her read two, which were "nearly word for word those he used to write to me." In one he mentioned plans to be at Glaston- bury, and Violet searched back to that time "to remember how he was with me . . . I know we sat together hand in hand in the Vic- toria—and went & saw the buried village together. I do remember I was a little bored with him & thought a week was rather long. I was not very well. Yet we were happy. It rained. And he was writing ardent letters to May all that time. I cried. I felt faint. May B. had to give me port wine. 'I would lie to you if I could,' May said, 'to make you happier! And so I might if the letters were not these.' "

The last refuge of a failed love affair is friendship, which she now sought "for the sake of both our reputations." To Violet, the only basis for a liaison with an unmarried woman was absolute, unquestionable fidelity, which she had had little of since 1891. During the winter of 1899 they ran into each other at social func- tions, but Crawfurd no longer wrote, and Lita avoided those parties where she might see Violet. On New Year's Eve, Violet attended a Royal Academy private view and cried into her punch cup as everyone sang "Auld Lang Syne."

When Crawfurd decided to stop paying for the flat, Violet retrieved her coffeepot ("it is mine and I love it") and fled to Paris to visit her friend Agnes Farley. There she met Alys Bosanquet, a friend of Crawfurd's, whom she begged to intercede on her behalf.

He did so, telling her that Crawfurd had agreed to a friendship and meetings in public. Bosanquet said she was "wrong to say he bears resentment—and if you will accept this half loaf, *you would be more than wise . . .* you have the future. He will not hurt you ever *if you will leave things alone.* He never said one unkind thing of you, and to the world is your friend, if *you* are not a little fool (don't hate me) and make it public. Let it die out. The world is busy, and forgets if apparent facts are all right. Go out and cheer up."

In another letter Bosanquet warned that while Crawfurd was infatuated with Lita, Violet would only harm herself by "letting him think you want anything of him. It will come to an end one day, and then he may turn to the woman who loves him well enough to let him behave as *he* likes." Violet wanted to believe this. In Paris, she and Agnes Farley decided—appropriately enough—to collaborate on a translation of the memoirs of Casanova.

Returning to Tor Villa in September 1899, Violet learned that Crawfurd's wife had recently died, leaving him a substantial legacy of £45,000 ($225,000). "What will happen now?" she asked all her friends. "Everything and nothing," they replied. Violet, of course, was free to marry immediately. But, if Lita Browne was to be his choice, she must divorce, not a pleasant procedure at that time: secular divorce was based on guilt, and guilt was based on evidence of adultery, easy enough to document in this situation. Hoping to be the second Mrs. Crawfurd, Violet waited—passively for a change—spending her free time cycling around the country-side with the faithful Cholmeley.

Henry James, whom Violet had known as an acquaintance since 1882, was now a friend. To James, she was the "woman about town." He met her at "the haunt of the beflounced," as he called the Adelphi Terrace Club, and she fed his hidden Rabelaisian nature. "I used to enjoy shocking him," Violet bragged. "He had set me up as the Medusa-head by which he envisaged the less refined happenings of life. I was the weak prop by whose help he made his little cautious descents into reality . . . the violet ray in his so pure spectrum." When Violet went off to Paris, James told her: "You will evidently come back saturated with romance, of which you will find me a sympathetic devourer."

She started her sixth novel, *Affairs of the Heart,* as her fifth,

The Human Interest (published by Methuen, following Crawfurd's departure from Chapman & Hall), was still being reviewed. It got good notices, but Violet took no pleasure in this, for she knew Crawfurd, who had plotted its course, would not read it. Henry James wrote that he was "extremely struck with its cleverness & expertness—your acuteness of mind & skill of hand." _The Standard's_ critic found the heroine, Phoebe Elles, a modern woman, "who is all nerves, and pose, and self-conscious egotism, with a certain amount of superficial cleverness and an inexhaustible interest in her own emotions . . . incapable of a _grand passion,_ but so anxious to have one"—a not inaccurate description of Violet, for her heroines were always versions of herself.

In the novel, Phoebe's father is a landscape painter so deeply absorbed in his art that he is dead to all "human interests." The critic advised Violet to "dispense with the grey-haired middle-aged artist or archaeologist, whom every woman adores . . . at best a melodramatic creation, and Miss Hunt does not shine in melo-drama. Her strength is in the satirical presentment of character and the vivacities of dialogue."

At year's end, she pondered: "This book [_Affairs of the Heart_] will soon be written and I then begin one where there is no A [Crawfurd]—Can I? I don't believe I can live without the idea of him & the dreams of him. That is all I have." On New Year's Eve, 1899, she wrote hopefully, "I can't believe that A will let the year die without giving a sign?" and she vowed that her new diary would not include the letter "A." But he never wrote, and they saw each other only once again, in 1908, six months before his death, when he took tea at South Lodge. Violet's diary did record that before Lita Browne was granted an uncontested divorce on January 16, 1902, her husband, Ralph, declared bankruptcy. Lita wed Crawfurd on September 18 of the same year, and thereafter the couple lived mostly abroad.

It is interesting to speculate on what Lita Browne offered Crawfurd that Violet did not. To be sure, Violet had become tire-some, but there was still a strong physical attraction between them, and she certainly overshadowed Lita socially and professionally. But Crawfurd probably yearned for a quiet, unaggressive woman. Violet and Crawfurd were not a mismatched couple; indeed, they were too much alike: possessive and passionate. Seven years of life on the fringes of Victorian morality, however, did little to make them a committed couple; they clashed in many ways and disappointed each other in many other ways. Although Crawfurd had been an able instructor in forbidden pleasures, he had withheld respectability, which Violet—unafraid—now sought in the new century.

8

South Lodge

IN DECEMBER 1896, seven months after her husband's death, Margaret Hunt took a forty-year lease on a three-story, semi-detached house across the street from Tor Villa. The house was called South Lodge after the astronomer Sir James South, who had lived there in the 1830s. It was smaller and more economical for a widow and her unmarried daughter, although Alfred, who so feared poverty, had left a substantial estate of £25,958 (about $130,000). South Lodge was not on the grand scale of the houses and gardens of its neighbors, like the Alexanders, who were patrons of Whistler; the Rawlinsons, who had a fine collection of Turners; and the Colvins, who displayed prints and drawings. But it was a home with Italianate charm, imbued with the spirit of Alfred Hunt and the Pre-Raphaelites.

A high wall surrounded the stolid gray-stucco house, and a flagstone path led to the front door, painted dark green. There was a small front garden, overhung with trees and lush with lilacs in the spring, and a larger back garden, where Violet bred her smoke-gray Persian cats in cages. (At one of her parties Henry James was so involved in a monologue that he squeezed a kitten—placed on his lap by Violet—like an accordion. Violet adored her animals and presented beribboned fluffy kittens to reluctant caretakers such as Arnold Bennett and Thomas Hardy.)

The large front drawing room was decorated with William Morris' pink-and-blue-flowered wallpaper, chintz-covered chairs and curtains embroidered with a Morris climbing-plant design; the rear room seated twelve comfortably for dinner, which was always black-tie. On the second floor was Margaret's bedroom with an adjacent dressing room, and a library; Violet's bedroom, a guest room and a bathroom were on the top floor. The walls were hung with memories: portraits of Violet in Victorian and Greek dress by George Boughton, a pen-and-ink drawing of her at seven done by Alfred and a red-chalk drawing of an adolescent Violet sketched by a classmate in art school.

The doyenne of the household, Margaret Hunt, was entering her seventies with diminished energy for writing. (Her most recent novel, *Black Squire,* had been published in 1894.) She now preferred the *grande dame* role, letting Violet be the hostess of South Lodge, assisted by Annie Child, the parlormaid who would serve the family for half a century. But Margaret also expected her unmarried daughter to be a nurse and companion, a stifling Victorian role that Violet evaded by escaping to Paris to work with Agnes Farley on their Casanova translation.* While in Paris, Violet also translated Berthe Tosti's *The Heart of Ruby* and started another novel, *The Celebrity at Home,* a satire on high society. Working with a vengeance, she would average a novel a year from 1900 to 1918. Since Crawfurd, she had become a more prolific writer: lovers always interfered with her output. Cholmeley remained the ever-faithful platonic escort, but MacColl had married in 1897.

On April 30, 1902, the name of W. Somerset Maugham first appeared in Violet's diary. A dapper young man of twenty-nine, Maugham was poised and worldly, still unsure of his sexuality. He had achieved modest success with his novel *Mrs. Craddock* and was editing the short-lived art and literary magazine *The Venture,* to which Violet contributed before it folded in 1904. They most likely met through this magazine and subsequently had a brief affair. In 1905 they met again in Paris.

---

*This two-volume translation was published in 1902 without credit. (The British Library catalogue, however, now lists Violet Hunt as co-translator.) After Violet's death, Douglas Goldring found in her copy a statement explaining that her father had objected to her signing the translation "of such a man": "I should like to get Messrs. Chapman & Hall to place it on record that I, Violet Hunt, am responsible for the translation [she also wrote the introduction], and now that I am seventy-four the impropriety of it would hardly 'lie' as they say of winter snow."

That year was the apogee of *La Belle Époque*—the Paris of Degas and Lautrec, of the Moulin Rouge and the cancan. The English pound yielded twenty-five francs, and a good dinner cost two francs fifty. Russian grand dukes drank champagne out of slippers, young girls played croquet on lush lawns and sailor-suited children rolled hoops in the Bois de Boulogne.

Known as the First Gentleman of Europe, King Edward VII was the true father of *La Belle Époque,* or the Edwardian Era as it was called in Britain, setting sartorial style with red neckties and socks, purple ties and pink carnations, Tyrolean hats, and the homburg, which he introduced to England at the Ascot races. Extravagant parties, elegant manners, conspicuous consumption and marital infidelities characterized Edward's court, which was exotic with princes and maharajahs from the far reaches of the Empire.

Addicted to gossip, Violet and Maugham liked to dissect the British colony in Paris; they both found it difficult to hold their tongues when there was something clever to say. On October 31, 1905, as they parted on the Left Bank, Maugham saw Arnold Bennett and ran down the boulevard to catch him and introduce him to Violet. Bennett had been in Paris for two years, living in Montmartre, working on what would be his finest novel, *The Old Wives' Tale*. He still used his first name, Enoch, and Parisian life had not obscured his provincial origins. Born in 1867 in the industrial Midlands region known as the Five Towns, Bennett was the son of a potter who advanced himself to become a lawyer. He first published in *The Yellow Book* and edited the magazine *Woman,* which had as its motto "Forward but not too fast."

Bennett found Violet attractive and was impressed that she had read all of Casanova by the age of sixteen. When Maugham was away from Paris, Bennett escorted her to some of his favorite haunts. Violet later recalled him as "a charming, patient, erudite, and sporting companion, and there was not a sight or sound of Paris with which he was not acquainted." She enjoyed the thirty-eight-year-old bachelor's company but did not fancy him as a sexual conquest; she said Bennett found her "just clever and modern without much knowledge or interest in any traditional matters—my walk of life being too purely sexual for him."

Although Bennett's French was not so correct as Violet's, he was an enthusiastic cicerone around Montmartre. They ate potatoes and haddock on the rue d'Amsterdam, dropped in at the Moulin Rouge and drank beer in the dance halls. Bennett did not dance, but he loved watching others, sometimes exclaiming, "Passion! Perfect passion! Did you ever see anything like it? They might be going round and round in one of the circles of Hell—or Heaven! It would be all the same to them." After dining out (and splitting the bill), they returned to Bennett's apartment on the rue de Calais, filled with imitation Empire furniture, and drank glasses of hot milk while he played Chopin on the piano.

Or they dined with Violet's chaperon, Agnes Farley, a vivacious Irishwoman married to an American dentist with a Parisian practice; "the great *piocheuse* in localities and scandals in old Paris and London," Violet called her. Agnes introduced Bennett to a charming eighteen-year-old named Eleanor Green, to whom he shortly became engaged; but she capriciously canceled the wedding at the last moment.

It was a terrible humiliation for Bennett. He tried to be philosophical, telling Violet that "such was life," which she knew only too well. "In spite of everything," he wrote her, "I wouldn't blot out the last six months even if I could. I knew a devil of a lot about women before. I know more now, and I have never yet bought knowledge too dearly. Besides that, I know more about myself, and can write infinitely better books. And I am a writer first; all the rest comes afterwards." (Drawing on his impressions of Violet and other women novelists, Bennett created Carlotta Peel, the heroine of *Sacred and Profane Love,* a sheltered young girl who has affairs with married men, writes novels, gets involved with the underclass of Paris and bizarrely dies of appendicitis brought on by swallowing strawberry seeds.)

Candid about her previous affairs with Boughton and Crawfurd, Violet was curiously reticent about Maugham; her autobiographical notes—written sometime in the 1930s—included two cryptic comments: "He is a fearfully emotional man, sexually," and "I never saw Maugham moved except one other time in Paris and the it [*sic*] was me." The intimacy was brief, and years later she told Rebecca West "the painful tale" of how she had seduced the young author; it was "one of the few documented instances of an affair with a woman," according to a Maugham biographer.

First as a lover and then as a friend, Maugham was to have a permanent place in Violet's life. They had a lively correspondence over the years, and in 1908 she dedicated to him *White Rose of Weary Leaf,* the novel that established her reputation; he reciprocated with his travel book on Spain, *The Land of the Blessed Virgin,* which did not please her. Maugham later explained that "she could not imagine what the hell would be her business in such a country."

When Maugham wrote *The Moon and Sixpence* in 1919, he used Violet as the original for Rose Waterford, a Pre-Raphaelite beauty who wore sage green, carried a lily and looked upon life as an opportunity for writing novels. Rose "combined a masculine intelligence with a feminine perversity, and the novels she wrote were original and disconcerting," Maugham wrote, adding that she had "a blistering tongue, no one could say such bitter things; on the other hand, no one could do more charming ones"—an apt description of Violet.

He was one of the first to read *Sooner or Later,* Violet's *roman à clef* published shortly after they met. Written out of her unresolved anger at Crawfurd, the book, like the affair, flickers, burns brightly, dies to embers and shows the world how loathsome men can be. Maugham was surprised at how good it was, admitting he had underestimated her talent. It "explores undiscovered country," he wrote. "I do not think, in English at least, that the relationship between a married man & his mistress, a *jeune fille,* has ever been analyzed before. I think you have done it with very great skill. I confess I should have liked a little more 'obscenity,' because Assheton's [Crawfurd's] charm is obviously sexual, but I recognise that this was impossible."

Violet had asked Maugham about public reaction. "Of course the work has an autobiographical ring about it," he replied, "& you must expect to hear a good deal of disagreeable things—however what does it matter? My own impression is that most of what one writes is to a great or less degree autobiographical, not the actual incidents always, but always the emotions. Anyhow we are able to *fouter* ourselves of the world at large—when one has to suffer so much it is only fair that one should have the consolation of writing books about it."

Sooner or Later is the story of Rosette Newall (Violet), an "ingenious ingenue" who, bored by proper, dull suitors, has an affair with Robert Assheton (Crawfurd), an elderly rake attracted to her because she likes "irregular situations." They go through a mock wedding ceremony (a plot twist foreshadowing Violet's fake marriage with Ford Madox Ford) and set up house together. Eventually Rosette becomes possessive, demanding, accusatory, like "an unpaid bill in the room." In the tradition of French realism, Violet traced the revulsion between disillusioned lovers, echoing her own painful sexual wisdom, often transcribing phrases directly from her diaries.

When the novel was published in 1904, with a dedication to Henry James, one reviewer called it "a story of passion and disillusionment, full of strong character-drawing and intense true feeling." Marie Lowndes, sister of author Hilaire Belloc, thought it Violet's "most important book . . . the first modern novel which dealt, in a serious sense, with the problem of illicit love." After writing *Sooner or Later,* Violet had purged some but not all of her anger.

In late 1906, while still seeing Maugham, James and Bennett socially, Violet began a year-long affair with H. G. Wells, four years her junior. Wells was then married to his second wife, Jane, and also was sleeping with the writer Dorothy Richardson. Wells and Violet met as fellow contributors to *Black and White,* the *Pall Mall Gazette* and the *Saturday Review.* By then Wells had written *The Time Machine, The Invisible Man* and *The War of the Worlds* (its radio dramatization by Orson Welles ignited the famous Martian invasion panic of 1938).

Wells practiced "free love"—dalliances were solely for mutual physical release. In the midst of his flirtation with Violet, Dorothy announced that she was pregnant, and then that she had miscarried—a fact Wells never believed, calling the pregnancy hysterical, an excuse to get free of him sexually.

A stocky panda bear of a man, with penetrating bright-blue beady eyes, a bushy mustache and a grating, high-pitched Cockney accent, Wells, though not handsome, had a beguiling manner. "Be nice to a very melancholy man . . . I'm rather down, cross and feeble," he wrote Violet, inviting her to lunch at Torino's, noting suggestively that his afternoon was free. "Do you know of any convenient place for sin in Kensington?" he inquired on another occasion. "If so, write here and tell me and I'll wire you if I can get away." Indeed, after seven years with Crawfurd, Violet knew quite a few places perfect for sinning.

With women, Wells sought what he called the "transitory ecstatic physical realization of his _persona_." When he looked back on his numerous infidelities, he said they "never entered intimately and deeply into my emotional life. . . . My impression is that I got nothing better than I gave. I was loved as I loved. . . . The exchanges were fairly equal—two libertines meet—and when I _got_ a woman, a woman _got_ a man."

Violet's "nervous lively wit laced with threads of French" attracted him. She was also vulnerable, mourning the recent death of George Boughton and, Wells said, "full just then of the same restless craving for the clasp of an appreciative body as myself. So we came to an understanding . . . we lunched and dined together and found great satisfaction in each other's embraces." Violet introduced Wells to the "mysteries of Soho and Pimlico," where they explored "the world of convenient little restaurants with private rooms upstairs, and the struggling lodging-houses which are only too happy to let rooms permanently to intermittent occupants." Best of all, Wells said, "there was little or no pretense of an exclusive preoccupation."

In 1900 Wells had built himself an imposing mansion (with central heating and modern plumbing) called Spade House, at Sandgate near Folkestone. Violet was a frequent houseguest, sometimes accompanied by her attractive niece Rosamond (called "The Beauty" by her aunt); Violet was shepherding Silvia's daughter through her first London season. Spade House weekends were frivolous and jolly, with many attractive women to surround and flatter the attention-craving Wells. His long-suffering wife was content to be a motherly organizer, allowing him to womanize without interference. Violet observed that Jane no longer looked pretty: "to save trouble she does her hair in a knot on the top of her head which doesn't suit her, makes her look scanny . . . I ventured to tell her so. I don't think she likes me. I don't see, all things considered, why she should. I should not, in her place. I am her Mrs. Ralph Browne," a reference to Lita Browne. Here Violet overstated Wells's feelings for her, or for any of his many lovers; he never considered leaving Jane and his children.

In August 1907, at Spade House, Violet attracted attention

by playing tennis in her bare feet and flirting outrageously with Wells; she was thrilled by the obvious jealousy of Dorothy Richardson, with her "half sulky moonface and drab fawn clothes shapeless over a shapeless figure." At one point Wells lured Violet, who was wearing a lace-trimmed white-and-green-dotted dress, into a tool shed, which he called his study. Later they arranged to meet in some bushes, "encompassing us but not quite," with Wells in "continual terror of Dorothy's sharp eyes . . . and I am such a devil that I am only nice to him *outside*. He is getting cross with me."

Still childish at forty-five, Violet enjoyed manipulating Wells, who soon moved on to Rosamund Bland, and Amber Reeves, who bore him a daughter. Wells and Violet remained friends through the years, and he said she inspired Beatrice in *Tono-Bungay,* described by Violet as "the pert, aristocratic lure of the enquiring, pathetic, and pushful Wells boy who was the hero."

By the time of her affair with Maugham, Violet had syphilis, thanks to Oswald Crawfurd. She did not realize the seriousness of her condition (apparently none of her sexual partners contracted the disease). The course of syphilis is different for each individual; secondary symptoms include malaise, fever, headaches, joint pain, depression and skin lesions. Violet had all these ailments from time to time, but mostly she complained of "spots" on her face. As early as 1893, nineteen months after their first ardent night in Gravesend, there was a hint in her diary of some medical problem: "I am really ill. He [Crawfurd] says he will take me to a doctor, some doctor whom my people won't know and to whom I can speak freely as a married woman."

In September 1896 she wrote that she was "hideous with spots." Crawfurd recommended Carter's Pills; in *Their Hearts,* Violet draws attention to a prescription bottle labeled Mrs. Barker (a spelling variation on Barber, a name used by Crawfurd when renting rooms). Violet was taking arsenic, a common cosmetic treatment, to freshen her skin; it was prescribed by Cholmeley, but there is no evidence that she continued to use it for more than a few months. At this time there were few means of treating syphilis, only bichloride of mercury injections and potassium iodide; no successful treatment was available until 1909, when Dr. Paul Ehrlich developed his "magic bullet," Salvarsan, an arsenic-based drug.

In 1907, during a weekend in Norwich, Violet's skin problems were noticed by her hostess, Ethel Brunner, who said her own spotty face had been cured by a Dr. Payne. Violet went to this physician, but he was unable to help. "Perhaps hers aren't caused by the same cause as mine," she wrote. "He *said* mine was my hair [which Violet chose to believe]. But [Dr.] Stephen Paget didn't. He was beastly to me I remember. He cut about eight [spots] and left me bleeding. . . . I hated Paget so, to whom Cholmeley had recommended me, that I could not tell him all about the row with OC which was the cause of it all." Around the same time she wrote to Marie Belloc Lowndes, inviting her to tea at the New Reform Club, noting, ambiguously, that "it is hard that suspense should express itself in spots!"

Judging from this diary entry, Violet must have suspected something was wrong in 1905, when she saw Paget, but it is doubtful that he prescribed any medical treatment; this is further documented in an autobiographical fragment dated August 1936, six years before her death, when she recalled how Cholmeley came to lunch at her club, "with tears in his eyes [and] told me to my face and of my face (and my wrist) that I had a disgraceful illness in fact tertiaries [and in this stage incurable] only he did not name it or do more than hint. But I had had warnings. Archie Propert [a suitor] looked at me at the Monds [Alfred and Angela Mond] and my spots on my forehead and said, 'You ought not to be out' ie. going about. (He said, 'you ought to be in bed,' actually)." Cholmeley sent her to Paget, who "looked at me and spoke to me as to something unclean. I never went again . . . as he looked upon me with disgust and loathing, as I could see. It was the most inglorious moment of my life. And of course Archie Propert, being a doctor, did not propose, as everyone thought he would." At the end of this typed page Violet added in her own hand, "Now I know what fallen women may feel."

Arthur Mizener, Ford's biographer, interpreted this statement as "remarkably honest and at the same time naïve. 'Fallen women'— the socially superior and personally charming, if not morally impeccable, company of Pinero's Paula Tanqueray, of Wilde's Lady Windemere and Rachel Arbuthnot, of Violet's own autobiographical heroine in *Sooner or Later*. She had transformed the drab and humiliating life of venereal disease's slow dulling of the mind and destruction of the body into the romantically interesting situation of some Dame aux Camélias."

Perhaps, but this ignores Violet's Pre-Raphaelite heritage: she had grown up with the "fallen woman" image, a popular subject in early nineteenth-century British painting. She had seen Holman Hunt's *The Awakening Conscience* and Rossetti's *Found,* pictorial studies of women trapped by the lust of men. At the end of her days she probably felt closer to these women than to a consumptive Parisian courtesan.

When Douglas Goldring, a friend of Violet's from 1908 until her death, first wrote about her condition, he never specified syphilis. He noted only that Crawfurd had helped Violet professionally, but also did her an "appalling injury . . . which undoubtedly embittered her whole life and lent to all her subsequent novels their valuable 'Brontë-esque' qualities, their strain of 'nastiness' and their rich flavour of the macabre." (Oscar Wilde's biographer Richard Ellmann makes a similar claim. Convinced that Wilde contracted syphilis as an Oxford student and died from it, he maintains that the disease played a crucial role in his life, giving his early poetry a dark, self-destructive tone.)

In the summer of 1907 Violet faced a new sexual quandary, posed by a woman eighteen years her junior. Marguerite Radclyffe Hall, who would write the infamous lesbian novel *The Well of Loneliness,* made advances, which Violet rebuffed. Sexual inversion, as the Victorians termed homosexuality, was not shocking to Violet; she accepted it as yet another kind of sexual excitement. So she explained it to a woman friend who asked her about lesbians, trying "to lighten just a little her astounding innocence, but she stopped her pretty ears. 'Do you know, dear Violet—I don't think I'll hear any more.' It all had the effect of a heavy snub. These so-called innocent women have a way of bringing you to the water of revelation and letting you drink and reveal out of kindness what you know and then pulling you up sharp."

Born to a philandering father and a quarrelsome mother, Radclyffe Hall grew up in a prosperous Catholic family, lonely and poorly educated. During her youth she pursued women who ended up at the altar. Her first long relationship was with Mrs. Mabel "Ladye" Batten, whose male admirers included the Prince of Wales and the poet-adventurer Wilfred Scawen Blunt. The affair began after her interest in Violet waned and lasted until Ladye's death in 1915; then followed a twenty-eight-year liaison with the sculptor Una Troubridge, wife of an admiral.

Violet observed that Radclyffe Hall did not have "a bit of romantic feeling about her. Her heart only goes out to physical geography sort of things like sunsets and autumn tints. Man is vile to her and I believe that is why she will never marry." Radclyffe Hall wrote Violet a long letter offering friendship and affection: "I do not know just how much you are likely to be bored by my affection which you never after all sought, for perhaps even now you are thinking me impertinent, as you read this letter. I can't help it Violet I must risk that, if I can't always say the things I am feeling when we are together it is because you have built a brick wall around yourself and I must not venture to get inside it. No doubt you have many good reasons for wishing it to be there. I have never met any one who could so repulse affection as you can in your quiet sweet way. If you are angry with me, what can I say except that I am so fond of you? I will never bother you to read this sort of thing again. Forgive it this once. Don't bother to answer. I will call for you Thursday unless you stop me."

Violet did not end the friendship. The two women shopped (Radclyffe Hall made Violet order a purple tweed dress and a purple greatcoat, which inspired Henry James's nickname, "Purple Patch") and they lunched, but Violet noticed a "coolness only because she loved me so hotly, poor darling. She was good to me. But she is so strong and has put it behind her and now, like Rossetti's girl, 'Her eyes looked on me from an emptied heart,' because my heart had *never* been full of her. She used to write and say that I erected a *brick* wall between her and me. Why brick? I would say nervously, but I knew. I was always full of someone else."

They traveled to Malvern Wells in Worcestershire to stay at Radclyffe Hall's rambling gabled house called Highfield. "I was tetchy about the food and gave myself the airs of a Sultana," Violet wrote. "It is her fault for being so at my feet, poor dear. She is a stately intent sort of body, her poetry is her only sex outlet. I behave like a minx, shows how easily one is corrupted by adoration." In the evenings Radclyffe Hall came to her bedroom wearing a Japanese kimono from Liberty's "with a streak of blue on the collar and her fine sandy auburn hair in a plait."

They talked of love, and Violet pressed her to repeat any gossip about Crawfurd: Radclyffe Hall revealed that people said Violet once "had made a great mistake," and Violet marveled at the "hypocritical English way of alluding to a seduction." Afterward they went to Bedburn to visit Silvia. Her husband, Walton, was impressed with how Radclyffe Hall shouldered a gun, and insisted on hunting rabbits with her. Surprisingly, Walton, with his roving eye, did not try to seduce her. "M [Radclyffe Hall] is rather a tough proposition," Violet concluded, "so cold and manly."

Violet was earning a reputation as a literary hostess. At the Writers' Club on Bruton Street she held bimonthly luncheons for twelve, never spending more than a couple of pounds, with a "good" house wine. Among the guests were Bram Stoker, Radclyffe Hall, Arnold Bennett, the hostess Gwen Otter, Jane and H. G. Wells, Angela Mond, the playwright H. H. Davis, Somerset Maugham, Provost Battersby (foreign correspondent for the *Morning Post*), Agnes Farley, Austin Harrison of the *Daily Mail,* and her old friend Edward Heron Allen and his wife. Violet's other club was the New Reform on Adelphi Terrace overlooking the Thames, where members drank bananas and eggs beaten up in glasses. "I know exactly where to put myself now, to dominate the room," she wrote of the club's lounge.

During the cold, chilly January of 1907, Violet invited her nieces, Amerye and Rosamond, to South Lodge. First Rosamond got the flu, then Amerye developed such severe pneumonia that the doctor feared for her life. Unwisely, Violet did not inform Silvia until Amerye's temperature shot up to 103 degrees, and then shifted the blame, explaining that Amerye had arrived with a cold. Silvia said that South Lodge was too cold, and that Bedburn, her home, was a warm house. Violet described her nieces as "pampered." Silvia angrily replied, "I suppose you would say we were *pampered* at Tor Villa, sleeping in an attic at 70 degrees, breaking the ice in our jugs—very seldom hot water except to get up with—no bedroom slippers, or dressing gowns or jackets." Arguments often flared up between the sisters, mostly over Violet's need to have Rosamond visit London so frequently.

Obsessive about showing off the seventeen-year-old Rosamond, Violet gave luncheons in her honor and hoped to make a splendid match. Arnold Bennett admired Rosamond's beauty, which had a Pre-Raphaelite patina, but thought her a bit "mad." Violet kept track of everyone who did or did not admire "my Rosamond." Henry James was quite taken with her country-bred healthiness and asked Violet for a photograph, which disappointed him, although he kept it on his mantelpiece. "No photograph does much more than rather civilly extinguish the life and gloom (so exquisite a thing) in a happy child's face," he wrote to Violet. Douglas Goldring, summoned as a dancing partner, found Rosamond "rather dumb . . . with an odd little habit of gasping in the middle of her not over bright remarks. Violet was possessed," he said, "by a devouring maternal affection for Rosamond which was almost painful to witness." More than that, Violet was reliving her successes of the past, when her own dance card was always filled.

But her sisters challenged any good intentions. Venice disapproved, Violet said, of her "having charge of an innocent girl after my record & my life _now_." Silvia told her the neighbors "know too much about you. . . . I have pondered all this, & have trusted you very much, & I feel confident you will be most awfully discreet about the child, & guard against the slightest breath of scandal or talk. Forgive my plain speaking, but it is better to speak out & you will be sensible enough to see my point of view."

Silvia agreed to Rosamond's visits at this time only because her existence at Bedburn had turned nasty. Walton, used to sleeping with the maid, now took as a mistress an orphaned friend of his wife's who was a houseguest, a Miss Eames. At the best of times, Silvia's life had never been happy. She had grown up unloved, been traumatized as a child by a middle-aged beachcomber who fondled her, suffered a painful childbirth and now had to endure her husband's infidelities.

One New Year's Eve, Silvia found her husband in Miss Eames's bed. Utterly calm at being interrupted, Walton ordered Silvia to leave, saying he would return in a minute. After dressing, he entered their bedchamber and admonished her for making a fuss: the girl was an orphan and her guest, he whined, and he was only helping her see in the New Year!

Violet said Walton liked Miss Eames because she was common, and urged her sister to divorce the brute, or at least repulse him, which Silvia preferred, for she had never cared much for men or sex. To defend his behavior, Walton complained to Violet that after he made love to Silvia, she would get up and put on "a clean nightgown," an act he interpreted as mockery, not modesty.

Even though Violet had endured an unfaithful lover, she proclaimed her sister weak for putting up with the same treatment from a tyrannical husband. But she cared mostly about Rosamond, the "ugly, long yellow legged rickety baby" whose appearance had repulsed her after her birth in the summer of 1890. Her niece had grown into a swan, but Violet was quick to point out flaws: Rosamond was wooden and thickset ("I mean a pelvic circumference which points to a large curate's family which in effect is what she desires"), as well as pathetically English, with "a veiled antagonism between her and her mother which makes me feel she is glad at all costs to be away from her." No matter how much stardust Violet sprinkled around, Rosamond remained an ingenuous North Country girl unable to dazzle men with sparkling epigrams. "She will marry the first person who offers first to have a baby," her mother accurately warned Violet.

After much debate, Rosamond's parents decided that she would come out in the winter of 1909, after a year of finishing in Paris. She needed French discipline, they said, for she had transgressed class boundaries (she gave household matches and soap to the hired help and cared for the lodgekeeper's baby). In October 1908, Rosamond arrived in Paris, accompanied by mother and aunt. Silvia placed her with an elderly spinster in the suburbs, where, Violet argued, she would learn only bourgeois French and bourgeois marketing. Violet made sure she was enrolled in a course at the Sorbonne, and Agnes Farley offered to show her the city.

During this trip Violet saw the "La Femme Nue" revue at the Moulin Rouge. "It was for me a great experience, a revelation of the sanctity of the human body," she wrote, "*sans voiles* of tights and sashes and maillots." She was moved by one performer, "naked except for a sort of gold lace with huge reticulations from her neck to her knees . . . which allowed the brown hair to show very faintly. . . . There was no suggestion of meretriciousness about her and yet . . . she had absolutely nothing on under the wide diagonals of the gold netting—three inches square I should have said—and she had not shaved anywhere," an ingenuous reaction for such a worldly woman, but typical of Violet's simplistic honesty, a trait that fascinated her admirers.

With Rosamond settled in Paris, Violet returned to the routine of South Lodge. She saw little of Venice, who visited only when forced to pay the interest on Margaret's £4,500 loan to her husband. Once there, however, she snooped around, interviewing the servants about Violet's care of their mother. Since Violet lived rent-free, Venice felt she should devote more time to Margaret. Then, too, Venice worried about Margaret making additional bequests to Violet if she did; Violet was already the beneficiary under a 1902 codicil leaving her £3,000 whether married or not. Venice once threatened her sister: "If Mammy has made any fresh bequests in your favour—altered things materially—it would be infamous and I'll fight." When told this, Margaret replied, "Yes, but I'll circumvent them."

Margaret Hunt was increasingly cranky and censorious. She was writing her last novel, _The Governess,_ but had lost her touch. _Black and White_'s reviewer noted that her "admirable" novel _Thornicroft's Model_ had "a good deal of analysis and psychology," but in her recent books there was "little or none of these things." She refused to dress for dinner and wandered off by herself. Violet, to her credit, took her out ("she had the habit of society and kept it to the last"). But as often happens with elderly people, Margaret became suspicious of kindnesses, seeing Venice's visits, for example, as attempts to obtain more money for her husband. (In 1901, Venice and her husband, Willie Benson, had asked the family physician to commit Margaret to an asylum; Dr. Barton refused, explaining that she suffered only lapses of memory, common for anyone her age, and to remove her from home would be even more deleterious.)

For solace Violet turned to Henry James, whose friendship was now an important part of her life. He praised her "heroism and valour," and counseled her not to allow "domestic chill," referring to problems with her sisters, to "tax all the daily resources of your genius . . . These are terrible mortal hours, but sit tight, hold on, & deal with them day to day as you can." Another time, he hoped her "brave life [was] winning most of its battles. You strike me always in the thick of the fray, & I look at you through a hole in the curtain of a broken-down ambulance—pulled off into a distant field," which was James's way of sympathizing, but from a safe perspective.

Violet was a frequent visitor to Lamb House at Rye in Sussex, the one real home of James's roving life. There he wrote his last three novels, *The Ambassadors, The Wings of the Dove* and *The Golden Bowl,* and lived until 1914, two years before his death. James met his guests with ceremonial gaiety at the railway station—accompanied by his frisky, ruby-colored dachshund, Max, on a long lead which the playful dog wrapped around lampposts. James escorted his visitors through the winding cobblestoned streets of the ancient town and pointed out Romney Marsh (acres of sheep-dotted, silvery grasslands threaded with canals) on the way to Lamb House (now part of the National Trust). After breakfasting with his guests, James disappeared—weather permitting—into the garden study (destroyed in a 1940 German air raid), where his booming voice could be heard for some four hours dictating to his amanuensis as he paced up and down.

Although James himself almost certainly was never intimate with either sex, he was indeed a voyeur of the sex lives of others. He eagerly devoured details on the latest divorces, and the Oscar Wilde scandal moved him to write that Wilde's fall was "hideously tragic, and the squalid violence of it gives him an interest (of misery) that he never had for me, in any degree, before." When Wilde read *The Turn of the Screw,* he said, "James is developing, but he will never arrive at passion, I fear." Nor would James allow himself to be emotionally involved in the travails of others, often interrupting a story by extending a finger and saying, "Thank you, I've got as much—all I want."

To James, Violet was "society." When she entertained him with gossip, she was the "Improper Person of Babylon," "the lady about town," but when she tried to lure him from his writing desk at Lamb House to celebrate life in London, he refused, calling her the "great Devourer," explaining that the city was "spasms & dashes, all made up of appointments, adjustments, dense memoranda and rattling cab journeys. . . . You *are* Society, and I am more and more contemplative, detachment—hanging on to the world after the fashion of a very obese spider by a thin thread of my own independent weaving."

He refused with good reason for he was struggling with editing the New York Edition (twenty-four volumes of his collected works), but when he had a hiatus from deadlines he invited Violet to Rye for a November weekend. She wore the purple coat and packed a Chinese dressing gown (chosen for her by Radclyffe Hall during one of their shopping sprees) and a red-and-white chiffon dress she had purchased in Paris.

At dinner James's cook served a bisque that made her ill; she rushed to her room and vomited, soiling her new dress. Feeling better around nine o'clock, and in a flirtatious mood (she was the only guest), she donned her Chinese dressing gown and "drifted as I know how" into the drawing room, but James disappointed her by wanting only to discuss the merits of Mrs. Humphry Ward's books. Violet complained that he never critiqued her novels, and James admitted that he read women's books reluctantly, if at all. What he wanted, Violet said bitterly, was her gossip, "but never more than half of it, always getting bored or delicately offended."

The next morning at breakfast, still unsettled by the bisque, Violet gingerly sampled her food and had to watch James "Fletcherize" (a health fad of masticating food into liquid) his breakfast cereal, topped with a poached egg. This was too disgusting to endure and, perversely, she chose this inappropriate time to discuss her feelings for Oswald Crawfurd. How could someone with "such a thin mentality," James asked his queasy guest, have achieved such conquests? Insulted, Violet blurted out, "I loved him!" James got up from the table "like a dog that has had enough of his bone, and closed the discussion, for it was becoming too intimate, too little academic for him. He 'skoots' from passion as if he had been once bitten by it and yet I am sure that in _my_ sense of the word he never has—he is incapable—a glance at a photograph I once saw in a drawer in my room at The Lamb House convinced me of that. It was the face of a lad sealed in eternal ignorance of one side of emotion . . . and yet a powerful head . . . of the type that goes Nap [to the limit] on passion, if the physical nature had been according . . . I don't know how to put it."

Later that day, after their tense breakfast, frisky Max and his dour master escorted Violet to the station. "We walked about on the platform, I felt he was content to get back to work, but pleased with my visit and my purple get-up, motor veil on a little purple velour hat and the big coat." He told her that the "weekend was a purple patch on his existence. I shall call you The Purple Patch—you are so vivid." It was a sobriquet Violet would cherish.

□

Celebrating her forty-fifth birthday in 1907, Violet was no nearer marriage or emotional fulfillment than she had been seventeen years earlier when she first met Crawfurd. At year's end she had a bittersweet finale. Cholmeley visited South Lodge and asked her to sing; she tried a tune, but her voice was gone. Then her "faithful" suitor finally spoke. As she recorded in her diary, he "did not want to marry her; he had given it all up," realizing that they could never be happy. It was the first time in the eighteen years of their friendship that he had talked to her of marriage. "I did not ask him to love me and if I had given in it would have killed him since I *hated* his touch," she later recalled.

In the end the good, faithful Dr. Cholmeley with his leather-bound books and his green-dyed carnations was too boring for any witty woman and too much of a mama's boy ever to have taken a wife. Still, Violet took him for granted, anticipated his proposal, counted on it as a last resort. Now it was over—and she was alone. "Somehow," she wrote, "I was just beginning to think as Mamma says that I have 'run my rig' and want as Silvia says 'something kind and strong.'"

PART THREE

1908-1914

9

The English Review

VIOLET NEEDED a cause, a diversion. Always a feminist in her thinking, she now acted like one and joined the Women's Social and Political Union, led by the fiery militant Emmeline Pankhurst and her daughter Christabel. In the nascent days of the equal rights movement, launched in Britain in the 1880s by Charles Bradlaugh and Annie Besant (who linked the cause with birth control and socialism), Margaret Hunt had had Browning, Millais and Burne-Jones sign petitions. Violet enlisted support from other well-known artists and writers, attended mass demonstrations, offered South Lodge as a place for meetings and lent her name to fundraisers, where the women begged and pleaded to collect donations.

"It was most dramatic," she wrote of one. "Women stood up in their places and offered odd 100 pounds. I took my cousin George Raine. He was full of the voluptuous appeal of the Pankhurst—her lazy outspread palm and so on. Then we went to Roman's and supped with a large and disreputable party." The contrast appealed to Violet, though her advocacy was sincere.

The marches, arrests and confrontations filled a lonely, loverless life and provided drama, though Violet managed to avoid the brutality endured by many other ardent suffragists. Parliament had debated the Votes for Women question no fewer than eighteen times by 1905, and by 1909 a militant faction of the movement had emerged. Women set fire to buildings, smashed shop windows, tore the clothes off cabinet ministers, jabbed their ten-inch steel hatpins into police horses and raked policemen's faces with their fingernails.*

Protesters were hauled off to Holloway Prison, where they lived for three months with hardened criminals; during hunger strikes they were force-fed through tubes in their mouths, a painful and humiliating experience. Violet claimed she too would have gone to prison had she not had the responsibility of caring for an invalid mother and a young niece. "Mrs. Pankhurst and Christabel kindly dispensed with my services *in extremis*," she wrote. "So my nose remains in its own shape, not squashed against the flank of a horse— voted by Miss Evelyn Sharp as the safest place of all when the mounted police were turned out to disperse us—or torn in the efforts of the doctors to forcibly feed us."

She avoided physical harm, but received unwarranted recognition for collecting money for three days in February 1908 outside the Kensington High Street railway station: her photograph appeared in *Black and White* next to a picture of Emmeline Pankhurst being arrested for attempting to present a resolution to the House of Commons. "Much has been said of our heroism," she snobbishly bragged, "in standing outside to beg, and I fancy she [the writer May Sinclair, who collected with Violet] felt as I did—as if we had suddenly been stripped naked with a cross-sensation of being drowned in a tank and gasping for breath. We had asked all our friends and editors and readers to come and cheer us up as we stood there pilloried, and they backed us up splendidly. Mr. John Galsworthy sauntered along and tipped us immeasurably and gallantly— everyone in fact, who wished the movement well."

And if the literary elite did not support suffrage, Violet worked to change their minds. G. K. Chesterton testily wrote her: "I am not a supporter of female suffrage. I believe in women as despots, but not as democrats. I obey them individually but not collectively. Therefore I submit to my wife and as she is against female suffrage, I follow meekly in her footsteps." Although sympathetic, George Meredith felt that women were "erratic in policy. They are quite unaware of the sturdy hostility they are exciting."

*One woman slashed a Velásquez painting in the National Gallery, and Emily Wilding Davison, wearing the white, purple and green suffragist colors, ran out on the Epsom Downs racecourse in the middle of the 1913 Derby and was trampled to death by Anmer, the king's horse. All women did not receive the vote in Britain until 1928.

Henry James was tentative, but did agree to sign a copy of the _English Review_ containing an article for a suffrage fund-raiser. "No— I confess I am not eager for the _avènement_ [advent] of multitudinous & overwhelming female electorate," he wrote to Violet, "& don't see how any man in his senses _can_ be: I am eager at present only for dreadnoughts or aeroplanes & people to man—not woman— them!" James's attitude was not a surprise: he was, after all, a great friend of Mrs. Humphry Ward, who was a celebrity supporter of the Anti-Suffrage League (Rudyard Kipling also supported it). It was a constant irritant to Violet that James kept Mrs. Ward's books on a shelf above his writing table and gave her advice that contributed to her phenomenal success. Ward's uncle Matthew Arnold once huffed: "Written a novel has she? No Arnold can write a novel. If they could, _I_ should have written one long ago!" This was the kind of gossip Henry James loved to hear from his "Purple Patch."

Though still a "sensualist of the emotions," Violet, in her maturity, learned to temper the adolescent behavior that had hastened the end of the Crawfurd affair. She would always be an unconventional conventional woman, but at this time she seriously considered settling down. To "society," she was the respectable aunt chaperoning her niece through her first London season and the dutiful unmarried daughter caring for an aged parent. But how boring it all was, when what she wanted was a lover.

Violet had completed _White Rose of Weary Leaf_, a retelling of the classic governess story, and her journalism was read in _The Sphere, The Tatler, The Sketch_ and the _Daily Chronicle_. She was "one of the outstanding women writers of the period," the writer Douglas Goldring later observed, "and, within the limitations of her particular world, she 'knew everyone' and 'went everywhere,' " and ranked "as one of the most exciting figures in the Edwardian capital. Fashionable, brilliant, daring. . . . She was glamour personified."

Violet knew that few women writers of the time surpassed her flair for clever dialogue, but her prose style, never pellucid, was sometimes sloppy and ungrammatical. She often wrote with a litter of newborn kittens on her lap, which did not inspire careful work. She admitted that her books "were haphazard and inspired with a great amount of pains bestowed on revision. There I am supreme. I don't care _how often_ I rewrite but so carelessly generally I leave a bad sentence where I found it." When Maugham read _White Rose_, which was dedicated to him, he found "slovenly sentences" and advised her not to attempt long ones. "Your style is always better when they are short. The full stop does away with any number of obscurities and makes the dragging subsidiary clause which is apparently so dear to you impossible."

Maugham told her to leave Chapman & Hall; it was a good idea, he suggested, to start a new association and leave behind the memories of Crawfurd's mentorship. Violet asked her agent, James Brand Pinker, whom Wells had recommended, to send *White Rose* to Maugham's publisher, William Heinemann. He agreed to take the novel if she changed the ending; the public, he said, would not accept a pregnant woman accidentally killed by bricks from a crumbling chimney stack. Heinemann gave her a generous £100 advance with a 20 percent royalty (10 to 15 percent was the norm) on the six-shilling price up to 5,000 copies and 25 percent thereafter.

After a meeting with Heinemann on April 25, 1907, Violet ran into Ford Madox Hueffer on the street. She had met him a month earlier at a dinner party at John Galworthy's, where they had reminisced about their Pre-Raphaelite childhood and exchanged notes on women's suffrage, which Hueffer publicly supported in lectures and articles. He was a reviewer for the *Tribune,* and Violet, chattering away, finally asked him to notice her book. "He looked very red and golden against the dark grey wall," she said, "and smiled down at me—he is very tall—and said he would. He was awfully amused at my 'brass.' I always do ask for what I want—of a man and especially of a man with reddish hair."

According to Ford's later version of the meeting, he was walking up Bedford Street when Violet "suddenly jumped out at me from the door of No. 32, and exclaimed: 'I say: Mr. H.....n, the publisher, says that you have made the fortune of So-and-So by writing a Literary Portrait of him. Why don't you do one of me?' This, you will observe, is the direct method. I had at that date (except for passages in a pre-Raphaelite infancy) only met the lady once—the day [actually the month] before—and I didn't, to tell the truth, very exactly fix the author's identity in my mind. Still it was the direct, the pagan method of attack, whether for extracting notices from a slightly bemused critic or for writing striking fictions; and I should certainly have 'done' the portrait if the *Tribune* had not stopped."

"As a rule," said Ford, astounded by Violet's assertiveness, "whether you approach a critic or a 'subject,' you are vastly apologetic, vague, conditional. But there is never any of these qualities about Miss Hunt's work: What she thinks she may require she goes and takes—the same as me!" Violet had made a favorable impression, but it would be nearly a year before they met again.

Joseph Leopold Ford Hermann Madox Hueffer, to use his full baptismal name, which he eventually shortened to Ford Madox Ford, was the son of Franz Carl Christoph Johannes Hüffer, a German journalist with distinguished academic credentials, who had emigrated to England, anglicized his name to Francis Hueffer, become _The Times'_ music critic and introduced Wagner to England; he championed Schopenhauer and wrote the standard work on the Provençal poets. Ford's mother, Catherine, was the daughter of the Pre-Raphaelite painter Ford Madox Brown and Brown's model, Emma Hill, a fifteen-year-old farm girl whom he secretly wed three years after Catherine's birth. (Brown's first wife had died young, leaving a daughter, Lucy, later the wife of William Michael Rossetti, Gabriel's brother.)

Born in Merton, Surrey (now a part of London), in 1873, Ford, like Violet, spent much of his youth in the company of the era's thinkers, poets and painters. As children they first met at a party, where Violet recalled swatting Ford's hand for playing ball with the penny buns. She thrived in this heady intellectual atmosphere, but he felt cowed and insecure, forever hearing his father calling him "the patient but extremely stupid donkey."

When he was sixteen, an age when a young boy needs his father's guidance and approval, Francis Hueffer died, leaving the family impoverished. Ford was yanked out of Praetorius, a progressive private school in Folkestone (which he later elevated to Winchester or sometimes Eton). With his mother and younger brother, Oliver, he went to live with his widowed maternal grandfather in London. He spent less than a year at London's University College School, finishing off his education in the cafés near the British Museum, arguing with the anarchists and pseudo-intellectuals and wondering what to do with his life.

Ford adored his capricious but saintly grandfather—a formidable figure to any adolescent boy seeking a surrogate father—who humorously signed his letters to his grandson "MAD-OX." Brown was a generous man, ever ready to help his fellow artists. He told Ford never to refuse assistance to anyone "whose genius you think shows promise of being greater than your own," advice Ford never forgot. But lack of parental love left its scars, and Ford grew into manhood with more than the usual neurotic problems: depressions and free-floating anxiety (called neurasthenia in Victorian times), recurring bouts of debilitating agoraphobia, thoughts of suicide and fantasies of grand proportions.

Ford was a self-mythologizer or, as some bluntly said, a liar. Throughout his life, he reinvented himself. Not born and bred an English country gentleman, he decided to act and dress like one or to create fictional characters, such as John Dowell and Edward Ashburnham in *The Good Soldier* and Christopher Tietjens in *Parade's End,* to satisfy this self-image. When ambivalent about his Anglo-German-French heritage, he adopted another: "I am a Cockney myself and so is Mr. Charles Chaplin and so was Keats," Ford boasted, ignoring the fact that the sound of Bow bells would be faint indeed in Merton. He bragged that his Prussian heritage made him the Baron von Aschendorff, while during World War I he claimed a Russian or Dutch background to escape the stigma of being German.

At Praetorius School, Ford met and courted Elsie Martindale, the daughter of a prosperous pharmacist; her sister Mary, a beautiful girl of delicate health, also fell in love with him. When Ford asked for Elsie's hand in marriage, the Martindales, fearful of Mary's reaction, refused. "We can always cut our throats and have it over," he wrote Elsie, making grand opera out of their thwarted desires. They eloped in 1894, when Elsie was seventeen; six years later there were two daughters, Christina and Katharine. Ford, who had joined the church at nineteen to please his German relatives, insisted they be raised as Catholics.

Most of Ford and Elsie's married life together would be spent in Kent and Sussex, in the company of James, Wells, Stephen Crane, Edward Garnett, the astute publisher's reader, and Arthur Marwood, the Yorkshire gentleman of Ford's fantasies. These were pleasant years. All the writers lived close by, and after a chilly walk or bicycle ride over Romney Marsh they would drop by Ford's home for a cup of his special punch.

Although his in-laws thought his prospects dim, Ford was not bereft of credentials. He had published three children's stories, a volume of poems and a novel, and was completing a biography of his grandfather. And then, in 1898, Garnett introduced him to Joseph Conrad.* Shortly thereafter, Conrad wrote Ford to suggest that they collaborate on a revision of Ford's current book _Seraphina,_ which Garnett said was unpublishable. Since leaving his life at sea, Conrad had spent four years writing _Almayer's Folly_ and _An Outcast of the Islands,_ and was completing _The Nigger of the Narcissus._

Conrad explained that he wrote slowly and with difficulty and doubted his command of English. Working together sounded like a fine idea: Ford, at twenty-four, was still searching for a father figure and a writing style; Conrad, at forty, had lived a full life and had many tales to tell about his adventurous years spent in exotic locales. In particular, Ford welcomed the arrangement because he had "unchanging affection and admiration for [Conrad's] almost miraculous gifts."

Born Teodor Józef Konrad Korzeniowski of a Polish family in the Ukraine, Conrad had lost both his parents by age twelve. He was twenty-one before he spoke English, which he first learned on the ship _Skimmer of the Seas,_ plying between Lowestoft and Newcastle. Sixteen years older than Ford, Conrad could be authoritarian, but Henry James, for one, was baffled by what they had in common. "To me this is like a bad dream which one relates at breakfast!" James exclaimed. "Their traditions and their gifts are so dissimilar. Collaboration between them is to me inconceivable."

But Ford did more than edit and correct Conrad's language errors. He bolstered Conrad's ego by assuring him that he was the

*Edward Garnett was the scion of a famed literary family. His grandfather Richard Garnett was assistant librarian to Antonio Panizzi, who planned the British Museum; his father, also Richard, was the museum's keeper of printed books and wrote the highly regarded _Twilight of the Gods._ Edward and his five siblings grew up among the book stacks; he became a book editor and discovered Conrad when he read _Almayer's Folly_ in 1894. Few novelists of the time did not profit by Garnett's criticism. His wife, Constance, was the first to make complete translations into English of Turgenev, Dostoevsky and Tolstoy. His son David, a novelist and publisher, became a Bloomsburyite and took as his second wife Angelica Bell, twenty-six years his junior, the illegitimate daughter of the painters Vanessa Bell and Duncan Grant and the niece of Virginia Woolf. (David had had a youthful romance with Grant, and had unsuccessfully tried to seduce Vanessa Bell.)

greater writer; he saw him through times of self-doubt and despair, and tidied up his muddled life by organizing his financial affairs. Their partnership worked as well as any in literary history, and for a decade they plotted, wrote and edited novels with what Ford said was an "absolute one-ness of purpose and with absolute absence of rivalry," producing (under a shared byline) *The Inheritors, Romance* (from *Seraphina*) and *The Nature of the Crime.*

In 1903, depressed over the lukewarm reception of *Romance* and his stale marriage, Ford complicated his life by starting an affair with Mary Martindale, his sister-in-law, a Pre-Raphaelite "stunner" with golden-red hair and liberated sexual views. Elsie shortly discovered the liaison, but they continued to meet. Violet met Mary in 1909 and found her "beautiful in a simple way, like clear water and primroses," with "a ringing laugh, rather like the cuckoo's note"; they became close friends.

Although Ford had yet to write a book the critics admired, he kept at his craft. When he met Violet at the Galsworthys' dinner party in 1907, he was completing his twenty-fourth work, *The Fifth Queen Crowned,* the last of three historical novels about Henry VIII's wife Catherine Howard. As he emerged from a two-year depression that had kept him in Germany convalescing for six months in 1904, his outlook was more optimistic. But his finances, always a problem, were worse than ever, and he was borrowing against future work.

Elsie had been ill for some time; for three years her family thought her complaints imaginary, until doctors correctly diagnosed a tubercular kidney. The marriage was troubled, and Ford later wrote that Elsie had "intermittently" asked him for a divorce "for a number of years previous to 1908." Her illness intruded on his life and work in the country and, as was typical of Ford, he wanted to escape—to London and the life of a literary gentleman.

In 1907 Ford rented a maisonette above a poulterer's shop at 84 Holland Park Avenue in Kensington, where the stench of slaughtered chickens seeped through the drafty doors. There was a large drawing room and bathroom on the first floor, and two small bedrooms, a dining room and a tiny kitchen on the second. Ford made the bleak place comfortable, with the desk on which Christina Rossetti had written her poems, an old Spanish cabinet overflowing with manuscripts, his grandfather's portrait of him as "William Tell's son," a bookshelf devoted to Constance Garnett's translations of Turgenev, overstuffed lounging chairs and a piano.

Into this hodgepodge roamed, by Violet's account, the landlord's rabbits, burglars (one took all of Ford's hats) and Russian anarchists (who ransacked his desk). The address, she said, "seemed to be a mark for all sorts of Communist, Bolshevik attempts, a regular danger-spot. On the pavement outside a man had been sandbagged and left for dead; and Mr. Chandler, the poulterer, his landlord, and a big, hefty man, carried his own takings to the bank every day, but went continually in fear of a knife in his back. The editor rather liked it."

In this unorthodox atmosphere Ford launched the *English Review*. He had previously discussed the concept of publishing imaginative literature with Conrad, Wells, Garnett and Marwood during their long fireside evenings together in the country. But needing more than a magazine, he called for a "movement": a group of writers orbiting around him, all searching for *le mot juste*. "He who wants to persuade should put trust, not in the right argument, but in the right word," Ford said. "Give me the right word and the right accent and I will move the world."

Ford wanted to promote good writing, and good writing was what *he* thought was good. He felt, for instance, that W. H. Hudson, author of *Green Mansions,* wrote "as simply as the grass grows." He followed his grandfather's dictum to help others, even those more talented than himself. He coaxed Conrad to write *Some Reminiscences* and printed Thomas Hardy's poem "A Sunday Morning Tragedy," on a death resulting from an illegal abortion, which had been refused by another magazine. But in his search for the right word, Ford rejected bad writing from influential critics, a demand for quality that some thought hindered the recognition of his own work. Through the *Review,* he had hoped to bolster his career, to be noticed in literary London, to throw off the cloak of the "stupid donkey."

To raise money for his magazine, Ford turned to his new friend Arthur Pierson Marwood. Descendant of a Yorkshire family named in the Doomsday book (William the Conqueror's survey of English lands), Marwood was an expert in English Tory law and a mathematical genius. He was also, along with Conrad, Ford's closest friend and an object of his envy: for here was the country gentleman, the last Great Tory of Ford's fiction. Marwood contributed £2,200, and Ford scraped together £2,800, soliciting funds from his European relatives, "the money of cohorts of relations—German Hueffers, Dutch Hueffers, Paris Hueffers: tremendously rich, these Paris Hueffers," Violet said. For his assistant he hired Douglas Goldring, a twenty-one-year-old Oxford dropout who became his Boswell during the *Review* years.

Just as Rossetti and the Pre-Raphaelite Brotherhood had plotted how they would change the look of British art, Ford and his friends longed for an Edwardian literary revival. In October 1907, Ford, Goldring and Ford's secretary, Olive Thomas, descended on the Conrads at their gloomy farmhouse, Someries, outside Luton, for a planning session. The trio demanded separate rooms, and Conrad's wife, Jessie, was not pleased with the intrusion. "No birth," she said, "could have been more painful or more expensive in the matter of food and light and output of nervous energy."

Goldring recalled Ford and Conrad talking in a mixture of French and English in the candlelit study after dinner. Ford lounged in an armchair, "his light-pitched, drawling tones mingling with Conrad's deeper, more staccato notes. After a while they started booming about Flaubert, hurling great chunks of *Madame Bovary* and *Un Coeur Simple* at one another, with ever-growing excitement." At evening's end they had thrashed out the editorial policy, that "sweet and fatuous circular," as Violet called it.*

The first issue of the *English Review,* dated December 1908, had 192 pages bound in blue paper and sold for two shillings, six pence. In addition to Conrad's reminiscences, there was the first part of a serialization of Wells's new novel, *Tono-Bungay,* and contributions from Hardy, James, Hudson and Galsworthy. Subse-

---

*The manifesto read: "The only qualification for admission to the pages of the *Review* will be—in the view of the Editors—either distinction of individuality or force of conviction, either literary gifts or earnestness of purpose, whatever the purpose may be—the criterion of inclusion being the clarity of diction, the force or the illuminative value of the views expressed. What will be avoided will be superficiality of the specially modern kind which is the inevitable consequence when nothing but brevity of statement is aimed at. The *English Review* will treat its readers, not as spoiled children who must be amused by a variety of games, but with the respectful consideration due to grown-up minds whose leisure can be interested by something else than the crispness and glitter of a popular statement."

quent issues were equally stellar, with works by Arnold Bennett, D. H. Lawrence, G. K. Chesterton, W. B. Yeats, R. B. Cunninghame Graham, Hilaire Belloc, Vernon Lee, Norman Douglas, E. M. Forster, Ezra Pound, Percy Wyndham Lewis, George Moore, Rupert Brooke—and President William Howard Taft. Ford mixed the immortals and the unknowns. And it was this flair, this inspired choice of writers, that made the *Review* so memorable.

The editor wanted his writers to be idealists, not money grubbers, and offered to pay them under a profit-sharing plan, but no more than a guinea a page. Ford was insulted when Bennett sent stories through his agent, J. B. Pinker, demanding his usual rate of £40 to £50. "Oh hang!" he wrote Bennett. "If you negotiate through Pinker what can you expect? . . . I am running a philanthropic institution for the benefit of the better letters: I am perfectly resigned to bankruptcy." Bennett got his £40 for *The Matador of the Five Towns,* and other writers, including James and Conrad, received generous checks. So much for philanthropy. Ford ended up spending far too much for articles—some £300 an issue.

Financially, the *Review* was struggling. The first two issues sold around 2,000 copies, bringing in £200; advertisements added £140 for four issues. After paying the printer and other bills, Ford was losing from £400 to £500 an issue, a figure Goldring said must have staggered even the press baron Viscount Northcliffe. Bankruptcy seemed more than an idle jest and any notion of profit-sharing a pipe dream. Wells, who had been offered one-fifth of the profits (calculated at £600) for the serial rights to *Tono-Bungay,* was enraged by the financial facts and worried that remaindered copies would limit the sale of his novel.

The critical response was immediate for this extraordinary magazine. It filled a void. Those publications that did exist—notably *The Athenaeum,* the *Quarterly Review,* the *Times Literary Supplement* and *Blackwood's*—seldom made a point of publishing unknown writers. "It proved to us that magic was still practised," Rebecca West recalled, "and every issue had that harmony of content, that mixture of variety and unity, which is the hallmark of a great editor." It was the first time, said Frank Swinnerton, "that English literature was treated as something that was as important and exciting as politics and sports."

To save money, Ford had tried—with Bennett and others—

to bypass J. B. Pinker, who was the literary agent for most of the elite Edwardian writers, including Violet. Affectionately known as "Jy Bee," Pinker was a Jewish Scotsman who started his career on the *Levant Herald* in Constantinople, moved to *Black and White,* where he met Violet (they fought over the foreign stamps thrown into the editor's wastepaper basket), and then to *Pearson's Magazine.* He left publishing in 1896 and set himself up as an agent in Arundel Street, off the Strand, eventually representing James, Conrad, Wells, Maugham and later D. H. Lawrence and Rebecca West.

Pinker thoroughly enjoyed his work and his life. He spent his fees on horses, drove a four-in-hand and married above his station. An astute judge of talent and a shrewd negotiator, he was also generous to those he admired, investing heavily in Conrad and advancing Bennett money to go to Paris. Lawrence called him "that little parvenu snob of a procurer of books" when Pinker refused him a loan. To Violet, Pinker was the "prince of agents."

Sometime in the summer of 1908 Violet sent Pinker three of her *Tales of the Uneasy.* He was unable to place them, so she showed them to H. G. Wells. "Send them to the *English Review*," her former lover said. "It's *It* this year!" So on a cold, rainy October afternoon Violet walked from South Lodge to Holland Park Avenue to sell her stories to the editor.

Ford was thirty-five, tall and thin and fair-haired, with a blond mustache that failed to conceal defective front teeth and a mouth that always hung open. Rather gaunt, he had not yet ballooned into what Wyndham Lewis would call a "flabby lemon and pink giant, who hung his mouth open as though he were an animal at the zoo inviting buns—especially when ladies were present." A habit of not breathing through his nose had distorted the shape of his mouth, giving his speech a whispered quality; his *sotto voce* stories told to ladies were so hard to hear that he had to lean into their décolletage in search of an ear. Around London Ford affected an important manner in "a grey-blue swallow-tail coat of uncertain cut, and carried a leather dispatch case."

Violet was forty-six, eleven years older than Ford, still a handsome, vibrant woman, but no longer the delicate beauty who had attracted Oscar Wilde and Oswald Crawfurd. She was, in her own words, "a woman at a loose end of life, with a visiting list of notabilities as long as your arm and some experience of literature, especially of the genus review!" Violet was looking for a respectability thus far denied her and, perhaps, a last grand, passionate fling, if not marriage.

As Douglas Goldring observed, Violet had "inherited and built up . . . a 'position in Society' which to a Victorian woman, even one as advanced and emancipated as herself, was of immense importance to her life and happiness. Although she enjoyed the friendship of writers and artists, she was in no sense a Bohemian and dreaded being ostracized by all the solid and respectable people who formed her real background."

Clutching her stories, Violet arrived at the *Review* office, pushed past suspended carcasses of rabbits, fowls and game birds, and sloshed through a mixture of blood and sawdust to the stairway leading to the editorial department. There she found the editor dressed in a brown velvet jacket once owned by Rossetti, sorting through manuscripts carelessly stuffed into a cabinet that had once belonged to the Duke of Medina-Sidonia. Ford gallantly ushered her to an overstuffed chair by the tea table. She was uncharacteristically shy and quiet. As they chatted about mutual friends, Violet scrutinized him: he was not a handsome man, but she sensed a compelling charm. When not distracted by an anxiety to be admired, Violet later said, Ford could be gentle and understanding.

After a lingering tea he politely flipped through the pages of the three stories, pausing at the second one. "I'll take this," he said, selecting "The Coach," an eerie tale of ghosts riding through the countryside in a phantom carriage with a headless coachman. Violet protested his snap selection, but Ford was an instinctive judge of writing, and this story does not depend on clever dialogue—it has style.* (Ford later peevishly wrote that Violet's work was charac-

---

*"The Coach" appeared in the fourth issue of the *Review,* in March 1909. In this story Violet breaks out of her trademark—witty conversation—and demonstrates her descriptive skills: "At a certain point on the line of way, a tall, spare, respectable-looking man in a well-fitting grey frock-coat stood waiting. The rain ran down the back of his coat collar, and dripped off the rim of his tall hat. His attitude suggested some weary foredone clerk waiting at the corner of the city street for the omnibus that was to carry him home to his slippered comfort and sober pipe of peace. He wore no muffler, but then it was summer—St. John's Eve. He leaned on an ivory-headed ebony stick of which he seemed fond, and peered, not very eagerly, along the road, which now lay in dazzling rain-washed clarity under the

terized by "pure irresponsible Gothic and macabre genius, without a trace of selection, of self-consciousness, of idealism.")

Following this encounter, she was asked to tea again, and he was invited to South Lodge for lunch with Margaret Hunt. When the first issue of the *Review* came out in December, Violet was at the office for a splendid Christmas party with plum pudding and roasted chestnuts. In fact, there was always some kind of party going on above the poulterer's shop as writers dropped off manuscripts and stayed to gossip. When Ford attempted to interest the American publisher S. S. McClure in financing the *Review,* he insisted on Violet's company, signing his invitation to join him at the Empire Music Hall "Yours until death and after." Violet enjoyed Ford's admiration, but she was wary of a third affair with a married man.

With the publication of *White Rose of Weary Leaf* by Heinemann in 1908, Violet's career peaked: she was a popular novelist, if not one of stature. Some critics found the story depressing (*The Spectator* called it "squalidly dreary"), but others compared it favorably to Charlotte Brontë's *Jane Eyre.*

In the mold of *Anna Karenina* and *Madame Bovary, White Rose* tells the story of Amy Steevens, a waif-woman who reaches out for independence only to die for her presumption. A governess for the Dands, a British family living in Paris, Amy loses her post by aiding a co-respondent in a divorce suit who threatens to shoot himself. He takes her to London as his secretary, where she lives in his house, further compromising herself. Although lacking in beauty and passion, Amy nonetheless attracts men, including Jeremy Dand, whose household she transforms. When Dand's wife is injured in a railway accident, they become lovers. Amy discovers she is pregnant and runs away (to save his marriage). She dies in childbirth, leaving him a daughter, whom he acknowledges as his heir.

Violet had changed the ending as Heinemann requested. Still, Boots, which kept circulating libraries in their thousand-odd shops to induce customers to buy pharmaceuticals, refused—as they had

---

struggling moon. There was a lull in the storm. He had no luggage, no umbrella, yet his grey coat looked neat, and his hat shiny." May Sinclair would speculate: "What wild turn [her] talent might have taken if she had never lived in London, never seen Fleet Street, but had been brought up, like Emily Brontë, in the Yorkshire country of her people and had never left the moors."

with *Sooner or Later*—to stock the book. Violet protested the ban and sent Boots her photograph, asking if they thought she looked like the author of an "improper novel."

May Sinclair called Jeremy Dand "the one entirely successful male figure" that Violet ever created, praising her for doing "what Hardy only tried to do when he wrote 'Tess.' It took a woman to do it!" Violet's old friend Raffalovitch said that the story approached "the unsexual novel towards which the talents of the world are bending."

H. G. Wells told her it was her best book, George Meredith said Amy was "fashioned to live in memory," and Thomas Hardy felt she had "tapped a curious and little worked section of society. . . . Not a stratum of nice people altogether: but you must use what you can find and be thankful for the find. . . . You are a bit slip-shod in your English in the early pages, by-the-way, but get more facile and masterly as you get on."

She was disappointed that Henry James did not respond. "In all my intercourse with him, I kept well in my mind, that as far as he was concerned, the eccentricities of my feminine personality and the light I was enabled to cast for him on various side-shows of London life were my only contribution to his entertainment," she complained, "while the little fact that I 'wrote' was to him *la moindre des choses* [the least of things]."

Ford also praised *White Rose* and, to her, he was the most important of critics. In the early months of 1909, Ford was needy and lonely, and he was "most susceptible when he was unhappy," says Arthur Mizener, his biographer. "He found the excitement of sexual exploration irresistible and the sympathy of an attractive woman necessary to the dramatization of himself as the unjustly suffering man." With Violet's help, Ford was confident that he could make the *Review* a paying proposition. He metamorphosed her into his ideal woman.

Conrad's biographer Frederick Karl sees a more sinister side, observing that Ford's "need to be worshipped either by much younger or much older women, reflects an infantilism that was connected to a hatred of the sex altogether. It is a harem-and-slave mentality." But, says Ford scholar Sondra Stang: Ford "seems to have sought not power over [women] but imaginative identification with them. To read [his] novels is to see how far it is possible for a man writing about women to project himself imaginatively into male and female selves."

As for Violet, she was available and equally vulnerable, for Oswald Crawfurd had died in Montreux on January 31, 1909. When she "heard of the death, far away in Switzerland, of such a one as we women, roughly, and tenderly speaking, choose to call 'the only man we have ever loved,' " she was deeply depressed. She turned to Silvia, who refused her sympathy, saying she had "no good feeling for O.C. He has ruined your life & spoilt our friendship, & made fearful difficulties." (Crawfurd's obituary made the delicate point that he had helped "many young writers of both sexes to their first chance in life.")

Impatiently Ford courted her, rushing the relationship. Violet was cautious. One day at Holland Park he made "an astounding, romantic, nonsensical proposition, over the luncheon-table among crumbled bread and smoking Irish stew: 'Will you marry me if ever I am a divorced man?' he asked. 'It was too sudden,' as Victorian ladies used to say, and I did not really think he was serious. And, besides, I was thinking at that time—all the time—of a freshly made grave at Clarens."

Enduring, as Violet put it, "the slings and arrows of literary fate," they cooked comforting dinners for each other at the *Review*'s office, ordering meringues from the confectionery shop next door. On June 10, 1909, Violet arrived at half past six to find Ford cooking cutlets, oblivious to the fact that he was burning them and spattering grease over his silk Japanese dressing gown. Pale and unhealthy, he puffed away at cigarette after cigarette, looking "white like a stick of asparagus grown in the cellar"; he sat on "a hideous red plush Victorian armchair, the one blot on the room, and I on a *chaise-longue* that an invalid had used."

Ford read passages from his new novel, *A Call* (in which an unmarried couple go abroad and return saying they have just married, a harbinger of things to come!), and talked intermittently about suicide. He would escape his torment, he explained, by swallowing poison and throwing himself in front of a bus; no one would do an autopsy of a mangled corpse, and his children would collect the insurance. "The depression was as one might say of a fog—so thick you could cut it with a knife," Violet said when she described the scene in her memoirs, indulging in some melodrama. "Was it a cry for help from the intimate thought-reserve of another human being?" She thought so.

Violet asked for some lemonade. When Ford returned carrying the glass, she got up and took it from his hand and put it on the table. "Don't look so unhappy!" she cried, as she took hold of his coat lapel with one hand while the other, directed "by the will of Providence," crept to the loose, open pocket of the brown velvet jacket and "fished out a dark, fluted bottle, inscribed in the Futurist colours of danger, POISON. The blunt letters were like the head of a cobra suddenly reared. I took it to the light, and he waited like a condemned criminal."

"Were you?" she asked darkly.

"I was," he admitted.

"Donkey!" she chided, throwing on her cloak.

"Do you mean to give it back to me?" he asked anxiously.

"No!" she said firmly.

Violet had berated him for being a "donkey," a hateful echo of his father calling him that "stupid donkey." And for the first time after one of their dinners, Ford escorted her home to South Lodge, the blue poison bottle in the pocket of her coat.

10

Brewing Scandal

Convinced that she had rescued a genius from destruction, Violet felt more in control than ever before in a relationship. She told her diary, "Dined FMH," with the phrase "the threatened suicide" crossed out and ambiguously replaced by "Final." At this moment, she "was ready to commit the eternal error," she said. "I was full, not of Love, but of Loving-kindness, and obsessed by the permanent illusion of all women that they can Save . . . it is well known that the shipwrecked mariner turns against his rescuer: and sailors, wise and primitive men, will let a man drown lest he live to do them an injury."

The next evening she returned to Holland Park, and they became lovers. The following day she wrote Ford, "What happened last night made me know that I loved you. Never regret it & I won't fail you." Ford thanked her for "the tenderness that has saved one's reason and one's life." Her romanticism and his optimism were at once satisfied. They were wildly happy as only new lovers can be.

With Rosamond's debut season approaching, Violet brought her to Oxford to meet some well-bred undergraduates at All Souls College. Rosamond had met Ford and had a crush on him, which she confided to her aunt, who severely told her that he was not for her. On the train, Violet wrote Ford a love poem:

> There's a witch upon the hill
> *Give me a kiss*

There's a dragon I must kill
And there's this.
The danger signal's up
Give me another kiss
There's poison in the cup
But there's this.

There's the night comes long and deep
Give me another kiss
When you and I must sleep
But first there's this.

Ah me there's sin and shame
Give me another kiss
Joy by another name
This! This! This!

She was giddy; he was smitten. "My dear, all of the Shaws, Galsworthys, Grahames and fine noble creatures [are] slow witted fools when it comes to real brain work beside you and me," he wrote her, "and you—well, Helen of Troy and Semiramis, The Blessed Damozel and Becky Sharp, St. Catherine and Christina of Milan could not, all together extract from me the emotion and devotion that are yours." Ford was like a gangling adolescent, babbling idiotically at the beginning of a love affair. He told Violet how he kissed her letters all over and was observed slobbering over one by a cab driver.

They made a "goodly couple," he said. It is unclear how much Violet told Ford about her previous lovers beyond Crawfurd, but she did worry about the age difference. Ford assured her that he was not jealous of her past memories, even as he found them intriguing and intimidating. Violet said he was like her big cat Puck. "I ought to keep *you* in a shed in the garden as a 'dangerous male' as I have to do him. I thought of that once, the other night." In another letter, she teased, "I've got your letter between me and my stays. Do you like that? I wish it was you—or even your hand. The thought does make me thrill as I sit here, though, you must believe it." Violet was euphoric.

With bewitching candor she told him, "I run for the post like a schoolgirl. No dear, I can't say I do enjoy being away and cut off from you—now. And yet it is just the same as it used to be in past years, when I was contented and resigned and enjoyed my life—

yes, really! *Something* turned *up—somebody* came into my little orbit and was affected by me—didn't as a rule, fall in love with me—so it was just nice and what Angela [Mond] calls '*moussie*' for me. That was my interest in life, affecting people—men *and* women, making myself count with them one way or other." Part of Violet's enchantment was believing that time could not "wither her nor custom stale her infinite variety," as Shakespeare wrote of Cleopatra, also a consummate flirt.

At first they met in those places so familiar to Violet, rented private rooms away from Kensington; then they stayed at his flat, or at South Lodge, but she was uneasy at home with her mother and the servants about. "How is your room that I love?" she wrote. "I like it so much better than my own at South Lodge. I am a little apprehensive there all the time and I do believe that I prefer it to be me to get up and go!" Violet's attitude was far ahead of her time on this issue and she realized it, adding, "I feel it for you—isn't it absurd of me! I hate and feel so many things that are not in my province."

No matter how Violet flouted convention, she still wanted the approval of "society" and her family. In July she asked Ford to escort the infirm Margaret Hunt to Bedburn for her summer stay with Silvia, who believed that he was already divorced. When she discovered otherwise, the ill-fated visit edged toward disaster, additionally provoked by Rosamond's flirting with a flattered—and probably receptive—Ford. The fair Rosamond took dictation from Ford and was so nervous that her hands trembled. Also at Bedburn was the faithful, milquetoasty Cholmeley, who had transferred his limited affections to Silvia. Ford tried to fit in but lamented to Violet, "*How* they bore me!" He caught four trout, rolled lawns, played tennis and talked to the local gentry. Still, his dislike of country ways did not go unnoticed. Silvia huffed that "Mr. Hueffer was not a success—simply because the whole house was annoyed at R's hero-worship of him. It was so very plain. She sat on a stool at his feet—as it were—and adored him—I confess I like him better in his own milieu," adding that she would help Violet only when Ford was free to marry.

"I agree, he & Walton are miles apart," Silvia continued, "but as I respect W's intellect more than you do—& also believe in the husband being master in his own house, & declining to have visitors who despise him, & he does not like well—in this case I am *not* buckling under to him. Either Mr. H found it restful to rest his brain & rather play the fool—or he tried to adapt himself to *our* intellects— He was really very dull & on a few occasions—interesting . . . a baffling puzzle. How is he going to get a divorce?" she asked. "It is an ambiguous position at present."

Violet urged Ford to be honorable, to say he was "taking steps" but that she was a "little half hearted about it all," being nearly eleven years older. She suggested he ask Silvia to invite them both to Bedburn so the two couples could get to know each other better. But Ford had had enough of the North. "I don't wonder," he wrote, "after seeing the character of the country and its inmates that 'Wuthering Heights' was written." As for the age difference, he assured her that she was his ideal woman, lively and vivid, the only one for him. In return, Violet promised never to be dull just because they were engaged. "I love you so very desperately . . . I never thought there was anybody in the world like you." On August 16, 1909, Violet told her diary that Ford had promised to marry her.

Ford and the *English Review* now became the focus of her life, with less time given to her mother or Rosamond or to suffrage activities. Arthur Marwood approved Violet's appointment as "reader, occasional sub-editor, contributor, but above all a 'society hand' and touter for rich, influential subscribers." A Victorian woman of Violet's class never worked in an office, so being the "quasi-mistress" of the magazine's business and housekeeping needs challenged her. She observed that Ford was "a babe unborn in the guiding of mere worldly matters. He seemed like an infant in charge of a motor-car."

Gracious and gregarious, the couple adored entertaining. "These intellectual hosts," said Wyndham Lewis, "were of that valuable kind of human, who shuns solitude as the dread symbol of unsuccess, is happiest when his rooms are jammed with people (for preference of note)." Douglas Goldring observed that the society of South Lodge "had few connections with the fox-hunting aristocracy and the naval, military, and diplomatic caste formed by its offshoots," but "it was probably the most amusing, the most intelligent and the most worthwhile that late Victorian London had to offer."

For special parties at Holland Park, Annie Child brought over

Violet's best silver and a butler was borrowed, though these events were far from stuffy, even with a few lords and ladies or a member of Parliament sprinkled about. Violet recalled how the grown-ups "were made to play the most childish of games—Clumps, Honey-pots, not stopping short at Hunt-the-slipper. I knew we all seemed to be sitting on the floor . . . There was no one to curb the editor and his German instinct for games." At one all-poets party, Ezra Pound, Hilaire Belloc and others competed for a crown of bay leaves by writing *bouts-rimés* [rhyming last lines].

Flaunting his newfound fame with a fur coat and shiny top hat, Ford was seen alighting from hired carriages at the Square Club in Fleet Street and the Mont Blanc restaurant on Gerrard Street. "His fresh features, the colour of raw veal, his prominent blue eyes and rabbit teeth smiled benevolently and patronisingly upon all gatherings of literary lions," recalled David Garnett.

But when Olive Thomas and Goldring left at the end of the day and Violet returned to South Lodge, Ford was alone to indulge in self-pity, as only he knew how. "Like Cinderella's pumpkin carriage and its mice footmen, all this glory vanished at dusk," Violet recalled, "and the editor was left with a few broken sandwiches and half cups of tea . . . sitting by his dying fire and an empty coal-scuttle that he was too lazy to go out and replenish, or thumping his piano and shouting 'Madam, will you walk?' for his own dreary amusement and company."

Somehow the manuscripts, if they did not get lost, got edited. The real work began on those nights when Ford escaped to the Shepherd's Bush Empire Theatre, where he sat in the orchestra and during the more boring parts of the music-hall entertainment told Goldring, who had brought along the day's submissions, which to reject. This frantic pace kept Ford's mind off the news that his recent books, *An English Girl*, *Mr. Apollo*, even *The Fifth Queen Crowned*, had not sold as well as expected.

Shortly after Violet started as a reader, there arrived, in reply to a notice in the *Review* asking for unpublished work, a short story called "The Odour of Chrysanthemums," which began, "The small locomotive engine, Number 4, came clanking, stumbling down from Selston with seven full waggons. It appeared round the corner with loud threats of speed but the colt that it startled from among the gorse which still flickered indistinctly in the raw afternoon, outdistanced it in a canter. A woman walking up the railway line to Underwood, held her basket aside and watched the footplate of the engine advancing."

Ford recognized immediately that the author knew how to write a euphonious sentence and how to structure a paragraph. His name was D. H. Lawrence. "That *was* a Moment!" Violet exclaimed. "The first blush—the blowing—of Mr. Lawrence's flower of genius. I was, at that time, reader. The editor handed me some manuscript poems written in pencil and very close, which had come to him from a young schoolmistress in the Midlands. . . . She had copied out some of his poems, and would the editor give them a glance? They were perfectly wonderful. The editor was beside himself with pleasure at his discovery." (For many years Violet gave the impression that she had read the poems first, thus discovering Lawrence, but later revealed that "the sheaf of pencil scrawled poems I hardly could be bothered to read. I said [to Ford] 'People *ought* to have things typed!' 'Let's see!' said the Editor, *et puis, violà!* Lawrence's fame.")

That evening Ford attended a literary dinner at the Pall Mall restaurant; seated at a table with Wells, Belloc and Chesterton, he proudly bellowed that he had discovered a genius. Wells turned around and shouted the news to the next table: "Hooray, Fordie's discovered another genius! Called D. H. Lawrence!" Next Ford invited his genius to visit. The son of a coal miner and a possessive mother, the shy and awkward twenty-four-year-old arrived unannounced one Saturday afternoon at Holland Park, looking, Ford recalled, rather like a russet-haired human fox.

"This isn't my idea, Sir, of an editor's office," he said, eyeing the homey atmosphere. Ford defended the antique clutter. "That's all very well," Lawrence replied, "but it doesn't look like a place in which one would make money." "Oh, we don't make money here. We spend it," quipped Ford with an amused grin, but Lawrence failed to see the humor. When Ford asked not to be called "sir," Lawrence retorted, "But you are, aren't you, everybody's blessed Uncle and Headmaster?"—not the first time that Ford was cast as a mentor to unrecognized literary genius.

Lawrence thought Ford "the kindest man on earth," Violet wrote. She admired Lawrence's eyes, "very blue, his lips very red, and his face very white—sinisterly so, for he looked consumptive," and thought him "more conversant with decadent poetry (he read Verlaine and Baudelaire to Jessie)" than either she or Ford. In fact, she said, he "had studied it too deeply."

In November, Jessie Chambers (the Miriam of *Sons and Lovers*), who had sent Lawrence's work to the *Review*, was coaxed down to London from the Midlands, where she and Lawrence had grown up. A luncheon was planned at South Lodge, with Ezra Pound among the guests. A farm girl with a keen intellect but no sophistication (she asked the maid if she should keep her gloves on while eating), Jessie thoroughly enjoyed the feast of fish, roast beef, brussels sprouts, plum pudding and champagne. She admired "the genial warmth" of Ford, Violet's gentle kindness, and the "amiable buffoon" Pound, who startled her by bowing from the waist like a mechanical toy.

Conflicts with Arthur Marwood, Ford's business partner, soon overshadowed the discovery of Lawrence. Ford believed that he was responsible for the *Review*'s critical acclaim (and he was), and accused Marwood (who in addition to funding the *Review* had loaned Ford £440 for Elsie's kidney operation) of not only taking credit for the magazine's success, but also of blaming Ford for its financial ills. Then the rivalry accelerated: Elsie told her estranged husband that Marwood had written her incriminating letters and had made advances. Whatever the truth, Ford believed this story— or wanted to.

The Conrads sided with Marwood. Conrad admonished Ford for his lack of tact, his "Olympian severity" toward "men who *were* your admiring friends. . . . You will find yourself at forty with only the wrecks of friendship at your feet." Violet said Ford "adored" Conrad and Conrad "loved" Ford. It was a complex relationship on both sides; it eventually ruptured for a number of reasons, but Ford's relationship with Violet was certainly prominent among them. Conrad said he could not breathe in such unclear situations. Ford never again found a masculine friend as inspiring. (Conrad's prophesy was fulfilled, for Conrad, Marwood, Elsie and Violet were past tense by 1913, but with *The Good Soldier*, sifted from the embers of these loves, Ford established himself as an author.)

Ford was being irrational about Marwood, whom Violet called "the brave and gentle Yorkshire squire, the best, most loving friend an editor ever had—and wasted." The upshot of Elsie's accusations was a temporary reconciliation between her and Ford, and an estrangement between Ford and Conrad. Conrad complained to Pinker about Ford's "impossible" conduct, calling him a "megalomaniac who imagines that he is managing the Universe and that everybody treats him with the blackest ingratitude. A fierce and exasperating vanity is hidden under his calm manner which misleads people . . . I do not hesitate to say that there are cases, not quite as bad, under medical treatment. Generally he is behaving like a spoilt kid—and not a nice kid either."

Ford saw his life as a terrible muddle: his beloved *Review* was financially ailing; his male friends were attacking him; he was in love with another woman, and getting a divorce was far from easy. Recent evidence suggests that Ford had considered—and refused—Elsie's earlier requests for a divorce; but things change, and now he wanted to be free to marry. (See note on page 314.) Easily convinced, Violet wrote that "the plangent, languid, tenor voice overcame my north-country sensibleness, hypnotised me into folly, as it was meant it should do." Violet's solicitor offered Elsie £400 a year (of Violet's money) if she agreed to a divorce. She refused, although Ford later claimed that she wanted one.

The only option left was to set up grounds for adultery. The victim could not be Violet; she would not sully her reputation again. Besides, their relationship was still relatively secret. But they had the perfect co-respondent waiting in the wings: Gertrud Schablowsky, the seventeen-year-old daughter of a Königsberg tailor, whom Ford had befriended in the Empire Theatre lounge. Violet described the girl as a "lazy, Slav type" with a "white, heavy moonface . . . short Calmuck nose, wide red mouth, and loops of black hair falling over a rather brutish forehead." At one Holland Park party, when Gertrud wore a gray fake-fur dress borrowed from Violet, May Sinclair said she looked like a "beautiful, pale, Russian princess." Enraged at Ford's interest in the young woman, Violet sent him a poem, entitled "To Gertrud," and signed it "George Angel":

> *Stir up the fire, draw out your chair:*
> *Kick off the shoes: let down the hair:*
> *Your white kimono, now disclose*
> *The little budget of your woes:*

Then snuggle down and let us doze
It's very late: It's very cold:
And you're too young and I'm so old.
You shall have both my hands to hold:
It's very late: It's very cold. . . .
And both with a most ancient work to do,
You selling worthless love: I modern rhyme,
Sitting beside your hearth in wintertime
Cheer on, I know, each other. Yes. I know. . . .

It is uncertain whether Ford and Gertrud were ever lovers, but Ford certainly had a promiscuous side to his self-proclaimed Tory-gentleman nature. What mattered for the scheme, though, was that Gertrud had stayed overnight at Holland Park and traveled with Ford as his "secretary," giving the impression that they *were* sleeping together. With this script in mind, the desperate couple drafted a letter to Elsie, outlining this sexual outrage, and when Edmée van der Noot, the governess for Ford's children, came to London, Ford gave her the letter to deliver to Elsie. (In an unsigned legal deposition written in 1913, Ford reversed the facts, indulging in the revisionist history he excelled at: thus Elsie sent Edmée to ask him for a divorce. Violet's account that Edmée was sent by Ford to Elsie seems more plausible in view of Elsie's feelings about divorce.)

That evening, about the time Elsie was opening the letter, Violet prepared a celebratory supper at Holland Park. The confident couple lifted champagne glasses to a future seemingly secure and talked the night through. Ford valued conversation, and Violet had earned a well-deserved reputation for being wickedly chatty. Early in their courtship Ford expressed the view that talking was more enjoyable than sex. "Don't you see all it means to me to be certain, only of knowing one can talk to you for the rest of one's life! That, alone, would be heaven. And then there's you, in addition." In *Parade's End*, Ford's alter ego Christopher Tietjens observes that one "seduced a young woman in order to be able to finish your talks with her. You could not live with her without seducing her: but that was the by-product. The point is that you can't otherwise talk. You can't finish talks at street corners; in museums; even in drawing-rooms. You mayn't be in the mood when she is in the mood—for the intimate conversation that means the final communion of your souls."

As anticipated, after Elsie read the letter she consulted her London solicitor, who wrote the necessary overture to divorce: a petition for restitution of conjugal rights. Gertrud had served her purpose, and Violet shortly shipped the "bored, pining, discontented" girl back to Germany with funds to emigrate to New South Wales, Australia.

In August the lovers spent a golf weekend at Sheringham; Violet wrote Annie Child (who cared for her like a mother and to whom she dedicated her animal biography _The Cat_) that "Mr. Hueffer has had the letter from Mrs. Hueffer that means it will be perhaps only six months or eight months hence. So we are both very happy." Violet later wrote on a copy of the letter, "We took a turn in the shrubberies to read it. Ford was very quiet about it—I was shy. I could not somehow express my gladness and I don't quite feel that he felt any." Perhaps Ford's elation was tempered by the letter's ending: a plea from Elsie for Ford to "come back and be the loving husband you always have been."

Earlier Ford had told Annie Child, who was considered a member of the family, that it was his "intention—as it is the most earnest desire that I have—to marry Miss Hunt as soon as my wife divorces me. . . . So do not have any doubt about it." By this time Violet had met Elsie and her two daughters, as well as Ford's mother and Mary Martindale, his sister-in-law and former mistress. Ford had captivated the young Rosamond and entertained Margaret Hunt, but Violet's inflexible sisters never accepted him.

By the autumn of 1909 their liaison _was_ serious gossip, and the resulting problems eventually gave Ford "a fresh attack of neurasthenia that lasted three whole years, and was responsible for many things, and much private and particular misery," said Violet. Ford indignantly wrote his mother that the only thing Elsie could say against him "with any shadow of proof and absolutely the only wrong I will admit having done is having a housekeeper [Gertrud] younger than convention demands." He asked his mother to make Elsie stop slandering him. "Without exaggeration Elsie has ruined me so that I am mentally a wreck. My work is going all to pieces and I cannot even place the last book but one that I wrote [_The "Half Moon"_], incredible as that seems."

Utterly confused about her position, Elsie blindly followed the advice of relatives and solicitors. "Oh dear, if people had not stepped in," she later recalled. "Of course it would have been better for me if I had divorced him." Violet, too, would admit that managing Ford's life had been a mistake. "The male must not depend on the female, even in business; but if love comes in the situation becomes more than impossible. F.M.H. would have done very well without me; perhaps better, as I have come to see now. But the octopus tentacle of the extreme need of the artist-egotist for an Egeria—any number of Egerias—won. He got his way."

And for a year or so Violet had what she wanted: a loving man who loved her, for there was a strong physical attraction between them. When Violet decided they needed time alone, she arranged to visit William and Agnes Farley, who had a villa at Beaumont-le-Roger in Normandy, a place where, Violet said, Madame Bovary might have lived and been bored. Here she celebrated her forty-seventh birthday on September 28, 1909, in an ebullient mood for once. In the morning Ford dictated *The Portrait* alternately to Violet and Agnes; in the afternoon the lovers walked—cautiously—in the boar-infested woods, visited the nearby cathedral and châteaux, and returned to a roaring fire and a hearty meal of chicken flavored with the local Calvados. They traveled to Evreux to witness a ceremony honoring the canonization of Joan of Arc, staying at a hotel with "silver taps, lace pin-cushions, fancy soaps . . . a bower of bliss." For two weeks, it was like a honeymoon.

They had planned to return by the night boat from Le Havre to Southampton, but Violet suddenly took ill and they rescheduled their departure for the next day, wiring Annie Child and Olive Thomas to meet them at Charing Cross Station on Friday night rather than Thursday morning. Unfortunately, Elsie and Edmée arrived at Holland Park on Wednesday inquiring—and then demanding—to know Ford's whereabouts, and after much badgering Olive showed them the telegram. When the lovers alighted from the 10:45 P.M. train, they were met by the icy stares of Elsie and her solicitor, William Sturgis.

"It's all up, old girl!" Ford said to Violet as they separated. "You will see. There'll be no divorce." As the more experienced in romantic deception, Violet blamed herself, obsessing about why she did not get off at Hither Green and Ford at Charing Cross. "We were so good we were careless," she lamented, "and I, so neatly chaperoned while I was in France, *tant soit peu* [somewhat] relaxed when I set foot on the shores of England."

1

2

3

ANCESTORS: Alfred Hunt's parents, Sarah Sanderson, 1, and Alfred Hunt, 2, an artist, on their wedding day in January 1824. 3, Violet's maternal grandfather, the Rev. James Raine, the Durham antiquarian who took his family to live in a haunted medieval mansion called Crook Hall. Violet preferred her North Country heritage over her father's Liverpool roots.

PARENTS: 4, Violet as an infant with her mother, Margaret Raine Hunt; 5, Violet's mother; 6, her father, the painter Alfred William Hunt, photographed in a reflective, dreamy mood, which characterized his personality. 7, This 1889 watercolor of Windsor Castle shows his affinity to Turner's landscapes, which he emulated by holding a watercolor under running water to reduce the finish, and then scrubbing it with a stiff brush to eliminate detail.

4

5

6

INFLUENCES: Violet's youth was shaped by many eminent Victorians, including (from left to right) in this 1863 photograph the artist William B. Scott, her mother's art teacher; the critic John Ruskin (in his favorite gray suit), her sister Venice's godfather; and Dante Gabriel Rossetti (with the smoldering eyes), whose personal life became an obsession with Violet, and the subject of her last book, *The Wife of Rossetti.*

9

FIRST LOVE: The studio of George Henry Boughton at West House on Campden Hill. Three years younger than Violet's father and a friend of the family, he became her first lover when she was twenty-two. Violet said the cluttered studio where she posed for Boughton's demure maidens (a Violet type is on his easel) reminded her of a church.

10

11

ARTIST'S MODEL: A photographic study of Violet taken between the ages of nineteen and twenty-four when she modeled for the Pre-Raphaelite painter Edward Burne-Jones, who admired her heavy-lidded eyes. Although other women claimed to have sat for the virgin in Burne-Jones's "King Cophetua and the Beggar Maid," Violet's features are evident.

12

LOVER AND WOULD-BE LOVERS: 13, Violet's first conquest, Oscar Wilde, here in a photo taken during his American tour in 1882, was said to have proposed marriage. 14, The diplomat dabbler, Oswald Crawfurd, made Violet one of his mistresses for seven tumultuous years. 15, The art critic D. S. MacColl was a steadfast but unsuccessful suitor; she found him boring.

13

14

15

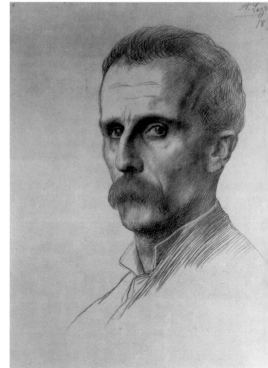

HOME: The Hunts' first London home, 1 Tor Villas, later named 10 Tor Gardens (16). Built in 1851 by the artist James Clarke Hook (who designed the square studio tower to give maximum light), it was occupied by the Pre-Raphaelite painter William Hol-

16

17

man Hunt before the Hunts leased it in 1866. It was destroyed during a bombing raid in 1941. After Alfred Hunt died in 1896, Violet and her mother moved across the street to South Lodge (17), where they lived out their lives. The house is pictured at the turn of the century. Today it is marked with a plaque commemorating the fact that Ford Madox Ford lived there, without mention of Violet Hunt.

FAMILY: From left to right, Violet's sister Silvia with her country-squire husband, Walton Fogg-Elliot, her sister Venice, and a friend identified only as Alice. The photograph was probably taken at Bedburn, the Fogg-Elliot country estate south of Durham.

18

19

20

MENTORS AND LOVERS: 19, Violet in 1894 when she was thirty-two. 20, H. G. Wells, who seduced Violet; 22, Somerset Maugham, whom Violet seduced. Both remained her lifelong friends. 21, Ford Madox Ford around 1910, the year he and Violet became lovers.

21

22

FRIENDS AND ACQUAINTANCES: 23, Henry James, in a picture he inscribed to Violet during her November 1907 visit to Rye; 24, Ezra Pound in 1909, the year he arrived in London and first met Violet. 25, Margaret Radclyffe Hall, who had a crush on Violet in 1907, before Hall became a well-known lesbian and wrote *The Well of Loneliness*.

23

24

25

PROTÉGÉS: Violet was in stellar company in the *English Review,* Ford's outstanding literary magazine that he launched to great acclaim in 1908; the March 1909 issue, 26, published her short story "The Coach." 28, Percy Wyndham Lewis, "the incipient madman," as Violet called him, was one of Ford's *Review* discoveries, as was the young D. H. Lawrence, 27, shown here at age twenty-three.

THE

ENGLISH

REVIEW

MARCH 1909

EMILE VERHAEREN : HENRY
JAMES : JOSEPH CONRAD
VIOLET HUNT : H. GRAN-
VILLE BARKER : ETHEL
CLIFFORD : J. W. ALLEN
H. G. WELLS : H. BELLOC
G. K. CHESTERTON

Subscriptions cannot be accepted for the supply of Magazines and Reviews only
W. H. SMITH & SON'S LIBRARY
186 STRAND, LONDON, W.C. AND BRANCHES
Subscribers are respectfully requested not to retain this publication
longer than three days, and to return it earlier if possible

LONDON : DUCKWORTH & CO.
PUBLISHED MONTHLY 2/6 NET

26

27

28

The LIBRARY: WEEK by WEEK.
By FRANK A. MUMBY.

A Link with the Past. Messrs. Chatto and Windus have in the press a book which forms an interesting link between the modern school of fiction and that of a generation or so ago, in the waning days of the three volume novel—those good old days as they are now regarded in the book trade, though the three volume novel, be it remembered, had just as many critics in its own time as the six-shilling novel of to-day. The forthcoming book is a romance entitled "The Governess," by Mrs. Alfred Hunt, one of the popular novelists of the old days, and her daughter, Miss Violet Hunt (now Mrs. Ford Madox Hueffer) one of the successful of the modern school.

Hills and Saunders.   *Elliott and Fry.*

On the left, Mrs. Alfred Hunt, who is joint authoress with her daughter, Miss Violet Hunt (Mrs. Ford Madox Hueffer) (right), of a forthcoming novel, "The Governess," which links the modern school of fiction with the old three-volume days.

29

CATALYST: The innocent-enough announcement in *The Throne* which referred to Violet as "Mrs. Ford Madox Hueffer" and ignited the libel trial.

TRIUMPH AND SHAME: Elsie Hueffer on the front page of a tabloid, dressed in fur and royal purple, after winning £300 in damages from *The Throne*. Ford fled to France during the trial, while Violet waited it out in London. Both were surprised that the jury did not believe their story about a German divorce and remarriage.

The Daily Mirror

THE MORNING JOURNAL WITH THE SECOND LARGEST NET SALE.

No. 2,900.   SATURDAY, FEBRUARY 8, 1913.   One Halfpenny.

IN THE COURTS YESTERDAY: MRS. HUEFFER WINS HER LIBEL ACTION AND CHAUFFEUR IN "GREY CAR CASE" IS ACQUITTED.

Mr. Roe reading a letter in court at Hove yesterday, where the inquiry was adjourned after Mr. Muir had stated that two witnesses had refused to come. The small photograph shows Dr. Baines, Mr. Trevanion's medical attendant, who was recalled to reply to certain statements which were made by Nurse Rice at the last hearing. Interest in the case showed no sign of abatement, and the court was again crowded.

Mrs. Elsie Hueffer (wife of Mr. Ford Madox Hueffer, the novelist) leaving the Law Courts yesterday, where she was awarded £300 damages for libel. The portraits are of Miss Violet Hunt, the authoress, who was frequently mentioned during the case, and Mr. Ford Madox Hueffer.—(*Daily Mirror* and Elliott and Fry.)

Chauffeur John A. Sallows, who was acquitted at the Old Bailey yesterday on a charge of the manslaughter of Miss Amy Chillingworth. He was arrested in connection with what is known as "the grey car case."

What happened on board the steamer Hardy, which foundered after leaving Treport, was related during the hearing of a remarkable case yesterday. There was some sodium included in the cargo, explained counsel, and the water, getting to one of the cases, set it on fire. The captain, who did not understand the nature of the substance, played the hose on the cases, setting fire to the contents. A series of explosions followed, and when the cases were thrown overboard several jumped back. (1) Captain Cooper. (2) The Hardy, which broke her back and sank.

31

32

SELSEY SUMMERS: During the Ford years, when Violet rented Knap Cottage on the southern coast near Portsmouth, the couple entertained constantly. 31, Ford, Violet, and H. G. Wells relax outside the Knap; 32, Rebecca West (here in a 1932 portrait by Wyndham Lewis), was also a visitor. 33, Violet in her mid-forties.

33

34

THE FORD SAGA: 34, Some of the South Lodge Group at the Selsey Hotel in 1913. Brigit Patmore (Ford's new distraction) is seated at left next to Violet; Ford is seated at center. 35, Ford and Violet at the Selsey Hotel. 36, Ford in his World War I uniform.

35

36

37

STOIC PROFILES: 37, Violet, left, at a literary event (H. G. Wells is seated opposite her). In profile she photographed badly, appearing severe and haughty. 38, A study done by the photographer E. O. Hoppé around 1910.

38

When Ford arrived at Holland Park, he had another shock: John Galsworthy was sitting in his editor's chair. Ford's brother-in-law, David Soskice, who had been asked by Ford to raise money for the *Review* after the Marwood incident, assumed that Ford and Violet had run off and decided to replace him. From the start, Soskice was a bad choice as publisher. He wanted a magazine of politics, not literature.* Ford called him a "revolutionary extremist" and asked Violet to convince her friend Sir Alfred Mond (later Lord Melchett), a millionaire munitions magnate, to buy the *Review*.

Mond took over the magazine in December 1909, but did not reinstate Ford as editor. Instead, he hired the uninspired Austin Harrison, a former correspondent of the *Daily Mail*. After directing thirteen issues, Ford was no longer in control; the last issue he produced was that of February 1910 (which carried the first installment of Violet's latest novel, *The Wife of Altamont*, a convoluted and improbably plotted story of murder, suicide, lust and betrayal—another unhappy love story), but material he selected continued to run (Lawrence's "Odour of Chrysanthemums" appearing in June 1911).

Ford's depression deepened. "And we walked as usual in the Park," Violet sadly recounted, "treading the dead leaves like faded hopes under our feet, in silence. For a week of mornings he did not address more than three words to me." Violet mourned with Ford the loss of his beloved magazine, but she had her own private terrors. After the Charing Cross debacle, she thought she might be named co-respondent, "the greatest misfortune that could, at that still stringently Victorian epoch, befall an unmarried woman with a mother to take care of, and a girl to chaperone; and a large circle of friends and relations to placate and keep in a good humour."

According to their plan, Gertrud's name was the one to be tarnished—not Violet's. They lived with the greatest rectitude. Vi-

---

*David Vladimirovich Soskice, a Russian-born Jewish revolutionary and lawyer, spent three years in various Russian prisons before fleeing to Switzerland and then to London in 1895, where he became a journalist and through the Edward Garnetts met Ford's sister Juliet, whom he married in 1902. In 1917 he returned to Russia as a correspondent for the *Manchester Guardian*, serving as Alexander Kerensky's private secretary in the short-lived provisional government. (Soskice was born in the same Ukrainian city of Berdichev as Joseph Conrad, but Conrad did not want his reminiscences, including his account of Czarist Russia's cruelty to his parents, appearing in a journal run by a Russian.)

olet no longer visited Holland Park; Ford dined at South Lodge always in the company of Margaret Hunt, with whom he played the card game piquet, and following a few tunes on the piano departed promptly at eleven. When Ford's literary agent J. B. Pinker heard about Elsie meeting the boat train, he repeated the story to his client Wells, who wrote Violet that he hoped she wasn't "going to get into another mess—any mess—a particular mess he had heard of?"

Pinker was a busybody, and Ford angrily told him so: "I know how inveterate a gossip you are. But don't bring me—and still more don't bring third parties—up against little animals like Wells. I don't know him; I don't want to know him and I try to forget that I ever made the mistake of knowing him." This was Ford's deranged way of talking when he realized that he was in trouble—and trouble of his own making. He was also still angry at Wells for his "treacheries" during the launching of the *Review*. But did he know about Wells's affair with Violet? Rebecca West told Arthur Mizener she thought not, at least not from Violet, who evidently decided that if Ford had heard the common gossip about Boughton and Crawfurd, more sexual statistics would not enhance her mystique.

What stunned Violet, though, was Henry James's rejection. The "Purple Patch" had continued to make the elderly author's life more vivid, more vicarious (with him watching—safely—as he once wrote her, through the curtains of a retreating ambulance); she had expanded his social circle, introducing him to, among others, R. B. Cunninghame Graham, "the uncrowned king of Scotland," an adventurer who traveled extensively in nineteenth-century South America, claimed descent from Robert II of Scotland, and as a liberal MP was suspended for saying "damn" in the House of Commons in 1886.

When James was ill during the early spring of 1909, he wrote Violet from Lamb House to think of him "in the pleasing & unaggressive minor key." He advised her to marry off the "Dancing Girl" Rosamond and "recover your rest." Violet offered to come to Rye and cheer him up, and in October James extended an invitation, writing, "I am more and more aged, infirm and unattractive, but I make such a stand as I can, and shall be very glad to see you if you can brave the adventure or face such a tiresome *déplacement* on such meagre terms. We can have a long jaw (with lots of arrears to make up) and, weather permitting, eke a short walk."

The rules of hospitality demanded honesty, so Violet and Ford separately wrote James explaining the impending divorce. To their astonishment, James promptly withdrew Violet's invitation. That news, James told her (formally addressing her as "Dear Violet Hunt"), made impossible "our projected occasion of indispensable elements of frankness and pleasantness," adding, "I deeply regret and deplore the lamentable position in which I gather you have put yourself in respect to divorce proceedings about to be taken by Mrs. Hueffer; it affects me as painfully unedifying, and that compels me to regard all agreeable or unembarrassed communications between us impossible." Although James genuinely liked Violet, he was not fond of Ford and had in the past taken pains to avoid the braggart's company. Why, then, should he now become involved in Ford's unsavory problems?

James's attitude toward this potentially messy situation stemmed not from a repressed New Englander's abhorrence of adultery, but from the fear of being linked—in any way whatsoever— with someone publicly involved in a court action. The first commandment of the Edwardian code of morality was "Thou shalt not be found out." Discreet affairs were tolerated, but to feature in the newspapers, to end up in court, was unforgivable. No matter what their social station, women could not survive the lingering Victorian taboo that no respectable woman could possibly enjoy sex. Moreover, there had to be a distinction between women who acted disreputably and those whose reputation was untarnished. If no lines were drawn, then why be good?

Violet realized her situation only too well. When scandal had threatened with George Boughton, her mother had sent her to Paris, but the years with Crawfurd had given Violet a false security since Crawfurd's wife tolerated infidelity. To maintain her dignity and her friendship with James, Violet lied to him. "I am not in a 'lamentable position' at all as regards Mrs. Hueffer's divorce proceedings," she replied, noting that she was only Ford's editorial assistant, but if her name were involved she could only "speak the truth, and defend myself. That is why it seems very hard that my old friend should turn against me—unless indeed [it is] the fact of marrying a divorcee that he so deplores . . . if you were ever in the least interested in me, could you not come to see me in town, and let me tell you how I stand."

James answered that his concern was not with Violet's illicit relationship with Ford, which was "none of my business at all," but with her "position, as a result of those relations." If Violet's name figured in divorce proceedings, "I really don't see how an old friend of yours could feel or pronounce your being in a position to permit of this anything but 'lamentable—lamentable—oh lamentable!' "

Although Violet had explained that Elsie and Ford had lived separately for several years, James was not persuaded. "I neither knew or know anything whatever of the [separation] matter," he added, "so it was exactly because I didn't wish to that I found conversing with you at all to be in prospect impossible. That was the light in which I didn't—your term is harsh!—forbid you my house; but deprecated the idea of what would otherwise have been so interesting and welcome a tête à tête with you. I am very sorry to have had to lose it, and am yours in this regret."

Three months later James softened his attitude, when Violet inquired about his health and received a friendly reply. "It was a charming charity in you to write," he said. "Everything you tell me [is] a breath of your roaring London world (gracefully & considerately bedimmed a little) wafted into a sick room that at the end of six or seven weeks has become dismally tedious. . . . I rejoice in your brace account of your own heroisms. They come to me like vague infused strains & boom-booms of a Wagner opera—that there are women of confirmed genius who take ravenous nieces to London balls." Violet certainly must have cherished the phrase "confirmed genius." James expanded his good will by requesting a copy of *The Wife of Altamont*, which he heard was "very strange & fine & fierce." This was praise indeed, for Violet knew that he read Mrs. Humphry Ward's and Lucy Clifford's books in preference to hers. When *Tales of the Uneasy* was published the next year, James was particularly enthusiastic. He even helped select the title.*

At last "The Master" had acknowledged her literary worth. "I have always tried to get a handsome, well grown bush for my wine— a personable godfather for my literary children," she said. "And I

---

*Initially James suggested she call the collection "Ghostly Stories of a Worldly Woman," which indeed they were. As a fictional character, shades of the "Purple Patch" are found in James's final collection of short stories, *The Finer Grain* (published in 1910), particularly the character of Mrs. Worthingham, a disturbingly modern woman, in "Crapy Cornelia." Ford believed he was the model for Merton Densher in James's *Wings of the Dove*.

have succeeded in getting at least four out of the big five—Mr. Conrad, Mr. Hudson, H. G. [Wells] and Mr. James—Mr. Bennett has, hitherto, firmly refused to sanction any of my works, but I have it on his spoken word that he does not utterly disapprove of my literary progeny." Still, she was hurt that James would not deal with her personal problems, that he only "wanted to see the game— as much of it as was likely to be useful to him—from the stadium reserved for spectators, with good strong railings between tragedy and him." In the end, it would be his loss, for the story of Violet and Ford matches any Jamesian plot.

II

German Overtures

ANEW GENERATION of artists and writers gathered at South Lodge, replacing the old guard of Wells, Conrad, Galsworthy and James. Ford christened them *les jeunes*. During the prewar years the names and faces changed, but the indubitable leader was the irrepressible American Ezra Pound, who, from the day he landed in London in 1909, shocked the Edwardians with his wild antics. His dress was eccentric, his social behavior (eating centerpieces of roses and tulips) startling and his energy (breaking fragile chairs) disconcerting.

Pound lived at 10 Church Walk, a cul-de-sac near the church of St. Mary Abbots, a short walk from South Lodge, in a minuscule room hopelessly cluttered with books, manuscripts and sketches. This part of Kensington, he wrote, was "SWARming with writers and intellectuals." Violet lent him some of Alfred's paintings and odd bits of furniture, including an overstuffed armchair in which D. H. Lawrence had often slept after missing the last train to Croydon. Pound enjoyed his snug quarters but loathed the tidal regularity of the church bells.

Ford recalled how Pound "would approach with the steps of a dancer, making passes with a cane at an imaginary opponent. He would wear trousers made of green billiard cloth, a pink coat, a blue shirt, a tie hand-painted by a Japanese friend, an immense sombrero, a flaming beard cut to a point and a single, large blue ear-ring." Violet's parrots—part of a menagerie that included an owl (named Anne Veronica after Wells's novel), a bulldog and nine Persian cats—shrieked "Ezra! Ezra!" whenever they saw him bouncing up the walk.

Before he became arrogant and tiresome, Pound was a curiosity, sweeping away Victorian cobwebs with his outrageous behavior. Wyndham Lewis called him a drop of oil in water, refusing to mix, wanting only to impress. As connoisseurs of eccentricity, Violet and Ford were fascinated by the young poet and impressed with his talent. The first to publish him in England, Ford put "Sestina: Altaforte" into the *Review* of June 1909. Eventually Pound, like Ford, saw himself as a self-proclaimed missionary of culture, offering food, clothing and advice with a generous heart to artists and writers. He championed, with impeccable taste, Robert Frost, T. S. Eliot, Conrad Aiken, William Carlos Williams and, in particular, James Joyce.

The frantic epicenter of the afternoon tennis games held on the grass court in the communal garden across from South Lodge, Pound was frequently paired with Ford against Mary Martindale and Grace Crawford, a Michigan girl whose father was Buffalo Bill's business manager. Pound played tennis, said Violet, "like a demon or a trick pony, sitting down composedly in his square and jumping up in time to receive his adversary's ball, which he competently returned, the flaps of his polychrome shirt flying out like the petals of some flower and his red beard like a flaming pistil in the middle of it."

Watching small, agile Pound compete against tall, hefty Ford was a show all its own (like playing against "an inebriated kangaroo," said Ford). Brigit Patmore, another of the South Lodge group, described them as "crouched-for-action players, readier to spring at each other's throats than the ball, the service of which was very free. It seemed to matter little how often they served fault after fault. They just went on till the ball was where they wanted, then one or other cried 'Game' or 'Hard luck,' 'My set' or 'That's love-all' or 'Six sets to one'! It was beyond anyone to umpire or score. A voice murmured as the two sportive gentlemen walked haughtily off the court, 'Quite a new sort of game, isn't it?' "

During these tennis parties and at tea time, the elderly Margaret Hunt, wrapped in a white woolen shawl, enjoyed harassing the young people. Grace Crawford recalled that she was "very eccentric and apt to come out with the most surprising and irrelevant remarks which Violet always received with complete calm. Once on being handed a cup of tea, the old lady sniffed it suspiciously and then in a deep and tragic voice said: 'What is this, poison? Well, never mind, I'll drink it if you like'; downing it all in a single hearty gulp." Another time, Crawford said, she asked everyone, including Ford, whom she saw every day, what they did. Violet interrupted, saying, " 'You know quite well who they are, Mother, and that they are all poets.' Mrs. Hunt's only answer was a loud snort; for the rest of tea she fixed poor Lawrence with a basilisk stare, occasionally muttering under her breath: 'All poets indeed. Ha! All poets, indeed. Ha!' "

Margaret particularly disliked Ford and Pound and would hide their tennis rackets and shoes (which they kept at South Lodge) in a different place every day; all this tumult delayed the game while exasperated, shoeless players searched the house for their gear. D. H. Lawrence, who came to watch, keep score and retrieve balls, laughed himself silly at this treasure hunt. He confided to Crawford that he was glad not to play, for he was sure Violet's mother cared less for him than the other two and would have burned, not hidden, his things.

On January 11, 1910, Violet's life crashed: while walking down Kensington High Street she saw a bedraggled man shuffling along the gutter wearing a sandwich board emblazoned with the words MR. HUEFFER TO GO BACK IN FOURTEEN DAYS. The petition for the restitution of conjugal rights had reached the divorce court, and Ford was ordered to return to his wife in a fortnight. Violet's name was not mentioned, but she was nonetheless ashamed; she had never been associated with anyone who had "been in the papers." She worried about how the servants would greet Ford when he arrived that evening for dinner, but he wisely stayed away from South Lodge that night and for many nights to come. Instead, he tucked up at Holland Park, editing Violet's novel *The Wife of Altamont* (dedicated to Mary Martindale, Ford's sister-in-law and former mistress). Violet had befriended Mary in her peculiar penchant for keeping her lovers' former lovers within her social orbit.

When Ford refused to return in fourteen days, the court ordered him to pay £25 in alimony within three weeks and £3/3s a week thereafter (in addition to paying clothing and education bills for his children). Since Ford (more likely, Violet) had already been paying £3/10s weekly since December, he refused. The order created the impression, he claimed, that he had not provided for his family. Charged with contempt of court, he was sentenced to ten days in Brixton Gaol commuted to eight days because the first day fell on a weekend.

Violet consigned to a dealer Ford's Holland Park furnishings and personal possessions, raising £1,500. With the help of Mary Martindale, she sold most of his books and moved everything else to South Lodge, where he would live, paying Margaret Hunt £3 a week—for appearances. Thus Violet took financial control of Ford's life, paid off his debts and sent money to Elsie and the children. But Elsie took no further steps toward a legal separation or divorce. Religion and relatives were factors in her decision, as well as apprehension that her sister still loved Ford. Ford had converted to Catholicism to please his German relatives, and his children had been baptized Catholics at his insistence. An Anglican but often labeled a Catholic, Elsie worried that a divorce would stigmatize her daughters, or that Ford might abduct the girls, thus forcing a divorce on his own terms. There was simply too much pressure from the European Hüffers and the Martindales for her to proceed.

Ford's time in prison was disagreeable but illuminating. He ate little, read one prison book, _A Story for Girls_ by Mrs. L. T. Meade, made mailbags, talked with the burglars and embezzlers and, when bored, rolled his socks into three balls and practiced curling them off his back and arms at the same time—a pastime consistent with Ford's childlike love of games. Following his release, he ate a big steak at the Continental and Violet took him—along with her mother and Gertrud Schablowsky (soon on her way to Australia via Königsberg)—to the Bell Inn, in the village of Fordingbridge. Contented and tranquil, all his needs attended to, Ford began the book he dedicated to Violet, _Ladies Whose Bright Eyes_, using Rosamond as a model for its heroine, the Lady Dionissia.

Rosamond had been living at South Lodge, preparing for her debut season, but all plans were canceled when Silvia learned of Ford's problems. It is "impossible for any of us to stay with you whilst this legal business is on," she wrote. Violet pleaded for her niece to stay, but her sister was firm: "Nothing you say will make me change my mind. I consider it *most* harmful in every way for R to be with you in town . . . and your love for her which you say is so strong—should make you see that I am right." But Violet would not accept that her scorning of convention reflected in any way on Rosamond's matrimonial prospects.

How could anyone question her reputation when she had invited Ford's mother and Mary Martindale to stay at South Lodge when Ford was there? The young David Garnett, son of Richard and Constance, recalled how intent Ford and Violet were "on singeing Mrs. Grundy's beard," once accompanying them in a hired open carriage to leave cards and pay formal calls, Ford with his top hat upon his knee, Violet "all veils and tocque and parasol beside him, the card-cases at hand."

On May 6, 1910, the Edwardian Era ended abruptly with the death of Edward VII, the playboy king. The new king, George V, found himself siding with the House of Commons, which sought reforms favoring the working classes, and against the House of Lords, which defended the power of the aristocracy. The old order was crumbling. Ortega y Gasset identified the year as the turning point between the age of reason and the age of existentialism. Roger Fry's Post-Impressionist exhibition that year at London's Grafton Galleries with its geometric Cézannes and sensual Gauguins shocked viewers (the *Morning Post*'s critic said all the paintings should be burned). Diaghilev's Russian Ballet with Nijinsky and the Russian opera with Chaliapin in *Boris Godunov* came to London, changing forever British attitudes toward dance, staging and costume.

In this time of political and cultural ferment, Violet was too busy to take notice. As she worried about what Elsie might (or might not) do, she was suddenly accused of misappropriating her mother's money. Aunt Jane, to whom Margaret sent a monthly stipend, claimed Violet was beautifying South Lodge (whose lease she had purchased from her mother in 1908 for £1,200) at her sister's expense. Violet had recently repapered the upstairs rooms with Morris designs (at six shillings a yard) and installed a much-needed bathroom on the second floor—improvements that Aunt Jane thought frivolous. Needing little encouragement, Silvia and Venice joined the fray and asked their sister for a full accounting.

At such moments, Violet's tough North Country spirit normally propelled her through chaos, but now she felt overwhelmed, unable to deal with practical problems or with Ford's depression. Ford looked in the mirror, wanting to see the man of good will, the chivalrous Tory gentleman, but instead he saw the failed editor, husband, father and writer. "With Ford, nothing was of real importance in comparison with his work," Goldring observed. "If he could shut his door on 'writs and duns, bores and viragos,' he could be happy. 'He refused absolutely with his intellect to face them'— the problems of existence"; whereas Violet, as she said, needed "to live always in the boiling middle of things or, to mix metaphors, in a world of thin ice and broken eggs that will never make an omelette." She was rushing toward disaster.

During that hectic summer of 1910, in one of his splendid descriptions, Lawrence saw Violet "tremendous in a lace gown and a hat writhed with blue feathers as if it were some python. Indeed she looked very handsome. She had on her best society manners. She is very dexterous: flicks a bright question, lifts her eyebrows in deep concern, glances from the man on her right to the lady on her left, smiles, bows, and suddenly—quick curtain—she is gone, and is utterly somebody else's, she who was altogether ours a brief second before."

Even as Violet peppered Ford with questions—what was to happen to them? would they ever marry?—she fatefully decided they should visit his German relatives. To put herself in the right mood, she shed a Francophile cocoon and emerged a German butterfly, full of hyperbole for a country she had never considered worth visiting. She wanted to see "decently, sensibly arranged German things, German customs, German institutions, everything but German cooking. The *décor* of Germany was to me like the background of a fairy-tale—a familiar one of Grimm's."

For a chaperon she asked, of all people, Oswald Crawfurd's widow, Lita, who was then living in Bad Nauheim. To pay for the trip, she sold one of her father's paintings to the City of Liverpool for £150, and later—to finance Ford's German stay—sold more paintings (including one of her father's favorite oils, *Brignal Banks*, for £75 to Liverpool's Walker Art Gallery). She also sold the first volume of Ford Madox Brown's diary to the Pierpont Morgan Museum in New York for £200. Violet was investing heavily in her future—and in Ford's comfort.

☐

They took a slow boat up the Rhine to Assmannshausen, not far from Boppard, where Ford's Aunt Emma lived; his Aunt Laura had died while he was in prison, and her long-awaited legacy was contingent on Ford's good behavior. They hoped the visit would eradicate this concern, after Ford explained his position. Violet never discounted the mercenary aspect of the journey: they had visions "of a villa on the Rhine [which they would rent for the summer] and where money, that Germans adore, would be his for the asking and a little deference and kowtowing to an ancient and influential relative." With each cathedral spire and promontory castle that came into view, the embroidered fairy tale grew more opulent.

The trip was long and ultimately dull. Even a people-watcher like Violet grew tired of witnessing Aubrey Beardsley's mother ("all turquoises and lace") scurrying about the decks. But there was much for Violet and Lita to discuss; they had not seen each other for eight years. To Violet's annoyance, though, Ford spent hours playing patience, which he said helped him organize the day's writing.

In early September David Garnett visited them in Boppard, where they were paying court to the relatives. Soon Lita Crawfurd was bored, needing "the hectic joys of her cure" at Nauheim, and they accompanied her there. Lita and Violet checked into Bittong's, a swank hotel, while Ford bunked at the less smart Hotel Alexandre. During their stay Tsar Nicholas II and his wife visited to take the waters, and were observed shopping and walking about the town. The Tzaritza "looked stupid, incompetent, haughty, dejected," said Violet, cattily dismissing the image of Russian royalty, "the morbid shadow of a queen" in "black with pearls," with the disconsolate Nicholas a figure "marked down for destruction." Other spa delights also displeased: a champagne bath was overrated, and one drink of the waters upset her stomach for days. (The languid ennui of Nauheim is vividly re-created by Ford in *The Good Soldier* and by Violet in *The Desirable Alien*.)

On their return to Boppard, Aunt Emma, who felt the family name had been dishonored by Elsie's suit, encouraged her nephew to obtain German citizenship and divorce Elsie in that country. On the recommendation of Lita Crawfurd, Ford consulted Rechtsanwalt Ludwig Leun, a lawyer with a practice in the town of Giessen, located between Frankfurt and Marburg. Would the fact that his father took out naturalization papers in Britain in the 1870s affect his right to German citizenship? he asked. "No, indeed," said Leun. All that Ford needed to do was live for six months or so in Germany and be accepted by the town elders as a man of worth and credit. It sounded so simple.

Most of September passed pleasantly at Marburg, where they stayed at Ford's favorite hotel, the Hotel zum Ritter. They were avid sightseers, delighting in the beer gardens, and every evening after dining they promenaded to Marchesi's, the town's most popular café, to drink coffee and eat large slabs of fruitcake while Ford translated news from the local newspaper. On September 2, a local holiday, they joined the parade of little boys with Chinese lanterns going up and down the narrow streets. As they "did" Marburg, they contrasted Germany with conditions in England. Violet thought Marburg more romantic than Oxford, not so many "dreaming spires"; in fact, it was reminiscent of her birthplace, Durham. They found the German waiter superior to his British counterpart, but viewed the student rite of inflicting dueling scars uncivilized.

The main topic under discussion was the divorce plan, and they realized that they would have to give up their British citizenship. Their joint book *The Desirable Alien* (dedicated by Violet to "Mrs. Oswald Crawfurd who led me into Germany") was testimony of their affection—at that time—for Germany. Here Violet recorded her impressions of customs, costumes, ceremonies and conspicuous consumption. Striking a false note for such an avid Francophile, she confessed that she had "taken to German cookery as no alien could even have hoped to do. I care nothing for what my grandfather probably called French 'kickshaws'—all grandfathers did. I detest the eternal omelette of France, the eternal *pommes frites* [french fries], the same good sauce—I don't say it isn't good—disposed over everything." Also an ailurophile, Violet observed that she never saw any grown cats in Germany, only kittens. "I suppose you eat them as soon as they are fat enough?" she teased Ford. "Something in that!" Ford replied. "But the real reason," he said, "is that they eat the birds. Germans love birds, and would sooner have an aviary than a cattery like yours," adding with typical Fordian self-importance, "I am a German, and *I* love birds."

While in Germany, Violet saw her first motion picture. "I was then told that England abounded in them, and this wild joy was at hand, and had been at hand for years in the two main streets that bounded my dwelling. I had never, so far, discovered them— never known this famous form of amusement," adding with ingenuous hyperbole: "Yes, I consider the advent of the Boy Scouts, the invention of picture postcards, and the rage for picture theatres, as the three most important developments of this age of brass and iron."

One day they made a pilgrimage to Marburg Castle to see Luther's Protest. Ford was in one of his brooding religious moods, mourning the loss of Germany's Catholic churches to the Protestants, making Violet drink, as she put it, "the Protestant cup of bitterness to the dregs." After riding an hour in a "clumsy, old-fashioned landau" to the castle, a custodian, irritatingly rattling his keys, ushered them "into the large Ritter Saal with the painted ceiling, with the immense fireplace, and the wide window-seats cut in the thickness of the wall."

Passing through a corridor lined with suits of armor made for dwarfs, they entered a room with glass cases "containing sheets of parchment written in crabbed characters—the handwriting used in Shakespeare's three authentic signatures, which are actually written in German characters." Violet circled the room, looked at the discolored parchments, listened to Ford's proselytizing, and then saw "the unpretending signature of Martin Luther, and the warrant that gave Protestantism to the world!"

"That bit of paper *is* Protestantism," Ford pronounced. "It all began with the signing of that bit of paper. That is what you mean when you say you are a Protestant!" he said, thrusting his finger at Violet. "But I don't say it," Violet replied helplessly. "I even deny it. Useless! A 'Prot' I am, and seemingly must remain so in the eyes of this black Papist." Out of this encounter Ford drew the pivotal scene in *The Good Soldier* where Florence lectures on the glories of the Protest with her hand on Edward Ashburnham's arm and her eyes on his, until her husband became "aware of something treacherous, something frightful, something evil in the day."

In the midst of touring, Violet suffered vaginal bleeding and was bedridden for several days, during which she took dictation from Ford for *Ancient Lights* (published as *Memories and Impressions* in America). When she was able to walk around, she returned to England to answer the legal action concerning her mother's finances.

Ford accompanied her as far as Cologne and then returned to Giessen to establish residency and be close to his lawyer. Back in London, she signed the papers making her receiver of her mother's estate, which put her, more than ever, under the scrutiny of her sisters. As she left Temple Bar and walked along Fleet Street, she felt like the "sparrow, hopping off the pavement . . . in dread now of the great hoofs." But it was the wrong time for Violet to consider living a righteous life.

Ever since her childhood when she had helped her mother translate Grimm and collected fairy tales for Andrew Lang, Violet had been an accomplished researcher. The burning topic now was German divorces. She took notes on *The Life and Letters of Sir Hubert von Herkomer*; he was the artist who usurped Alfred Hunt's place as president of the Royal Water-Colour Society, and a naturalized citizen who had resumed his German nationality in order to marry his sister-in-law. Holman Hunt's predicament was already a familiar story. He too wanted to wed his deceased wife's sister and circumvented the law forbidding this (it was considered incest until 1907) by marrying in Switzerland.

The "German plan" was discussed with absolutely everyone who would listen: two friends, Dollie Radford and Ethel Colburn Mayne, were skeptical and sought more information from legal expert R. Ellis Roberts. He was not optimistic. Yes, Ford could acquire German citizenship, divorce his wife and wed Violet, but the marriage would be legal only in Germany, he said. In England, Violet would still be Miss Hunt—Ford's mistress. When she heard this, Violet decided to trust the opinion of Ford's German lawyer.

But the more she sought approval, the more she heard unpleasant truths. Henry James's friend Lucy Clifford, whom Violet called "a female Kipling," bluntly asked why she had traveled to Germany with Lita Crawfurd, her former lover's widow. Violet defended her behavior, arguing that it showed her generosity. Still, she had broken most of the rules and now wanted to stretch the rest to the limit. Respectable people did not depend on foreign divorces and remarriages.

"Elsie will, I think, succeed in ruining us *socially*," Violet wrote Ford in Germany. "Dear darling, do you like my letters?" she continued. "Aren't they like myself, patchy and scrappy, and altogether wild and disconcerting?" Although spunky on the outside, she was distracted, unable to start a new novel ("I can't do creative work . . . when I'm worried"). Even a short story seemed an effort. She said she wanted to do reviews and journalism but without signing her name, which Ford—like Crawfurd—vetoed as unseemly considering her position. By doing hack work, Violet estimated she could earn a steady £2/2s a week to keep them in cabs and cigarettes. And perhaps chocolate. "I'm nibbling chocolate. It is become my craze like smoking with you." She did write stories for *Lady's World*, which had published her autobiographical plots for more than eight years.*

Alone in London, Violet looked after Ford's affairs, forwarding his mail, keeping him informed of the London news (particularly the *Review*'s progress), typing and organizing his novel *Ladies Whose Bright Eyes* and badgering Pinker about getting more money for him. In Giessen, Ford lived a spartan but far from miserable life, constantly complaining. At least he was healthy and well fed, ballooning to 224 pounds. Violet, though, was not well, and when she had another siege of bleeding and was hospitalized, Mary Martindale wired Ford. He arrived "incognito" from Germany to be by her side when she came out of the anesthetic in the nursing home.

The operation was probably a D and C, possibly caused by the onset of menopause (her doctor's version) or complications from syphilis. In any case, she did not recover quickly, and once home the hemorrhages recurred. "I am afraid it will happen again just about when I go to you. Then you'll have a wife and not a wife," she wrote. She also had an abscessed tooth that had to be extracted. "Can it be true what he [the dentist] hints at, that it may be because of the spots, and the lip, and the sore throat I always wake with?" she asked Ford. (It is unclear what Violet had told Ford about early medical opinion regarding her spots.)

---

*In *The Novelist's Revenge*, published in March 1910, Violet describes her alter ego: "She was clever, too clever to keep a man; that is what her friends said, stupid women are best at that. Men hate clever women, especially clever women who write. It is a most unromantic accomplishment, and unless one is a George Sand or a George Eliot, is sure to lead to a division when of interest in the eyes of the critical male." This story is a thinly veiled account of her emotional state when she wrote *Sooner or Later*, following the Crawfurd affair.

During 1910, Ford's first year of exile to establish residency in Germany, their letters crisscrossed the English Channel. As Violet raced about London, she noted her thoughts: "I can feel things far better than I can visualize them. I don't see you so much as I feel you—your mouth and your beautiful hands!" Lonely and needing approval, she asked him about "The Tiger Skin," which she was writing for _Tales of the Uneasy_. "I wonder if it's good? Alter it any way you can for me." Ford liked it, and his praise made her "glow all over, makes me want to deserve it better." No matter how bedeviled their relationship, Ford approached Violet's work as an editor, not a lover: her five novels written during their affair have a clarity only Ford could have helped to craft. _Tales of the Uneasy_ was favorably reviewed. _The Bookman_ said the author knew "as well as any living English writer how to write a short story."*

After several months it was evident that German bureaucracy would detain Ford for up to eighteen months rather than six months. This news raised the question of whether Ford (or rather Violet) need pay Elsie's alimony during this time since Ford was domiciled abroad. Violet suggested leaving Elsie "absolutely alone all the winter—no light whatever on the situation—no money paid her at all—not even for maintenance of children at Xmas—or clothes, an absolute silence from you—[so] that she would want to begin to stir up the pool again & perhaps divorce you after all." By an earlier court order Ford had paid Elsie £3/3s a week, but Violet wanted to wriggle out from this commitment because her finances were now under court scrutiny. After legal consultations, she advised Ford to seek a reduction to £1 a week, pleading reduced

---

*"The Tiger Skin," echoing the frustrations of the Ford relationship, was praised by _The Athenaeum_ as a "grim study in morbid psychology which displays the author's remarkable gifts to the utmost. It is virtually a picture, painted with signal power and restraint, of a woman's unnatural cruelty towards her child [believing in the survival of the fittest, a mother murders her deformed child]; and so brilliant is the handling that we are led almost without reluctance through the phases of the horrible history. . . . Miss Hunt has gained greatly in craftsmanship during the last few years: her style is excellent, her grip of her subjects sure, and her insight exceptionally clear and sane." These tales, more carefully plotted and seamlessly written than her novels, explore Violet's preoccupation with dependent, diffident men like Ford and willful women like herself who make the wrong choices and end up in unequal relationships. Another tale, "The Coach," which brought Violet and Ford together, was later anthologized in _Georgian Stories_ of 1922, and by Somerset Maugham in _Tellers of Tales_ in 1939.

circumstances while living abroad. No finagling, however, budged Elsie from her married state.

While Violet focused on money or the lack of it, Ford had second thoughts about his self-imposed exile. Could he become a German citizen without serving in the military or performing other national obligations? Already there was talk of war. He might be asked to fight against his beloved France. And why should he bury himself in Germany, ruining his reputation and career, when he was a British writer? Why was he living a dull life in a dull manufacturing town? The answer rankled: he was doing it to please Violet, not himself.

Deprived of London life and Violet's companionship, which he sincerely did miss, Ford became more critical of his environment. His letters whined loudly. He said children set off percussion caps outside his lodging house and climbed up to grin at him while he worked in his ground-floor room, yelling, "*Tag! Englander!*" Ford's surroundings were always important to him, and he loathed his two-room prison, decorated with "about two hundred and fifty ornaments, ranging from bits of coral like human brains to gilded busts of Lohengrin." His landlady was a deaf mute who stuffed him with heavy soups; the house reeked of onions; the bathroom was an outhouse.

He bemoaned his writer's cramp: "When I write legible the pain is bad; when I don't take trouble, and write illegible, nothing to speak of." He grumbled so frequently about his decaying teeth that Violet spent her £60 royalties from *The Wife of Altamont* for emergency dental work, telling him that she was "glad to spend it on such a good object—I *must*, and you can repay me—bless you! Don't just muff it. You get indigestion from not having the proper amount of grinders." Additional money arrived promptly to pay his bills; it was critical for their plan, Violet warned, for him to appear a prosperous author and never owe money to shopkeepers.

If life was monotonous for Ford, it was not dramatically different for Violet, who kept a low profile. Wooing Ford's relatives, she visited Mary Martindale and dedicated her new novel, *The Doll* (featuring a character, Isabel Agate, modeled on Radclyffe Hall), to Ford's mother. At South Lodge, she entertained René Byles, a likable fellow who as managing director of Alston Rivers had published Ford's *The Soul of London* and *The Fifth Queen*, and spent so much on advertising the two books that the firm ended up with no profits. After that Byles lived for a while in Japan and ran a mineral-water business there before returning to London in 1909.

Meanwhile Ford, claustrophobic in his shabby rooms, suggested Violet meet him in Berlin for Christmas. But Violet was too financially and emotionally invested in the success of the divorce scheme to risk any setbacks. Could he legally leave his residence to travel anywhere? she asked. Wasn't Berlin "too far" and "too expensive"? Eventually they compromised on Spa, Belgium, where Violet had friends. She was still bleeding and not able to take long walks, but urged Ford to have knickerbockers made in Germany for hiking, Spa's only attraction.

Thus three months after Ford kissed Violet good-bye at the Cologne train station, they again embraced on the Spa platform. They prudently stayed in separate lodgings, and during the day collaborated on _The Desirable Alien_; in the book Violet calls him Joseph Leopold, his German-Catholic baptismal name. "We are very sociable here," she wrote his mother, "the people at Spa are so dull, they welcome new additions." When Ford saw Spa, he said it was "the quietest place . . . that God ever forgot to finish."

On New Year's Eve "the snow hung on the trees in a solid wall of white over the red roofs of Spa," Violet recalled, "and we all went over to supper at Alighans's, and Joseph Leopold made his famous punch. And when day dawned on what was to prove a year of bitter, continuous litigation, he fetched me early, and we took the train. At eleven o'clock on New Year's Day, 1911, he and I, kneeling painfully on the stones of the Cathedral at Aix la Chapelle, over the tomb of Charlemagne, in the company of other godly Germans, in the colored darkness of the great rose window, smelling the bitter-sweet of the incense, heard Mass." For Violet, it was an emotional ceremony, but Ford, the "cold, patient man, without fire, lazy of habit: his heart, dull-beating, was perhaps more faint about it all than he was willing to let it appear."

During that winter of 1911, though, Ford was optimistic. There "is every chance of the authorities recognising me soon . . . and if they don't I shall appeal to the Emperor," he wrote. But he needed to improve his image, to exchange his cheap student rooms for impressive quarters with his own furniture. Violet agreed but

insisted he take furnished rooms to save money, provoking the first
of many battles over Ford's use of her income. Ultimately, he rented
a furnished apartment in a new building at 15 Friedrichstrasse, hired
a man and his wife to care for him and concentrated on writing
The New Humpty-Dumpty.

In April Ford escaped to London for a few days, and returned
to Giessen with his mother. Violet planned to join them for Easter,
but inquired, "Could you leave your mother in Giessen for a fortnight in your flat? *Never*, I suppose!" At Ford's request, she arrived
wearing a harem skirt, the latest fashion fad. "It will be good business if you bring the harem skirt; the whole town is agog about
this new fashion," he wrote, "and I will ask some local swells in to
tea to see you in it." Invited to a professor's home, Violet noted
"little tables bearing the novels of John Galsworthy and H. G. Wells,
and on the wall, plates, and on the mantel, peacock's feathers in
the style recommended by Wilde." The host was suitably impressed
when she told him that Oscar Wilde had proposed to her.

Working to solidify Ford's standing in the community, Violet
and Ford's mother made social calls, and Mrs. Hueffer took her
chaperon duties seriously: Violet complained that she and her lover
scarcely had ten minutes to themselves. But the visit was successful,
and all three returned to London with Leun, Ford's lawyer, and
another German friend to see the coronation of King George V on
June 22.

Introduced to Windsor, Oxford and the English countryside,
the German contingent returned with "their minds properly full of
the importance of Joseph Leopold in the sorry scheme of things,"
said Violet. Ford left briefly, returning to England on June 29 for
Violet's South Lodge party celebrating the publication of *Ladies
Whose Bright Eyes*, his medieval fantasy inspired by the uncompli-
cated days of their early courtship, particularly their visit to Fordingbridge after his release from prison.

On Ford's return to Germany, Violet received—to her dis-
pleasure—letters posted outside of Giessen. Why was Ford traipsing
around Germany instead of being in his drawing room when the
burgomasters called? she demanded. "Surely sky-larking about the
Duchy was a mark of frivolity that would disgust Their Profund-
ities?" Ford was obdurate and made more demands. When he asked
Violet to buy a pony and trap for his children, she exploded: "That

set the match to me. It was the last straw." She would not be obligated for an unnecessary pony cart; her mother, she told him, "walked miles to save a twopenny bus fare so as to be able to afford the very best blankets . . . The idea of debt stands at my bedside like a spectre."

In response to this lecture, Ford sent good news—perhaps too quickly?—assuring her that the naturalization seemed certain. "Isn't it jolly?" he exclaimed. But Violet insisted on "quite a formal statement." She wanted tangible proof and rushed to Paris, where she met Ford at the Gare du Nord, "toothless and feckless" without a "grinder in his head," and "limited in expression." Agnes Farley's husband was replacing all his teeth at £8 apiece. "It seemed to me," Violet said bitterly, "that he could have inserted diamonds."

Without his teeth, Ford refused to see his lawyer to obtain proof, then, with his teeth in place, claimed Leun had mislaid the papers. Finally crumbling before Violet's constant interrogation, he admitted there were no papers, no multipage legal documents, only a "big card" which had to be inscribed. Ford's naturalization was pure fantasy, but he lied convincingly enough for Violet to believe that a wedding was imminent, and they happily vacationed for several weeks in Hildesheim and Münster, visiting Hüffer relatives. In late July, Ezra Pound arrived and climbed with them to the terraced convent of Schiffenberg. Pound scaled the fluted pillars, tottering about on an elevated wooden stage and chanting his poetry at the top of his lungs, then crashed to the floor, dusty, bruised and grinning. Pound stayed several days while Ford critiqued his *Canzoni* poems. "I would rather talk about poetry with Ford Madox Hueffer than with any man in London," he said afterward. During their travels, Violet and Ford could not ignore the foreboding sight of military reservists crowding the train stations.

In September they returned to Paris, and Ford's dental work was completed. Violet wrote his mother that he was ill and cross after having four teeth pulled, adding, "I believe the German business is all right, but the naturalization did not come in time for the divorce to be pronounced before the courts rose for six weeks holiday. So that would make it deferred till they sit again in October. Anyhow, no one will see me or Ford again till we are married."

Violet returned briefly to London to pick up some clothes and rejoined Ford; they moved on to Trier, where her bleeding started again. "Three years of constant agitation had done their work," she said. At Spa she had another operation, and they stayed on while she recuperated. One day as they prepared for a trip to the fairy-tale town of Montjoie to buy cigars and marquetry furniture, a reporter from the *Daily Mirror* asked to see Ford. Taking her lover aside, Violet cautioned against any publicity, even though "both of us had new books out. It is simply an odious literary 'wheeze' unworthy of either of us." That evening, though, the reporter found Ford at Houtermans, where he played billiards with the visiting nobility. In this atmosphere of male clubbiness, bragging and pontificating, Ford destroyed forever Violet's dream of respectability.

12

Marriage Mirage

On October 21, 1911, based on information that Ford egoistically had babbied to the *Daily Mirror*, there appeared on page three the following announcement:

AUTHOR WEDS

Mr. Ford Madox Hueffer Married Abroad
to Well-known Lady Novelist.

The Daily Mirror is able to announce that Mr. Ford Madox Hueffer, the famous novelist, has been married on the Continent to Miss Violet Hunt, the well-known authoress.

Although still in the thirties, Mr. Hueffer has published many novels. One of his most remarkable successes was "The Fifth Queen," which was universally regarded as reaching the highest standard of literary workmanship. . . .

Mr. Hueffer was seen at the Red House, Spa, Belgium, yesterday before starting for his daily motorcar ride with the second Mrs. Hueffer.

"I don't want to advertise myself," he told *The Daily Mirror*, "but it happens that both my wife and myself have books appearing today. Messrs. Duckworth published mine [*The Critical Attitude*] and hers [*The Governess*] is published by Stanley Paul in her maiden name, Violet Hunt.

"I married her in Germany after divorcing my former wife on a technical ground, desertion, as I had a perfect right to do, being domiciled in Germany.

"I am heir to large entailed estates in Prussia, and have therefore retained my German nationality. . . . I offered myself for service with the German army, but was not required to serve, and I attended Bonn University.

"My former wife brought an action against me for restitution of conjugal rights. Then we agreed upon a separation order, she having the custody of our two daughters, now fifteen and sixteen. . . ."

Like her husband, Miss Violet Hunt is now well known in England as a writer, having published a number of novels and other books, including "The Cat," "Unkist! Unkind!" "Affairs of the Heart," and "The Wife of Altamont." . . . Miss Hunt began her literary career early for several lyrics written when she was only twelve were published in the "Century Magazine." . . . Miss Hunt was one of the early members of the women's suffrage movement.

Ford's enrollment at Bonn University was an invention, as were the grounds for divorce and the German marriage. Again Ford had entrapped himself with lies. The following week Violet's old friend Clement Shorter compounded the damage by publishing an announcement of the marriage in *The Sphere* and *The Sketch*. By this time Elsie's solicitors had threatened to sue the *Daily Mirror* for libel. In *London Opinion*, the "Round The Town" columnist speculated on the bigamous implications of the marriage, "alleged to be valid [in Germany], but not in England! . . . According to British law, the first wife is still married to her husband. According to the law of the husband's native country, the second wife is married to him. The result is that the happy man has two legal wives."

Douglas Goldring hypothesized that, in a fit of exasperation, Ford probably exclaimed, "Hang it all. What does it matter? Let's go home and *say* we've been married. No one will ever find out." And whatever the fabrication, Violet "agreed to it with her eyes open," Goldring said. "Her courage amounted to recklessness, but as she admits, she was 'the New Woman they used to write about in 1890's' and that young person, although emancipated by comparison with her predecessors, had not yet reached the point of disregarding appearances."

With war approaching, Violet realized that Ford could no longer stay in Germany, and she surely knew that there were no divorce papers and there never would be, but she decided to seize the moment for married respectability. Apparently a ceremony was

staged a month before the _Mirror_ interview, for years later she sent
Ford's longtime friend Edgar Jepson a draft of a letter written to
Ford, stating that she had lived as his "supposed wife for eight years
counting from the fifth of September 1911 till the twenty-ninth of
March 1919."

But where were they married? Violet told René Byles that the
ceremony took place in Hanover, and then confided to Rebecca
West that there was a mock ceremony performed by a defrocked
priest in a hotel room in Rheims, a scene already rehearsed by Violet,
who has Rosette Newall and Robert Assheton in _Sooner or Later_
go through a bogus service and set up house together. Perhaps they
were deliberately trying to confuse the issue to protect Ford from
bigamy charges. (In the American edition of her memoirs, _I Have
This to Say_, Violet admitted that she "never did become a legal
wife," that is, with a marriage certificate, and in a final taunt claimed
that the "whole truth [was] at the bottom of the well at Selsey
[Violet's summer home] where it may appropriately lie until the
Peninsula is all at sea." The "whole truth" probably meaning the
facts of the untruth.)*

Violet immediately changed her listings in the telephone di-
rectory and _Who's Who_ to Mrs. Ford Madox Hueffer. Still living
at South Lodge, they made one of their first appearances as man
and wife on December 3, 1911, at a party honoring H. G. Wells
at the home of the journalist Eliza Aria. That same month Lady
Lucy Byron (Poppy Houston) lent them her Sandgate cottage.
Knowing how Ford missed Conrad, who was living nearby, Violet

---

*Douglas Goldring, who inherited Violet's library, said that as late as July 1930
she had written in the flyleaf of _Memories of John Westlake_ "a final statement
regarding her German 'marriage,' which may be held to contain a belated admission
on her part that, as most of her friends already knew, it never took place." It went:
"John Westlake was, with Leonard Courtney, Joseph Chamberlain and Dilke in
a lesser degree, my father's most intimate and earliest friend, apart from art friends.
And when I contemplated an international marriage, complicated by a divorce—
the man divorcing the wife for causes valid in Germany but not in this country—
I asked him if it were possible. He said it was but he wished I wouldn't. The plan
was defeated by the inertia—or malice—of the male protagonist." Janice Biala,
Ford's last mistress-wife, who lives in Paris, told this author that the marriage
took place in Germany. When asked about Rebecca West's version, and not eager
to discuss Violet, she snapped, "Well, then, it was France," saying it would not
have mattered to Ford whether the priest was defrocked or not. "If he said he was
married, then he was married!"

plotted to reunite them. "The way to Conrad's heart just then was a motorcar," she recalled, "so we used to get one from Clayson's and go out to Orlestone to bring the Conrads and the little boy, Jackolo, back to lunch."

The charade appeared to be working. Then Annie Child returned to Sandgate from London with an hysterical story: on the railway platform she had observed "an Implacable Face" watching her. While serving dinner, she gibbered on about "Those Eyes!" until Ford's pink face turned white. Knowing the truth of his lies, he feared any number of process servers. Late that evening he burst into Violet's room demanding to know whether she had heard the doorbell pealing. She shook her head, but Ford was too agitated, insisting that someone was outside the cottage. He locked the servants in their rooms, tied up the doors with odd straps, strings and dog leads, and blocked the front entrance with a bicycle. He slept not a wink.

With Ford apprehensive about the uninvited, Violet made sure they were surrounded by familiar faces. René Byles, now business manager for a society weekly called *The Throne*, and the conduit for Ford's alimony payments (he wrote Elsie a weekly check for £3/3s with Violet's money), was a regular visitor. Arthur Marwood, Ford's estranged partner from the *Review* days, also dropped by, acting as though Elsie had never accused him of sexual advances. Even Jessie Conrad, who loathed Ford, appeared friendly, probably for the wrong reasons. "She knew all the people who indirectly swayed my fortunes," Violet said of Jessie, and "hinted at some shadowy horror, some 'catastrophe' or other which was preparing for me. Can a catastrophe—which is usually the Will of God—be prepared for a particular person? I then thought kind Mrs. Conrad wool-gathering . . . fallacious . . . trying her hand at her husband's métier. I little knew." If the Conrads and Marwood knew anything of Elsie's plans, they gave no warning.

The new Mr. and Mrs. Hueffer were seen parading about London. Lawrence ran into them in the winter of 1912 and gleefully reported to Edward Garnett: "Do you know, I rather like her—she's such a real assassin. I evoked the memory of various friends that were her friends twelve months ago. Behold, she nicely showed me the effigies of these folk in her heart, each of them blemishes marked with a red asterisk like a dagger hole. I saluted her, she did the business so artistically: there was no loathsome gore spilt over the murdered friends."

Since that luncheon two years before at South Lodge when the shy Lawrence had been intimidated by Violet, the future author of *Lady Chatterley's Lover* had mellowed: he now appreciated Violet's strengths, telling Garnett that she "looked old, yet she was gay— she was gay, she laughed, she bent and fluttered in the wind of joy. She coquetted and played beautifully with Hueffer: she loves him distractedly—she was charming, and I loved her. But my God, she looked old. . . . Fordy . . . feels, poor fish, the hooks are through his gills this time—and they *are*. Yet he's lucky to be so well caught—she'll handle him with marvellous skill." In this glorious description, Lawrence captured Violet's joy of possession.

While Violet and Ford played the radiant newlyweds, Margaret Hunt gradually slipped into senility, laid down her pen and asked them to finish her final novel, *The Governess* (the retelling of a familiar story except with a murder-mystery twist). It was published on April 18, 1912, with a joint mother-and-daughter byline and a preface by Ford, who noted that "from the seventies to the nineties," Margaret was one of the "wittiest women in London": no one, he said, was "sharper at repartee of a sort, at quick characterisation, and at a sort of verbal sword-play."

For her byline, Violet had urged Chatto & Windus to use "Violet Hueffer," but they wisely insisted on her maiden name (or they would have been in court). Aunt Jane, Margaret's sister, called *The Governess* a "nice, quiet book"; but Venice and Silvia filed an injunction to stop publication, claiming the book was unauthorized because their mother had not been in her right mind when she relinquished editorial control. Accompanied by Ford ("sulky, top-hatted and loathing it"), Violet attended hearings on her mother's estate at Temple Bar, eventually abdicating in disgust, in favor of her greedy sisters.

When *The Governess* came out, René Byles praised it in *The Throne*, publishing a stern profile photograph of Margaret and an unflattering full-face study of Violet in an extravagant hat that obscured her eyes. The blurb, lifted from the preface, announced that "the forthcoming book is a romance . . . by Mrs. Alfred Hunt, one of the popular novelists of the old [three-volume] days, and her daughter, Miss Violet Hunt (now Mrs. Ford Madox Hueffer), one of the successful of the modern school."

Byles's good intentions had ricocheted. By the time Elsie read the *Throne* article, she had already threatened a suit against the *Mirror*, which was dropped when they published "A Withdrawal and Apology," retracting Ford's quote that he had divorced his wife on grounds of desertion. Next Elsie sued Byles and his publication for libel: Violet had called herself Mrs. Hueffer when it was Elsie who was the legal wife. The case was placed on the docket for February 1913. "All through the year I watched the case creeping up the List in the *Telegraph* . . . nearer . . . nearer!" said Violet.

Ford took to his bed, dictating an occasional letter and depending on Violet to keep South Lodge humming. It was not a happy time. Violet worried that her sisters might conspire to send Margaret to a nursing home, and Ford's financial state bordered on bankruptcy. She dreamed she was dragged backward and forward by Silvia, sometimes by her hair, up and down the stone floors of the law courts. For solace, they gulped "that nice new German drug" Adalin (a hypnotic). "I was useless," Violet said, "living in a dream, full of the kind drug which we were both taking."

To forget their troubles, they frolicked at the Cave of the Golden Calf, London's first nightclub, also known as the Cabaret Theatre Club, which opened in a basement on Hedden Street, off Regent, in June 1912. Its proprietor, Frieda Strindberg, was an Austrian journalist who, after a two-year marriage to the Swedish dramatist August Strindberg, had lived with the German poet Frank Wedekind, who spurred her interest in cabaret entertainment. Moving to London with an inheritance to spend, Frida stayed at the Savoy Hotel with a menagerie of monkeys.

By all accounts Frieda Strindberg was a remarkable eccentric. Called the "walking hell-bitch of the Western World" by the portrait painter Augustus John, she was renowned for her ravenous sexual appetites and penchant for suicide attempts (usually swallowing Veronal washed down with Bovril). At the club, the faded Viennese beauty, draped in coral necklaces (Violet said she wore a hundred), greeted customers with a pet monkey on her shoulder. Austrian cooks and waiters provided a mittel-European ambience; frenzied Hungarian gypsy fiddlers played until dawn and couples danced the Turkey Trot and the Bunny Hug. The poet Osbert Sitwell, a frequent visitor, recalled that in the early morning hours the club became "a super-heated vorticist garden of gesticulating figures, dancing and talking, while the rhythm of the primitive forms of ragtime throbbed through the wide room."

The cave was expensive but democratic, with impoverished writers, artists and models feeding off the largesse of well-heeled aristocrats and American millionaires. Frieda maintained her own table where interesting people, such as Ford and Violet, ate gratis. At dinner one evening, Frieda—wrapped in an immense fur coat which slipped off her alabaster shoulders, her dark hair crowned with enormous pearls—scrutinized each Carlsbad plum before crushing it between her perfect white teeth. "I do not let a waiter here serve an anchovy without inspecting it," she imperiously told Ford.

The decor was rococo caravanserai, an inspired hallucination. The New York–born sculptor Jacob Epstein covered iron columns with plaster, sculpting them in the form of hawks, cats and camels, which gave the impression of holding up the low ceiling. Wyndham Lewis, a recent graduate of the Slade School, frescoed the walls with what Violet called "Bismarckian images, severings, disembowellings, mixed pell-mell with iron shards that did it, splashed with the pale blood of exhausted heroes"—a prophetic scene inspired by the nearness of war. Ford recalled "menlike objects colored slate-green with faces of enlarged ants and blue, reticulated limbs like rolled paper cylinders set in scarlet landscapes." Edith Sitwell called it "hideously but relevantly frescoed."

For entertainment, there were veil dances, jesters, masks, gypsy folklore, readings and songs by guests and that cabaret staple, the shadow play, inaugurated at the Chat Noir in Paris, where cabarets first began in 1881. Chinese-inspired, the shadow play (which Ford uses as a locus for character development in *The Marsden Case*) employs silhouettes or shadows projected by means of a light source onto a screen to act out a story; performances later evolved into cutouts animated by a puppeteer.

The Cave beamed brightly for two years but was never in the same league as the cabarets of Paris, Vienna, Berlin and other continental cities. With war imminent, Frieda Strindberg closed the doors, stripped the club of everything she could carry and sailed off to New York, leaving behind memories of dazzling nights that became a minor legend in British cultural history. Before her club, the Café Royal on Regent Street and the Café Vienna on New Oxford Street were London's only continental cafés. At the famed Royal saloon, with its gilded caryatids, red-plush banquettes and marble tables, conversation hummed into the early morning hours accompanied by the click of dominoes. More subdued than the Royal, the Vienna had a triangular first floor with a glass ceiling to reflect the comings and goings of European émigrés, artists and writers, and readers from the nearby British Museum. Ezra Pound was introduced to Wyndham Lewis there, and fondly recalled the coffee served with real cream.

Violet met the "incipient mad man," as she called Wyndham Lewis, at the Cave of the Golden Calf. Ford knew him from the *Review* days, when, as one story goes, Lewis arrived at Holland Park and found Ford in his bath, soaping himself. Declaring himself a writer of worth, Lewis asked if he could read his story, a character sketch called "The Pole." While Ford soaked, Lewis read; Ford said he would print it. Emotional, unpredictable, brimming with ideas, but taciturn, Lewis intrigued Violet. Here was an Italian-bandit type like Oswald Crawfurd, but Lewis, twenty years younger and a devotee of youth, saw Violet only as a diverting mother figure, certainly a new role for her. She recalled his dark eyes looking out of a "buzz of hair flanking on either side the upturned collar of an Inverness cape," which he insisted on wearing even at the most crowded indoor events.

Born on a yacht docked at Nova Scotia of an American father and an English mother, Percy Wyndham Lewis fit right into South Lodge's international atmosphere. His father ran off with the house-maid when Lewis was eleven, setting a standard of irresponsibility that his son surpassed by fathering at least five illegitimate children, with whom he had little or no contact. In background and ap-pearance, the South Lodge group were disparate indeed. Most shared a foreign heritage and lacked the Oxbridge ties so necessary for acceptance into British society; Lewis, a Rugby boy, was the only one with public school polish.

Another member of the group was Brigit Patmore, a literary dabbler, with reddish-gold hair, gray eyes and a flawless complexion, a luminous Irish beauty whom most men and some women found irresistible. She was married to a boring businessman, John Deigh-ton Patmore, grandson of the Victorian poet Coventry Patmore, known for his long poem on the joys of married love, "The Angel in the House." Twenty years younger than Violet, Brigit was "in-stantly charmed" by Violet's "uncommon beauty, her dreamy but meticulously considerate manners," and greeted this "representative of the modern times with enthusiasm."

Violet found Brigit "very beautiful, with a queer, large, tor-tured mouth that said the wittiest things, eyes that tore your soul out of your body for pity and yet danced. She had no physique, as doctors would say; no health, as women would say; and—as no woman would ever admit except me—charm enough to damn a regiment." Violet called her Princess Maleine [*sic*], after a heroine of the Belgian dramatist Maeterlinck, who was imprisoned in a tower and dug herself out with her nails.

But often Violet, the "verbal dragon-fly," shocked the proper Brigit, who said Violet described "people as if she were a latter-day portraitist, their faces sliding down the canvas in alarming colours and out of line, at their best Modiglianis, recognizable but out of proportion and all their features a little distorted." When Ford criticized her malicious stories, Violet quipped, "But Ford, I've always had the name of being—not exactly spiteful—no, not at *all* spiteful, but *sharp-spoken*. My friends would think me dull if I weren't."

One afternoon at South Lodge, Violet fluttered over to Brigit and pointed out a guest leaning back in an armchair. "The young man like a Renaissance portrait is Ezra Pound," she said. "A poet, very good. *Punch* makes fun of his name—calls him 'Ezekiel Tun'— rather rude and schoolboyish, I think, but I suppose it impresses the facts on the public. He's just been roaming round Provence like a troubadour." Brigit thought him more like Paderewski, the pi-anist.

Through Pound, Brigit met the poets Richard Aldington and Hilda Doolittle. H.D. had known Pound in America and was un-officially engaged to him. Aldington recalled that Pound was so excited by H.D.'s poems that one day while the three of them were having coffee in a pastry shop, Pound removed his pince-nez and announced that they were Imagists. Pound's new school of English poetry eschewed abstraction and iambic pentameter to stress accurate imagery and a musical rhythm flowing from line to line. By 1913 Imagism was being widely discussed, and the following year when Pound edited an anthology of Imagist verse, he laid the foundation for modernism. (Ultimately his movement was appropriated by the wealthy, cigar-smoking American poet Amy Lowell.)

Violet spent the summer of 1912 in Selsey, a peninsular retreat of remote charm on the southern coast below Chichester, where she leased Knap Cottage from Edward Heron Allen, whom she had known since the 1890s. Flanked by towering trees, Knap Cottage was an ordinary three-bedroom stucco house, with leaded-glass windows its only distinguishing feature. Through the years, Allen, a man of eclectic interests (marine biologist, zoologist, expert on violins and palmistry, translator of Omar Khayyám), had flirted with Violet, finally settling for the role of confidant; Violet called him "gentle, clever, caressing and souless." Her next-door neighbors were Charles (C.F.G.) Masterman, politician, editor and author of the acclaimed *Condition of England*, and his wife, Lucy, who were close friends of Ford's.

With them that summer was Brigit Patmore. Beguiled by her charm, Ford fell in love; whether Brigit succumbed, as Violet believed, is uncertain. Brigit claimed to admire only his intellect. "I confess I had thought of the ultimate cataclysm as, alone in the mornings while the dictation [probably *Mr. Fleight*] was going on," said Violet, "I wandered round one or other of the three beaches of Selsey, conscious of the drone of a sad sea line on the two other sides, pacing on the edge, without looking where I was going."

Returning late for lunch one day, she met Ford rushing hatless down the village street, wanting to know if she "had committed suicide." With increased foreboding, Violet identified with Sibella, her heroine in *Unkist, Unkind!*, who poisons herself with amyl nitrate hidden in a ring, similar to Violet's own jeweled toad-head poison ring, which held, at this time, only a nonlethal tablet, kept there, she said, to "unnerve the man who took me in to dinner."

Violet asked Ford to write a poem for her. "You say you believe in a heaven," she declared. "I wish you'd write one for me. I want no beauty; I want no damned optimism; I want just a plain, workaday heaven that I can go to some day and enjoy it when I'm there."

Several days later Violet and Brigit listened to him read what would be his best-known poem "con amore, sans façon, tactlessly evincing his honest joy in his work." In the poem, "On Heaven," set in Provence, God makes everything work out for Ford; Violet joins him in a "swift red car"; the Blessed Virgin promises them a son if they will make a pilgrimage to Lourdes; and they embrace, undisturbed by the turmoil left behind on earth.

Dedicated "To V.H. who asked me for a Working Heaven," the poem was a disappointment. She thought "A Frivolous Heaven" or "A Baby Heaven" or "A Doll's Heaven" would have been a better title. "My Poem turned out as profane a piece of work as Grimm's _Kinder Märchen_ or the Bible itself at times. The introduction of earthly love into heaven could not but be profane according to the usual canons." It was, she sniffed, "love without breadth, depth, or thickness, without dimension. Subjective, purely. . . . Not . . . the love that moves mountains, faces the seven deaths of boredom, but the mild, watery variety." It was the kind of love that Ford gave.

In September, using the pseudonym Daniel Chaucer, Ford published _The New Humpty-Dumpty_, a novel that savages Elsie, H. G. Wells and Ford's brother-in-law David Soskice, and puts Ford and Violet on a pedestal, echoing the episodes and emotions surrounding their affair, as well as Ford's problems with the _Review_. The Fordian hero, Count Sergius Mihailovitch Macdonald, has a charming nobility that enables him to manage others effortlessly (a trait Ford certainly lacked); Lady Aldington (Violet) is bored with her rich, brutal husband and finds her first happiness with Count Macdonald, whose quarrels with the Countess (Elsie) reverberate with real-life passion. (At one point, the Countess describes her husband as "a man who leaves his wife when she is ill to go and revel in the luxuries of the smart set.")

An eighteen-year-old critic named Rebecca West wrote an incisive review, Violet said: "a whole column of wit and innuendo— as destructive as a prairie fire." West identified the author as Ford, because the novel "deals with aristocrats that Mr. Hueffer, the Mediaevalist, loves, because aristocrats can so often produce convincing proof that they have been in England since the Middle Ages." Tantalized by fresh wit, Violet invited West to South Lodge to meet the other rambunctious _les jeunes_.

After an Edinburgh education, West (born Cicily Fairfield) had moved to London determined to be an actress, studying at the

Royal Academy of Dramatic Art before dropping out and entering journalism. When her first article, on the anti-suffragist writer Mrs. Humphry Ward, was accepted by *The Freewoman*, she took the name of Rebecca West, a "new woman" character in Ibsen's *Rosmersholm*, to avoid embarrassing her family. Rebecca was a complicated child-woman, a born writer and critic, and her tough-minded articles about the disenfranchisement of women quickly built her a reputation on Fleet Street, making "not so much a splash," Violet said, "as a definite hole in the world."

Few women impressed Violet as much as this *enfant terrible* who arrived at South Lodge wearing a pink dress with a wide-brimmed "country-girlish straw hat that hid her splendid liquid eyes. Her voice was like milk and honey," Violet recalled, "something mellifluous, soothing, like sweet bells rung in tune, quite superiorly, ostentatiously, young—the ineffable schoolgirl!"

Although Rebecca admired Ford as an editor and writer, she (unlike most women) was not charmed by the man, finding him "stout, gangling, albinoish." His embraces made her feel like "the toast under a poached egg." She liked Pound and persuaded him to be literary editor of the *New Freewoman*, which published James Joyce after Pound changed its name to *The Egoist*.

In October, after closing Knap Cottage, Violet and Ford traveled to Durham for a week. At Bedburn Violet found her sister "a little ill, and surprised her into almost cordiality." Silvia ordered Rosamond to give her aunt a cup of tea and then dismissed Violet, saying, "Let the lawyers thrash it out!" In Violet's opinion that was the problem: while Venice and Silvia tried to document her excessive spending, escalating legal fees were eroding Margaret's estate. Anticipating a sizable legacy from her godfather, Canon Greenwell, Violet and Ford entertained him one evening with their lively London stories and made, she felt, a good impression.

When they returned to South Lodge, Margaret Hunt had bronchitis. In recent months she had been tiresome, peevish, melancholy, irresponsible, "dothery" as she called herself in North Country parlance. Ford and Violet took turns nursing her, and played some rounds of piquet, her favorite card game, looking on helplessly as Margaret gasped for each breath. "My mother had been a tall, large, wide-faced woman," Violet said, and now "she seemed a small, brown, wizened changeling. Her grey hair, matted and damp, had the effect of a black hood round her shrunken face with her mouth like a small, round O in it."

On November 1, 1912, two weeks after her eighty-second birthday, Margaret Hunt's temperature soared to 110 degrees. Within minutes she was dead. Summoned to South Lodge, Venice arrived before Silvia and refused Violet's request for a reconciliation. "Oh, we Northerners!" Violet exclaimed. The estranged sisters buried their mother at Brookwood Cemetery next to Alfred, but for some reason never had her name engraved on the headstone.

Margaret's estate was valued at £23,589 (then the equivalent of $118,000); after payment of debts and probate expenses, Violet received one-third of it as well as Margaret's personal possessions and a cash bequest of £3,300 (previously the £3,000 had been in trust, with the income payable until Violet married or died, but in 1902, two years after drafting the original will, Margaret added a codicil, giving Violet the sum outright). Venice and Silvia contested the will at once. Her sisters, Violet said, masqueraded as strangers, their "heads averted . . . the sneer courteous . . . macabre scenes such as one reads of in Victorian novels," or as Ford put it, they were "setting little devil-kites adrift in each other's skies."

Violet was mistress of South Lodge at last. She could entertain whomever she wished; she could live more intimately with Ford; she was free of responsibility, except for her cats. But she had no money, and it would be four years until she received her mother's legacy. She sold some of Ford's Pre-Raphaelite mementos to the Pierpont Morgan Library in New York, accumulating £300 for Ford Madox Brown's diary for 1856–1868, a Christmas card with an original poem from Swinburne to Ford and a Rossetti sketch of Ford Madox Brown.

Violet could not imagine Christmas at South Lodge without her mother, so she and Ford borrowed a cottage at Farnham Common near Burnham Beeches and invited Pound, Mary Martindale, Ford's nephew Frank Soskice and the Compton Mackenzies to join the celebration. Faith Mackenzie brought a Sudbury ham, which Pound attacked with greedy enthusiasm, and Ford, depressed because Elsie refused to let him spend the holiday with his daughters, withdrew and "could only be approached through the keyhole of his bedroom, in which he was firmly locked against all comers." His absence, Faith observed, "gave a spice to the party, since Violet was continually running upstairs to entreat him, speculating loudly as to why he was up there at all, and giving a touch of drama to the whole affair."

With typical jocundity, Pound delivered an endless monologue, and Ford finally came downstairs the next day, "with his store of intellectual energy unimpaired by festive excesses, full of benevolence, good cheer, and lively conversation; in short, he was himself again," said Faith. "And Violet, her great eyes blazing, carved the turkey [Violet said it was a suckling pig] and what remained of the ham with more than her usual dexterity, her cheeks flushed at the excitement of his restoration."

The men played chess and discussed writing. Pound wrote his mother that they stayed "in a dingy old cottage that belonged to Milton. F.M.H. and I being the two people who couldn't be in the least impressed by the fact, makes it a bit more ironical . . . Impossible to get any writing done here. Atmosphere too literary. 'Kreators' all in one ancient cottage *is* a bit thick."

As 1913 approached, the libel action brought by Elsie Hueffer against *The Throne* for identifying Violet as Ford's wife had climbed to the top of the list, scheduled for February 7. "I was glad my mother was dead," Violet said bitterly. "Her 'nice, quiet book' had been a boomerang, and had returned to me. It had not even done for me what she had intended since it had been ordered that the money it earned should be paid into court." What actually had backfired, though, was not *The Governess* or its publicity in *The Throne*, but Violet's insistence on being called Mrs. Ford Madox Hueffer.

13

The Two Mrs. Hueffers

Lsie's suit against the *Daily Mirror* objected to Ford's statement that he had divorced his wife on the technical ground of desertion. She dropped the charges after the paper printed an apology and paid her £350 in damages. But the issue in *The Throne* case was libel: Violet had called herself Mrs. Hueffer, which was Elsie's legal name. An apology from *The Throne* would not suffice: if Violet were the rightful Mrs. Hueffer, then she might bring her own libel suit. If, on the other hand, Violet denied she was Mrs. Hueffer, she would negate everything—Ford's alleged German naturalization, his ostensible divorce and their foreign marriage. Violet and Ford decided to brazen it out, without concern for personal repercussions or for their friend Byles's stake in the outcome. *The Throne*'s finances were precarious and it would fold if ordered to pay substantial damages, but Byles assured his editor, Comyns Beaumont, that his friend Ford was indeed divorced and had wed Violet in Hanover, Germany.

Since no scrap of paper existed to document the divorce, much less the marriage, the defense, such as it was, hinged on the jury believing Violet and Ford's trumped-up story. To enhance their credibility, they falsely assured Byles that they would give evidence in court to support the case, if necessary. Shortly before the trial, though, Ford had his doctor certify that he was being treated for neurasthenia and was not fit for any court appearance—all in all, a dismal trick to play on the steadfast Byles. The guilty couple slipped away to Boulogne, where Violet left Ford at the depressing Hotel Dervaux and recrossed the Channel in a bad storm. She had to be in London to learn the verdict.

The two-day trial began on February 7 in the Court of King's Bench before Justice Avory and a jury. Elsie's solicitor told the court that Ford had deserted his wife and had for some time refused to pay alimony and child support, that the legal Mrs. Hueffer had refused to obtain a divorce because the children were Catholic. As to Ford's German divorce and remarriage, the solicitor said, "no papers were ever served on the plaintiff and inquiries had elicited no particulars of any divorce proceedings in Germany," adding that his client sought not heavy damages but only to establish in the eyes of the public her sole right to be called Mrs. Ford Madox Hueffer.

In an emotional appeal, Elsie's counsel told the jury, "Think of the position in which this placed the plaintiff. Since 1894 she had moved in Society and in literary circles as the wife of Mr. Ford Madox Hueffer. In April 1912, the *Throne* said that somebody else was entitled to that position. People reading it would think either that the plaintiff was not his wife at all or that she was divorced. She, poor lady, who had suffered enough in this world at the hands of her husband, stood to be persecuted by people announcing to the world in their periodicals that she had no right to the title of Mrs. Hueffer at all. This exposed her to ridicule, hatred, and contempt, in the language of the law, and was a libel."

When court reconvened the following day, Elsie wore royal purple, Violet's favorite color. The *Daily Mirror* photographed her standing outside the court in a fur-trimmed coat, hat and muff, and ran this picture with insert photos of Violet (looking innocent and wide-eyed) and Ford (looking starchy and Edwardian). Elsie testified that the *Mirror* had apologized for their story, that *Lady* magazine had also apologized for running an announcement that Mr. and Mrs. Hueffer attended a dinner held by the Women Writers' League, that she also had sued some weekly and provincial newspapers that referred to the alleged marriage in Germany, that the Postmaster General promised "to have the matter [of Violet's listing as Mrs. Hueffer] attended to." (Even so, it remained the same until Violet's death.) Asked if she knew that Violet was living with her husband as his wife at South Lodge, Elsie replied, "I do not know it as a fact. I suppose so. I have no definite proof." Asked if she had read Violet's new novel *The Celebrity's Daughter*, she replied indignantly, "I do not read her books."

Witnesses for the defense testified that they had known Violet and Ford as a "married" couple. Frank Mumby, author of the offending column, said that as literary editor he "was supplied by Messrs. Chatto and Windus with an advance copy of the preface of the book he was reviewing, written by Mr. Ford Madox Hueffer, in which he spoke of Miss Violet Hunt as Mrs. Hueffer. He [Mumby] had read the announcement of the wedding and it never entered his head that it had not taken place."

The Throne's editor, Comyns Beaumont, also took the stand. "When I was in the witness-box," Beaumont recalled in his memoirs, Justice Avory asked, "rather on the same lines as the old tag, 'When did you last beat your wife?' 'If you had known that Miss X was not Mr. Hueffer's wife would you so have described her?' I tried to parry the question by replying, 'I can't say what I might have done. The point never arose.' Pressed for a more explicit answer, I said, 'I should probably have evaded the subject. The private relationship of these two persons was merely a side issue to a literary critique. We only quoted the book.' "

Sir Arthur Legge testified that Violet, whom he had known for many years, told him in 1911 that she was engaged to be married, and he sent her a silver cream jug as a wedding present. When the judge asked if it had been returned, he replied, "Never," instigating laughter. Brigit Patmore and other friends told the jury that Violet and Ford appeared in public as man and wife and, as Mr. and Mrs. Hueffer, had invited a hundred people to a South Lodge garden party. Not seeing this as relevant, the judge commented that "people can always get 100 people to a garden party if they send out enough invitations."

Playing the victimized wife, Elsie said she had received no money since June (which Violet privately denied). In his summation, Elsie's solicitor maintained that his client had suffered enough trying to rear and educate two children on £3/3s a week. Without leaving the box, the jury agreed: Elsie had been held up to ridicule by the implication that she was a divorcee; they awarded her £300 plus costs, which came to £1,000. *The Throne* paid the levy and ceased publication.

□

Violet spent the first day of the trial at Mary Martindale's house. Ford's mother was also there, with her smelling salts. Storry Deans, Violet's solicitor, called and told her that "dreadful things were being said." He asked to read a statement at the end of the trial. After the verdict was announced, Deans rose and said, "I am instructed on behalf of a lady whose name has frequently been mentioned in this case—Miss Violet Hunt. She wishes me to say that she believes herself to be Mrs. Ford Madox Hueffer and intends to continue—"

"I have nothing to do with her belief," interrupted Justice Avory.

"Derogatory statements have been made about her," said Deans, "and neither side has called her."

"I can hear you no further," declared the judge, "because I am not in a position to decide, and it is useless for you to make an ex-parte statement with no one here to contradict you. I decline to allow this court to be made a medium of advertisement."

On the final day of the trial, Violet returned to South Lodge before Deans called with the verdict. Unable to find an afternoon paper anywhere in Kensington, she sat in the darkened dining room while the servants moved quietly about the house. When no one came and no one phoned, she frantically rang up friends, reaching only her accountant, who divulged the bad news. She was shocked. She had truly believed in the success of their sham.

The decision alienated her godfather, who changed his will in favor of his nurse and verger, and it gave her sisters added ammunition for their legal battles. For the moment, though, Violet denied that her social prestige had been hurt, admitting only her underestimation of "the English synthesis of morality, but one must bear in mind that it is Mr. and Mrs. Grundy . . . You never know the way the cat bearing the standard of British virtue will jump. . . . Everything in England, especially feeling, it seems, can be reduced to terms of musical comedy. Crowds listen with tears in their eyes to that song, so cynical and touching, 'If you were the only girl in the world, and I were the only boy.' But she isn't and he isn't; he knows it and she knows it; and when the apple-cart upsets, the courts are there to adjust matters."

A bitter Comyns Beaumont recalled later that the "laws of libel have been so strained and the damages awarded against a newspaper can be so preposterous that to-day newspapers insure against actions for libel. This case seemed a particularly dangerous trap, for after all a newspaper, like an individual, can only accept the relationships between private persons as they are known generally to the world. Hueffer and his lady lived in good surroundings as husband and wife and the ass had gone to the length of publicly labeling her as wife in the introduction to her novel. The only way to ascertain such relationships, as our counsel suggested, would be to ask persons for their marriage certificates, which was absurd. Why Hueffer stirred up mud and victimized us I never ascertained."

Richard Aldington blamed Ford's arrogance. "He was not only conceited, but an incorrigible exhibitionist," who had to give "a pretentious interview" about his marriage to the *Daily Mirror*. Aldington sympathized with Violet, who had to see the High Street filled with newspaper placards reading "Libel Action against Famous Novelist" and "Verdict against Woman Novelist." Calling Violet one of the last victims of the expiring Victorian conventions, Douglas Goldring wrote: "It was a disaster which even the excitement of figuring in a *cause célèbre*, since she herself was a Victorian, made no easier to bear. For Ford it was simply the *comble* [culmination] of a long series of misfortunes. His code made it obligatory for him to bear it in dignified silence." Violet's did not.

Immediately after hearing the verdict, she left for France to tell Ford. Mary Martindale saw her off at Charing Cross Station, where newsstands hawked papers with her picture. Violet gave Mary half a crown and told her, "Buy them all." Moments later Mary returned, "her red lips trembling, her large white face like a rock with the rain running down it," with sheaves of papers and pushed them through the window as the train pulled out. Violet observed that five people opposite her were reading papers on the back sheet of which was her photograph. She was glad that the photo was "not in the least" like her. No one in the compartment recognized the second Mrs. Hueffer.

"My apparent non-recognisability," Violet recalled, "struck me as quite a good tip for a story—a shocker—and I began to invent a plot. It might soothe me, and make me a cheerful companion to the person I was going to, more stricken than I, and who now had need of me. I was to be nursetender to the sore heart—sore about a variety of things . . . not about me any more." Life is "always a sad affair," said Ford, who believed that "the heart of another is a dark forest."

When the train pulled into Boulogne, a light rain was falling. Ford met her at the station, silently helped her into a carriage, and they drove up the steep street to the hotel without exchanging a word. Violet was not impatient to tell him the verdict or that Elsie had testified to his neglect of his children. In their room, Ford revealed he had laryngitis, more from nerves than anything else, and crawled back into his sickbed, where he lay gloomily sipping his medicine. Violet hid the offending newspapers in the bottom of her trunk and waited for him to ask about the trial.

The next morning she entered the breakfast room and saw an Englishwoman to whom she had loaned *The Celebrity's Daughter* before she left the hotel for the trial. As she was cutting into her filet of sole, the woman walked over and threw the book on the table. "There's your book, Miss Hunt!" Thereafter they stayed in their room, until Ford was well enough to travel south. He drank heavily and sulked. Violet forgot about her humiliation trying to breach his depression.

Violet had never been farther south than Paris, so they went to Montpellier because Conrad had raved about the villages perched on conical hills, standing out against "the great and weeping lines of violet ranges as if in an enchanted country." The visit, however, was disappointing, memorable only "as the place where we lost our luggage," Violet said. They continued on to the walled city of Carcassonne, arriving in the midst of a rabies epidemic. Ford put a lid on the bathtub and used it as a writing desk. Violet listened to the February mistral shaking the plane trees outside the window and wondered what kind of reception to expect when they returned to London.

In an optimistic letter written from Carcassonne to Ford's mother, Violet sounded like her old spunky self. "One must put one's back to the wall & let 'Egypt stand where it did,' " she said. "The only thing for Ford & me to do is to wipe the unjustifiable mud Elsie has thrown off our faces, make ourselves presentable & go on as if nothing had happened. I have heaps of nice letters—making light of it & invitations!! I'm glad I can't accept them—it would embarrass kind hostesses just now—but later expect to see me with a very stiff upper lip—knocking about as usual. After all Ford did divorce Elsie. . . . And Ford did marry me—& we spent nearly £500 on it & I've got all Leun's [the lawyer's] bills." If Violet really had such documentation, why did she withhold it during the trial?

Violet answered this question in a subsequent reply to what was probably a stern admonition from her "mother-in-law." "I can't forget your eyes on that awful day when Elsie was swearing away all my reputation & I could do *nothing*," she wrote. "That she *proved* nothing doesn't make it less of a public exposé." Violet stressed that she knew only what Ford told her: "the divorce—that is his affair. Of course the marriage is mine & no one contested that, for of course Elsie wants to try and get Ford for bigamy." Then she explained that she did not appear in court because she "might have been made to give date & place & witnesses. Now—nobody, not even you knows them."

Following visits to Arles, Avignon and St. Rémy, Violet and Ford took a boat to Corsica to search out Violet's Corsican governesses, Reine and Catherine Dausoigne. They had returned to their village in 1874, after Margaret Hunt failed as a matchmaker. Reine had married an impoverished French aristocrat and on his death entered a convent; Catherine had wed the elderly widowed mayor of Vivario and still lived there. They found "a demure, white-haired woman, with the husband she had procured for herself according to the custom of her country, in her decline looking no longer like a rose but a tall stalk of the white heather that grew all over her native hills, wilting, withering, with the vestiges of her past all around her. . . . The walls of her parlour were hung with drawings and paintings, with signatures, respectful and affectionate: 'to Catherine, from Hers ever, D. G. Rossetti,' and 'To the Fair Lady, Respectfully, Ford Madox Brown.' "

Violet frequently had fantasies or dreams about blood, perhaps because of her hemorrhages, perhaps because she felt vulnerable, unprotected. In 1909 on the train from Selsey to London, she saw a field of buttercups passing by and saw blood blanketing the flowers. No one else saw it. "But I—morbid fool!—saw a third primary colour. Flakes and splashes and pools of red lying, as it were on the yellow pile of a Maple carpet of flowers, as if an army had bled to death on it . . . Always the oiliness, the thickness, the glutinousness of blood appalls me when I see it flow, even from a finger."

Similarly, in Corsica one morning, when she walked onto the wooden balcony adjoining her bedroom, the view reminded her of a recurrent nightmare: below her was an old horse tied to a stake set in a dung heap; in the middle distance, a red smock, the color of blood, was spread out to dry on the mountainside; above her, the snow-capped Monte Rotondo. "The whole island of Corsica was poised high in air," she said, "the mattress of my dream."

In this dream, Violet and her lover of the moment are "placed" on a mattress that is lying in ether. It is quiet, the blue of a chemist's bottle surrounds them, the bedclothes are neatly tucked in: "we are as safe as if we were in our own bed at home," she recounted, "only we must not fall out! There is no more reason why we should fall out of bed into the ether than on to the floor; all we have to do is not realise our position. If we do, we are certain to wriggle and look over the edge . . ."

A revealing account: Violet may be saying that as long as she and her lover denied the relationship's dangers they were safe, but if they realized the situation and fell into the ether, they lost all sensation, becoming patients on a table, not lovers on a bed.

Shortly the distractions of travel waned; the return to London could not be postponed forever. Violet tallied up the friends who would rally around her: the novelist May Sinclair and Ethel Colburn Mayne, a translator, novelist and Byron scholar; her bohemian friends, but not her relatives or those aristocrats whose opinions she valued. Keeping his distance, Henry James advised her to "patch with purple if you must, so long as the piece holds." An ailing Arthur Marwood, who was putting his affairs in order, called in his loan of £440 for Elsie's kidney operation. Violet claimed the debt was paid immediately, but where she got the money is a mystery, for Margaret Hunt's estate was still not settled.

If only Violet had been content to be a mistress in the mold of a George Eliot or an Ellen Terry, she could have faced down her detractors; but she wanted respectability as well, to be accepted as Mrs. Hueffer. That the marriage charade made headlines mattered less than Violet's determination to continue the fabrication. The Mrs. Grundys refused to let her have it both ways; propriety demanded that her name be stricken from elite invitation lists. Years later she confided to Ethel Mayne that if she had demonstrated her "*bona fides*, Ford would only be decried for having committed a bigamous attempt for love of me! Not anything for a man to be ashamed of."

As far as Ford was concerned, they should act as if nothing had happened, no apologies, no explanations. "I hold very strongly," he said, "the view that friends are people before whom one does not need to justify oneself and, personally, I am absolutely determined to speak to no-one about these matters." But Violet needed to flaunt her elevated position. She had cards printed for Ford with South Lodge and Knap Cottage as addresses. Her stationery read "From Mrs. Ford Madox Hueffer (Violet Hunt)."

No one was more loyal to Violet than May Sinclair. Their friendship—built on a mutual interest in feminism, cats and gothic tales—survived despite differing attitudes toward sex and morality. May was the consummate unmarried woman, prim and proper, with black, emotionless eyes that exuded a Buddha-like calm. A more astute writer than Violet (she was the first to examine the Brontë sisters from a psychological angle), she attracted attention in 1904 with *The Divine Fire*, a novel about a young bookseller which Jack London termed "colossal."

May was a no-nonsense pragmatist. Earlier, when Elsie brought the suit for restoration of conjugal relations, May wrote Ford, "I'm sick of the world we live in, with its cowardice and hypocrisy, and abominable, poisonous sham morality." Equally passionate about their present predicament, she wrote Violet that she didn't "care two straws whether your marriage holds good in this country or not, and should *not* care if it had never taken place," but she cautioned that others did not share her opinion, and advised them to remain in Europe for at least six months.

Lucy Clifford, a close friend of Henry James's, was harsher. "I don't think you know *how strong* the feeling about you is," she warned, "and it would be *impossible* for you to go about and be received without first asking what sort of reception you would get or whether you would get any at all. I would do a good deal for you but I simply should quake if you came here on Sundays, and I believe other people would walk out." Lucy told them to stay away for three years!

Violet rushed to the parapets. "No," she brusquely replied, "I can't say I do understand what my friends are so upset about. The mud flung at me in the course of the attempt to . . . drag me into a Court, where I was prohibited by the law from putting in an appearance, was of course disagreeable enough to bear but it did not alter the situation for people who had accepted the fact of the legality of my German marriage. I expected all my friends to treat the attack with contempt and not help . . . to make it impossible for me to live in England."

She had letters from a great many friends, she told Lucy, mentioning Henry James, Lucy Masterman, all of Ford's relations. Everyone, she said, expected her back, including those "who entertained me and backed me up in my rescue of Ford from a state far worse than death, which indeed he did contemplate . . . And that is why I am so surprised at your advice. Of course, I should not have thought of entering your drawing-room on Sundays without a very pressing invitation from you . . . I should expect all my real friends to accept my version of the affair naturally and easily— and if other friends walked out, let them!" When incited, Violet was a North Country spitfire, but referring to Ford's so-called suicide threat in this context was a bit melodramatic.

Lucy's reply should have shamed Violet. "I think it is so foolish not to have courage to tell you what it is people *do* say—not what *I* say, mind, nor what just a few others say:—they say it is impossible to believe that Ford had definite reason for divorcing his wife or that he did divorce her, or that he thought he had divorced her, that you went through no marriage ceremony, and that you have no reason for believing yourself legally married to Ford." She advised Violet to have her solicitor draft a statement giving exact dates and places for the divorce and wedding ceremony. "Do this," she said, "and you'll get back all the friends you had." Unfortunately, this was the one thing Violet would never do.

Aimlessly they toured France until the end of May 1913. In Paris they had tea with Gertrude Stein and Alice B. Toklas. Intrigued by unconventional couplings, which Violet and Ford indeed were, Alice confessed a weakness for Ford, in later years boasting that she had known him "intimately" through his three "marriages"; she found Violet attractive, amusing and eccentric.

When they returned to London, Elsie brought suit against Ford for £93 in back alimony. The two Mrs. Hueffers were at it again.

René Byles had found a job at a new publishing firm, Howard Latimer, and to make amends for the shabby treatment he had received, Ford offered him—without an advance—his next book, *Mr. Fleight* (the book includes a tough, sexy editor, Augusta McPhail, as the Violet character). Ford probably hoped that Byles would boom it the way he did *The Soul of London*. That did not happen. Shortly after its publication, the undercapitalized firm folded. During this time Ford wrote a pamphlet, *The Monstrous Regiment of Women*, for the Women's Freedom League. He was proud of this effort, a curious, weakly argued pitch to expand women's rights, in which he discusses Elizabeth I and Victoria as rulers, seeking by extension to prove a woman's administrative abilities.

Intent at felling the philistines, Violet sent out engraved invitations to her annual garden party on July 1. "Home, and my yearly garden-party never so well attended," she noted with forced effervescence. "Cabinet Ministers, by Jove! Dinners in the House. *Fêtes champêtres* at the Monds' in Lowndes Square, Henley with the Harmsworths, the Cabaret Club and all the charming artist rabble who were on the top of the vogue." But their social life was not that exciting, and the party was not the success she pretended. Their old friend Charles Masterman was probably the only cabinet minister present. The gentry sent regrets.

Some old friends and relatives wrote lengthy excuses, ranging from "I am not strait-laced, and I care for you for your father's sake, who was really good and dear to me and who was so proud and fond of you. . . . I *am* sorry, dear Violet, for you, but I cannot visit you until you have vindicated your position publicly," to "I am very sorry that I cannot come to your party. And I am *more* than grieved for the sad troubles that have come to you. I feel sure there must be *some* explanation of the difficult position into which you have been drawn."

Concerned about keeping her "society" friends, Violet ignored the effect on her relationship with Ford. They still stepped out proudly, but Violet's compulsion to explain their "marriage" was boring Ford, who needed to be admired, to have his wounded pride soothed; what he did not want was a woman who competed with him as a public personality. And Violet was becoming just that, establishing herself as *the* literary hostess to a new generation of writers.

Kathleen Cannell, wife of the American poet Skipwith Cannell, described South Lodge in the summer of 1913 as "big, comfortably worn," with a "large, beautifully appointed table" laden with "lavish crumpets and sandwiches, nut bread and plum cake," which were gobbled up by the young writers, probably their only meal that day. "Authors on every rung of the literary ladder were apt to drop in," recalled Cannell, "from Lady Gregory to Frank Stewart Flint, who spoke 10 languages, and his surprising Cockney wife who practically spoke none."

Meanwhile, a marvelous romance was developing: South Lodge regular Rebecca West was in love with H. G. Wells. Violet advised her on the inherent problems of loving her former lover, a man who, no matter what, would never divorce his wife. Wells met Rebecca in the same manner that Violet and Ford had met her: she reviewed Wells's novel *Marriage* in *The Freewoman*, calling him "the Old Maid among novelists." Wells knew Rebecca by name only. He and his current mistress, Elizabeth von Arnim, author of *Elizabeth and Her German Garden*, had recently made love under the trees on a copy of *The Times* containing a morally indignant letter from Mrs. Humphry Ward denouncing Rebecca's journalism. Afterward, they showed their support for the young critic by burning the paper in protest.

Rebecca and Wells met and were immediately attracted to each other; despite a twenty-six-year age difference, they became lovers. Being in his company, Rebecca recalled years later, was "on a level with seeing Nureyev dance or hearing Tito Gobbi sing." The second time they slept together she became pregnant. In the beginning of what would be a tumultuous ten years they were happy and devoted. He called her Panther; she called him Jaguar.

Violet was the first to hear about the affair; Rebecca told her during a Christmas visit to Selsey. At that time Rebecca suspected she was pregnant, but did not discuss this complication, fearful that the talkative Violet would babble the news all over town. Rebecca did not want people saying she was the Free Woman wanting to be the Mother of the Superman. But she shortly wrote Violet explaining why she had made love to Wells ("I think it was the only honest thing to do"), then went to Selsey to be "your ever so depressing and sallow guest." When she returned to London she went to a doctor, who confirmed that she was pregnant.

□

In September, accompanied by the Mastermans, Violet and Ford toured the Rhineland. Masterman, who was largely responsible for the Insurance Act the Liberals had passed, wanted to see how a similar program was working in Germany, and to visit the battlefields of the Franco-Prussian War. Preparations for a new war had escalated since Violet and Ford were last there. People were hoarding gold; recruits swelled the German Army; children pointed to planes in the sky; workers erected barracks and zeppelin sheds and built railroad tracks. Creating some personal drama, Violet believed that the German secret service thought the Mastermans to be the Churchills and had them followed—an unlikely confusion, said Lucy Masterman, unless they had no idea what the Churchills looked like.

The Rhine boat trip recalled Violet's optimism of two years before, when she and Ford set out to be desirable aliens. At Düsseldorf, Ford and the Mastermans left the steamer to tour the industrial area of Duisburg and Essen while Violet went on with the luggage to find a hotel in Rüdesheim. She savored the pragmatic aspect of travel and insisted that their hotel rooms have armchairs and eiderdowns. This time, however, she settled for two rooms in an old barracks run by a Dutchman, ate some tasteless food and walked around the embankment meditating on the failed fairy tale of living in a castle with her medieval knight. To make herself more miserable, she reread *The Desirable Alien*, with its prodigal portrayal of a nation that no longer existed. Germany was "sulky," she said angrily, admitting that she "had never liked Germans, never felt at home with them, I hated them, in fact." After this trip, Violet never returned to Germany.

Back in London, she gave tennis parties and dinner parties and tea parties. Ford debated with *les jeunes* on *le mot juste* in poetry just as he had done with Conrad on prose. But they were living beyond their means. Pinker paid royalties from Ford's *Young Lovall* directly to Violet, and she economized by serving stewed rabbit and ginger beer instead of Ford's favorite Rhine wine. Despite a frenetic pace, it was not the South Lodge of old. Richard Aldington said Violet's "gossiping made many enemies, and the scandal cut off most social callers"; her parties "were nearly all made up of Ford's Bohemian friends and very few loyalists among the respectable."

Unlike Violet, whose self-worth came from invitations to the right parties, Ford could reinvent himself through his writing. He was working on *The Good Soldier*, which Violet snidely commented was going "to contain something quite unusual for him: there would be 'heart' in it." In January, Brigit Patmore joined the couple in Selsey to take dictation on the first part of what would be Ford's most enduring novel: a brilliant examination of marriage, sexual passion, social taboos, possession and loss.

Ford had been infatuated with Brigit two summers before when she stayed at Knap Cottage, and his feelings had not changed. Violet was intensely jealous. "To see his happy face when she came down to breakfast the next morning," she sneered, "ought to have told me" what was going on. Violet claimed that Brigit gave Ford the pectoral cross that dangled from his neck when they made love, an infuriating symbol of his unfaithfulness. Brigit certainly inspired Ford in the writing of *The Good Soldier*, but Ford's relationship with Violet, the libel trial and the subsequent scandal produced the state of mind for this emotional story of modern love.

One day Ezra Pound brought a new friend around to South Lodge. He was a twenty-two-year-old French sculptor named Henri Gaudier-Brzeska, a carpenter's son who had studied in England and Germany on scholarship and wanted to be an artist. At nineteen he had met Sophie Brzeska, a Polish émigrée twenty years his senior, who convinced him to pursue his dream. They moved to London, where his demanding mistress, who treated him like a son, supported them with itinerant teaching positions while Gaudier learned his craft by studying collections in the British Museum. He called Sophie his sister, and to make her happy adopted her name and signed both to his work.

Not a typical South Lodge habitué, Gaudier was slight with an ascetic, hawklike face, thin lips and nose and long dark hair. He always looked wan and authentically underfed. Richard Aldington said he was "probably the dirtiest human being" he had ever seen and "gave off horrid effluvia in hot weather." He stole pieces of stone from a mason's yard near the Tate Gallery and coveted the headstones in the cemetery he passed on the bus going to his Putney home. With his purloined marble, Gaudier produced small statuettes and futuristic animals.

When Pound decided to immortalize himself, he asked Gaudier to be the sculptor. Pound bought him a half-ton block of marble (the largest he ever worked on) and specified that it be phallic (the overall silhouette suggests a circumcised penis). He posed on a rickety wooden chair in the artist's freezing, mud-floored studio under a Putney railway arch with the trains rushing overhead. The work went slowly, for Gaudier's tools were blunt and inadequate, but after four months there emerged a thirty-six-inch-high despotic head, later known as _Hieratic Head of Ezra Pound_, inspired in part by an Easter Island figure in the British Museum.

The critic Hugh Kenner described how "the incised narrow eyeslits gaze, without pupils, on the invisible; the asymmetric rhombic nose carries its flat thrust upward to the plane of the brow, overlapped by a flamelike forelock; the broad mouth is calm; the formalized goatee, as if clapped on, is from Egypt, as are the truncated shoulders rising as through illimitable sand."* The statue was first exhibited in May 1914 as part of the Whitechapel Art Gallery's survey of twentieth-century art (the gallery paid the transportation costs), but it was too heavy for frequent exhibition, so Pound plopped it on the lawn in front of South Lodge. There was no money to buy a pedestal.

Violet planted geraniums around the statue's base to prevent the gardener from slicing it with the lawnmower. Pound fussed over his likeness (one day Annie Child informed Violet, "Mr. Peaound iz ine garrden a-scrubbin his MONUMENT"). Having a marble phallus in the front yard did little to enhance Violet's respectability, but the plucky band of bohemians convinced her that its presence would guarantee immunity from German bombs. Neighbors suspected it was a German cache for papers and said it looked ghastly under a full moon.

To forget their troubled lives and tentative loves, the South Lodge group partied almost every night. Sometimes they were seen at the Cave of the Golden Calf, with Emilio Filippo Tommaso Marinetti, the Italian Futurist leader, or at the Café Royal or the

*John Russell, art critic of _The New York Times_, noted on November 15, 1987, that the head is "one of the most powerful works of art to have been produced in Britain during this century. . . . It stands for a key moment in the history of the cosmopolitan London that was to be dispersed and demoralized by the war."

Tour Eiffel restaurant at 1 Percy Street, next to Wyndham Lewis' flat. They danced till dawn whenever the mood struck them. Then, as Ford nostalgically recorded, "you turned into the house of someone who had gone before you from the dance to grill sausages and make coffee. Then you breakfasted—usually on the lead roof above a smoking-room, giving onto a deep garden. There would be birds there. Those who cannot remember London then do not know what life could hold. Alas . . ."

And at all hours there was talk about art and poetry, how to change it, modernize it. "Those young people," Ford said, "had done their best to make a man of me. They had dragged me around to conspiracies, night-clubs, lectures where Marinetti howled and made noises like machine-guns. . . . So they pranced and roared and blew blasts on their bugles and round them the monuments of London tottered." They called themselves Vorticists, Pound's word for the small band of artists—led by Lewis—who produced the first modernist paintings in England, between 1913 and 1915.

From Cubism they borrowed a schematization of forms and from Futurism a celebration of the machine and the city. England, a bastion of the machine age, should be first in its aesthetic glorification, said Lewis. The Vorticist artist was at the quiet center of a whirlpool, the point of maximum energy, said Pound. The resultant semi-abstract art featured dynamic forms and bright colors. "Lewis supplied the volcanic force, Brzeska the animal energy, and perhaps I had contributed a certain Confucian calm and reserve," Pound modestly averred.

The Vorticists eschewed the sentimental genre scenes favored by Augustus John and Walter Sickert and advocated art that reflected contemporary technology, particularly the dynamism and speed of cars and the new airplane. To make their point, in June 1914 they launched *Blast: The Review of the Great English Vortex*, which featured startling typography: bold sans-serif letters printed black on a magenta-colored cover. "We will convert the King, if possible. A Vorticist king! Why not?" they pledged. *Blast* carried the beginning of *The Good Soldier* under its original title, *The Saddest Story* ("My Great Auk's Egg," Ford called it).

Readers were reminded that the "Modern World is due almost entirely to Anglo-Saxon genius—its appearance and its spirit. Machinery, trains, steam-ships, all that distinguishes externally our time, came far more from here than anywhere else . . . But busy with this LIFE-EFFORT, [England] has been the last to become conscious of the Art that is an organism of this new Order and Will of Man." Harriet Monroe, editor of *Poetry*, put it more succinctly: *Blast* wanted "to blow away in thick black capitals half an inch high, the Victorian Vampire." The literary establishment was horrified. Ford observed that "these young fellows not only drove the old— oh, the horrible wearisome!—Academics out of the field, the market and the forum; they created for themselves also a 'public' that had never looked at a book otherwise than to be bored with it; or considered that an Art was an interesting, inspiring or amusing appearance."

Violet dressed in the vibrant palette of the Vorticists (she looked better in bold colors, Lewis said, instead of walking around like a "dying stag or a virgin in Greek dress picking daisies"). She decided to decorate her mother's old bedroom, now Ford's study, in the Vorticist style, and commissioned Lewis to do an abstract painting to go over the mantelpiece; the doors and moldings were painted red, and the windows draped with brick-red tapestry curtains. Ford Madox Brown's painting of Ford as William Tell's son and watercolors by Alfred Hunt remained on the walls. Rebecca West remembered Lewis' painting as "very violent and explosive." Ford, in his quizzical way, "found it extremely restful," she said.*

Late in July, Lewis was ill with recurring gonorrhea. He had his eye on a future mistress, Mary Borden, an American heiress and novelist, who was living with her second husband, a red-haired Scottish missionary, George Douglas Turner, in Berwickshire. In-

---

*It has never been verified whether Lewis did a fresco or a painting. A South Lodge inventory from 1926 lists a large oil painting by him, valued at £40, with this figure changed to £30. Was it sold for this price? Did it disappear? When South Lodge's furnishings were sold after Violet's death, it was not included. And there is no record of such a painting in any collection. The current residents of South Lodge found faint reddish colors when they stripped the wallpaper. One catalogue of Lewis' paintings describes the design as an "abstract panel over chimney piece, with red paint on the doors and skirting boards," suggesting it was a fresco similar to those Lewis did for the Cave of the Golden Calf and a Vorticist Room in the Tour Eiffel (destroyed when the restaurant was sold in 1938 and became the White Tower, a still fashionable Greek restaurant). Margaret Cooper Fogg, Violet's great-niece (the daughter of Amerye, Silvia's daughter), told this author that she remembered Lewis' extravaganza as "painted all around the fireplace."

vited to spend the weekend, Lewis brought along Ford and Violet; it was a last respite before war swept away Edwardian complacency. They sat on the manicured lawns, basking in the soft sunlight or turning their faces into the gentle Scottish rain. Ford read aloud the opening chapter of *The Good Soldier*, and Mary Borden read the work of a writer unknown to Ford whom Pound had published in *The Egoist*. His name was James Joyce, and what they heard was *A Portrait of the Artist as a Young Man*. Perhaps only Ford realized that soon the world was to be irrevocably changed.

PART FOUR

1914-1942

14

The Good Soldier

HORTLY AFTER war was declared on August 4, 1914, Violet and Ford left for Selsey, lugging three Persian cats onto trains jammed with escaping Londoners. They planted a vegetable garden in the rear of Knap Cottage and shivered at the sound of the Portsmouth guns practicing for air raids eighteen miles away. Outwardly they seemed a caring couple, but Violet was cautious, worried about Brigit Patmore, worried about any young woman attractive enough to distract Ford.

In truth, there was little passion left between them. Trapped in a worn-out romance, Ford had no place to escape, no available "ideal" woman to baby him—and no money. No wonder he saw the war as liberating. But was Ford German or British? This he surely knew. Even so, he consulted Charles Masterman, who assured him that he was a British subject in good standing. (He later admitted: "I never became a German for legal or illegal reasons or for any reason.")

But to Edward Heron Allen, Violet's landlord-friend, who had convinced many Selsey residents that the Germans planned to use Portsmouth as a submarine base, Ford was the enemy; soon his neighbors saw him as such, murmuring his German name: Hueffer. And when Allen read "The Scaremonger," a satirical sketch of him and his Selsey friends, published in the November issue of *The Bystander,* there was a terrible row. Ford had written—surely not out of vindictiveness—a silly, superficial story about a silly, hysterical man, who at the end is proved right when there is a small submarine invasion.

How could Ford attack "about the only Englishman who has ever been known to say a good word for him?" Allen asked Violet. He told her that her lover had "not only lived for years largely on your means, but 'pays for his keep' by being uniformly rude & brutal to you in public (&, presumably, in private also) & openly contemptuous about you behind your back." Allen wanted Ford out of Knap Cottage. "I have spent a great deal of money there to carry out his various whims," he continued, "only because as a friend of yours I wanted to put him under future obligation (if that were possible) to *you*."

Brigit Patmore was also shocked. "It seems to me artistically and—well, socially—a low thing," she told Violet. "I hated the little 'hits' against Richard [Aldington] and Hilda [Doolittle] that used to appear in the *Outlook* articles [written by Ford], but after all, they were only apparent to a very few, but the attack on Ned is flagrant, & all the more astounding as Ford always pretended to like Ned. Why did he do it?" Violet noted on a copy of this letter that Ford wrote it in a morning for £10: "We were hard up." She probably meant that Ford had written a quick piece on the first idea that came into his head, and without thinking how Allen would be offended. Ford was often surprised when accused of insulting people, which he frequently did. Although he apologized, Allen never forgave him, and it was probably he who asked the chief constable of West Sussex to write an official letter demanding that Ford leave the county (an order canceled through Masterman's intervention).

Disgruntled and distrustful of each other, they returned to their writing desks. Violet finished *The House of Many Mirrors*; Ford contributed weekly articles to *The Outlook* and wrote books for Masterman, now in charge of the Foreign Ministry's counter-propaganda office. To help with dictation, Ford hired Richard Aldington,* who found Violet amusing and often walked with

*Both Brigit and Aldington took dictation for *The Good Soldier*, and their lives were inexorably intermingled. Aldington married Hilda Doolittle (H.D.) in 1913. They separated in 1919, and six years later he and Brigit (who had had an intimate relationship with H.D. during the war years) began an affair that lasted for ten happy years until Aldington ran off with his lover's daughter-in-law. In 1938 Aldington divorced H.D. and married Netta Patmore. (Michael Patmore, Netta's her in Kensington Gardens. Once when they came to a long, secluded avenue of trees, she "suddenly broke off her tragical declamations, smiled coquettishly, and said: 'This is where I used to meet Andrew Lang by permission of his wife.' " Indeed, Violet cherished her halcyon days of outrageous flirting. Aldington also recalled how Ford would imitate her talking on the telephone: "Yes, this is Violet Hunt. Who is it speaking? Oh, Lady de Lammermoor—how *are* you? What! What? I said you had a baby before you were married? Oh, nonsense, I said that about Lady Bridlington."

Aldington snidely noted in *The Egoist* that Violet "writes like a woman better than any other woman," and her wit is "her most valuable quality." *The Celebrity at Home,* he said, was "as real as Cinderella." In his 1929 novel *Death of a Hero,* Aldington brutally satirized the couple. Shobbe (Ford) is the fat but talented editor who runs a review, a "literary Falstaff," living off his wife's money. His wife (Violet) is a "soft, kind grey moth, for ever fluttering with kindly intent and for ever fluttering wrong." She had, he wrote, that "sweet exasperating gentleness and refined incompetence which marked so many women of the wealthier class whose youth was blighted by Ruskin and Morris."

As Violet predicted, Ford put "heart" into *The Good Soldier.* Out of his personal chaos came a journey through self-doubt, greed, death and suicide. It was, as the original title indicated, the saddest story. Ford wanted to show the literary world something different in form, narration, time shifts, dialogue; he wanted to reimagine himself, to work out his private demons.

The male protagonists, John Dowell and Edward Ashburnham, embody two sides of Ford's character: generosity and ineffectiveness. Violet said they were his Jekyll and Hyde, or two Mr. Jekylls, "for neither is really wicked." Leonora Ashburnham's shrewd pragmatism and Florence Dowell's cold sensuality personify Violet's duality. Nancy Rufford, the unattainable beauty, repre-

---

former husband, told this author that his mother, Brigit, was probably bisexual. "She was a very passionate woman," he said, "attracted to both sexes," but he doubted that she ever had an affair with Ford. Rebecca West, however, told Arthur Mizener that she had never questioned that Ford was Brigit's lover for a while. In her 1917 diary Violet said that Brigit didn't care "a pin for F. She succumbed from the flattery of his suit—his plausibility.")

sents aspects of Brigit Patmore and Violet's niece Rosamond. Leonora's privileged background and her managing of Edward's affairs also recall Violet. "I have to support the character of Leonora, the sportswoman, 'clean run,' " Violet said, "but doing evil that good may come, and incidentally driving the poor Girl mad." However, in Florence, Ford created a more clearly defined Violet type, a woman without natural feelings, only lust, filled with vanity and deceit.

"Florence was a personality of paper," Ford wrote. "She represented a real human being with a heart, with feelings, with sympathies, and with emotions only as a bank note represents a certain quantity of gold. . . . She wasn't real; she was just a mass of talk out of guide-books, of drawings out of fashion-plates"—a harsh indictment of Violet, even though she superficially embraced "society's" trends. Of the three heroines, Violet noted, "Florence is a cat, Nancy is nothing, Leonora, so Rebecca [West] said, is 'a Northern Light among women to whom marriage meant an appearance of loyalty before the world.' " This comes from John Dowell's prediction that "Leonora will burn, clear and serene, a northern light," which Violet interpreted as a reference to her North Country roots. But West also saw the other side of her friend, telling Violet that she was "a sensitive piece of beauty created in studios and drawing rooms and ballrooms," while she herself was a "thickskinned product of a Victorian Scotch home."

Mouthing Ford's philosophic need for a devoted, dependent, ultimately satisfying woman, Dowell says that "there is no man who loves a woman that does not desire to come to her for the renewal of his courage, for the cutting asunder of his difficulties. And that will be the mainspring of his desire for her. We are all so afraid, we are all so alone, we all so need from the outside the assurance of our own worthiness to exist."

But such reassurance was lacking in Ford's life, and he no longer cared to struggle for it with Violet. Now fifty-three, she was becoming more possessive and demanding—reminiscent of the years with Crawfurd. The situation was exacerbated when Ford learned about her syphilis, sometime in 1914. (Later Violet confided to Rebecca West that Ford was "somewhat repelled" by her after that. West told Ford's biographer Arthur Mizener that Violet went to a doctor who treated and arrested the disease, but insisted on examining her "husband," and this was how Ford discovered she had tertiary syphilis. "It put an end," said West, "to the 'marriage,' and was the real cause of their breakup.")

Ford also doubted himself as a writer, and never more so than when he read the first reviews of *The Good Soldier*. Although West called the novel a "supreme triumph of art . . . a much, much better book than any of us deserve," most critics thought the story sordid and the structure confusing, although later reviewers applauded its inventive structure, style and characterization, and today the novel is considered his masterpiece.

Happy men who are over the age limit do not volunteer to go to war. But Ford was not happy with his career or with his love life, and when he had to face up to unpleasant facts about his life, he usually suffered a nervous collapse: this time, to escape the emptiness of love, but also out of patriotism, he enlisted. After receiving his commission in August 1915, he wrote his mother that "if one has enjoyed the privileges of the ruling class of a country all one's life, there seems to be no alternative to fighting for that country if necessary." Violet, who viewed the war as a personal inconvenience, knew nothing of his decision. "I wanted," he told his mother, "to get a commission without talking about it, & a commission in the regular army, not in any of the fancy services which are only a form of shirking."

Their intimacy strained, Violet and Ford lived a work-centered life, collaborating on *Zeppelin Nights: A London Entertainment,* a confection of twenty-four historical vignettes, written by Ford and reprinted from the *Daily News* and *The Outlook*. Violet wrote the connecting tissue linking the *Decameron*-style tales, told in wartime London to fortify readers against the threat of German zeppelins flying overhead.

Doubtless to improve relations between Ford and his onetime friend, Violet dedicated *The House of Many Mirrors*, published that June, to Joseph Conrad, who responded with an atypical exuberance, pronouncing the book "delightful in expression, poignant in matter with a general amenity of treatment." *The Outlook*'s critic (probably a friend of the couple) heralded Violet's "return from the literary shallows, where she has been straying too long," to produce "a true picture of ante-bellum London . . . all as painful as it is brilliant."*

In the novel, Alfy Pleydell is a Fordian character of good manners and gentility, whose older wife, Rosamond (Violet), supports him out of desire, but also guilt, because Alfy's uncle disinherited him when they married (echoing the disinheritance by Violet's godfather and Ford's aunt). Later, Ford told her he thought Alfy hurt him socially in London; he disliked any thought of his being seen as a "kept" man.

As the South Lodge men—Lewis, Aldington and Gaudier-Brzeska—donned uniforms, they expected to be home in several months. No one imagined the war would last four years. Wyndham Lewis trained as a gunner and bombardier and, through Masterman's influence, was commissioned and shipped to France in May 1915. A month later Gaudier was killed in France. When Pound, who had become W. B. Yeats's secretary in Sussex, learned of Gaudier's death, he was so enraged that he volunteered, but was rejected for reasons unknown. "We have lost the best of the young sculptors and the most promising," said Pound. "The arts will incur no worse loss from the war than this."

Ford was the last to go. He used the Selsey incident and Violet's association with those who had denounced him as a German agent as a convenient excuse for his decision to enlist. "Violet's course seemed to me," he explained to Masterman, "to be so radical a disloyalty to any form of joint life that I saw no other way open than to retire from the scene." He joined the Third Battalion of the Welch Regiment stationed at Cardiff Castle. "I have never felt such an entire peace of mind as I have felt since I wore the King's

---

*The critic of *The Times* of London was less enthusiastic, complaining that Violet is "always seeking the striking phrase, the illuminating word, but a strained inaptness is all that is usually achieved. One wonders, for example, what Mrs. Pleydell's 'irregragable eyes' could have been like, and how anything could have pleased her husband in a 'curious ricochetty way.' How impossible, too, are such phrases as 'her state of absolute, pitiful disequilibrium' and 'she uttered a little noise of denegation.'" The review noted that "long-windedness and the florid style which weaken the book are serious faults that might well have wrecked it; but Miss Hunt's brilliant, untidy cleverness undoubtedly overcomes them," even though "one has neither hopes nor fears" for the characters. As usual, Violet was applauded for being clever: "it is only when one has quite finished the book that one fully realizes its immense cleverness."

uniform," he wrote his mother. When Violet heard the news, she became hysterical, flinging herself on the bed, crying and carrying on for three days. Ford hated scenes, but these tears were mild compared to the tantrums she would have thrown if he had told her beforehand of his enlistment. Violet "takes it rather hard, poor dear," he told his mother, "but I hope she will get used to the idea."

Also caught up in the war effort was Henry James, who had decided to become a British citizen. When Violet asked him why, he said, "My dear Purple Patch, chiefly because I wanted to be able to say *We*—with a capital—when I talked about an Advance." One day while James was polishing a speech for the Anglo-French Parliamentary Committee, Violet dropped by his Chelsea flat, where he had moved from Rye. "Perhaps you would be kind enough to tell me if I am comprehensible? They tell me," he said, turning his head away, "that I am obscure."

James walked up and down the drawing room and read, with a voice "strong, resonant—the wonderful voice that old invalid men can muster when put to it—trembled, not from feebleness, but from emotion." Violet was greatly moved by the words. "Mr. James, I did not know you could be so—*passionate!*" she exclaimed. "Ah, my dear Purple Patch, you must not forget that I am addressing— not a woman but a nation!"

Before receiving his orders to report to Tenby on August 15, 1915, Ford muddled through another unfortunate incident. In 1912 D. H. Lawrence had run off to Europe with Frieda von Richthofen Weekley, wife of a Nottingham professor, and they married two years later. The Lawrences contended they were persecuted in Greatham (as Ford said he was in Selsey) because of Frieda's German origins. To sort things out, Violet and Ford drove down to Sussex with Jane Wells (H. G.'s wife), and what started as a friendly visit ended with recriminations on all sides. At issue was whether Frieda made anti-Belgian remarks, insulted Ford's uniform and forced him to take refuge in an outhouse. Violet had made some remark about Ford's poem "Antwerp," inspired by the sight of Belgian refugees at Charing Cross Station, when, by Violet's account, Frieda shouted in her German accent: "Dirty Belgians! Who cares for them!" By Ford's account, it was Jane Wells and Frieda who were arguing about the merits of the Belgians.

The incident took on a *Rashomon* quality when Frieda claimed years later that Ford had never been in uniform, that there was no outhouse, that Lawrence was not there and that Violet spent the visit claiming Ford was not German, but Russian, and then Dutch. It ended up, Violet recalled, being "a regular mill between me and the Valkyrie." When they left, Violet told Frieda that she hoped they never met again. They never did: a sad ending to a friendship begun so optimistically in the bygone days of the *English Review*.*

The day before he reported for duty, Ford and Violet's friends gathered at South Lodge for whiskey and sandwiches, knowing this was probably the last time they would be entertained by Mr. and Mrs. Hueffer. "The evening was a hectic one," Douglas Goldring recalled. "Violet was always lavish with her drinks—but the departing guests did not take Ford with them, as seemed to be anticipated. He lingered behind, finished off the remaining whiskey . . . and after a violent quarrel was finally 'hoofed out,' in an advanced state of what is politely called 'fatigue.' "

Before leaving London, Ford legally changed his name, dropping Joseph Leopold Hermann to become Second Lieutenant Ford Madox Hueffer. Initially army life agreed with him, as did his absence from South Lodge. Convinced that she had lost Ford, Violet broadcast her unhappiness to all her friends, even publishing a love poem, "Merciful Aphasia," which describes her personal battle to keep Ford's love.

> *When you are with me it is Life.*
>
> *Réveillés, alarms.*
> *The thrust, the parry, the séance in the trenches—*
> *The violent shell encounters—*
> *Hail and missile of words—*
> *Retreats and advances—*
> *Ambushes—*
> *Feints of passion*
> *Too starved, too ill-equipped to succeed.*

*In 1925, when Lawrence was living in New Mexico, he told an American journalist, "Why the devil he [Ford] ever married Violet Hunt! Why, she's too devilishly clever for a man ever to want to marry." The reporter asked who Violet was, and Lawrence replied that she was a novelist, not fully appreciated, and much better than May Sinclair. "Why do you like Sinclair so much over here?" he asked, continuing to praise Violet's writing.

Then the wounds
Starting red
That kisses after the fight staunch not after the fight
Nor prevent from bleeding
Silently, through their bandages, in the night. . . .
But still we are washed and laid out, and our eyelids
    closed.
At peace. . . .
It is a merciful dispensation.

Yet you'll come back?

Violet even exhibited her hurt feelings in theater reviews. In a critique of Arthur Wing Pinero's *The Big Drum,* she berated the playwright for trying to make a hero out of a novelist who can only be interesting when "he is something else!" She mocked any writer (and thereby Ford) who throws down his pen, shoulders a rifle and puts "himself into the hands of his colonel instead of his publisher," who "purges his sorrow in pages of close print," and who stands "at attention, under fire, with the solid wedge of note-book over the heart, with a set of proof-sheets for a shield, guaranteeing the wearer from the after-effects of direct and poignant experience."

But even in sadness, Violet kept life percolating with her scrappy North Country optimism. She told Faith Compton Mac-kenzie that she tried to think of a "new dress or new figure or new life or new man, far more to the point. I say new man but I've only the old one—& he is a dear dull thing—not because he is stupid, but because he has lost interest in such an unattainable possession as befalls me to be."

When Rebecca West wanted to escape country life, Violet offered her and nine-month-old Anthony (H. G. Wells's son) the shelter of South Lodge. Rebecca liked the proposal. South Lodge held many happy memories for her, and her "secret" motherhood had kept her away from London literary life far too long. Wells, however, was apprehensive. How could Rebecca endure Violet's constant talk and questions? he asked. If she lived at South Lodge as an unwed mother, he worried, wouldn't everyone know the truth? (It was already known and whispered about.)

Anthony West later said that his father feared Rebecca would "step out into stage center, shameful bundle and all, to make herself maximally visible to a packed house. Everybody in London who was anybody knew Violet, and if there was any more compulsive and irresponsibly inventive gossip in the literary swim than Ford himself, she was most certainly it. She loved gossip passionately, and she was as unable to refrain from asking personal questions as she was from passing on the answers. If my mother wanted to advertise the reasons for her prolonged absence from the London scene, moving into South Lodge with Violet and a baby would be her best way of doing it. She would not be able to keep any secrets once she was living there, and what was more she would be associating herself with someone who had already been the subject of a public scandal." Under pressure from Wells, Rebecca declined Violet's invitation, and remained in her East Hertfordshire farmhouse.

Alone with the faithful but censorious Annie Child, Violet was unable to entice anyone—even during wartime—to South Lodge; so she turned to Rosamond, the only relative she cared for. Rosamond had married a minister, the Rev. George Robert Wilkinson, in 1911 (Violet was not invited to the wedding), and was raising a family at Fingleton, Barnard Castle, not far from Durham. Violet sought an invitation to visit, but her niece rebuffed her, explaining that she could not entertain someone whose life the church did not sanction. Violet made a copy of Rosamond's letter and on it wrote a note to Ford blaming him for this reproach. Goldring found the letter inside a copy of *The Good Soldier* after Violet's death.

"This is what you have brought on me, dear Ford, and you are happy in Cardiff and leaving me to bear it alone," she lamented. "It is this sort of thing all the time—and loneliness—and I wish now I was out of this world you have made for me, or that you'll say we made, so that we could live together. That's the joke! And this is the last straw, more than I can bear. Don't write to Rosamond on any account. You have done me enough harm already." More family problems followed. The Fogg-Elliots were finally breaking up. Silvia, fed up with Walton's infidelities, had started divorce proceedings.*

*In 1915 Silvia brought suit for restoration of conjugal rights, and after a divorce the following year, Walton married Frances Ellis, a widow with two children. Walton and Frances had a son who died in World War II, and thus Walton's stepson, John Roland Ellis, inherited Bedburn and took the Fogg-Elliot name.

By the end of 1915 Ford was finding military life at Cardiff tiresome. He regularly complained to friends about the paperwork, but still played golf every Sunday and saw Violet on weekends. When he dedicated a poem to a Mrs. Percy (Eleanor) Jackson, Violet smelled infidelity and unwisely asked Wells to intercede, which he did. Feigning innocence, Ford replied, "I haven't the least idea that there was any difference between Violet & myself—or at least anything to make her face the necessity of talking about it. I, at any rate, haven't any grievance against her and want nothing better than to live with her the life of a peaceable regimental officer with a peaceable wife. Of course that is not very exciting for her & enjoyment of life depends so much on excitement. But one's preoccupations can't, now, be what they were in the 90's—or even three or two years ago. That, I suppose, is the tragedy—but it is the tragedy—isn't it?—of the whole of Europe."

He urged Wells to convince Violet that "short of absence without leave or cutting parades, I shall always be and am—at her disposal," adding that he had "the greatest possible affection & esteem for her; there isn't anyone else (but I don't know what she has got into her always romantic head) and I am frightfully sorry that these bad years are such bad years for her." Of course, Mrs. Jackson was a passing fancy for Ford, as Violet had been for Wells; but clearly the good soldier, no longer emotionally committed, was looking for a rejuvenating womanly muse.

Before his battalion left for France in July 1916, Ford put his affairs in order. He asked Joseph Conrad and Violet to be his literary executors; for some time he had wanted to bring Conrad back into his orbit. Conrad could hardly refuse such a patriotic request, particularly when Ford asked to carry his old binoculars with him to the front. Ford invited his daughters—Katharine, fifteen, and Christina, seventeen—to London, where they lunched at a Lyons café. Christina wanted to enter a convent against her parents' wishes, and Ford's attempts to postpone her decision failed. Following this awkward meeting, he never saw his daughters again.

Though not at the front, Ford was still under fire with the first-line transport of the Ninth Welch Battalion, stationed behind Bécourt Wood. Like all soldiers he missed news from home and in late July complained to Lucy Masterman that Violet had not written. "I don't know what psychological vagary or manoeuvre it implies," he wrote. "But it is a queer way to set to work." He asked Lucy not to repeat anything to Violet, for she seemed "very queer." Ford assumed Violet was deliberately ignoring him, which was not her style.

In fact, Violet was busy finishing her autobiographical novel *Their Lives,* which ranks (along with *White Rose*) as her most enduring work. Ford corrected the proofs in September while watching the gas shells bursting in Poperinge, Belgium. He wrote a short preface illuminated by the images of war and signed it "Miles Ignotus." The novel was selfish history, he concluded, for "that horrible family [the Radmalls, that is, the Hunts] of this author's recording explains to me why to-day, millions of us, as it were, on a raft of far-reaching land, are enduring torture it is not fit that human beings should endure, in order that—outside that raft— other eloquent human beings should proclaim that they will go on fighting to the last drop of *our* blood."

What did he mean? Ford said he wanted to awaken the sleeping reader "to the fact that selfishness does create misery . . . and see that the selfishness of the Eighties—of the Victoria and Albert Era— is the direct Ancestor of . . . Armageddon." Ford also wanted to attack effete Pre-Raphaelite sensibilities, which he despised more than Violet. Ford wrote Lucy Masterman that "V's novel . . . is really very good," noting that she "seems to be absolutely untouched, mentally, by the war—wh[ich] is no doubt a blessed state."

When Violet complained about the equivocal reviews, Ford counseled that all an author needed for confidence was approval from one or two discriminating people. Sufficient praise came from Rebecca West, a discerning critic, if a close friend. "*Their Lives* is a work of art," she wrote. "It gives a cold, white vision of reality that recalls Maupassant; it is a valuable historical document; it is a study of adolescence. . . . Meticulously, with the controlled garrulity of Jane Austen, she describes the horsehair texture of their home life. Their lovable father was so deeply absorbed in his painting that he was of no more use to them than a gentle dove fluttering above their roof. . . . Their mother, a hard, noble Yorkshire woman, was afflicted with a bleak inability to live suavely and gracefully; she was unable to conceal from her children that she disliked two of them."

Placing Violet's novel alongside Dostoevsky's *A Raw Youth*, West observed that the Pre-Raphaelite and aesthetic movements described in the book "with such gentle malice had nothing more to do with a woman than put her on a brocade settee with a sunflower. So all a girl could do was to sit up in the 'Trust' position till a husband was given one, and one could drop into the happy relaxation of 'Paid For.' " (More than sixty years later, Rebecca West still recalled *Their Lives,* saying, "There is nothing quite like it.")

After two weeks at the front, Ford was knocked out by a near miss, which damaged his precious new teeth. Sent to a field station at Corbie, he lost his memory and could not recall his name for thirty-six hours, and not much more for a month. He later admitted that he did not get "over the nerve tangle of the war" until 1923. At forty-two, Ford knew he was neither a hero nor a leader of men. He returned to duty a tense soldier, terrified of losing his sanity; to make matters worse, his commanding officer told him he was inefficient, lacking the confidence needed to inspire the troops. He asked Ford to resign his commission and said he could not recommend him for home service. Again Masterman saved the day, using his influence to have Ford sent back to Wales. But Ford was still unhappy: he needed the extra pay for serving abroad. Expecting him to support himself, Violet had withdrawn her financial guarantee in July 1916.

When he realized he might have to beg for money, Ford angrily blamed Violet for all his problems, including those with publishers. "I rather suspect V (though I may be unjust) of suppressing them [his poems] for ends of her own," he wrote Lucy Masterman. He *was* unjust on this point, for Violet always pushed their agent Pinker to find publishers for Ford. But his frustration was justifiable. Ford had failed to be the Edward Ashburnham of his fantasies; doubts plagued him and failures, real and imagined, tormented him.

In late November he was sent back to France and was so worried about confronting his old commanding officer that he suffered another nervous breakdown. "I am in short rather ill & sometimes doubt my own sanity," he wrote Lucy Masterman. To Violet, he ominously confided his fear that they would never meet again in this life.

Obsessed about losing Ford, Violet sought support from women friends: Rebecca West (who was at odds with Wells) and Radclyffe Hall (who was grieving over the death of her lover Mabel Batten); she renewed her friendship with Rose Ferguson (née Cumberbatch), to whom she had written adoring adolescent letters. "Cheer up!" Rebecca said. "The only people who are really well treated by life are people like Mrs H[umphry] Ward and Mrs J[oseph] C[onrad] . . . and that's too heavy a price to pay." May Sinclair and Ethel Colburn Mayne were still her literary friends, but their experience with men was limited (Ethel's grand passion was Byron). They could not appreciate tales about Ford's supposed infidelities or join Violet in her speculation about his patronage of whorehouses in Rouen or his *passade* with a "garrison hack."

Violet tracked down Eleanor Jackson, to whom Ford had dedicated a poem and to whom Violet dedicated *Their Lives*—perhaps out of spite. On February 26, 1917, the two women lunched at the Kardomah Café. Violet was sad and preoccupied as she listened to Eleanor blackening Ford's character with tales of his flirtations. As the woman scorned, Violet said Ford had "not one single gentleman's impulse, only savage, secret furtive animal ones." Perhaps so. Suffering from insomnia, Violet dosed herself with barbiturates and visited Richmond for water therapy. In happier moments, she learned to fox-trot at the popular ragtime parties.

Although Ford wanted to remain in France, his health did not permit even limited service. He was sent back to England in March 1917, where he was given light duties with the King's Liverpool Regiment at Kinmel Park; he regained some of his self-esteem through the encouragement of a new commanding officer, who praised his ability as a lecturer. During his first leave, Ford planned to stay at the YMCA at Grosvenor Gardens. He wrote Violet of his arrival and asked to see her, but she ignored the invitation until Lucy Masterman told her to see Ford or lose her hold over him. That night Violet went to a dinner party, and after one too many glasses of champagne had the courage to call the Y and leave a message. Ford telephoned, and they met the following day at the London Library. The day started off well. They lunched, had tea with friends and attended the popular revue *The Other Bing Boys* at the London Opera House.

Violet kept her mouth shut—for a while—but eventually could

not resist asking about his Cardiff girlfriend, whom Violet called "Miss Ross." Ford admitted only to a continuing infatuation with Brigit Patmore. They talked until 2:00 A.M., and when he suggested that she put him up, she agreed. But Ford wanted a warm bed to himself, not with Violet, and they fought and slammed doors for three days before leaving for Selsey. At Knap Cottage, a "spasm of regret, of sexual rage" overcame Violet. She went to Ford's room and told him she was lonely. They argued. But Ford evaded the real issue—their relationship—by demanding that she cease seeing those he saw as his enemies: René Byles, Kenneth Dolleymore (Violet's solicitor) and Ernest Sims, a member of Ford's regiment from whom Violet obtained information about Ford's sexual activities at camp.

"Then he became abusive," Violet wrote, "& asked me not to speak in a whining voice, like the creaking of a door! . . . I said 'Well let us settle it . . . are you in love with Brigit?' 'Of course I am!' he retorted. What else c[ou]ld a churl like him have said?" Ford retreated from the room. Violet threw herself on his bed "& lay alone & cold for 2 minutes," then went back to her own bed. For the rest of the stay, they did not "meet after saying Goodnight again."

Violet went up to London for two days, and when she returned to Selsey Ford was in a seductive mood. "It was an historic evening," she wrote. "Something changed. I sat on his knee & he débitéd extraordinary fatuities—so much so that he stopped & in the midst of my silence said, 'I may seem very fatuous. . . .' I did not deny it but lay with my head on his shoulder. . . . My unusual silence & lack of combativeness brought it out."

Explaining that he loved Brigit and would go to her in a moment if she asked, Ford said he still cared for Violet but complained that she was never kind to him like these other women. "You were—are—stimulating if you like. B[rigit] means to me quiet appreciation—praise . . . encouragement. . . . You never praised me—never once!" He was a misunderstood soldier, he said, who cared only that England win the war, not about making love to women. "I would sacrifice *even* Brigit to the army!" he pledged heroically.

Then he maliciously added, "I admire you, for your intellect—no, not your intellect but character & personality—but no, you never waked in me the feeling you speak of. . . . Good god, my dear, take what you can get, like other women. If you want me to take your hand: put out yours—if you want to attract be attractive. It's the lot of all women!"

"My dear, you're too clever by half," Violet said. "That's the matter with you."

"Don't be a silly woman . . . come to my bed if you will. . . ."

"I went & stayed a moment. He embraced me dully—then slept. . . . I began to go away."

"What are you doing? Can't you stay here?"

"No. I can't sleep . . . you just bore me."

"That's that!" Ford said.

Back at South Lodge there were more scenes. Violet demanded real affection, but Ford would not be bound by the feeling of the moment. He bellowed that she "was a most irritating person to live with," that "domesticity had killed the feeling." When Violet suggested they live apart and she would send on his things, he pleaded poverty and demanded the right to a room since his furnishings and pictures were there. If he stayed, things might get better, Violet reasoned, so she unwisely gave in.

15

Lying and Spying

SHALL I COME IN when I come back & say Good-night?" Ford asked one evening after he had settled in at South Lodge. "No, not anything unless you love me," Violet huffed. When he failed to appear, she was so enraged that she hurriedly dressed and fled, in the middle of the night, to the hydrotherapy spa in Richmond. Ford accused her of having "a bed room mind." The following evening when he inquired, "Shall I come & sleep with you?" she agreed, but his attentions were not what she desired: he "lay like a log & groused—groused blue & deep. He *is* awfully disappointed & unhappy & needy. He never kissed me—one of those awful lie-a-beds when one lies & thinks & wonders when the other person is going to speak." Ford's mind was probably far away—in Brighton, where Brigit Patmore was recuperating from surgery.

During a frightful row before he left at the end of March, Ford hammered away at his favorite theme: Violet's indiscreet talk had ruined him. As appeasement, she offered to have no confidants if he would love her as before, but he shook his head: no promises. When she saw him off at Euston Station, he murmured, "Wait & see what happens." In a moment of weakness, Violet whispered, "I will be very glad if you come back to South Lodge even if you *don't* love me." He replied, "That is nice of you, dear."

Now both were lying about themselves and others. Violet was slowly unraveling. "Oh what is the good of my life, hanging *in ribbons* round a man who does not care for me!" she told her diary. "I can't hold out against loneliness, & neglect. Besides, there's no time." Examining her behavior, as she often did in her diaries, she admitted treating Ford shabbily, which she realized did not inspire him to "be eternally grateful. He paid as he went along: in caresses. And now I can no longer *subvenir* [meet] his wants: give him pleasurable sensations of opulence, of flattery, of consequence. I am not doing my part & he does not give me anything at all."

Eleanor Jackson sat her down for a heart-to-heart. When Ford told Violet to make herself attractive, her new friend pointed out, he did not mean dye her hair or make love: all he wanted was money and for Violet to make South Lodge pleasant. Although oversimplifying the issue, her argument made sense, and Violet decided to write what she facetiously termed her "first 'non-calculated' letter for a year & a half." Noting that Ford's indifference to her had begun when she withdrew financial support in July 1916, Violet offered him an unspecified allowance.

Ford had wanted to return to France for the additional service pay, and also to be a hero, for which he had to be at the front, but his two nervous breakdowns while in uniform were marks against him. The medical board refused him a transfer, and when he answered Violet's letter he gloomily suggested relinquishing his commission, for he could not "stand the merciless financial strain." (He wasn't that poor: he had £23, Violet said.) "The idea of once more chancing a hold on my Frankenstein monster" made Violet optimistic that they would resume their life as man and wife at South Lodge. Ford, however, did not resign; instead, he was promoted to lieutenant in July. Violet panicked. She told Ezra Pound she wanted Ford back so badly that she was willing to be his housekeeper at South Lodge and ask for nothing more, an empty vow she could never keep.

Violet wanted to maintain the illusion of marriage, and Ford wanted, as she bitterly wrote, only "to find a quiet woman, who will sleep in his arms & ask not so many questions. Then she must be a woman he loves—as I was, when I did." Ford also wanted love to be a mood, not a state, which, Violet said, demanded "wifely quiescence & passivity." She longed to confess that she had no love and no respect for Ford, only "an unholy passion that will last till I die . . . I don't want his mere society—that's love. I want his manifestations—that's passion."

□

On May 2, 1917, Violet told her diary: "My first infidelity to F." Who was this? Her escort of the moment was an artist and caricaturist, A. G. Watts, twenty-one years her junior, but her entries indicated a platonic relationship, by her choice. Could it have been Edward Heron Allen—at last? Or perhaps René Byles—in a fit of remorse for the wrong she and Ford had done him (she had dined with him the previous night)? Or a total stranger? Whoever—he remains Violet's mystery lover.

Later that month she visited Ford at his battalion headquarters at Redcar, in Yorkshire. It was not an enjoyable visit. (A picture taken at this time shows Violet patting Rex II, the mascot goat.) "He is growing colder," she observed. "He has a toothache adroitly every night at 10—or thereabout. I don't care." Ford made no effort to conceal his flirtation with the wife of his commanding officer, who was helping him select poems for the volume _On Heaven and Poems Written on Active Service,_ published in April 1918. Because the title poem had been dedicated to her, Violet objected to the inclusion of some "cheap silly pieces," doubtless the poems written to Mrs. Jackson when Ford was at Cardiff.

One evening Violet challenged Ford to a "truth" game. When he was in the hospital, she asked, did he love Miss Ross or her? He evaded the question. Then she asked, "If you were very ill then and the doctor had said that someone should be sent for, would you have sent for me?"

"It depends," he replied thoughtfully, "one can't tell at supreme moments. I might have sent for you or Jane [Wells] or Nora [Haselden] or Brigit [Patmore] . . . it is interesting to speculate."

"I had asked for & got it," Violet said. "But how can one be devoted to a cruel jester like that!" Later Ford explained, "You see I _can not_ care for people with any constancy." She hated him at that moment and it gave her a surge of self-control.

But in the end, Violet bartered for affection: in exchange for a kiss, she gave Ford £18 to pay his mess bill and then fumed that her invitation to Redcar was primarily to pay his debts. Ford was a "_mental_ parasite," she exclaimed. "He will do all he can to get _mental_ ease—he exerted just as much emotional fluid to get me as was required & has now turned off the tap. Well, he can't hurt _me_ so much now—only my vanity & I must learn to let that go, or get others to satisfy it. Then age will come. So long as we don't lose each other but live on together inconvenienced but not solitary." Still, Ford was an expensive luxury. "I can't go near him but bang goes—much more than sixpence," she said.

That the realities of war—apart from air-raid annoyances—barely intruded on Violet's life irritated Ford, who flaunted his patriotism. Plucky May Sinclair was driving an ambulance in Belgium, and other women rolled bandages; even Henry James visited hospitals. But Violet was in Soho dining at Bellotti's with the wartime remnants of the South Lodge group. One evening at the restaurant Ezra Pound introduced her to Iris Barry, a cerebral poet of twenty-two, whom Pound had rescued from the industrial wasteland of Birmingham.* Iris recalled Violet chattering away "with a sublime disregard for practically everything, distraught golden hair, obviously a beauty of the Edwardian era," who disconcertingly asked too many sharp-tongued questions.

During visits to Rebecca West, isolated at Leigh-on-Sea (where frequent bombing raids terrified her), the two women sat amidst the teacups, complaining about their men. The "poetically scandalous" Rebecca was "as absorbed in H.G.'s noncontentment of her as I *was* in F's . . . of me. She runs on & sighs & groans & has got H.G. tight because of it," Violet noted. Wells had recently told Rebecca that she had turned what should "have been a love-adventure . . . into an utterly disagreeable story—which has become the basis for an entire hopelessness about anything yet to come."

A. G. Watts continued to escort Violet about town, to the Automobile Club and the Café Royal ("my gold hat & gold veil create sensation. I like it. . . . A W makes no love. I am glad. It *affermirs* me, though, to know"). One evening after an abstemious temperance dinner Violet returned early to South Lodge, downed a few whiskeys and wandered ghostlike around the house—through Ford's Vorticist study, into the sitting room with its Pre-Raphaelite

*Iris Barry would become Wyndham Lewis' mistress from 1918 to 1921 and the mother of two of his five illegitimate children. When she returned from the hospital with her second child, Lewis was having sex with Nancy Cunard in his studio and she had to wait outside, holding the baby, until he finished. Neither was a fit parent, and after Lewis deserted her, the daughter was adopted, happily, but the son spent six miserable years in an orphanage. They never knew Lewis was their father until they were adults, and they never saw him. In 1923 Iris Barry wrote the first serious film criticism in England for *The Spectator,* and in 1935 founded the film library at the Museum of Modern Art in New York.

memories. "Possessed with a sense of fellowship with those gone," she found herself saying, "(like Hamlet & his 'fellow in the cellarage')—'I'm only walking about on top a little bit longer & then.'— After all, one is dead in the best company. Is it real, being dead? If I died now—I should have no terrors. I am ill, but there is I believe no danger of a stroke—arteries all healthy. But I wonder? I don't love Ford—I am a queer side-bone of him." Violet pitched even morbid thoughts dramatically.

On July 20, 1917, Watts escorted her to a party, where she sullenly watched the dancing, which she no longer enjoyed at her age. "I felt as if A W & I were married & had got to _that_ stage of indifference & kind feeling," she wrote. "I want all the love I can get," she said of Watts, "and although he has the face of a gnome, he _is_ something." Ezra Pound arrived and introduced Violet to Stella Bowen, a twenty-four-year-old Australian painter enrolled at the Westminster School of Art.

Watching Stella and Watts dance, Violet admitted to jealousy. Yet why? she asked herself. "I could have him . . . I would if I liked him physically as well as F—whom I hate rather." As the party thinned out, Stella invited the group to continue dancing at her studio. Feeling old and petulant and admitting that she wanted to pique Watts, Violet declined. Everyone piled into a taxi and waved good-bye; she walked home and poured herself a solitary whiskey and soda. A week later she saw Stella again and met her roommate Phyllis Reid, an aspiring actress; the two newcomers joined the Bellotti's crowd and were invited to Selsey during Ford's next leave. "He asked for 'something young,'" Violet portentously told her diary.

Violet spent August in Redcar and initially found Ford more amorous, but still inadequate: "He permits himself to be passionate. He was not: only brutal & coarse." Violet was bored, bored, bored (a favorite word of her fictional alter ego Sylvia Tietjens). She wanted to be swept off her feet, carried in her lover's arms like a Pre-Raphaelite heroine along the sandy shore, her diaphanous nightdress billowing in the night breezes. Instead, she gave Ford the ice-maiden treatment. "Well, I'm tired & I'm going to my own bed!" she announced one evening. He kissed her and said, "All right, darling!"

But once alone in the big bed, Violet had second thoughts and asked him to sleep with her, peevishly telling him that Mrs. Powell, the colonel's wife with whom he had been flirting, had advised it. "Well-ell!" Ford replied. And it was all over in a minute—no satisfaction. "We did not quarrel or I cry, but it seemed *again* (it has happened twice before) as if the end of the world has come." "I didn't want you for *that*—just for quiet companionship," he told her. "That was no good to me!" Violet complained, and ordered him out of the room. There was nothing more to say.

Sexual frustration turned to rage, which she tried to contain, except in her diary, where she called Ford a "slug, or the cuttlefish that throws out venom to annoy & obscure the issue . . . He turns sleepy comatose & gets out of the discussion by saying that *I* am not serious." The rows always seemed worse on Saturday, the one night he can "afford to be passionate," Violet said, for there was no early parade on Sunday. At one point she "hit him & then took him to bed. His face is all scratched by me." Then Ford declared himself impotent.

The next morning, Ford came to Violet's room for morning tea. "Aren't you going to kiss me?" she demanded. "It depends on what terms we are on," Ford replied. Why, she said, "on the only terms that are possible for us—badly as we may interpret them." She said they "must be ineffectual lovers but lovers—or else part." Ford said she killed all feeling with her speeches, citing as an example: "I may as well sleep badly with you because you snore & take up the room as sleep badly because we are estranged."

Violet vowed to change: "It is absurd to break a butterfly—a tolerably substantial one—on the wheel & I shall learn not to." But the fights continued, and she decided to break her stay at Redcar with a trip to Durham, and was allowed to see Rosamond and her children. Perversely, she also visited her godfather, ninety-seven-year-old Canon Greenwell, who had disinherited her because of her relationship with Ford. It was a tribute to Violet's fighting spirit—and perhaps her need for money to placate Ford—that she subjected herself to this humiliation. Until the old verger, Wesley, shouted "Your goddaughter, Sir!" Greenwell did not recognize her; then his expression changed and he rasped, "Damn! I wish to have nothing to do with you. You are not his wife." He refused to look at Violet as she stood with her back to the roaring fire while Wesley gently argued with him. It was a final rebuke; she left quietly, maintaining her dignity and thinking: this "is the end of my mother's romance. That is how she & he broke—the reason why he was not my father!"

On her return to Redcar, nothing had changed. She refused Ford's request to live with her for "quiet companionship" only. "Ever since he told me that I 'made no effort to be attractive to him'—& that I ought 'to be more elusive' I am so awkward with him that *no* position is tenable." She wanted to return to South Lodge, but Ford begged her to stay: it would be an insult to him if she left.

Violet unpacked her bags for another week. One evening after entertaining all day, Ford wanted to sleep with her in "the literal sense 'cushy & agreeable'—I tried to arouse him: In vain. He said 'Do I worry you' & I said 'Well, rather.' The idea is that he is distressed at his impotence, which I don't believe in—how should I?—& I remind him. A fearful row—we still talk of parting, which is absurd as we neither of us mean to. 'The only way to end this quarrel,' Ford said, 'is for you to go quietly to your own bed & say no more about it in the morning.' " How could Ford ask such a silly thing of Violet? Morning recriminations were a favorite with her.

After a sleepless night mulling it over, Violet decided that money—again—was the issue. Although he said nothing specific, she knew that the regiment was talking about Ford's nonpayment of a £10 wager that the war would end by June 1917. When he accompanied her to Middlesbrough en route to London, she paid his 7s/6p fare; he had no money with him. At the station they parted friends. She held him for a moment and thought him "kinder than he has been for 5 weeks—in the train & *knew* it meant nothing but both our good will to part picturesquely." Back at South Lodge, Violet heard more about Ford's loss of face, and sent him a check made out to Grismond Phillips, the disgruntled winner. "A showerbath string pulled," she noted ruefully. But Ford denied the whole wager, even as Phillips cashed the check. Ford's mendacities on such occasions made him truly repugnant—"a malignant elf," Violet said.

In September, when London was frequently bombed, Violet celebrated her fifty-fifth birthday at an air-raid party. News reports predicted bombing over the city, so guests gathered in a top-floor kitchen with the windows wide open, watching and waiting. A man on a bicycle rode by ringing a bell for everyone to take cover, but the planes bypassed London that night, attacking the east and southeast coasts. At another party a few days later Violet made a grand entrance: "there will be a paragraph in the *Weekly Dispatch*—about my wearing Ford's tin helmet. I did. It *was* nice, no raid." Grace Crawford recalled that "Violet, with inspired sartorial genius, arrived wearing Ford's 'tin hat' firmly anchored to her head by a broad pink satin ribbon tied in a bow under her chin. Her entrance was hilariously greeted and she took this very well; but I have never been quite sure whether she wore the helmet as a joke or as a serious attempt at protection." Probably both.

Traveling during wartime was inconvenient, particularly to Selsey, but adverse conditions never stopped Violet from entertaining. On October 1 she sent Annie Child to Knap Cottage, laden with provisions. Three days later she arrived to find the water pipes broken, the kitchen a mess and three plumbers unable to make repairs in time for the arriving guests: Ford and Stella Bowen, Violet's new young friend. She wired Ford not to come and was so unnerved she hemorrhaged. Ford told her to have her doctor wire his commanding officer that she was dying so he could get a longer leave. She ignored this impudent suggestion.

On October 22 an angry Ford arrived on a forty-eight-hour pass, irritated because Violet had not provided the excuse for a longer absence. He greeted Stella Bowen curtly and after her hasty withdrawal embraced and kissed Violet. "I *could* not respond," she said. That night Ford said coldly, " 'Well, I'm going to bed'—(I had given him the big double bed & stayed in my own small bedroom). Then I made my first mistake. I exclaimed 'And is this all—you have come all this way for—after all this time!' No more amenity. Yet he makes me go to his bed & lie in his arms for a time. I hate it. He says he is *not* impotent, but he can't have *me*— 'I could have you through another woman.' That is simply to say he is tired of me. I realised it & had the sense not to say anything. I just went. He kissed me. I said 'Don't be rough because of my nose bleeding again' & he said with pride 'I *am* rough!' " The next day he explained: "I suppose I want adventure. If I could have another woman I might desire *you*. I was nice to you in the Brigit time." A not-so subtle admission that they had been lovers? Violet thought the whole conversation perverted.

The embattled lovers seldom strayed from discussing either sexual performance or lack of money. Ford said he could not "think of making love till he was no longer worried to death about money." He was overdrawn again, and Violet offered him a temporary guarantee. That evening in bed, a cold silence remained. He was only affectionate when he wanted money, Violet complained. When he told her to stop whining, she pummeled him with her fists. "He lies like a jelly fish instead of taking me by the wrists & stopping me," she angrily recorded. "It is contemptible. And *then* he said 'If you'll stop this disgusting exhibition & let me speak I'll tell you what I'll do. If I go away & have a quiet time for a couple of months I'll get leave at Xmas & then by that time I'll be able to make love to you.'" Violet stormed out of the room and slept in her own bed; she barely spoke to him when he left the next morning for London with Stella, who now knew quite a bit about her future lover's problems. She was intrigued.

Violet and Ford had moved from loneliness through lust and love to loathing. Now Violet wanted loyalty. After consulting with Byles and her old friend Marc-André Raffalovich, she decided that she needed—for society's sake—the illusion of a relationship. "It is the end of the world—that world at least," she wrote, "but I shall feel better, not in a false position, not sailing under the false flag." To her credit, she tried to keep her resolve, refusing to visit Ford at Redcar and declining his invitation to a New Year's Eve ball. "If he isn't ravenous for me, then there is no need to try & come together."

Violet felt only amusement when her escort Watts suddenly got married. She socialized with Stella Bowen (who was now corresponding with Ford) and worked on *The Last Ditch,* another clever novel, this time in the epistolary form, featuring letters written by, as one critic put it, "anaemic, selfish, thick-skinned" female aristocrats. Her nosebleeds persisted, until one day, she wrote, "the lump of mucous in my nose came away: I feel like a woman who has had a baby." The doctor told her she had no septum. "I will not tell Ford," she said. "It seems as if the author of all my *maux* was O.C. [Oswald Crawfurd]," a hint that the nosebleeds and this condition were caused by syphilis.

Although he denied her sexual satisfaction and tormented her emotionally, Ford was not ready to unyoke Violet, primarily because he was unsure of Stella Bowen's affections, and like most men was loath to sever a relationship without a new woman ready to comfort him. He sent Violet a love poem (originally written to Stella). For his birthday she sent him a box of preserved fruits, plants, tablecloths and some vests.

In January 1918, Ford came to South Lodge for a week, and Violet made a point of staying with his mother. It was a test to see if Ford was willing to accept hospitality without Violet's presence. He was. "He left perfectly pleased with himself," she said irritably, "annoyed with me & rather slavish. The test . . . had worked out. It makes him contemptible." Ford never forgave her, she said, for staying with Mrs. Hueffer while he was on leave. "That did it, finally," she wrote in her diary, adding a later note: "Did it? It was Stella . . . the new passion."

In May, Ford advised her not to visit Redcar. His commanding officer had questioned him about his loyalty to Germany and was assured that Ford had sworn allegiance to the king. Ford wrote Violet that such questions did not alter their marriage, which, after all, had taken place, he said, in France. But under the circumstances, Ford thought it best for Violet to stay at home. That he and Stella Bowen, whom he was now addressing in letters as "My dear darling," were getting to know each other was a better reason.

Meanwhile, Violet's family problems continued; no sooner was her mother's estate settled than she was embroiled in another sibling squabble. The executors of Margaret's will had given Oxford a collection of Alfred's paintings and drawings. To formalize this agreement, Venice's husband, Willie Benson, wrote to C. F. Bell, keeper of fine art at Oxford's Ashmolean Museum, specifying that the bequest was to be in the names of Venice and Silvia, only— even though Violet had ceded her one-third share.

At the same time, Violet told Bell that she would donate in the name of Mrs. Ford Madox Hueffer her personal collection of Alfred's early sketchbooks containing some drawings done when he was nine years old. An enthusiastic Bell replied that this addition would make "the collection more perfectly complete and greatly enhance its value and interest." He informed the Bensons of Violet's offer, only to be inundated with vitriolic letters from Willie Benson.

The genial Bell, who had known Violet as a child, read a litany of her misdeeds: the fake marriage, the libel case, even an accusation that she never appreciated her father's work. Bell asked the Bensons whether Violet was offering anything "of a type unrepresented in your own and Mrs. Fogg-Elliot's series of Mr. Hunt's sketches. For if you think that it does not then I think that I shall deprecate the gift. Firstly because I have no desire to involve myself and possibly the University in a quarrel with the veritable Mrs. Hueffer." Bell then wrote Violet suggesting that since her sisters' bequest would not be unpacked for some time, he would prefer that her gift be deferred for the time being.

An irate Benson answered Bell immediately. His sister-in-law, who "would sell anything saleable," was not likely to be "offering anything but discards," and he doubted that they "would be a *distinctive* addition" to their own gift. "In effect what she now proposes," Benson added, referring to Violet's questionable marital status, "is to obtain official recognition of a theory of life which certainly the university cannot condone and which would be utterly abhorrent to such a man as Mr. Hunt." Brought into the fray, Silvia said it would be "an insult to Papa" to catalogue the drawings as a gift from "Mrs. Hueffer."

But Violet saw no reason to postpone her donation. She defended her "knowledge gathered from my mother's recollections and the data preserved in diaries" as essential to arranging the entire collection. Bell dutifully reported this opinion to Benson, who shot back: if Violet had retained diaries, she was "in defiance of an order by the court to hand them over, and I shall have to take action." Moreover, how could Violet present herself as a paragon of accuracy, he challenged, when she had written that Tennyson's "Margaret," published in 1832, was addressed to her mother, who was born in 1831?*

Benson further accused Violet of selling Alfred's drawings "from the walls of her mother's room" and attacked her for "the

*Here Benson is correct, but this myth of Margaret and Tennyson has been taken as fact by Mizener and other biographers. Benson was referring to a series of poems addressed to women, including "Margaret." There is a Margaret in *Sea Dreams,* published in 1860. Although the Hunts knew Tennyson, there is scant evidence that Margaret ever inspired a poem. Ford compounds the error in the preface to the reprint of *Thornicroft's Model,* saying, "Tennyson had reputedly written a poem to her, 'O Rare Pale Margaret!' "—a reference to the second line of the 1832 poem.

infamous prefaces written by F. M. Hueffer" to *The Governess* and the reprint of *Thornicroft's Model*. "No, it is not her father's reputation," he concluded, "but her own she is out for—she wants to be recognized by reputable people in Oxford and to spite her sisters over the arrangement." In a separate letter, Venice asked, "Is it fair to him [her father], or to me, to associate with him a daughter who has disgraced him, & the name of a man whom he could never have tolerated in life? And for the sake of a most doubtful advantage to the University?"

It was true that Violet had sold some of Alfred's watercolors to finance Ford's German sojourn; it was also true that she needed public recognition of her status, and that she always enjoyed spiting her sisters, particularly Venice. But whether the saintly Alfred Hunt would have rejected Ford was pure speculation. By this time Bell realized that to accept Violet's offer was to invite trouble; he declined the bequest, explaining that "most if not all of the stages of her father's artistic development" were represented in her sisters' collection. Thus Oxford has 225 sketchbooks, more than 200 drawings and one oil painting given by Venice Benson and Silvia Fogg-Elliot, and not one donation from Mrs. Ford Madox Hueffer. Violet's collection of Alfred Hunt's early work was sold piecemeal over time.

Ford had long cherished the idea of abandoning literary life and moving to the country, where he would raise pigs, plant vegetables, even have a family, and never write another book. Stella, who had now fallen under his spell, seemed the ideal companion for such a rustic venture. Ford was, she said, "quite the most enthralling person" she had ever met, and his "tragic vulnerability was a walking temptation to any woman." Optimistic and undamaged by life's vicissitudes, she enthusiastically embraced his plans, realizing that he required a new woman to keep him young, to bolster his ego, to restore a belief in his manhood and talent. "I happened to be the 'new object' at a moment when Ford needed to be given a new lease of after-the-war life," she later observed, accurately noting that he needed "more reassurance than anyone I have ever met."

On Armistice Day, November 11, 1918, Ford wrote Stella, "Just a note to say I love you more than ever." Following his discharge on January 1, 1919, he moved into a single room in a small house at 20a Campden Hill Gardens, not far from South Lodge. He left the army a poor man, reduced to wearing his military overcoat as a dressing gown and sleeping on a cot. Over the decade of their relationship Violet had given him and his family thousands of pounds; he owed her, depending on how she calculated it, somewhere around £2,000.* Although Violet had possession of paintings by Madox Brown, and watercolors by George Boyce and Frederick Sandys, the demand for such art was yet to come: Brown's famous picture of his grandson as William Tell's son was appraised in 1926 at only £100.

Violet insisted Ford receive mail at South Lodge to maintain the appearance that he still lived there, but when letters arrived, she or Annie Child opened them (Ford cautioned Stella to write to him at the Authors' Club). Just as she had been when Crawfurd started up with Lita Browne, Violet was obsessed with Ford's whereabouts: it was vital that she know what he was doing. This prying so unnerved Ford that he accelerated his plans to escape to the country; he needed rest, to forget the war, to elude Violet and her spies. Stella rented a dilapidated, five-shilling-a-week cottage near Pulborough, Sussex. Built of red brick and red tiles, and tucked under a red sandstone cliff facing a meadow that sloped down to a stream, it was called, appropriately enough, Red Ford.

It needed a new roof, ceilings and support beams, and there was only one place in the kitchen where a person could stand to full height, but Ford convinced himself that it was perfect. At the end of May, Violet—audacious as always—asked Stella to make Ford visit her. "As far as I was concerned," Stella replied, "I would have no hand in keeping him from doing anything of this sort, that might make matters easier for you." Ford, however, did not agree, and told Stella to keep out of his affairs. "You begged me to protect him from the evil consequences of a public scandal," Stella contin-

---

*"It is possible that when I am dead," Violet worried in 1934, "that Ford's dependants could come down on my executors for family portraits, books, silver, furniture, etc. all ceded to me in lieu of debts. I have, or should have, documents to prove it all. First of all a letter from him stating that he owes me two thousand pounds. I wrote and said only fifteen hundred and left it at that. When he left me I sent him back several IOU's, some for five hundred pounds. Paid his debts in the Army, paid his children's school bills and their clothes and £3/3 a week alimony." While he was in the army, Violet said, Ford forged her name on two checks at Barclays. (Ford said she did the same. If true, one of them must have.)

ued. "But indeed this rests in your hands, rather than mine." Violet even wrote Stella's former roommate, Phyllis Reid, who refused to see her. "I regard this whole thing as inevitable," she answered.

When Ford started a new relationship, he was ecstatic, a burbling intellectual child. His letters to Stella at this time mimic the mood of those written to Violet in 1909 when he drooled over her loving phrases to the smirking delight of a taxi driver. A decade later he was still writing nonsense. He told Stella, who was isolated at the cottage, that he hoped she was fattening herself with cream and browning herself with sun, while he, the deranged lover, made grotesque faces at her letters and Stella—in his imagination—mocked him to stop taunting her.

On June 4, 1919, Ford changed his name to Ford Madox Ford. He wanted to avoid a third Mrs. Hueffer in his life (the village locals called Stella "Mrs. Ford") and to rid himself of a German name in postwar Britain. Violet was not amused. She wrote H. G. Wells, "So I am not now even the wife of his pen!" adding, "You see one's name seems to matter so much when one has to fight for it and been ruined for it."

Using Ethel Mayne as a go-between, Ford informed Violet that he was living with Stella but would make occasional visits to South Lodge if she wished (which she did). He warned Pinker not to give the Red Ford address "to anyone outside your office—I mean to *anyone whatever*." Violet turned up at Ford's club one day with a package containing his dress clothes and unsuccessfully tried to pry the Red Ford address from the secretary.

As a last resort Violet feigned illness, summoning Ford, who rushed to a bedside audience. After he left, Violet informed his mother: "I have been in bed since Friday—and I believe I have broken a small blood vessel. Now Ford has come up at another woman's petition . . . We have agreed to stay together without love." That was untrue, for Ford told Masterman: "I shan't appear again in London, except that, in order to spare Violet the mortification of the appearance of an official abandonment, I shall figure at her larger parties from time to time—as, for instance, Monday next [June 30]. I don't like doing it, but I take it to be a duty."

Admittedly Ford always had difficulty with the truth. To acknowledge that he was in love with another woman would tarnish the heroic image of himself as the last Pre-Raphaelite, the last Tory squire. So he told Masterman, his mother and others the familiar story that he had left South Lodge because Violet refused to break with Edward Heron Allen and the other Selsey intriguers who, Ford claimed, had denounced him to the police as a German agent. Ford told his mother in a heroic Fordian flourish: "I did stick to her during all the years when I knew perfectly well how she was calling me drunken & dirty & parasitic to everyone in London."

Red Ford was a far cry from South Lodge. It was literally falling down, but even with these perils there was a steady stream of guests, though none from the halcyon prewar days. Soon, however, the inconveniences outweighed the pioneer pleasures. When Pinker sold the movie rights to _Romance,_ Ford's collaboration with Joseph Conrad, Ford took his share plus some of Stella's inheritance and bought Coopers, a three-hundred-year-old cottage in the village of Bedham near Fittleworth, Sussex. They moved there in September 1920, and on November 20 their daughter, Esther Julia, was born in a London nursing home. Both were disappointed not to have a son.

Violet never accepted Ford's new life. After Ezra Pound visited Coopers that summer, Ford wrote him that Violet "had planted herself in the neighbourhood & runs about interrupting my workmen & generally making things lively. I fancy she had you followed by a detective when you came down & so got the address. But I may be wrong about that." Violet had driven down to the country with May Sinclair and spotted Ford feeding the pigs. She hired Mrs. R. Hunt, wife of the local carpenter, to send reports, which Mrs. Hunt did until December, when she informed Violet: "I am returning the Stamps as I am afraid of getting myself into trouble in sending you a wire." Violet continued to open Ford's mail and conjured up excuses to see him.

Although estranged from her relatives, Violet was shocked when her twenty-nine-year-old niece Rosamond, the mother of three young children, died on April 3, 1920, from measles complicated by pneumonia. Then her sister Silvia died only twenty days later, at the age of fifty-four, from pneumonia and heart failure.

Violet turned to Ford for advice about her second autobiographical novel. He answered through his solicitor; the advice of

Pinker and Stanley Paul, the publisher, concerning *Their Hearts* was "advantageous," he said, although he had not read the novel and would prefer not to. He suggested Violet consult H. G. Wells. Angered by her spying escapade at Bedham, Ford told her that he would not attend any South Lodge social event and would discuss business matters only in the presence of his attorney. At Violet's insistence, he signed over to her all his pictures and furnishings at South Lodge.

One person Violet had not yet pestered was Ford's wife, whom she now dropped in on unannounced. They had a long talk, and later Violet wrote Elsie (addressing her as Mrs. Hueffer) that she "felt a great peace" after their visit. "Your wonderful attitude towards F. made me feel how strong a virtue self-control is, and your dignity, when you spoke to me, brought out the best in me—who am still storm-tossed." Violet hinted that she planned to leave money to Ford's daughter Katharine (she did not) and asked Elsie to write to her "as Miss Violet Hunt, of course, now." Violet did not remain friendly: in 1922, she published a sketch based on this visit in the *Saturday Review*, ridiculing Elsie and Ford; afterward he vowed never to see her again—and this promise he apparently kept.

To her old friend Edgar Jepson, Violet sent a draft of a letter she had written Ford, one of the most pitiable letters she ever wrote and, fortunately, never sent. Unsure of the correct emphasis, she parenthetically noted alternative verb forms. "I have come to the conclusion at last that I want (I must see you) pretty often—for the present, at any rate. I don't suppose you will care to ask me (why I want this) for reasons. I just do (want this) and I have lived with you as your supposed wife for nine years [crossed out] eight years counting from the fifth of September 1911 till the twenty-ninth of March 1919. So you will (can surely) give me, say, an hour once a fortnight (if I ask for it). I have nothing (particular) to say to you—no points to make—I only want to see you and I will. Remember I have now, the way things have gone, nothing to manage, to save or to fear. I would take you to a matinee or any thing you liked. For parties I can't. I have been boycotted since I took you to the Anglo-French dinner."

Jepson called the draft "a truly hopeless production," the kind of thing that Elsie must have written frequently. "It sounds as if you just wanted to see him to have an unpleasant row with him; & human intercourse is not really conducted on those beastly lines," he wrote, not realizing that a row was exactly what Violet did want. Jepson offered a succinct revision: " 'I have come to the conclusion that I want to see you occasionally, or rather pretty often—say once a fortnight for an hour or two. I think that as I was your wife for eight years it is not very much to ask and you ought to try to manage it. If it is too much bother to come to Town, you might walk over and have lunch or tea with me.' " Jepson suggested she and Ford meet at an inn, in new surroundings, rather than at South Lodge.

Another adviser was R. A. (Rolfe Arnold) Scott-James, a successful journalist who in 1914 launched the *New Weekly,* a literary magazine that soon had all the bylines that once appeared in the *English Review.* Shortly after Stella and Ford set up housekeeping, Violet asked Scott-James to intervene on her behalf. Noting that Ford had stopped visiting and writing in the winter of 1920 and was not keeping his part of the bargain to appear as her husband, she complained: "If he was a gentleman he would pay me every consideration without prejudice to his faux ménage down there. I have never *asked* him to come back to *live* with me. I don't want it. But the tension lasting with aggravation for nearly five years, added to the tension of his 3½ years in the Army when I was alone is killing me and hurting my brain." She refused to deal with him through lawyers, demanding that he take her feelings into consideration. "If he doesn't uphold the validity of our union," Violet said truly, "I am but a cast-off mistress."

Wearily, Scott-James took up his pen and informed Ford that Violet was going through "more or less continuous mental suffering, which may not be very sensible but is a fact. She says she can't be at peace till she has 'something settled,' meaning, as she put it, an 'amicable agreement to live apart,' " to pay her a courtesy call at regular intervals and to give her advice about her books, an opportunity she missed most of all.

One way to escape Violet's net was to leave England, an idea that Ford and Stella found particularly appealing after two frigid winters at Coopers. At the end of 1922, flush with royalties from *The Marsden Case* (in which Marie Elizabeth's determination to change her name to Lady Mary echoes Violet's obsession to be known as Mrs. Hueffer), they went to live in a borrowed villa at Cap Ferrat. Ford began *Some Do Not . . .* , the first volume of *Parade's End,* and Stella returned to painting, exhibiting that year at the Salon d'Automne. They sold Coopers, hoping to buy a small house in Paris, but ultimately used the money to launch the *Transatlantic Review.* In the tradition of the *English Review,* it published the new generation's promising writers, including Joyce (*Finnegans Wake*), Hemingway (Ford and Stella are the Braddockses in *The Sun Also Rises*), Dos Passos and William Carlos Williams.

Settled in his new life, Ford wrote Violet a final message in January 1922 ("Ford's last letter to me," she scribbled on the envelope). In it, Ford tried to exit as a gentleman, but it was beyond him to make a clean break: he suggested that on his next visit to London they might meet at Edgar Jepson's. But they never did. Violet, of course, in her driven way kept track of Ford until his death in 1939. She pasted clippings of his book reviews into scrapbooks, and never tired of talking about how she had married the last Pre-Raphaelite. Ford and Violet's love affair and bogus marriage was certainly one of the saddest stories of Edwardian letters.*

---

*In 1924 Ford had a six-month affair in Paris with the novelist Jean Rhys; in 1927 he had an affair in New York with a wealthy American divorcée, Rene Wright (Elsie refused to divorce Ford to free him to marry Rene). Stella and Ford's affair ended by mutual agreement in 1928. Stella wanted to get on with her life. She supported herself by painting, spent a year in America, where she did portraits of Sinclair Lewis and his journalist wife Dorothy Thompson, and during World War II was an official painter for the Australian government. In 1930 Ford met the young Polish painter Janice Biala, with whom he spent the remaining nine years of his life.

16

Scoundrel Time

EVEN AFTER Ford abandoned Violet, the sexual tension that had defined her life did not cease. There would be evenings when flirting made her seem gay and attractive, when she felt youthful and bounteous, but no new man came forward to hold her hand in old age. Instead, she found satisfaction in writing her memoirs, in which she lambasted the selfishness of Ford (and all men) and her sisters (and most relatives), and in writing biographies that crucified the Pre-Raphaelite rogues Dante Gabriel Rossetti and Charles Augustus Howell. She had reveled in the company of men but now had to turn to women for comfort. And a disparate group they were: the asexual May Sinclair and Ethel Colburn Mayne, the sexually liberated Rebecca West and Radclyffe Hall, and the sexually repressed Dorothy Richardson.

During the prewar years when May Sinclair attended South Lodge parties, Violet and Ford's friends accepted her as a genial spinster who loved cats and wrote complex novels. Her 1919 novel *Mary Oliver* explored the subconscious in terms of sexual drives and dreams, presaging the novels of Virginia Woolf and contributing to the development of the modern novel.

But it took the curiously ordinary Dorothy Richardson, who had preceded Violet into H. G. Wells's bed, to perfect the stream-of-consciousness style. *Pilgrimage,* a twelve-volume history of her alter ego, Miriam, was twenty-five years in the writing. Ford called Richardson "the most abominably unknown contemporary writer," one of the great unread. Woolf admitted that she was the first novelist to create a method and a language for expressing the feminine consciousness.

The third of four daughters of a Berkshire tradesman who bankrupted his family with grandiose schemes, Dorothy worked as a teacher and governess before returning home at the age of twenty-two to care for her mentally ill mother. During a seaside holiday, while her mother napped one day, Dorothy escaped their claustrophobic rooming house for a walk along the pier. When she returned, her mother was lying on the floor in a pool of blood, her throat cut with a kitchen knife: a suicide. Following this tragedy Dorothy moved to London and became involved with Fabian socialism as preached by George Bernard Shaw. She also looked up an old school friend, Amy Catherine Robbins (called Jane), and her new husband, H. G. Wells, who became Dorothy's literary mentor and later seduced her. By the time Violet met Dorothy in 1907 at a Spade House garden party, Dorothy had known Wells for eleven years, although they had only recently become intimate.

Violet recorded no details about Wells as a lover, but Dorothy did. In *Pilgrimage* he appears as Hypo Wilson; in one scene they prepare for bed in a hotel room and Miriam (Dorothy) is disappointed by his nakedness: "The manly structure, the smooth, satiny sheen in place of her own velvety glow was interesting as partner and foil," she wrote, "but not desirable. It had no power to stir her as often she had been stirred by the sudden sight of him walking down a garden or entering a room. With the familiar clothes, something of his essential self seemed to have departed." Wells always loathed this portrayal.

After Dorothy suffered a miscarriage and the affair ended, she turned for comfort to a fellow lodger in her seedy London boarding house. Her soulmate was Alan Odle, a tubercular artist, fifteen years her junior. Odle was a painter of grotesques, with only some illustrations of Rabelais and *Candide* to his credit. Doctors had given him but a few years to live, so he spent his days walking and thinking and sometimes painting, and his nights drinking in West End pubs and the Café Royal. They married in 1917 (apparently increasing his longevity: for Odle lived to be sixty; Dorothy died nine years later at age eighty-four). They lived a peripatetic life, always short of money, moving back and forth from Cornwall to London, borrowing the cottages of friends, and all the time Dorothy was writing—under the most appalling conditions—her monumental inner life.

Another of Violet's friends was the novelist Mrs. C. A. "Sappho" Dawson Scott, who shared Violet's interest in the supernatural and the occult. Born in 1865 to alcoholic parents, Catherine Amy Dawson was reared by a large extended family and earned the nickname Sappho after publishing an epic poem about the poet not as a lesbian but as an independent artist. She married a doctor, Horace Scott, and settled down to dull domesticity, raising three children, writing novels, and eventually divorcing her philandering husband. Violet first met Sappho in the 1890s, and they saw each other again some fifteen years later when she and Ford attended a literary party at the Scotts' home on the outskirts of London.

Sappho recalled the "newly married" couple that evening: "Ford big, fair, flamboyant, she slender and lovely in a ripple of colour made by the opalescent sequins of a Paris frock. I think only the spirit of adventure could have made them come so far for so little." Violet's success as a hostess, wrote Sappho, was doubtless due to her quality of restlessness and an ability to live among relics of the past at South Lodge and still wear "her surroundings like a series of many-coloured veils." (When Sappho published these reminiscences in 1923, she identified Ford as Violet's husband and immediately had Elsie's solicitor after her.)

Because Sappho and Violet were both social and loved entertaining, Sappho suggested they inaugurate a writers' organization for people of repute, leaving out their dull wives and husbands and the tiresome guests who come only to stare at celebrities. In this matter-of-fact manner, PEN (for "poets, editors and novelists") was launched in 1921; it grew into a worldwide association, becoming an articulate voice supporting freedom of speech from the time of the World War II European dictatorships to the present day. The London center opened with considerable fanfare. John Galsworthy was president, and important writers from Thomas Hardy to Robert Graves joined PEN simply because Galsworthy was its leader.

As a PEN founder, Violet demanded the privileges of rank: she did not want to be seated next to anyone boring. And when she brought guests like Horace Liveright, the American publisher, or Herr Dr. Sester of the Tauchnitz Publishing Company, she asked Hermon Ould, who made the seating arrangements, to give "her an amusing man on the other side. I don't mind a woman so long as it isn't a *new* girl member or a dull old one!!" She asked that her name be printed on programs as Violet Hunt without any honorific. By this time, on her old stationery headed "From Mrs. Ford Madox Hueffer (Violet Hunt)," she had crossed out "Ford Madox."

At PEN's first dinner she arrived with Douglas Goldring, who never ceased to admire her spunk and social resilience. "Violet's passion for going about and meeting people was insatiable," he recalled, "and in the early twenties, when there was a positive mania for giving parties, she appeared to be having the time of her life. Most of her old friends—apart from those who had been shocked by the now forgotten 'scandal'—and many new ones were delighted to entertain her, while the traditional hospitality of South Lodge continued undiminished."

At parties, young men crowded around her. She could still be the center of attraction, "a regular 'honey-pot,' sparkling, flirtatious and lavishly endowed with sex appeal. 'The brave old dear!' murmured a man who had known her as long as I had," Goldring recalled, "as we watched her flash her still lovely eyes at the youth who was handing her a cocktail. 'She *does* keep her end up!' "

Still, Goldring observed that in spite of this surface gaiety, Violet's "tenacious, possessive and, to be frank, jealous nature, did not allow her to put Ford out of her mind and leave him alone." She never forgot Ford, but she never stopped trying to make new conquests, even in her sixties.

One evening after too much champagne at a PEN dinner, where she was seated with Galsworthy, May Sinclair and Austin Harrison, editor of the *English Review,* Violet gaily asked Harrison to publish an article on the "Art of Violet Hunt," and he pointed across the table to May. Even though they were close friends, Violet did not want May as a critic, which she promptly used as an excuse to write Ford. May "looks upon my rough-hewn work and its savage verities," she told him, "much as you do on 'Corpus Poeticum Boreale,' which I never could persuade you to read. I think somehow that she hits the mark when she describes my style as 'innocent.' I am mature now but it is all the style I shall ever have, isn't it?"*

---

*May Sinclair wrote an appreciative analysis of Violet's *oeuvre* in the *English Review* of February 1922. She praised the autobiographical novels, which she said present "the naked thoughts, the naked lives of people we have known," and the tales, noting, "I wish she would go on being grim and northern, I wish she would write more uncanny stories. The Tales and the novels are in different worlds."

Poor Ford probably sighed and tucked the letter under a pile of papers; it would not fall on him to tell Violet she would never approach May Sinclair or Dorothy Richardson as a writer, much less Rebecca West.

In fact, an article called "The Art of Violet Hunt" had already been written in the _Sunday Chronicle_ in 1919 by Rachel Ferguson, who debunked the frequent criticism of Violet's "cleverness" and sordid plots. "If her subject matter is 'in bad taste,' " she wrote, "it is only the bad taste of 'Mrs. Warren's Profession,' the Bible or any other classic." Her books are "those of an unhappy nature whose salvation is its brain. She writes to please nobody but her own fastidious self. . . . With all her chill brilliance and wit, you never receive the impression that Violet Hunt is either amused at her own conceits or anxious that you shall be."

On Violet's endurance, Ferguson was realistic: "I cannot guess if Violet will become a classic when she is dead. Probably not for she is seldom in advance of her time, as are Wells and Shaw, but just of her time, with the edge on. But of this I am sure: she is the first woman novelist of the day to those who appreciate intellect and style." Certainly this was one of Violet's more gratifying reviews.

It was true that Violet's writing had become more refined over time. _Their Hearts,_ published in 1921, completed her family tale of the Radmalls, ending with Mr. Radmall's (Alfred Hunt's) death. _The Times_ of London called the autobiographical novel a "peep into the world of women," offering "a clue to the meaning of that intent and serious look which we so often see upon the faces of women when they are engaged in purely feminine concerns; a look which is often incomprehensible to the male." Alec Waugh added his tribute, describing Violet's novels as "sad stories. Some of bitterness, some of resignation, always, though, of courage, always of unfulfillment, with, at the close, now and again a note of lonely triumph."

In the spring of 1922 Violet attended a luncheon with her old friend Somerset Maugham. The occasion was the publication of the anthology _Georgian Stories of 1922,_ which included her story "The Coach," the one chosen by Ford for the _English Review._ Maugham devoted his full attention to Violet, as if she were the one person in the room who mattered. She tried to return to book reviewing, and asked old friends for assignments. J. L. Garvin, at _The Observer,_ said he would like to have her review when he "sees something that suits your excellent hand. Do you remember the verve and sparkle of your dialogues in 'Black and White'? Can it be thirty years ago? I remember them like yesterday." It was not the reply she sought.

When Violet decided to write the account of her "flurried years" with Ford, she asked Goldring to help her clarify events between 1907 and 1919, for her memory was beginning its slow and steady decline, attributable as much to age as to syphilis. At the same time she had undertaken a biography of the sinister Charles Augustus Howell. As a child Violet had seen Howell at Burne-Jones's studio, had heard stories of his legendary wickedness, and was now friendly with his illegitimate daughter. Why Howell? Perhaps because she saw him as an easy target: a deceitful man. Perhaps she was intrigued by the connections to her own life: he was of Anglo-Portuguese origins (a reminder of Crawfurd), and had summered at Selsey (a reminder of happier times with Ford).

The flamboyant Charles Augustus Howell was a genial swindler who deceived a stellar group of artists and writers, including Ruskin, Swinburne, Rossetti, Madox Brown, Whistler, Burne-Jones, G. F. Watts and Frederick Sandys. Violet wanted to call the biography "The Foulest Soul That Lived" (a title taken from Swinburne), but T. J. Wise, the bibliographer, warned that although "a *good* title, & a telling one," it might "be regarded as malicious." But she set Howell aside for a few years and concentrated on getting even with Ford.

In 1925 Elsie and Violet, as Ford told Conrad, were "about to burst onto new and even more violent litigation as to their right to use my abandoned patronymic." The impetus for this was Violet's letter to the *Weekly Westminster,* which she signed Violet Hunt Hueffer. "May I point out to you an error in your list of Prize Poems," she wrote, "and the names of the volumes from which they are culled. My husband never published a book called *From Ireland and Other Poems* with Messrs. Duckworth. It ought to run *From Inland and Other Poems*. This book is now out of print."

Why did Violet want to replay the court scenes of 1913? Why did Elsie—who should have been weary of guarding the purity of her name—want to get into the fray again? Ethel Mayne wrote Ford in Paris about the proceedings, explaining that the reason "for this sudden outburst of malice is the fact of Violet's not having been covered for five years by your actual presence." Ethel (urged on, no doubt, by Violet) asked Ford to have the papers print something like "I married Miss Hunt in Germany in 1911, having previously assured her that I had fulfilled all necessary formalities."

Ford did not like to be reminded of unfinished business across the Channel. He told Ethel that, on approval of his solicitors, he might say that Violet was entitled to use his name or, at least, morally consider herself Mrs. Hueffer. Even so, "the two Mrs. Hueffers" were in the headlines again. Elsie testified to Violet's illicit use of her married name as she had twelve years earlier; but now Violet admitted as much, maintaining that this did not mean that Elsie was guilty of a matrimonial offense. Violet's solicitor, Storry Deans, again told the court that it was a mistake to say that his client had formed an unsanctioned association with the plaintiff's husband. "At the time she lived with him she believed she was married to him," Deans said, pointing out that the judge would know "the workings of the male heart, and how a woman who had an affection for a man would believe him and not make too close inquiries.

"But the man Hueffer," he said, "who, I understand, has now adopted another name and is living in another country, undoubtedly represented that he was a German, and had obtained a divorce in Germany, and purported to marry Miss Hunt. Miss Hunt now knows that she was not lawfully married to Mr. Hueffer. She had never intended to suggest, nor did she suggest, that Mrs. Hueffer was other than a virtuous woman in every sense." As an afterthought, Deans added that both women had been badly treated by Hueffer. The judge issued a perpetual injunction against Violet's using the Hueffer name. She ignored it.

That same year, _More Tales of the Uneasy_ was published. "The sinister brilliance of Violet Hunt's art has long been recognized by those who have a taste for the occult," trumpeted the dustjacket copy. "The three 'long-short' stories here published are as dramatic as those original _Tales of the Uneasy_ which won the praise of Henry James in 1911." Violet also wrote an insightful preface, her first (in years past Ford had written introductions for her mother's books _The Governess_ and _Thornicroft's Model,_ and for Violet's novel _Their_

Lives). She discussed the genre of the long short story and the gothic tale, which she described as tales told at twilight, "when plain folks went to bed at sundown in order to save fire and light . . . and contributed to each other's amusement, repeating what each had the luck or the intelligence to recollect."

Violet acknowledged her debt to Henry James as a master of the short story and singled out *The Turn of the Screw*, describing it as an anomaly, "a freak story which rose full-armed from the sub-liminal consciousness of—as the surface mind goes—a sexually un-sophisticated man," quite the opposite, certainly, of Violet's tales, which were the product of a sexually sophisticated woman. Violet had grown up with ghost stories and an interest in the supernatural. She fell asleep to stories of Crook Hall's kitchen ghost, and her imagination was stimulated by her mother's work on the translation of Grimm's *Household Tales* and the stories told her by the folklorist Andrew Lang as they sat before the fire at Tor Villa. "Ghosts in our homes were taken for granted," she said, "and permitted to cross the border-line till they became rather common."

Dedicated to Poppy Houston (Lady Lucy Byron), who had lent Violet money and her cottage near Sandgate, *More Tales of the Uneasy* has strong autobiographical shades, with most of the stories dramatizing the plight of a victimized woman. *The Corsican Sisters*, which *The Times* of London called the "best of the stories," tells of exploited women who are avenged through the ancient code of the vendetta; "the uneasy element is never absent, and the climax is quite horrible." The reviewer noted that the "secret of a book such as this one, is, of course, to take it in small doses, one tale at a time, and preferably read aloud."

The following year, with the publication of *The Flurried Years*, Violet reimagined the past and tried to lay the Ford years to rest; of course, she never could. Ford was in New York at the time and worried about his reputation. "If they are bad," he wrote Stella, referring to the memoirs, "they will make a pretty good stink and might make Boni's [his American publisher, Boni & Liveright] want to draw back." When he heard that Rebecca West (who had read the proofs) was championing Violet's right to kiss and tell, he complained to Stella that "Rebecca, naturally, has sailed in and made matters excruciatingly more disagreeable. She has told several people that V.H. is an admirable and martyrised saint and that every word of the book is true." Ford was not the only victim: there are unflattering portraits of her sisters, particularly Venice ("now a widow, alive & malevolent"), whom she calls Regan; Silvia is Goneril.

To tell this story, Violet must have turned to her diaries; it is clear from the existing, though sketchy, 1908 and 1909 typed diaries that she used them as a chronological guide to events. But what about 1910 through 1916? Were these lost or destroyed when South Lodge was bombed during World War II? Or did Violet dispose of them, because she had used the best material for publication or because she decided on some revisionist history? _The Flurried Years_ is often an angry—and suspect—chronicle since it was written out of Violet's sublime fury at Ford. Perhaps one day these diaries will also be found in a bookseller's warehouse, and then the facts may be compared with the emotions. There is no doubt, though, that Violet often let her feelings control the narrative.

All the literati knew Violet's memoirs focused on Ford; calling him Joseph Leopold did little to conceal his identity. Indeed, that name triggered more whispering about the couple who claimed to have been married in Germany. "The object of the book is not to give a detailed account of the facts," said _The Times_. "As Miss Hunt writes, 'There are some things no one tells, some things that no woman tells, some things I cannot tell, but people know them.' It is not easy, indeed, to say what is the object of the book. It is not an _apologia:_ but just in so far as it is obviously an outlet for the author's feelings, this, like any other intimately personal book, makes the reader feel uncomfortable."

The reviewer thought Violet should have taken the material and written a real novel of literary life, rather than a novelistic memoir: "The additional labour would have refined away a good deal of the soreness and the fretfulness that were inevitable in a book of this nature. We should have seen the heroine under the influence of other things than persecution. . . . The book's other claim upon attention cannot be illustrated by quotation. It is in its very spirit, as well as in its material that it exhibits—sometimes more clearly than its author knew—the incompatibility between ordinary life and what Miss Hunt calls genius, but is perhaps more safely called the temperament possessed by some novelists, dramatists and poets, whose reality is not the reality of the world in general."

In the American edition, called _I Have This to Say,_ Violet added an appendix with newspaper reports of the 1913 and 1925 court cases, and expanded some sections on personalities. *The New York Times* said her story "comes from too near to the heart of pain not to cause pangs in the hearts of those who have known its author intimately or have been protagonists in her ghastly struggle against litigious relatives and persecuting Grundys." Exactly the reaction Violet desired. And even with her capricious lack of objectivity, she does capture the atmosphere of literary London during the brief rise and fall of the *English Review,* composing an epitaph for the *mot juste,* the death of a literary style that did not survive the war to end all wars.

17

On Being Sylvia

As a novelist, Violet had difficulty creating believable male characters; strong women were her métier. Had she written a *roman à clef* about her years with Ford, she could have revealed so much more about their relationship. Ford with Violet was a far different person from Ford with Elsie or Ford with Stella. Ford put all his women into his novels, but Violet characters predominate; she is found in *A Call, The Portrait, Ladies Whose Bright Eyes, The New Humpty-Dumpty, Mr. Fleight, The Young Lovall, The Good Soldier, The Marsden Case* and, most dramatically, in *Parade's End,* as Sylvia, the manipulative wife of Christopher Tietjens, the disillusioned Fordian character, a man at odds with himself and his times, a virtuous and astute man who nonetheless has made a bad marriage.

Sylvia as Violet is obvious; there are the physical similarities: her auburn hair and slim figure, her wit and indifference to war, her place in London society, and many echoes of the affair with Ford. There is no doubt that in Violet's refusal to let Ford go she nourished his idea of Sylvia, a *belle dame sans merci,* alternately hating and loving her husband, but determined to ruin him. Tietjens' nobility, his flawlessness, drive Sylvia almost to madness, to nymphomania.

In the first volume, *Some Do Not . . . ,* the reader learns that Sylvia has left Christopher to live with another man; that she is four years older than her husband and more sophisticated; that they were wed (in a Paris hotel room!) after she thought (mistakenly) that she was pregnant by an earlier lover. As the story opens, Sylvia wants to return to married life, and Christopher is en route to Germany to see her. But first he stops off to play some golf at Rye, where he meets his future mistress, Valentine Wannop, who, although a suffragist like Violet, is clearly modeled on Stella Bowen.

Violet felt she had more in common with this sympathetically drawn heroine, whose mother is modeled on Margaret Hunt. "I have been asked several times last year how I liked being called Sylvia," she said. "I should rather sign myself Sylvia-Valentine, for my record suffrage experiences were those of Miss Valentine Wannop and, though my hair is not yellow nor my eyes blue, my nose has certainly more than a *soupçon* of the tilt of the nose of Dante."

Subsequent volumes explore Sylvia and Christopher's sham marriage; he (like Ford) escapes to the front lines of World War I, and she (like Violet) conspires to make his life miserable. Discharged after the armistice, Christopher (like Ford) returns to an impoverished life in London and sets up housekeeping with Valentine, who becomes pregnant. Unlike Violet, who focused solely on her emotional losses during the breakup, Sylvia eventually agrees to divorce Christopher so he can wed Valentine.

Contrary to what she told others, Violet could not have been overjoyed with the portrait of herself as Sylvia, particularly such passages as: "If you wanted something killed you'd go to Sylvia Tietjens in the sure faith that she would kill it: emotion, hope, ideal, kill it quick and sure. If you wanted something kept alive you'd go to Valentine: she'd find something to do for it." Violet wrote Ethel Mayne, "I do fancy, apart from her beauty, he has come to look on me as like that, and it seems rather terrible, but a matter of no importance really."

But Sylvia has style. She is a virago, yes, but an imposing personality, a memorable character: she is Violet, minus the warmheartedness that Rebecca West never failed to emphasize. And that portrait Violet liked. Ford called Sylvia a "thoroughbred," and Violet was certainly that. Never a stranger to herself she must have smiled at the accuracy of the characterization: Sylvia forever "talking: usually cleverly, with imbecility, with maddening inaccuracy, with wicked penetration, and clamouring to be contradicted"; Sylvia being bored, bored and again bored, and Sylvia having "the whole night in which luxuriously to torment the lump opposite her" (a scene right out of the 1917 diary at Redcar).

The Fordian character is flawless, for Tietjens is Ford's idealized self. Ford wanted to remold the embattled years with Violet into a happy memory, to show Christopher Tietjens accepting himself and living in the postwar world. At the same time Ford could romanticize his relationships, for he never fully comprehended why they failed to live up to his expectations; when things ended badly he was always hurt, bewildered, the intellectual baby crying for a new pacifier. It probably never occurred to Ford that he picked the wrong women: although he thought himself a feminist in his public actions, in private he wanted a slavish, quiet woman, an icon to worship; instead, he was attracted to women of talent and independence.

Sylvia is labeled a whore, but Tietjens' fidelity to his unfaithful wife is never questioned, a deviation from the Ford/Violet affair that should have made her furious: she had one lapse in the eight years of their "marriage," whereas Ford strayed at least three times. Tietjens refused to sleep with Valentine before he goes off to war because "we're the sort that . . . _do not!_" South Lodge is transformed into Groby; Tietjens supports Sylvia and her mother, a reverse of the reality. Ford's underscoring of Sylvia's promiscuity probably stemmed from his distaste for Violet's early affairs and the resultant stigma of venereal disease, of which he had recently learned.

In the real world, Elsie never gave him a divorce, and Violet said when he left that he "was no longer free like other men that if he found he couldn't bear to live with me, his only remedy before having led me into such an impasse was to cut his throat." Violet observed that Ford's characters in _Some Do Not . . ._ are "punished heavily for sexual offenses, and so I am being," adding that he was "simply born out of his time. I say he is and so said Stella once, 'a moral coward' who fears nothing so much as the dislocation of his mental attitude and being forced to see the world and men as others mostly see it. . . . Under the influence (of the) terror of being disturbed mentally he gets flabbergasted and ungrateful and like an animal bites the hand that fed him forgetting the informing and at least sheltered years he has to thank me for, and the romance of our wild marriage, which is after all, the only emotional incident

in his life and mine which will be remembered after we are dead."
On this prediction Violet was so right.

Throughout *Parade's End,* Ford detailed—often gleefully—
those aspects of his relationship with Violet that most angered him.
He recalls Violet's spying on him and Stella at their cottage; Sylvia
also hires a carpenter's wife as a spy. "For it is to be remembered
that one of the chief torments of the woman who has been abandoned by a man," he wrote, "is the sheer thirst of curiosity for
material details as to how that man subsequently lives. Sylvia Tietjens for a number of years had tormented her husband . . . been the
dominating influence. . . . Now, except for extraneous annoyances,
she was aware that she could no longer influence him either for evil
or for good."

Passionless, loyal to his own sense of himself as a gentleman,
Tietjens has an infuriating dignity that Sylvia seeks to destroy.
"If . . . you had once in our lives said to me: 'You whore! You
bitch! You killed my mother. May you rot in hell for it' . . . you
might have done something to bring us together," Sylvia cries,
echoing Violet's one-sided rows with Ford when she wanted some
combative reaction.

After *The Last Post,* the final volume of *Parade's End,* was published in 1928, Violet was no longer a fictional harridan but just
Violet Hueffer, fighting old age alone. She was on the Committee
of PEN (but was ousted that year in favor of a younger member);
she was a judge of the annual Fémina–Vie Heureuse Prize and
attended lectures at the Institut Français. She continued to amaze
friends by her agility. Sappho Dawson Scott recalled saying good-
bye to her one day on Oxford Street and watching her run across
the street to the tube station while the traffic was "rushing and
roaring along, like a river in flood; but she slipped quickly in and
out, her skirt lifted over young limbs, her slender shape appearing
and disappearing among the buses for all the world as if she were
only seventeen."

But Violet was tiresome; in fact, some saw her as a social
albatross. Rebecca West said she suffered from two handicaps: "She
had that strange quality that makes the born murderee. She was
also going out of her mind [a result of syphilis]. All the time that
I and my friends were learning to grow fond of her, Ophelia was
slowly taking over, and as we found her we lost her."

Goldring wrote that one could never be sure when Violet would unknowingly insult someone. At a party given by Alec Waugh, Violet was talking to Goldring and the writer Michael Arlen when she suddenly blurted out, "You know I used to see quite a lot of Michael Arlen, at one time, but he never comes to visit me now. He's really quite a nice young man—and extremely clever. I wonder why it is that his books are so *awful*." Arlen stared at her in amazement. Another time she told her hostess, Ethel Mannin, "You know, I so much enjoyed meeting Ethel Mannin. What charming manners she has! They say she was only educated at a public elementary school but, really, she might have been 'finished' in Paris."

Anthony West knew Violet as Rebecca's friend, "an eccentric old lady and a compulsive talker." He recalled her remark after the sinking of the British liner *Vestris* in 1928 off the Virginia coast: "Why don't they make those ocean liners travel in pairs—surely it would be so much safer if they did." When West became interested in art, Violet took him aside, confiding, "You must come to me for advice about art schools, I went to all the ones that matter." Violet, he said, would arrive to visit his mother at tea time and stay on and on—until two or three in the morning, "talking all the time."

Violet was thrilled to renew her friendship with Radclyffe Hall (now known as John), who had not seen her for some years. One day while Hall and her lover, Una Troubridge, were exercising their dogs in Hyde Park, they saw Violet, stopped to chat and asked her to dinner, an invitation Violet eagerly accepted, remaining past midnight to retell at length the Ford saga. Violet nominated Radclyffe Hall's novel *Adam's Breed* for the Prix Fémina of 1926. (The plot concerned a waiter who, disgusted with food, starves himself to death and finds God.) Inaugurated in 1904 by twenty-two contributors on a magazine called *Vie Heureuse,* the prize honored women laureates ignored by the new Académie Goncourt.

Hall's novel won, and Violet urged her not to neglect foreign-language editions, as many English authors did by asking for too much money. "Don't, for it really would be nice to see it in French dress," she wrote. "I want to see your new one [*Stephen,* later *The Well of Loneliness*]. I *believe* I shall like it better than A.B. You gave me an idea of it once." Two years later *The Well of Loneliness,* a transparent account of "John" and Una's life, was published to great controversy (the editor of the *Sunday Express* said, "I would rather give a healthy boy or a healthy girl a phial of prussic acid than this novel"). Violet and other writers supported Hall in her fight to block its suppression.

Around 1927 Violet began writing random notes on viaducts, railways, dikes, tube stations, horse buses, omnibuses, hackney cabs, hansoms, stagecoaches, steamboats, all manner of transportation, apparently to write about how people moved about London in different eras; but she never used the material, returning instead to her biography of Rossetti's wife, Lizzie Siddal. Like Rossetti, Lizzie wrote poetry and painted and was admired by Ruskin, who initially thought her talent superior to Rossetti's. Ruskin became Lizzie's patron, bought her drawings and financed trips abroad for her delicate health. As a model, she was Rossetti's artistic obsession— his Beatrice, his Guinevere—and inspired "The Blessed Damozel," one of the great verse sequences of English literature:

> The Blessed Damozel leaned out
> From the golden bar of heaven
> Her eyes were deeper than the depth
> Of waters stilled at even;
> She had three lilies in her hand,
> And the stars in her hair were seven.

Rossetti's talents as a painter and poet far exceeded his abilities to care for and love a woman. After a troubled ten-year courtship, he grudgingly married Lizzie in 1860, by which time she was addicted to laudanum (opium) and unable to bear living children. Rossetti, the British-born but consummate Latin personality, and Lizzie, the frail, pale wraith with dazzling green eyes and radiant golden-coppery hair, were temperamentally fated never to understand each other. After two years as a wife, Lizzie died of a drug overdose. A coroner's jury declared it accidental; Violet said it was suicide, maintaining that Lizzie, in despair over Rossetti's affair with another of his models, Fanny Cornforth, took her own life, leaving a note pinned to her nightgown, which Ford Madox Brown—eager to protect his friend's reputation—destroyed.

As a child, Violet had listened while her mother and the William Bell Scotts whispered about Lizzie's death and the suicide note.

Ford gave Violet the version he had overheard at his grandfather's house: that Swinburne and Lizzie were in love, and she killed herself because he did not care enough for her to quit drinking. Violet claimed the note said, "My life is so miserable that I wish for no more of it." At first, Helen Rossetti Angeli (Ford's cousin from his grandfather's second marriage) rejected Violet's theory. Later she admitted that Lizzie had left a note, but claimed that it only asked Gabriel to care for Harry, Lizzie's youngest, handicapped brother (which he would have done anyway). Although the existence of a note substantiates Violet's suicide theory, it still leaves the motivation a matter of conjecture.

Poor Lizzie was not even laid to rest in peace. Overcome by grief and remorse on the day of the funeral, Rossetti placed in the coffin a notebook containing the only copies of his unpublished poems, nestling it into the folds of her golden hair; she was buried in the family grave at that Victorian Valhalla, Highgate Cemetery, in North London. Seven years later, after Rossetti fell in love with William Morris' wife, Jane, he had second thoughts and wanted to exhume the coffin and recover the notebook—a gruesome chore undertaken by his factotum Charles Augustus Howell.

On an October night in 1869, Howell, along with the family solicitor and a doctor, watched by the light of a blazing bonfire, built to guard against infection, as two gravediggers unearthed Lizzie's coffin, which was buried next to Rossetti's father, Gabriele, a poet and medieval scholar. Howell plucked the gray calf-bound book from beneath Lizzie's hair (which he said was still golden and growing) and passed it to the doctor, who plunged it into disinfectant; then each leaf was separated and dried. When Rossetti received his poems, he was shocked: a worm had eaten a hole through the leaves of "Jenny," a poem written about a night spent with a prostitute. Thus ended one of the most ghoulish graveyard tales in all of literature.

Violet's loathing for Rossetti was not new. She had nurtured a hatred of him for years. "Dante Gabriel was a wicked man—half-man; half-devil," she wrote in 1891. "I have even heard Papa say that but my mother always said positively that she could have refused those eyes of his nothing. And yet once when in the darkness of the studio at Cheyne Walk he tried to kiss her, she flounced out,

by her own account and never went alone, without Papa again!'"
By the end of her life, Violet had become so confused that she came
to believe, as Ford scholar Thomas C. Moser points out, that she
had lived with and loved not Ford Madox Hueffer but Dante Gabriel Rossetti: Rossetti's mistreatment of Lizzie was the equivalent
of Ford's shabby conduct toward her.

Memories of bygone Pre-Raphaelite days comforted Violet and
she continued to publish magazine and newspaper articles about
this period. She wrote down her recollections of William Morris'
home, Kelmscott, for the *London Mercury;* published a five-part
series, "The Beginnings of the Pre-Raphaelites," in the *Saturday
Review;* and wrote an article on the women of the Pre-Raphaelite
movement for *Artwork,* as well as a charming essay on her father
for the *Old Water-Colour Society Annual* of 1925. Before her last
book, *The Wife of Rossetti,* was published in 1932, there was a ripple
of interest in her early novels. *The Bookman* called for reprints of
White Rose of Weary Leaf and *Sooner or Later,* citing her "strong
sense of courage" at a time when feminism was distraught.

The Wife of Rossetti was dedicated to T. J. Wise, who had
advised Violet on research problems. A widely respected book collector and bibliographer, Wise was also a forger, with a specialty
in nineteenth-century pamphlets and first editions of Shelley and
Browning (making sure they were placed in reputable libraries). He
mutilated more than two hundred books in the British Library,
ripping out pages to meld with other purloined pages, making new
books. He managed to elude detection until 1934. Violet corre-
sponded frequently with Wise to ask his advice, and when she was
rebuffed in her research complained that the Rossettis "have a peculiar enmity to me about Ford."

Violet was a painstaking researcher, visiting geographical locations, trying to authenticate small facts such as the difference
between "lunch" and "dinner" in the 1850s. One of her sources
was Lizzie Siddal's great-niece. But the biography—long on oral
history and atmosphere and short on documented facts—is an unreliable text for Rossetti scholars. At the time, though, critics found
it colorful, informed and slightly scandalous: it went through six
editions in America.

The New York Times Book Review called it "one of the most
expertly executed biographies of recent years. Miss Hunt has done

for Elizabeth Eleanor Siddal what 'The Barretts of Wimpole Street' did for Elizabeth Barrett or 'Ariel' did for Shelley." Virginia Woolf said how pleased she was that Violet's "wonderful heaps of information are now safe for the rest of time." Hilda Doolittle (H.D.) sent her congratulations from Switzerland, where she was staying with her lover Winifred Ellerman (known as Bryher). "How happy the book must make you! The style, the matter, the manner," H.D. gushed. Bryher added that it was "not simply the material—it is the magnificent way it is written."

All this praise renewed Violet's fighting spirit. She fantasized that respectability might yet be within reach. In her rose-colored daydreams, she envisioned Ford divorcing Elsie and marrying her; they would have a ceremony and be divorced immediately afterward, leaving her with the rightful married name not of Hueffer, this time, but of Ford. More realistically, she considered using her influence to be nominated for the title of "Dame," which automatically confers the status of a married woman. To achieve such an honorific, she set about being seen at the right places.

Like her father, Violet had a constant fear of poverty. There had never been enough money when her parents were alive or when Ford was at South Lodge; alone, Violet viewed each day's expenditures as a threat to her very existence. She refused to touch her investments, preferring to go into bank overdrafts, which eventually forced her to sell a painting or letter to cover the debt. In the thirties she decided to auction the most valuable picture she held of Ford's: his grandfather's portrait of him as William Tell's son. She offered it to Christie's, stipulating a £100 reserve, but the bidding stopped at £75 and the painting was returned.

Violet sought Wise's advice about selling typescripts of John Galsworthy's novel *The Country House* and short story "The Unfortunate," both corrected in the author's hand, leftovers from the *Review* days. Not wanting to bring attention to the fact that she was selling what could be construed as Ford's property, she thought these items, along with twenty-one Galsworthy letters, should be sold privately, even though they would bring less than at auction. Wise advised against a sale, warning that she risked getting her name used in "a manner unpleasant to yourself & you've had enough mud flung at you as it is."

Considering what Violet sold during her lifetime and what has been catalogued, she once owned literary materials that would be worth a fortune today. Of particular interest are the letters she received from D. H. Lawrence. "It's only the people who don't like to throw anything away who can hope to discover treasure-trove among their papers or leave them behind for other people to find," she wrote. "My tearing up of Lawrence's rather indecent letters to me when I was in the nursing home in Osnaburgh Terrace [in 1911] (filthy rather, complaining and sex-grovelling, not-re-me) was an act of business madness. Those others that I sold for hardly anything were fairly decent, but who has got them? The others were descriptions of his own physical states, sexual and rather grovelling and disgusting. I kept them for years, and then tore them up. I sold a good many *purer* ones to a man in Museum Street." She also told T. J. Wise, "I've got a signed copy of Lawrence's poems given to Ford *'who made me'* and 2 or three first Editions & all the letters of his *I didn't* burn. Some of them were so horrid."

After living in France for some years, Douglas Goldring and his Swedish second wife, Malin, returned to England in 1930. When Violet heard the news, she invited them to dine. England had changed, Goldring recalled, but South Lodge was preserved as in amber. Annie Child still opened the door. Proust, the cat, was as standoffish as ever. Violet talked nonstop, but her mind was confused. At one point during dinner, she turned to Malin and said, "I always think the Swedes are such *dull* people, so heavy and *stupid.* Don't you?" A minute later, after realizing her *faux pas,* she apologized. "I'm losing my wits. You'll never forgive me." Malin smiled and soothed the embarrassment; a friendship grew between the two women, and Goldring speculated that his wife was the last woman friend Violet made.

For the next six years, the Goldrings were frequent guests at South Lodge; he was the unofficial host, acting as butler and dispensing the drinks. Violet called him the "nice elder brother" she never had. Goldring enjoyed the role. "You & your home & surroundings mean so much to us," he wrote to her. "Dear Violet, this is really a love letter. And hang it all why shouldn't I send you one? I am hopelessly loyal, old friends, old associations mean more to me as every year slips by."

Soon the last vestige of South Lodge's halcyon days was gone: strong men arrived in green baize aprons to heave Ezra Pound's phallic head out of Violet's herbage. Pound had ordered Gaudier's bust of him dispatched to " 'appier climiks" in Rapallo, where it was erected on a plinth in the restaurant of the Albergo Majerna, where the Pounds frequently dined. "The Gaudier head was finally howked [*sic*] out of Violet's garden," Pound wrote a friend, "the worse only for a few lawn-mower scratches. It adorns the hotel dining-room on the sea level as the facchini didn't feel equal to hoisting it, and we weren't sure the structure of the terrace wd. hold it."

In the restaurant, the statue was something like an American Buddha to which in spirit all present bent the knee, one visitor recalled. Violet mourned its loss. Ezra's "sexual organ in extenso has been sent for at enormous cost," she told the writer Nina Hammett. "It has scared burglars away for long in my garden and given me an excuse to put a little hoarding in between the pillars so that the little boys should not jeer at me sitting beside it."*

In the thirties Ford visited London in an unsuccessful attempt to arrange an art exhibition for Janice Biala, his new mistress. Violet knew he was in town and lamented to Goldring, "I wish he'd come to see me. Why doesn't he? Won't she let him?" After reading *The Flurried Years,* Ford must have felt there was no point in pursuing the past.

Like many unhappy writers, Violet discovered the pleasures of sublimation, the distraction of projecting her disappointments onto a blank page. She picked up the folders with the Howell research and tried to settle her mind for the task. Prolonged concentration was difficult, and she worried constantly about the enormity of the project. She had written *The Wife of Rossetti* in Lady Lucy Byron's Sandgate cottage, and she pleaded with her friend to invite her for another visit. Her "magnum opus," as she called it, would be her

---

*From the restaurant, the head was moved to the terrace of Pound's rooftop apartment in Rapallo, where it gazed priapically seaward. In 1958, when Pound was released from a hospital into his wife's custody, the head followed him to Brunnenburg Castle, near the village of Tirolo in the Italian Alps. It was put in the garden, catching the rays of the setting sun. It was later sold to a private collector and for many years was on loan to the Tate Gallery in London.

last book, she said. "It is a biography—more fun to do, but more trouble, for one has to be accurate when one's hero is a descendant of Charles II and the Countess of Castlemaine."

Violet managed to put together a draft of some seven hundred pages, much of it rambling and disconnected. Nearly twenty years later when Helen Rossetti Angeli wrote Howell's story, she reviled Violet for humiliating not only her cousin, Ford, but her uncle, Garbriel. "Violet Hunt long cherished the scheme [of writing Howell's biography]," Angeli wrote, "and lurid results might have been expected from that pen and brain: but nothing materialized." When Violet asked Sir Edmund Gosse, who had been hoodwinked by Wise and his fake books, about the forger Howell, he replied that he had only a passing acquaintance with Howell, but knew him as "an arrant rascal, but on the principle that 'when the burglar is not occupied with burgling he may listen to the little brook agurgling,' he may have been kind to his aunts. . . . I should be sorry that anyone should white-wash his memory, for he was a cunning rogue."

The long-standing seeds of discord between the Rossetti family and Violet are evident in Angeli's rebuttal: "It is a pretty picture: Sir E.G. gallantly appealing to the authoress of *The Wife of Rossetti* not to sully her immaculate pen with the exploits of such a reprobate as Howell—the authoress who out-Howelled Howell in untruth, and fastened her malicious lies haphazard on one or another person (safely deceased) as the whim of fancy urged her."

Howell now joined Rossetti in Violet's tortured mind as the personification of all unfaithful, scheming men. Ford had been the first to tout the value of Howell's life, entertaining her with overheard tales of how he had explored sunken treasure ships and become a sheik of an Arab tribe. "The lady with whom Ford was at one time closely associated (with little benefit to either party)," Angeli noted, "was a different and more dangerous type of the romancer in biography. Violent Hunt*—who ought to have confined her talents to the writing of novels—was led by Ford

*Given Helen Angeli's dislike of Violet, this misspelling may be intentional; but it must have been a typo when it appeared in Violet's *The Times* of London obituary in 1942. The addition of that "n" made the image live on: one British respondent to a query about Violet wrote this author, "I noticed your letter concerning Violet Hunt (or Violent Hunt as I once saw it misprinted)."

Hueffer into the devious path of biography and 'reminiscences.' And, enlarging on his already fantastic raw material, with a background of special pleading and grievances, together with an irresistible bent for malice, she produced some really noxious work, which still holds its own with the ignorant. The psycho-analyst might trace in her black picture of D. G. Rossetti's treatment of his wife, the projection of a rooted grievance of her own against the man who did not see fit to devote the rest of his life to herself [meaning Ford]."

Who was this Howell? His antecedents are sketchy, but it is known that he was an adventurer of Anglo-Portuguese origins who shortly after arriving in London in the 1850s involved himself with the Pre-Raphaelites. He became John Ruskin's secretary and was taken up as a factotum by other artists, who later accused him of lying, stealing and forging paintings. In the lunatic days at 16 Cheyne Walk, Rossetti's Chelsea home after Lizzie's death, Howell, nicknamed "The Owl," was a controversial character indeed. Even his death was magnified by Wise and Violet into a Victorian scandal.

In her rough draft, Violet claimed that on the night of Howell's death, Oscar Wilde attended the Lyceum Theatre for a first night, saw Theodore Watts, Swinburne's friend, and asked, "What about your friend H: now? He's been found in the street outside a public house dying, with his throat cut and a ten shilling piece between his clenched teeth." This scene is followed by Violet's musings: "How had Oscar heard? It points to a Sadistic revenge. . . . Isn't there a Charlie Howell in the evidence of the Wilde case? There was a bordel in the Euston Road. I wonder if it was the one that C. F. Keary alluded to and which was swept away in 1900 or so. Rossetti and Swinburne and the rest of them used to frequent it. The Madame procured young and fresh girls."

It could only have been Wise who told Violet the apocryphal story of Howell's death, for the account is mentioned in the Swinburne Library Catalogue, printed by Wise for private circulation in 1925 (now at the British Library). Wise's version (without sources) claims that Howell was taken to the Home Hospital at Fitzroy Square, where he died; pneumonic phthisis, a disease he had suffered from at the time, was given as the cause of death—to avoid scandal. As far as Angeli was concerned, the sordid circumstances of Howell's death were a figment of Wise's imagination. Not seduced by the charm and chicanery of the "foulest soul that lived," Violet knew a good story when she heard it and would have sensationalized the circumstances of Howell's death had she completed the biography, but it was beyond her mental and physical powers to do so.

18

Leftover Life

URING THE COBWEB YEARS at South Lodge, Violet was obsessed with the remnants of her life. She wanted her diaries published, the Howell biography finished and her own story immortalized. Although Goldring said she saw few old friends after 1932, apart from him, and made few new ones, apart from his wife, the newly discovered diaries for these last years reveal a much fuller schedule, though not a dazzling one. As befits a woman who had been wooed and won by the notably creative, Violet wanted endless adoration.

But she expected too much. In her dotage, she had one asset: oft-told gossipy tales about eminent Victorians and elite Edwardians. Because she was witty and traded in scandal, her name appeared on many invitation lists—an interesting eccentric selected to fill out a party, welcomed when sober and not befuddled—and drinking *was* becoming a problem. Violet's former lovers Somerset Maugham and H. G. Wells never forgot her. In 1934 she toasted Wells and Moura Budberg's* symbolic marriage at the Quo Vadis restaurant in Soho, along with Max Beerbohm, Lady Emerald Cunard and Enid Bagnold.

Mostly, though, Violet entertained at home, cajoling for an

---

*Budberg was the widow of a Baltic nobleman who was shot by rebellious peasants on his Estonian estate. She had also been the mistress of Robert Bruce Lockhart, a British envoy to Moscow during the Bolshevik Revolution, and of Maxim Gorky.

evening those who, like herself, were at the tag end of life. South Lodge was no longer the place to be seen, no longer the literary hub. It was dreary and badly staffed. When Annie Child retired in 1936, she was replaced by Ann Owen, a young and sprightly Irish girl whose boyfriend hung around the kitchen interfering with Violet's urgent demands. With that change, traditional hospitality ended. Proust, that bully of a tomcat whom Violet had compared to Ford, was dead. "It is awful without a beast," she told her diary. "I loved that beast. He was my undeveloped idiot child."

For nine years, Violet had a paid companion-secretary, Irene Cochrane (Cochie), who answered letters, helped her with the Howell research, accompanied her to the theater and, on those evenings when other guests did not dine, appeared at South Lodge on command. The long-suffering Cochie was a convenient doormat for Violet's frustrated last years.

More and more Violet's cronelike appearance was matched by a bitchy attitude. She was as slim as ever, but thinness in a woman of seventy-four is not graceful. She looked like a scarecrow, angular, with long grasping fingers; deep wrinkles lined the once stunning eyes, and the vibrant voice had deepened to sounds from an empty cave. The powder grew thicker, the stories of Pre-Raphaelite lovers longer, the clothes more faded and frayed. She played to the last notes, the ghostly mistress of South Lodge. Her life was like a windowshade coming down at the slowest possible speed.

After one party, she "felt a skeleton at the feast: I cut no ice: no one pleased to see me. It is like being dead." She went to the Savoy Hotel to celebrate H. G. Wells's birthday and was seated with three others close to the high table where H.G. sat ("as near as the favourite can be to the Sultan!" she cracked), but she "felt so dead & dull . . . No one seemed *very* glad to see me." Sometimes she was alert, her old vivacious self, but at other times, as she put it, "I can't *sort* ideas or summon knowledge." Her doctor could do nothing about this "senile decay." In 1936 the faithful Dr. Cholmeley died, who had "loved me & died at my neglect."

At this irritable time of life, few lived up to Violet's expectations. She maintained a friendship with Eleanor Jackson (with whom Ford had flirted while in the army) and her husband, Percy, convincing herself that they could all share a love (or hatred) for Ford, but was disappointed when, after one evening together, they "hardly mentioned Ford. Dull—she is dull. But it's as well to knit up old ravellings & she is lonely & as I am." One evening when she dined with the Jacksons, she fell asleep after dinner ("They won't ask me again"). Another evening, at the Compton-Burnetts, she left her false teeth on the table ("This is the social end of me"). When the Graham Greenes visited South Lodge, there were dinner parties reminiscent of the old days. Greene found Violet "an interesting writer and perhaps an even more interesting woman," although at this time, he recalled, "she was apt to forget that not only had she invited one to dinner but also who one was."

"I can't bear to be alone in the evenings," Violet told Lady Lucy Byron. "Couldn't I come to Hampstead & see you in the dear old place and your room where you showed me how to use baby powder? I can't get Atkinson's Baby Powder any more and that was what you told me to use. Please write again and tell me I may go to see you? It would be such a pleasure. I went one day in the summer last & sat & had tea in the innyard of the Bull and Bush and looked up at Byron Cottage. If you don't answer this post sometime I shall think you are angry with me."

Violet lived in the present, caring little for the future of the world if it did not concern her, ignoring even the Nazi threat. What mattered was her afterlife. Ethel Mayne was reluctant to be her executor, and Dorothy Richardson refused the responsibility. "I can't think who could 'arrange' my material, my diaries & notes— rather priceless!" Violet mused. She told Ethel and Cochie one evening at dinner that she wanted her papers "published with the least amount of 'editing.' They are all right & I don't want anything toned except what is libelous. I want myself given quite raw and I shall be a poor and pretty figure." A wish granted.

At various times she wanted her papers left to Cambridge's Newnham College, to the London Library, to the British Library or to William Morris' Kelmscott House. She thought about consulting Lord Ponsonby, then the leading expert on English diaries, but never did. She kept all her papers, according to Goldring, in a locked room in the basement. "The effort required to make up her mind, and take appropriate action," said Goldring, "owing to the anaemia of the brain from which she suffered, was beyond her capacity." In her head, she daily changed literary executors, finally settling on Ethel Mayne, and Gerald Henderson, the librarian of St. Paul's Cathedral, as first alternate.

Her anger at her relatives never faded. Venice had been shut out long before, but still living were Katherine and Amerye, Silvia's children, as well as eight great-nieces. In 1937 Amerye visited South Lodge with a mission: she wanted her grandfather's paintings for the family. Violet noted that "she spoke plainly re my intentions of sending all AWH's to galleries." She had brought with her "3 spoiled watercolors," offering to sell them to Violet. "The carriage [trade] shops," she told her aunt, "would pay £2 10s or more." The meeting ended in a stalemate: "Neither of us wants to pay."

"Papa wouldn't want to be buried in mediocrity at Amerye's or Kathy's" was Violet's final verdict, although she did consider giving the paintings to the family for an annuity to ease her finances. She saw the galleries stacking the pictures in a damp cellar (as they had Turners). When her niece next came to tea, Violet "tried to do a sort of deal with Venice through Amerye—re pictures. No go. They want me to leave AWH's to them to stick in their measley little cottage homes in the Home Counties."

Violet may have given in on this request, for no Alfred Hunts were in the final South Lodge inventory, and Margaret Cooper Fogg, Amerye's daughter, says that the family owns many of them. Margaret has only a dim memory of South Lodge. When Violet first met the sixteen-year-old, she took one look at her great-niece and concluded that she had "all the insouciance of youth without the charm, the go without reason, the off-handedness that means a paucity of training instead of too much, the hardness without unselfishness and power of endurance that should go with it. She flings her legs about and indicates, I don't say, shows her private parts or the place where they ought to be, with callous, maybe nymphlike charm, but then modern nymphs have not brakes to get behind, but arm chairs so difficult to sit in decently." It was difficult for Violet to accept youth, particularly in women.

Ultimately, Violet pronounced Amerye and Katherine's progeny (never mentioning the late Rosamond's three children) as "unfit to possess or dispose of any article of *vertu* or association." She said Amerye would receive only the "ordinary furniture" of the drawing room, with all the fine pieces—Morris and Parisian—withheld. As it turned out, Violet left nothing to Silvia's descendants (Alfred Hunt's paintings now held by relations were acquired before Violet's death).

"This year the first bad year of my decadence," she wrote in

January 1938. "Not spry, not pretty, not up to snuff. Non productive. Hardly any friends, certainly no acquaintances . . . I'm a fox without the tail of good looks and quickness of intelligence. Bad-tempered, unresigned, unreceptive . . ." She complained constantly about others' hospitality: the cooking at Gwen and Harry Otter's house (Gwen had been a rival hostess during the pre–World War I years) was "null and dull"; dinner at Julie Soskice's (Ford's sister) new house was disappointing: "No wine! Nice house!" She stopped making diary entries after February 12, 1939.

The last time Goldring and his wife saw Violet was on a warm July evening in 1939. "Oh, my dears! How late you are! I was afraid you weren't coming. . . . I've been so lonely and wretched all day," Goldring recalled her saying. She stood at the "dark green door of South Lodge, a frail, witchlike figure, dressed in tattered chiffons, the assembled remains, no doubt, of some of her fluffiest frocks of bygone times."

Ford had died from uremia and heart failure the month before in Deauville, Normandy, and Goldring said Violet spoke of him "all passion spent, all bitterness forgotten." Only three people attended his funeral; a drunken gravedigger mistakenly buried him in the wrong plot, and he later had to be disinterred. A less than heroic finale for the last Pre-Raphaelite.

"You know, Douglas, you are the only one left who understands all this," Violet said, gesturing to the Pre-Raphaelite paintings around the house and "embarking on an _orgie_ [orgy] of reminiscence" of which Goldring could follow the threads only by long experience of the way her mind worked. "She would begin a sentence about what Matthew Arnold said to her when she was a girl of sixteen, digress to explain that Browning, when he became famous, 'only dined with duchesses,' and contented himself with leaving cards on her parents, add that she sold one of Browning's visiting cards to Mr. Wise for a guinea, and wind up with a reference to the recent divorce of someone young enough to be her grandson. Her habit of bridging half a century in a parenthesis was baffling to those who were not so used to it as I was."

During the late thirties Violet befriended a minor novelist, Norah Hoult (a "charming cat"), who frequently dined at South Lodge. Norah observed Violet at her witty best and her shoddy worst: a Miss Haversham character, her mind wandering, constantly repeating herself, bullying her servants and longing for a chance caller. After Violet's death, Hoult wrote it all down in *There Were No Windows,* a pathetic story detailing the tedious decline of Claire Temple, the last fictional heroine modeled on Violet. Goldring, Ethel Mayne, Cochie, the new cat, the servants; even the ghosts of Ford and other lovers are trotted out for a curtain call. It is an unpleasant, overwritten book, but allowing for novelistic hyperbole manages to capture the loneliness of the twilight years at South Lodge.

When England went to war, Violet was lethargic, out of touch with reality. To her, rationing meant no cream, and bombing meant World War I. During the Blitz, while Londoners huddled in tube stations (Tor Villa was destroyed in a 1941 raid), Violet's maid told Goldring her mistress imagined she was with her father in the Welsh mountains during a thunderstorm. It was against this background that Violet died at South Lodge at the age of seventy-nine on January 16, 1942. Pneumonia and senile dementia were given as the causes of death; her much-maligned niece Amerye was at her bedside.

The Times of London obituary noted that "certain types— especially of disagreeable worldly women—she drew with extreme skill, and she was seldom restrained by considerations of taste," adding, "Violent [*sic*] Hunt's path through life had not been easy, but she retained the affection of her friends, who knew that kindness of heart and feeling for the troubles of others lay behind her often acid speeches." Whoever wrote the notice singled out one of Violet's more endearing qualities.

More than most of her friends, Goldring knew how Violet hated the idea of being quickly forgotten. "There can be no doubt that, artist as she was," he said, "she realised to the full the literary value and dramatic possibilities of her innumerable imbroglios. She was a student of historical gossip, adored scandalous memoirs and devoted all her intelligence and imagination as a writer to the analysis of affairs of the heart."

When Goldring returned to South Lodge early in March, some weeks after Violet's death, the house had been "blitzed" and some of the front windows blown in. He helped Gerald Henderson, Violet's literary executor (Ethel Mayne, the first choice, had died the year before), sort out the books and papers, and on April 16, when the auctioneer disposed of South Lodge's possessions, many of the best items in the sale were originally Ford's property. "The house thus retained, to the last," Goldring said, "the impress of his personality, just as the owner retained to the last, her memories of him and her bruised affections." But nothing "could really have brought calm to her uneasy spirit except its final release," he said, referring to her venereal disease. "The poisons implanted in her by the emotional tragedy of her early youth made their torturing presence felt to the very end of her long life."

"For many years, Violet used to refer to the fact—if it _was_ a fact," Goldring recalled, "that she had a dose of poison, put away in a safe place, which she intended to take when existence became finally unbearable. She was not, however, the kind of woman of whom suicides are made: her hold on life, like her mother's, was far too tenacious. Sometimes, after 1937, I used to think it a pity, for her own sake, that she did not take the easy way out, but perhaps it was more fitting that her long, varied and tempestuous career should end, as it did, to the orchestral thunder of a dying age."

Violet left an estate valued at £8,665 (about $42,000). Henderson was specifically directed to edit and publish the diaries and letters, which he never did, apparently collecting only copyright fees. Annie Child and Irene Cochrane received annuities for life, with the residual estate divided equally among Dorothy Richardson, Grace Raine (a maternal cousin), Mary Martindale and Mabel Cole (a friend). Douglas Goldring inherited Violet's library, including French and English classical literature, volumes on the French Revolution, folklore, feminism, archaeology and sexual psychology (including the Marquis de Sade's _Justine_ and _Juliette_), a collection of French erotic novels, all the works of Colette, scandalous memoirs, volumes of the Newgate Calendar and accounts of murder trials.

Violet was cremated and her ashes placed in her parents' grave at Brookwood Cemetery. As she requested, the tombstone was inscribed "Violet, daughter of Alfred William Hunt." There is no record of any burial service. The cottage at Selsey survives, wedged in between a shopping mall and a Washeteria, abandoned and forlorn, recently for sale. The Greater London Council's blue plaque at South Lodge proclaims that Ford Madox Ford lived there, but does not mention Violet.

Her literary legacy was considerable. She published poetry from 1879 and seventeen novels from 1894, two collections of stories, her memoirs of the Ford years and the biography of Lizzie Siddal, in addition to six collaborations (two with Ford), two book translations, and countless critical articles and short stories that appeared in London newspapers and magazines. All her books are now out of print and difficult to locate in libraries.

Except for *Their Lives* and *Their Hearts* and one or two of the romantic novels, Violet's writing has not stood the test of time. Her characters are usually unsympathetic and forgettable; she wrote about the contemporary moment, but was a superficial social historian. Not a thinker or a stylist, Violet depended on plot and dialogue, eschewing imagery, symbolism and ambiguity. She broke no new ground—unlike Dorothy Richardson and May Sinclair—in the development of the modern novel, and she lacked the cerebral clarity of Rebecca West. But her two volumes of *Tales of the Uneasy* exhibit a different talent: these stories exude atmosphere, they stick in the mind, they move swiftly and effortlessly as a good short story should. They rank among the best of Victorian ghost stories and are still anthologized.

Violet had put most of her talent into living. It is a pity that the end should have been so sad, with no great love to mourn her, no final triumph, but she had had a long and often happy life, on her own terms. She was addicted to "irregular situations," and addicted to love. "Love seemed the only thing she cared about in this world," she wrote in one novel, "and she would go on caring about it, and it only, until her hair turned grey and her neck got thin and she ceased from sheer weight of years to be concerned about such things. Marriage for her would only be a mistake, for she would never in her life find a man that she could love, who would go on loving her, and care to live always at concert pitch, without at least some recuperative periods of inanity! [She] did not want periods of inanity!; she would call it being 'dull.' "

Violet desperately wanted to be happy. "I seemed to have drawn a blank . . . in happiness," she lamented. "No Rewards and Fairies for me, no hope of the romantic millennium of which I had dreamed, of sentimental and satisfactory adjustments of joy or, at least, amenity all round, that many indications had led me to hope."

Indeed, at the end of her life, alone and lonely at South Lodge,

Violet had forgotten the bygone days when she was the center of attention, when as a precocious teenager she intrigued Oscar Wilde, when she was scandalous and shocking. She is forever etched into literary history as Henry James's "Purple Patch," sweeping out of a first-class train carriage in an amethyst haze, ready to mesmerize the Master with naughty London tales, to be his "Improper Person of Babylon."

Violet traded on winsome ways and clever conversation, savoring her role as the splendid South Lodge hostess who introduced the voices of Ezra Pound, Wyndham Lewis and D. H. Lawrence into Edwardian London. She was a personality more than a writer, never fully comprehending—or appreciating—her influence on the writers who made love to her. In various novels, Maugham, Wells and Ford portrayed Violet as a paradigm for the strong-minded woman. Today she survives not only as an example of the "new woman" of the nineteenth century, but as a spunky forerunner of the twentieth-century feminist—a woman worth remembering.

Books by Violet Hunt (1862–1942)

The Great Poets Birthday Album (London: Eyre & Spottiswoode, 1892). Violet wrote the preface and notes on Shakespeare, Wordsworth, Milton, Scott, Burns, Byron and other poets.

Dialogues of the Day (London: Chapman & Hall, c. 1894). Edited by Oswald Crawfurd. Violet contributed four dialogues.

The Maiden's Progress (London: Osgood, McIlvaine & Co., 1894).

A Hard Woman (London: Chapman & Hall, 1895).

The Way of Marriage (London: Chapman & Hall, 1896).

Unkist, Unkind! (London: Chapman & Hall, 1897).

Stories and Play Stories (London: Chapman & Hall, 1897). Violet contributed three plays: "The Benefit of the Doubt," "Lost and Found" and "As You Were!"

The Human Interest (London: Methuen, 1899).

Affairs of the Heart (London: Freemantle, 1900).

The Memoirs of Jacques Casanova de Seingalt (London: Chapman & Hall, 1902). Violet Hunt and Agnes Farley translated this two-volume work. Violet wrote the introduction. The British Library's catalogue gives credit to the collaborators, although the title page does not carry their names. Alfred Hunt objected to his daughter's name being associated with such a reprobate. Violet also translated *The Heart of Ruby* by Berthe Tosti (London: Chapman & Hall, 1903).

The Celebrity at Home (London: Chapman & Hall, 1904).

Sooner or Later (London: Chapman & Hall, 1904). Dedicated to Henry James.

The Life Story of a Cat (London: A. & C. Black, 1905). Dedicated to Anne Child (the Hunts' longtime parlormaid), this animal biography was based on Violet's extensive knowledge of feline behavior. Written from the cat's point of view, it became a popular book for children; it was reprinted in 1910, 1914, 1923 and 1924.

The Workaday Woman (London: T. Werner Laurie, 1906).

White Rose of Weary Leaf (London: Heinemann, 1908). Dedicated to William Somerset Maugham.

The Wife of Altamont (London: Heinemann, 1910). Dedicated to Mary Martindale (Ford Madox Ford's sister-in-law and former mistress).

Tales of the Uneasy (London: Heinemann, 1911). Dedicated to R. B. Byles (business manager of *The Throne,* which folded after paying Elsie Hueffer libel damages).

The Doll (London: Stanley Paul, 1911). Dedicated to Mrs. Francis Hueffer (Ford's mother).

Golden String: A Day Book for Busy Men and Women (London: John Murray, 1912). Edited by Susan, Countess of Malmesbury and Violet Hunt.

Zeppelin Nights: A London Entertainment (London: Chatto & Windus, 1912). Written by Violet and Ford Madox Hueffer. Dedicated to Ford's mother.

The Governess (London: Chatto & Windus, 1912). By Mrs. Alfred Hunt and Violet Hunt. Preface by Ford Madox Hueffer. Dedicated to the memory of Alfred Hunt.

Thornicroft's Model (London: Chatto & Windus, 1912). Reprint of Margaret Hunt's first novel with a preface signed by Violet, who later said Ford wrote it.

The Desirable Alien (London: Chatto & Windus, 1913). Ford Madox Hueffer wrote the preface and two chapters. Dedicated to "Mrs. Oswald Crawfurd who led me into Germany" (the widowed Lita Browne, who supplanted Violet and married Crawfurd following his first wife's death).

The Celebrity's Daughter (London: Stanley Paul, 1913). Dedicated to "My Husband."

The House of Many Mirrors (London: Stanley Paul, 1915). Dedicated to Joseph Conrad.

Their Lives (London: Stanley Paul, 1916). Dedicated to Eleanor Jackson (Mrs. Percy Jackson), a love interest of Ford's.

Their Hearts (London: Stanley Paul, 1921). Dedicated to W. H. Hudson (close friend and author of *Green Mansions*).

The Last Ditch (London: Stanley Paul, 1918). Dedicated to Valerie Violet Marley, a friend.

The Tiger Skin (London: Heinemann, 1924). A story from *Tales of the Uneasy.*

More Tales of the Uneasy (London: Heinemann, 1925). Dedicated to Poppy Houston (Lady Lucy Byron, who lent Violet money and her cottage).

The Flurried Years (London: Hurst and Blackett, 1926). Published in the United States as *I Have This to Say: The Story of My Flurried Years* (New York: Boni & Liveright, 1926).

The Wife of Rossetti (London: John Lane, 1932). Published in the United States as *The Wife of Rossetti: Her Life and Death* (New York: E. P. Dutton, 1932). Dedicated to Thomas J. Wise (bookseller and antiquarian who helped Violet with her research).

For a discussion of Violet Hunt's novels and tales see Richard Aldington, "Violet Hunt," *The Egoist,* Jan. 1, 1914, pp. 17–18; May Sinclair, "The Novels of Violet Hunt," *English Review,* Feb. 12, 1922, pp. 106–118; Marie Secor, "Violet

Hunt, Novelist: A Reintroduction," *English Literature in Transition,* Vol. 19, 1976, pp. 25–34; Marie and Robert Secor, "Violet Hunt's *Tales of the Uneasy:* Ghost Stories of a Worldly Woman," *Women & Literature,* Vol. 6, Spring 1978, pp. 16–27; Robert and Marie Secor, "Lives and Hearts in Pre-Raphaelite England: The Autobiographical Novels of Violet Hunt," *Pre-Raphaelite Review,* Vol. 2, 1979, pp. 59–70.

Acknowledgments

Many people helped to make this book possible, and three in particular: my friends Alf and Berthe Wallis, to whom the book is dedicated, and whose Violet Hunt collection is described in the preface, and my daughter, Deborah Belford de Furia, who encouraged me to rescue Violet from oblivion.

My agent, Carol E. Rinzler, believed that I had a good story to tell and was endlessly enthusiastic; my editor at Simon and Schuster, Bob Bender, helped to mold and strengthen the manuscript, as did Professor Thomas C. Moser of Stanford University and my friend and colleague Zachary Sklar.

I am indebted to many librarians for their kind assistance in providing research material, in particular Donald Eddy, Lucy B. Burgess and Janet Carruthers at Cornell University's Olin Library; J. S. Mallam at the Durham County Library (England), Darlington Branch; Roger Norris at the Dean and Chapter Library, The College, Durham; D. J. Butler, county archivist, Durham County Council; Charles W. Mann at the Pattee Library, Pennsylvania State University; and Cathy Henderson of the Harry Ransom Humanities Research Center, the University of Texas at Austin.

For permission to inspect manuscripts, letters and paintings in their possession, I would like to thank the curators and directors of the Ashmolean Museum, Oxford University; the British (Library) Museum, London; Newnham College, Cambridge University; Princeton University Library; Huntington Library; University of Illinois Library at Urbana-Champaign; New York Public Library; University of Virginia Library; Beinecke Rare Book and Manuscript Library of Yale University; Whitby Literary and Philosophical Society; Friends of the Royal Society of Painters in Water-Colours; the Walker Art Gallery in Liverpool; and the Tate Gallery in London.

And I thank all holders of copyrighted material who generously granted permission to print extracts from unpublished papers. Janice Biala, Ford's final mistress and his literary executor, refused permission to quote from Ford's unpublished letters to Violet Hunt and others.

Much of the information about Violet Hunt's life is published here for the first time, from original research and material in the Wallis collection. I am indebted to Professors Robert Secor and Marie Secor, of Pennsylvania State University, who were the first to mine the Violet Hunt papers at Cornell University, publishing numerous articles in scholarly journals about Violet and her family. For Ford's life and work, I turned to Arthur Mizener's biography, *The Saddest Story,* and Thomas C. Moser's book, *The Life in the Fiction of Ford Madox Ford.*

I am grateful to many others who provided me with much useful information, either through correspondence or by interview: the late Anthony West, the late Michael Patmore, Oliver Soskice, Richard Thames, Graham Greene, Margaret Cooper Fogg, Julia Cowgill Howe and Lettice Strickland-Constable; and for many specific acts of kindness: Edward Naumburg, Jr., Georgina Hewitt, William Kutik, Miles Merwin and Mary Ellen Noonan.

Grants from the National Endowment for the Humanities and the Research Fund of the Graduate School of Journalism, Columbia University, financed my research trips.

Notes

The two main repositories of Violet Hunt material are the Olin Library, Cornell University, and the private collection of Alf and Berthe Wallis, London. The Wallis collection includes all (except one) of the existing handwritten diaries, which are identical six-and-three-quarter-by-eight-inch hard-bound notebooks with blue marbled endpapers, as well as typed versions of some diaries, with handwritten afterthoughts by Violet. There are also typed copies of much of her correspondence, with errors and dropped paragraphs (when compared to the originals), perhaps because a secretary helped in these transcriptions. To aid the reader I have corrected spelling and punctuation errors in typed manuscripts.

The following short titles are used in the notes:

Their Lives: Violet Hunt, _Their Lives,_ 2nd ed. (London: Stanley Paul, 1916).

The Flurried Years: Violet Hunt (London: Hurst & Blackett, 1926).

I Have This to Say: Violet Hunt (New York: Boni & Liveright, 1926).

Their Hearts: Violet Hunt (London: Stanley Paul, 1921; 3rd ed., 1926).

South Lodge: Douglas Goldring (London: Constable & Co., 1943).

Ludwig: Richard M. Ludwig, ed., _The Letters of Ford Madox Ford_ (Princeton, N.J.: Princeton University Press, 1965).

The Saddest Story: Arthur Mizener, _The Saddest Story: A Biography of Ford Madox Ford_ (New York: World Publishing Co., 1971).

Austin: Harry Ransom Humanities Research Center, University of Texas at Austin.

Berg: Henry W. and Albert A. Berg Collection, New York Public Library, Astor, Lenox and Tilden Foundations.

Cornell: Olin Library, Cornell University, Ithaca, New York.

Huntington: Henry E. Huntington Library, San Marino, California.

Pattee: Pattee Library, Pennsylvania State University, University Park, Pennsylvania.

Princeton: Princeton University Library, Edward Naumburg, Jr. Collection of Ford Madox Ford.

Stow Hill: The collection of Lord Stow Hill (grandson of Franz Hueffer and David Soskice), House of Lords, London.

University of Virginia: Henry James Collection, Clifton Waller Barrett Library, University of Virginia Library.

Wallis: private collection of Alf and Berthe Wallis.

PREFACE

12
"Does post-war woman": *The Flurried Years,* p. 80.
13
"the most possessed": Graham Greene, introduction to Volume 3 of *The Bodley Head Ford Madox Ford* (London, 1963), p. 6.

1. PREACHERS AND PAINTERS

18
"I have no": Douglas Pocock and Roy Gazzard, *Durham: Portrait of a Cathedral City* (Durham: City of Durham Trust and Department of Geography, University of Durham, 1983), pp. 25–43.
18
"persons of sound": Wallis, unpublished manuscript of James Raine's autobiography.
19
"It was weary": Fact sheet from the Dean and Chapter Library, The College, Durham.
19
"invented for interested": James Raine, *Saint Cuthbert* (Durham, 1828).
19
"no mere antiquarian": *Durham County Advertiser,* Dec. 10, 1858.
19
"reproof to vulgar": Ibid.
20
"a feature of": Cornell diaries, April 17, 1889.
20
"They talked about": Robert Secor, *John Ruskin and Alfred Hunt: New Letters and the Record of a Friendship* (Victoria, B.C.: University of Victoria, English Literary Studies, 1982), p. 26.
21
"I began . . . a": Cornell diaries, June 11, 1890.
21
"consummated the sacrifice": *Their Lives,* p. 108.
22
"Oxford is a": Wallis, Alfred Hunt to Maria Hunt, 1850.

22
"I hope Mama": Berg, Alfred Hunt to Andrew Hunt, Feb. 24, 1849.
22
"from obscurity to": Wallis, Alfred Hunt to Maria Hunt, 1857.
22
"It is the": Alfred Hunt, _Nineveh_ (Chiswick: C. Whittingham, 1851).
23
"It would have": Penelope Fitzgerald, _Edward Burne-Jones_ (London: Michael Joseph, 1975), p. 33.
23
"The first moment": Cornell, Alfred Hunt to Andrew Hunt, March 26, n.y.
23
"one is born": Cornell diaries, Sept. 30, 1890.
23
"insane dread of": Wallis, Alfred Hunt to Margaret Raine, Jan. 9, 1859.
23
"If I can": Wallis, Alfred Hunt to Margaret Raine, Oct. 15, 1859.
24
"I won't get": Wallis, Alfred Hunt to Margaret Raine, Dec. 9, 1859.
24
"To be an": Violet Hunt, preface to the reprint of Margaret Hunt's first novel, _Thornicroft's Model_ (London: Chatto & Windus, 1912), p. ix. (Violet later said that Ford Madox Ford wrote the preface.)
24
"the best landscape": Secor, _John Ruskin and Alfred Hunt,_ p. 14.
26
"I am willing": Wallis, Margaret Raine to Alfred Hunt, Jan. 6, 1861.
26
"hammer him into": Wallis, Margaret Raine to Alfred Hunt, Dec. 8, 1859.

2. Pre-Raphaelite Childhood

27
"the appreciation of": Wallis, William Greenwell to Margaret Raine, 1860.
27
"a very good": _Durham County Advertiser,_ Oct. 10, 1862, p. 5.
29
"the child what": Secor, _John Ruskin and Alfred Hunt,_ p. 29.
30
"My children's bread": _Their Lives,_ p. 157.
30
"Well gentlemen . . . we": Max Beerbohm, _Rossetti and His Circle,_ introduction by N. John Hall (New Haven: Yale University Press, 1987), p. 36.
30
"None of us": Secor, _John Ruskin and Alfred Hunt,_ p. 83.

31
"It was mamma's": *Their Lives,* p. 7.
31
"went her way": Ibid., p. 162.
33
"to get much": Robert Secor, "Robert Browning and the Hunts of South Kensington," *Browning Institute Studies,* Vol. 7 (New York: The Browning Institute
and the Graduate School and University Center CUNY, 1979), p. 117.
34
"I was in": Wallis, biographical sketch of Theophilus Marzials included in "The
Passion for Romance," described by Violet on the cover as "the adumbration of
a book which Bobby Ross (deceased) said I must write *and* publish. I haven't yet
but I hope I shall. It is the adumbration of my memoirs [covering her early years]."
Also written on the cover was "Tor Villa (For storing)," indicating that it was
started in the 1890s, before the Hunts moved to South Lodge. Violet added
material when it was typed in 1921, and continued to make changes up to 1936.
It was never published.
34
"I was drawn": Wallis, Violet Hunt, unpublished article, "Walks with Andrew
Lang," p. 1.
35
"I will not": Secor, *John Ruskin and Alfred Hunt,* p. 34.
35
"They had been": Violet Hunt, *The Outlook,* March 27, 1915, p. 406.
35
"lazy, hot-tempered": Ibid.
36
"I do not": Huntington, John Ruskin to Margaret Hunt, Jan. 26, 1872.
36
"He looked through": Wallis, "The Passion for Romance."
37
"It will be": Secor, *John Ruskin and Alfred Hunt,* p. 46.
37
"the center of": Ibid.
37
"He was *cruel*": Violet Hunt, "Ruskin as a Guide to Youth," *Westminster Gazette,*
Feb. 3, 1900, pp. 1–2; also, Cornell, "A Child's Memories of John Ruskin," draft
of *Gazette* article, p. 4.
38
"*temperament* which puzzles": Cornell, John Ruskin to Margaret Hunt, July 18,
1873.
38
"a cat that": *Their Lives,* p. 239.
38
"There is much": Cornell, John Ruskin to Alfred Hunt, July 19, 1873.
38
"not a child": Cornell, John Ruskin to Margaret Hunt, July 25, 1873.

38
"A great man": *Their Lives,* p. 45.
38
"Very curious to": Joan Evans and J. H. Whitehouse, *The Diaries of John Ruskin*
(London: Oxford University Press, 1958), Aug. 15, 1873.
39
"The cult of": Cornell, "A Child's Memories of John Ruskin," p. 11.
39
"If good fathers": Cornell, John Ruskin to Margaret Hunt, August 1873.
39
"I really think": Huntington, John Ruskin to Margaret Hunt, Feb. 24, 1875.

3. ADOLESCENT DREAMS

40
"Life is so": Cornell diaries, Nov. 13, 1890.
41
"good, quick, clever": *Their Lives,* p. 63.
41
"pretty, very distracting": Wallis, "The Passion for Romance."
41
"I feel as": Cornell, letters from Violet Hunt to Rose Cumberbatch, Sept. 1879.
41
"I would like": Cornell diaries, April 25, 1882.
41
"nasty, ugly, new-housed": Wallis diaries, May 23, 1876.
42
"*I could* draw": Cornell diaries, Nov. 20, 1890.
42
"The carefully shaded": *The Observer,* Dec. 2, 1931.
42
"She was gracefully": *Their Lives,* p. 111.
43
"a little in": Wallis and Cornell, "I Remember Oscar" and "My Oscar," versions
of unpublished stories.
43
"all the proposal": Ibid.
43
"as nearly as": *The Flurried Years,* p. 168.
43
"I believe that": Wallis diaries, July 30, 1891.
43
"the sweetest Violet": Oscar Wilde to Margaret Hunt, March 1, 1880, in Rupert
Hart-Davis, *The Letters of Oscar Wilde* (New York: Harcourt Brace & World,
1962), p. 64.

43
"would never give": *Their Lives,* p. 98.
43
"His full pouting": Ibid., p. 99.
44
"Out of Botticelli": Wallis diaries, Feb. 28, 1892; Cornell, autobiographical notes.
44
"a beautiful woman": Cornell diaries, July 28, 1884.
44
" 'naiveté' of a": Wallis diaries, April 17, 1893; Cornell, autobiographical notes.
44
"Do you know": Cornell, "My Oscar."
44
"Beautiful women like": Ibid.
44
"I hope that": Oscar Wilde to Margaret Hunt, March 1, 1880, in Hart-Davis, *The Letters of Oscar Wilde,* p. 64.
45
"I always enjoy": Ibid., May 20, 1880, p. 67.
45
"I hope she": Ibid., Aug. 25, 1880, p. 68.
45
"It is a": Ibid., Nov. 30, 1880, p. 73.
46
"Oh, Miss Violet": *The Flurried Years,* p. 13.
46
"Peacock feathers and": Wolf Von Eckardt, Sander L. Gilman and J. Edward Chamberlin, *Oscar Wilde's London* (New York: Doubleday, 1987), p. 6.
46
"Would you like": H. Montgomery Hyde, *Oscar Wilde* (New York: Farrar, Straus and Giroux, 1975), title page.
47
"I am not": Richard Ellmann, *Oscar Wilde* (New York: Alfred A. Knopf, 1988), p. 158.
47
"Lady Wilde sits": Cornell diaries, May 27, 1882.
47
"red-haired, with": Ibid., July 13.
47
"not prepossessing, short": Ibid.
47
"I am so": Ibid., April 28.
47
"every single partner": Ibid., June 16.
47
"the elevated language": Ibid., June 20.

_48_
"[He] obliges me": Ibid.
_48_
"There is something": Ibid., Aug. 16.
_48_
"Here in the": Wallis, "Walks with Andrew Lang," p. 2.
_49_
"most ill-tempered": Cornell diaries, Dec. 26, 1882.
_49_
"Do you know": Ibid., April 26, 1883.
_49_
"It is as": _The Times_ of London, Nov. 25, 1882.
_49_
"Papa got his": Cornell diaries, Nov. 22, 1882.
_50_
"His hair was": Wallis, "I Remember Oscar."

4. IRREGULAR SITUATIONS

_51_
"a human creature": Cornell, John Ruskin to Violet Hunt, June 4, 1879.
_51_
"queer sunbrowned face": _Their Lives,_ p. 193.
_52_
"There is a": A. L. Baldry, "George Henry Boughton, R.A.," _The Christmas Art Annual,_ December 1904, pp. 1–31.
_53_
"Lady Lindsay defied": Cornell diaries, April 29 and July 7, 1882.
_53_
"very hideous they": Ibid., Feb. 18–19, 1883.
_53_
"I did snub": Wallis, "The Passion for Romance."
_54_
"the sacredness of": Cornell diaries, May 16, 1907.
_54_
"still lives prettily": _H. G. Wells in Love,_ edited by G. P. Wells (Boston: Little, Brown, 1984), p. 63.
_54_
"a sort of": Cornell diaries, May 7, 1884.
_54_
"in autumn colors": Ibid., Nov. 6, 1884.
_54_
"Your letter was": Cornell, George Boughton to Violet Hunt, Sept. 1, 1886.
_54_
"came to say": Cornell diaries, Aug. 3, 1887.

55
"to wander about": *Their Lives,* p. 197.
55
"The loveliest thing": Wallis diaries, March 25, 1891.
56
"sent us all": Violet Hunt, "Alfred William Hunt, R.W.S.," *The Old Water-Colour Society Annual* (London, 1925), pp. 29–47.
56
"long nervous bird-like": Ibid.
56
"The attitude of": Ibid.
57
"He enjoyed it": Cornell diaries, Dec. 24, 1889.
57
"He fell in": Ibid., Aug. 24, 1887.
57
"a brutal place": Wallis, Euty Strickland to Violet Hunt, Jan. 30, 1888.
57
"It must have": Letter to author from Lettice Strickland-Constable, Feb. 18, 1987.
57
"your hair is": Wallis, Euty Strickland to Violet Hunt, Feb. 5, 1888.
58
"Are you very": Wallis, Euty Strickland to Violet Hunt, n.d.
58
"How funny it": Wallis, Euty Strickland to Violet Hunt, Sept. 1887.
58
"one thing darling": Ibid.
58
"No dear I": Wallis, Euty Strickland to Violet Hunt, Oct. 4, 1887.
59
"Yes, come down": Wallis, Euty Strickland to Violet Hunt, Feb. 5, 1888.
59
"I am *very*": Wallis, Euty Strickland to Violet Hunt, May 27, 1888, and 1888.
59
"a rather apathetic": Wallis diaries, Feb. 20, 1890.
59
"Euty is developing": Ibid., May 26, 1891.
59
"tall, with a": *Their Hearts,* 3rd ed., p. 31.
60
"progressive instinct, every": *Their Lives,* p. 123.
60
"extraordinary gift of": *The Times* of London, July 9, 1924, p. 16.
61
"pulpy, calm, white": *Their Lives,* p. 343.
61
"a useful discipline": Wallis diaries, Aug. 7, 1891.

_61_
"Visitors to the": obituary, _The Times_ of London, July 9, 1924, p. 16.
_62_
"_remembered yesterday_ and": Ibid., May 12, 1888.
_62_
"I thought he": Ibid., Sept. 7–14, 1888.
_62_
"I yielded, I": Ibid.
_63_
"armed with a": Ibid., Oct. 24.
_63_
"whole walk [was]": Ibid., Nov. 9.
_63_
"Like Oscar Wilde": Ibid., Nov. 20.
_63_
"H.D. came &": Ibid., Dec. 4.
_64_
"no asceticism, no": _Their Lives,_ p. 52.
_64_
"delicate, he did": Ibid., p. 53.
_64_
"not bad for": Cornell diaries, Aug. 4, 1889.
_65_
"not dangerously. I": Ibid., June 13, 1888.
_65_
"fat & pleasant": Ibid., Feb. 13 and April 9, 1889.
_65_
"mean featured and": Ibid., July 11.
_65_
"a woman made": Wallis diaries, July 11, 1891.
_65_
"extremely ugly, knows": Cornell diaries, May 11, 1884.
_66_
"He had not": _Their Lives,_ pp. 267–268.
_66_
"Why am I": Cornell diaries, Feb. 7, 1890.
_66_
"an example of": Ibid., Dec. 13 and 31, 1889.

5. THE RAKE'S PROGRESS

_69_
"little dramas were": Cornell diaries, Jan. 11, 1890.
_69_
"tumbles all his": Wallis diaries, Jan. 26, 1891.

69

"I know I": Ibid., Jan. 29, 1890.

69

"growing quiet and": Ibid., Jan. 22.

69

"Well, I *was*": Ibid., Feb. 6.

70

"neither shining as": Ibid., Dec. 7.

71

"tired & bored": Ibid., March 30.

71

"a hopeless passion": Ibid., March 31.

71

"I wish *I*": Ibid., April 27.

71

a "very goodlooking": Ibid., June 19 and 26.

71

"dark brown, with": *Their Hearts,* 3rd ed., p. 36.

73

"*passé* well-dressed": Wallis diaries, July 13, 1890.

73

"He is certainly": Ibid., July 23.

73

"tired of unreal": Ibid., July 19.

73

"It was all": Ibid., July 21.

73

"put dangerous sentiments": Ibid., July 22.

73

"half asleep state": Ibid., July 26.

73

"loved him for": Ibid.

74

"I must be": Ibid.

74

"He does not": Ibid., July 27.

75

"nice healthy stalwart": Ibid., July 30.

75

"masses of seafog": Bram Stoker, *Dracula* (New York: New American Library, 1965), p. 87.

75

"a pleasant change": Wallis diaries, Aug. 2, 1890.

75

"I think a": Ibid., Sept. 19.

76
"He has so": Ibid., Aug. 19.
76
"pounded away at": Ibid., Sept. 25.
76
"take him away": Ibid.
76
"long yellow legged": Ibid., Oct. 12.
76
"The history of": Ibid., Sept. 8.
76
"You've lost your": Ibid., Sept. 23.
76
"a woman cannot": Ibid.
77
"commonplace, tongue-tied": Ibid., Sept. 24.
77
"plenty of lovers": Ibid., Sept. 27.
77
"not looked into": Ibid., July 27.
77
"best blood in": Ibid., Oct. 27.
77
"living in the": Ibid., Dec. 6.
78
"out of sheer": Ibid., Dec. 10.
78
"no one shall": Ibid., Dec. 24.
78
"How I do": Ibid.
78
"No other man's": Ibid., Dec. 30.
78
"if it will": Ibid., Dec. 31.
78
"I've lost him": Ibid.
78
"Shall you come": Ibid., Jan. 1, 1891.
79
"He did not": Ibid., Jan. 16.
79
"I wish I": Ibid., Jan. 24.
79
"My spirits rose": Ibid., Jan. 27.
79
"I hate being": Ibid., Feb. 26.

80
"always that of": *The Athenaeum*, Feb. 6, 1909, p. 164.
81
"That is the": Wallis diaries, Jan. 28, 1891.
81
"I'd go anywhere": Ibid., Jan. 17.
81
"Miss Hunt, I": Ibid., Jan. 22.
82
"the dress was": Ibid.
82
"I got myself": Ibid., Feb. 12.
82
"Mamma knows I": Ibid., Feb. 10.
82
"a childish thinker": Ibid., Feb. 23.
82
"so curious of": Ibid., Feb. 28.
83
"Do you know": Ibid., March 27. Translated from French.
83
"I knew if": Ibid., May 14.
83
"I myself am": Ibid., April 26.
84
"only vegetate abroad": Ibid., March 29.
84
"It didn't look": Ibid., May 1.
84
"all the lovely": Ibid., Aug. 10.
84
"Old as he": Ibid., May 26.
84
"Ma Chérie, c'est": Ibid., Aug. 12.
84
"in a voice": Ibid.
85
"slept like a": Ibid., Aug. 13.

6. VICTORIAN SEX GAMES

86
"I have a": Wallis diaries, June 5, 1891.
87
"murmuring little moans": Ibid., May 6.

88
"Of course I": Ibid., May 9.
88
"weary heart away": Ibid., June 23.
88
"young not three": Ibid., June 30.
88
"the sensuous part": Ibid., July 6.
89
"I like champagne": Ibid., June 5.
89
"I am badly": Ibid.
89
"refreshment room and": Ibid., July 1.
89
"I have almost": Ibid., June 18.
89
"so wrongly in": Ibid., July 10.
90
"I have been": Ibid., July 28.
90
"Why can't people": Ibid., July 21.
91
"doesn't even pretend": Ibid., July 16.
91
"a very nice": Ibid., Dec. 17, 1893.
91
"very raw and": Ibid., Aug. 4, 1891.
91
"Of course he": Ibid., Aug. 26.
92
"one of us": Ibid., Aug. 3.
92
"He looked rather": Ibid., Aug. 18.
92
"Under these maddening": Ibid., Aug. 28.
93
"Lottie Collins has": Duncan Crow, *An Edwardian Woman* (London: Allen & Unwin, 1978), p. 118.
93
"Now he is": Wallis diaries, Aug. 20, 1891.
94
"You are really": Ibid., Sept. 4.
94
"It wasn't malice": Ibid., Sept. 8.
94
"Will she cry": Ibid.

94
"to assume the": Ibid., Nov. 20.
94
"I must stick": Ibid., Nov. 22.
94
"Darling, it would": Ibid., Sept. 17.
95
"out of simplicity": Ibid.
95
"in almost indecent": Ibid., Aug. 23–26, 1892.
95
"I see how": Ibid.
96
"a new relationship": Ibid.
96
"It is ridiculous": Ibid.
96
"Dearest, it is": Ibid., Aug. 21.
96
"that in the": Ibid., May 11, 1891.
96
"Darling, I don't": Ibid., July 14, 1892.
97
"a few months": Ibid., April 28.
97
"merit as a": Ibid., April 23.
97
"plain linen nightgown": Ibid., Sept. 8.
98
"spirit of George": Ibid.
98
"lost its savour": Ibid., Oct. 14.

7. Errant Daughter

99
"the four-wheeler": Violet Hunt, "Alfred William Hunt, R.W.S.," *The Old Water-Colour Society Annual* (London, 1925), pp. 29–47.
99
"It was like": Wallis diaries, July 1893.
100
"one of the": South Lodge, pp. 5–6.
100
"You don't know": Wallis diaries, March 1, 1893.

101
"only one of": Ibid., March 25.
101
"You know, darling": Ibid., Jan. 17, 1895.
101
"It is such": Ibid., Feb. 9.
102
"dreariest of plays": Ibid., Jan. 5.
102
"It was like": *I Have This to Say,* p. 41.
102
"an act of": Grant Richards, *Memories of a Misspent Youth* (London: William Heinemann, 1932), p. 212.
102
"much of her": Ibid., p. 211.
103
"I'm sure he": Violet Wyndham, *The Sphinx and Her Circle* (London: Andre Deutsch, 1963), p. 24.
103
"a good woman": Wallis diaries, Nov. 4, 1895.
103
"coarse and plain": Wyndham, *The Sphinx and Her Circle,* pp. 35–36.
104
"I understand the": Wallis diaries, Sept. 8, 1895.
104
"domino-gray—accordion": Ibid., Feb. 18, 1896.
104
"a very real": Cornell, Alfred Hunt to Margaret Hunt, June 30, 1895.
104
"Mind, I think": Cornell, Alfred Hunt to Margaret Hunt, July 14, 1895.
105
"wanted to make": *Their Hearts,* 3rd ed., p. 294.
106
"Mr. Hunt was": Cornell diaries, Oct. 5, 1907.
106
"My idea of": Wallis diaries, May 18, 1896.
107
"How often I": Ibid., July 17.
107
"the most selfish": Ibid., Sept. 24, 1897.
107
"What of it": Ibid., June 20.
107
"or does he": Ibid., June 21.
107
"I want to": Ibid., July 10.

108
"I cannot imagine": Ibid., Sept. 30.
108
"What is the": Ibid., Nov. 29.
108
"disappointed in it": Cornell, Oswald Crawfurd to Violet Hunt, Sept. 21 [1898?].
108
"You need not": Cornell, Oswald Crawfurd to Violet Hunt, Oct. 23 [1898?].
109
"I love you": Cornell, Oswald Crawfurd to Violet Hunt, Nov. 3, 1898.
109
"You have no": Cornell, Oswald Crawfurd to Violet Hunt, n.d. [1898?].
109
"Do you really": Ibid.
109
"nearly word for": Wallis diaries, Nov. 28, 1898.
109
"to remember how": Ibid.
109
"for the sake": Ibid., Dec. 31.
110
"wrong to say": Cornell, Alys Bosanquet to Violet Hunt, n.d. [1899?].
110
"letting him think": Ibid.
110
"I used to": *I Have This to Say,* p. 45.
110
"You will evidently": University of Virginia, Henry James to Violet Hunt, March 18, 1901.
111
"extremely struck with": University of Virginia, Henry James to Violet Hunt, April 1, 1900.
111
"who is all": *The Standard,* Oct. 11, 1899.
111
"This book will!": Wallis diaries, Dec. 26, 1899.
111
"I can't believe": Ibid., Dec. 31.

8. SOUTH LODGE

114
"of such a": *South Lodge,* p. 238.
115
"a charming, patient": *The Bookman,* August 1932, p. 346.

115
"just clever and": Cornell diaries, Jan. 4, 1907.
116
"Passion! Perfect passion!": _The Bookman,_ August 1932, p. 346.
116
"the great _piocheuse_": _South Lodge,_ p. 238.
116
"In spite of": Margaret Drabble, _Arnold Bennett_ (New York: Alfred A. Knopf, 1974), p. 132.
116
"He is a": Cornell, autobiographical notes.
116
"the painful tale": Ted Morgan, _Maugham_ (New York: Simon and Schuster, 1980), p. 95.
116
"one of the": Ibid.
117
"she could not": Ibid.
117
"combined a masculine": W. Somerset Maugham, _The Moon and Sixpence_ (London: Pan Books, 1974), pp. 14 and 20.
117
"explores undiscovered country": Morgan, _Maugham,_ p. 96.
118
"a story of": _The Outlook,_ Oct. 1, 1904.
118
"most important book": Mrs. Belloc Lowndes, _The Merry Wives of Westminster_ (London: Macmillan, 1946), p. 151.
118
"Be nice to": Cornell, H. G. Wells to Violet Hunt, Feb. 12, 1907.
118
"Do you know": Cornell, H. G. Wells to Violet Hunt, n.d. (By permission of A. P. Watt Ltd. on behalf of the literary executors of the estate of H. G. Wells.)
119
"transitory ecstatic physical": G. P. Wells, ed., _H. G. Wells in Love_ (Boston: Little, Brown, 1984), p. 57.
119
"never entered intimately": Ibid., p. 61.
119
"nervous lively wit": Ibid., p. 63.
119
"full just then": Ibid.
119
"mysteries of Soho": Ibid.
119
"to save trouble": Wallis diaries, Aug. 20, 1907.

120
"half sulky moonface": Ibid., Aug. 16.
120
"the pert, aristocratic": *The Flurried Years,* p. 43.
120
"I am really": Wallis diaries, March 3, 1893.
120
"hideous with spots": Ibid., Sept. 20, 1896.
121
"Perhaps hers aren't": Ibid., Aug. 24 and 27, 1907.
121
"it is hard": Austin, Violet Hunt to Marie Belloc Lowndes, n.d.
121
"with tears in": Cornell diaries, fragment dated Aug. 1936.
121
"remarkably honest and": *The Saddest Story,* p. 149.
122
"appalling injury . . . which": *South Lodge,* p. 80.
122
"to lighten just": Wallis diaries, June 13, 1907.
123
"a bit of": Ibid., Oct. 7.
123
"I do not": Cornell, Marguerite Radclyffe Hall to Violet Hunt, letter marked private, n.d. [1907?] (By permission of the copyright holder, the estate of Radclyffe Hall. All rights reserved.)
123
"coolness only because": Wallis diaries, May 13, 1907.
123
"I was tetchy": Ibid., July 30.
124
"had made a": Ibid., Aug. 6.
124
"I know exactly": Ibid., April 29.
124
"I suppose you": Cornell, Silvia Hunt Fogg-Elliot to Violet Hunt, Jan. 1907.
125
"No photograph does": University of Virginia, Henry James to Violet Hunt, Aug. 16, 1903.
125
"rather dumb . . . with": *South Lodge,* p. 46.
125
"having charge of": Cornell diaries, June 8, 1903.
125
"know too much": Cornell, Silvia Hunt Fogg-Elliot to Violet Hunt, n.d. [1907?].
126
"I mean a": Wallis diaries, Oct. 19, 1907.

126

"a veiled antagonism": Ibid., Oct. 26.

126

"She will marry": Cornell, Silvia Hunt Fogg-Elliot to Violet Hunt, Nov. 14, 1907.

126

"It was for": Wallis diaries, Oct. 21, 1907.

127

"If Mammy has": Wallis document, typed and dated statements from Violet, apparently drafted during battles with her sisters over the care of Margaret Hunt, April 13, 1901.

127

"a good deal": *Black and White,* Jan. 14, 1893.

127

"she had the": Wallis document, 1909.

127

"heroism and valour": University of Virginia, Henry James to Violet Hunt, Aug. 22, 1904.

127

"brave life [was]": University of Virginia, Henry James to Violet Hunt, Nov. 5, 1902.

128

"hideously tragic, and": H. Montgomery Hyde, *Henry James at Home* (New York: Farrar, Straus & Giroux, 1969), p. 51.

128

"James is developing": Ibid., p. 52.

128

"spasms & dashes": University of Virginia, Henry James to Violet Hunt, Aug. 28, 1907.

129

"but never more": Wallis diaries, Nov. 2, 1907.

129

"like a dog": Ibid., Nov. 3.

129

"We walked about": Ibid., Nov. 4.

130

"did not want": Ibid., Dec. 12.

130

"I did not": Cornell, diary fragment, Nov. 1936.

9. THE *ENGLISH REVIEW*

133

"It was most": Wallis diaries, May 30, 1907.

134

"Mrs. Pankhurst and": *The Flurried Years,* p. 14.

134

"Much has been": Ibid., p. 42.

134

"I am not": Cornell, G. K. Chesterton to Violet Hunt, April 30, 1909. (By permission of A. P. Watt Ltd. on behalf of the executors of the estate of Miss D. E. Collins.)

134

"erratic in policy": George Meredith to Violet Hunt, Feb. 26, 1908, Beinecke Rare Book and Manuscript Library, Yale University.

135

"No—I confess": University of Virginia, Henry James to Violet Hunt, April 6, 1909.

135

"Written a novel": Cornell diaries, April 1, 1888.

135

"one of the": *South Lodge,* p. 78, and Douglas Goldring, *Life Interests* (London: MacDonald, 1948), p. 171.

135

"were haphazard and": Wallis diaries, Dec. 3, 1907.

136

"Your style is": Ted Morgan, *Maugham* (New York: Simon and Schuster, 1980), p. 97.

136

"He looked very": Wallis diaries, April 25, 1907.

136

"suddenly jumped out": Ford Madox Ford, "Literary Portraits," *The Outlook,* Oct. 11, 1913, p. 497. This is the literary portrait Ford finally wrote on Violet, but when their relationship was troubled.

137

"As a rule": Ibid.

137

"the patient but": *The Saddest Story,* p. 5.

138

"whose genius you": Nicholas Delbanco, *Group Portraits* (New York: William Morrow, 1982), p. 93.

138

"I am a": Ford Madox Ford, *Portraits from Life* (New York: Houghton, 1937), p. 113.

138

"We can always": *The Saddest Story,* p. 23.

139

"unchanging affection and": Ibid., p. 46.

139

"To me this": David Garnett, *The Golden Echo* (London: Chatto & Windus, 1953), p. 64.

140
"absolute one-ness of": *The Saddest Story,* p. 48.
140
"beautiful in a": *The Flurried Years,* p. 50.
140
"for a number": See paraphrased document on page 314.
141
"seemed to be": *The Flurried Years,* p. 20.
141
"He who wants": Joseph Conrad, *Some Reminiscences,* 2nd ed. (London: Eveleigh Nash, 1912), p. 7.
141
"as simply as": *South Lodge,* p. 27.
142
"the money of": *The Flurried Years,* p. 27.
142
"No birth could": *South Lodge,* p. 23.
142
"his light-pitched": Ibid., p. 25.
142
"The only qualification": Ibid., p. 24.
143
"Oh hang! If": Ford Madox Ford to Arnold Bennett, *The Saddest Story,* p. 158.
143
"It proved to": *Sunday Telegraph,* May 7, 1972.
143
"that English literature": Frank Swinnerton, *Georgian Literary Scene* (New York: Farrar & Rinehart, 1934), p. 187.
144
"that little parvenu": *The Saddest Story,* p. 66.
144
"flabby lemon and": Wyndham Lewis, *Rude Assignment* (London: Hutchinson, 1950), p. 122.
144
"a grey-blue swallow-tail": *South Lodge,* p. 15.
144
"a woman at": *The Flurried Years,* p. 26.
145
"inherited and built": *South Lodge,* p. 106.
145
"At a certain": Violet Hunt, *Tales of the Uneasy* (London: Heinemann, 1911), p. 132.
146
"What wild turn": May Sinclair, "The Novels of Violet Hunt," *English Review,* February 1922, p. 117.

146
"pure irresponsible Gothic": Ford Madox Ford, "Literary Portraits," *The Outlook,*
Oct. 11, 1913, p. 497.
147
"the one entirely": Sinclair, "The Novels of Violet Hunt," *English Review,* February
1922, p. 110; also Cornell, May Sinclair to Violet Hunt, March 24, 1908.
147
"the unsexual novel": Cornell, Marc-André Raffalovitch to Violet Hunt,
1908.
147
"tapped a curious": Cornell, Thomas Hardy to Violet Hunt, n.d.
147
"In all my": Violet Hunt, *More Tales of the Uneasy* (London: Heinemann, 1925),
p. xiii.
147
"most susceptible when": *The Saddest Story,* p. 177.
147
"need to be": Frederick Karl, *Joseph Conrad: The Three Lives* (London: Faber &
Faber, 1979), p. 482.
147
"seems to have": Sondra J. Stang, ed., *The Ford Madox Ford Reader* (Manchester:
Carcanet Press, 1986), p. xvi.
148
"heard of the": *The Flurried Years,* p. 54.
148
"no good feeling": Cornell, Silvia Hunt Fogg-Elliot to Violet Hunt, Feb. 1909.
148
"many young writers": *The Athenaeum,* Feb. 6, 1909, p. 163.
148
"an astounding, romantic": *The Flurried Years,* p. 59.
148
"white like a": Ibid., p. 55.
148
"The depression was": Ibid.

10. BREWING SCANDAL

150
"Dined FMH": Cornell diaries, June 10, 1909.
150
"was ready to": *The Flurried Years,* p. 66.
150
"What happened last": Cornell, Violet Hunt to Ford Madox Ford, June 12, 1909.
150
"the tenderness that": *The Saddest Story,* p. 179.

150
"There's a witch": Cornell, Violet Hunt to Ford Madox Ford, June 12, 1909.
151
"My dear, all": *The Saddest Story,* p. 189.
151
"I ought to": Cornell, Violet Hunt to Ford Madox Ford, 1909.
151
"I've got your": Cornell, Violet Hunt to Ford Madox Ford, Aug. 5, 1909.
151
"I run for": Ibid.
152
"How is your": Cornell, Violet Hunt to Ford Madox Ford, Aug. 3, 1909.
152
"*How* they bore": *The Saddest Story,* p. 191.
152
"Mr. Hueffer was": Cornell, Silvia Hunt Fogg-Elliot to Violet Hunt, fragment, 1909.
153
"a baffling puzzle": Cornell, Silvia Hunt Fogg-Elliot to Violet Hunt, July 1909.
153
"little half hearted": Cornell, Violet Hunt to Ford Madox Ford, Aug. 3, 1909.
153
"I don't wonder": *The Saddest Story,* p. 191.
153
"reader, occasional sub-editor": *The Flurried Years,* p. 28.
153
"a babe unborn": Ibid., p. 45.
153
"These intellectual hosts": Wyndham Lewis, *Rude Assignment* (London: Hutchinson), p. 122.
153
"had few connections": Douglas Goldring, *Life Interests* (London: MacDonald, 1948), p. 172.
154
"were made to": *The Flurried Years,* p. 44.
154
"His fresh features": David Garnett, *The Golden Echo* (New York: Harcourt, Brace, 1954), p. 129.
154
"Like Cinderella's pumpkin": *The Flurried Years,* p. 49.
154
"The small locomotive": Ford Madox Ford, *Portraits from Life* (New York: Houghton, 1937), p. 70.
155
"That *was* a": *The Flurried Years,* p. 47.
155
"the sheaf of": Princeton, Violet Hunt to Catherine Carswell, n.d.

155
"Hooray, Fordie's discovered": Ford, *Portraits from Life,* p. 71.
155
"This isn't my": Ibid., p. 78.
155
"the kindest man": *The Saddest Story,* p. 171.
155
"very blue, his": *The Flurried Years,* p. 48.
156
"more conversant with": Ibid.
156
"the genial warmth": E. T. (Jessie Chambers), *D. H. Lawrence: A Personal Record,* 2nd ed. (New York: Barnes & Noble, 1965), pp. 172–175.
156
"men who *were*": *The Saddest Story,* p. 184.
156
"the brave and": *The Flurried Years,* p. 28.
157
"megalomaniac who imagines": *The Saddest Story,* p. 185.
157
In the Wallis collection there is an unsigned fifteen-page typed document that appears to be a statement prepared by Ford for his solicitor during the time of *The Throne* libel trial; it is dated S[outh] L[odge] May 27, 1913, but deals with the years 1906 to 1910. It is noteworthy for hitherto unknown aspects of Ford and Elsie's marriage, with some facts in conflict with Ford and Violet's accounts and Elsie's. In it Ford claims that when Elsie accompanied him to the United States in 1906, she went primarily to divorce him in that country but changed her mind, which seems farfetched. Also startling is his description of Elsie as violent. He cites an incident when Elsie asked whether she should use her maiden name or Hueffer to publish her book, probably the novel *Margaret Hever,* published in 1909. When Ford arrogantly told her to use his name because of its prestige, a fight ensued and she struck him with a wood log and threatened his life with a gun. Later, Elsie again sought a divorce and sent the children's governess, Edmée van der Noot, with the message. (Violet's version is that Ford gave Edmée a letter with grounds for divorce.) The document also states that Ford was surprised at Elsie's request, but said he would agree to consider the proposal if Elsie asked again, though he felt that the eventuality would never arise. In fact, he noted that he was considering suicide and told the story of the prussic acid incident, also related by Violet in *The Flurried Years.* The thrust of Ford's argument—obviously written to put him in a favorable light—was that Elsie had always wanted a divorce, that he was the unwilling party, and after agreeing to end the marriage he was surprised when she did not follow through, as he wanted to answer the charges she had brought against him for known and unknown vices. He does document the scheme to give Elsie grounds for divorce, but emphasizes his charitable nature, explaining that as a German in England he frequently assisted his countrymen—or -women—falsely adding that he gave Gertrud sufficient funds to set her up in business abroad. Violet paid to get rid of her.

157
"the plangent, languid": *The Flurried Years,* p. 63.
157
"lazy, Slav type": Ibid., p. 50.
157
"Stir up the": Cornell, n.d.
158
"Don't you see": *The Saddest Story,* p. 188.
158
"seduced a young": Ford Madox Ford, *Parade's End* (New York: Vintage Books, 1979), p. 629.
159
"Mr. Hueffer has": Cornell, Violet Hunt to Annie Child, Aug. 1909.
159
"intention—as it": *The Saddest Story,* p. 190.
159
"a fresh attack": *The Flurried Years,* p. 202.
159
"with any shadow": *The Saddest Story,* p. 192.
159
"Oh dear, if": Ibid., p. 191.
160
"The male must": *The Flurried Years,* p. 25.
160
"silver taps, lace": Ibid., p. 77.
160
"It's all up": Ibid., p. 80.
160
"We were so": Ibid., p. 78.
161
"And we walked": Ibid., p. 91.
161
"the greatest misfortune": Ibid., p. 80.
162
"going to get": Ibid., p. 87.
162
"I know how": *The Saddest Story,* p. 196.
162
"in the pleasing": University of Virginia, Henry James to Violet Hunt, March 16, 1909.
162
"I am more": University of Virginia, Henry James to Violet Hunt, Oct. 31, 1909.
163
"our projected occasion": University of Virginia, Henry James to Violet Hunt, Nov. 2, 1909.
163
"I am not": Cornell, Violet Hunt to Henry James, n.d.

164

"none of my": University of Virginia, Henry James to Violet Hunt, Nov. 5, 1909.

164

"I neither knew": Ibid.

164

"It was a": University of Virginia, Henry James to Violet Hunt, Feb. 14, 1910.

164

"I have always": Violet Hunt, *More Tales of the Uneasy* (London: Heinemann, 1925), p. xiii.

165

"wanted to see": Ibid., p. xv.

11. GERMAN OVERTURES

166

"SWARming with writers": Brita Lindberg-Seyersted, ed., *Pound/Ford: The Story of a Literary Friendship* (New York: New Directions, 1982), p. 5.

166

"would approach with": Peter Ackroyd, *Ezra Pound and His World* (London: Thames & Hudson, 1980), p. 21.

167

"like a demon": *The Flurried Years,* p. 108.

167

"crouched-for-action": Brigit Patmore, *My Friends When Young* (London: Heinemann, 1968), p. 55.

167

"very eccentric and": Grace Lovat Fraser, *In the Days of My Youth* (London: Cassell, 1970), p. 128.

168

" 'You know quite' ": Ibid., p. 141.

169

"impossible for any": Cornell, Silvia Hunt Fogg-Elliot to Violet Hunt, n.d. [c. 1909].

170

"Nothing you say": Cornell, Silvia Hunt Fogg-Elliot to Violet Hunt, Nov. 3, 1909.

170

"on singeing Mrs.": David Garnett, *The Golden Echo* (New York: Harcourt Brace, 1954), p. 183.

171

"With Ford, nothing": *South Lodge,* p. 95.

171

"to live always": *The Flurried Years,* p. 123.

171

"tremendous in a": Fraser, *In the Days of My Youth,* p. 146.

171
"decently, sensibly arranged": *The Flurried Years,* p. 116.
172
"of a villa": Ibid., 167.
172
"looked stupid, incompetent": Ibid., p. 133.
173
"taken to German": Violet Hunt, *The Desirable Alien: At Home in Germany,* with preface and two additional chapters by Ford Madox Hueffer (London: Chatto & Windus, 1913), p. 164.
173
"I suppose you": Ibid., p. 194.
173
"I was then": Ibid., pp. 281 and 287.
174
"the Protestant cup": Ibid., p. 157.
174
"containing sheets of": Ibid., pp. 158–160.
174
"aware of something": *The Saddest Story,* p. 203.
175
"sparrow, hopping off": *The Flurried Years,* p. 145.
175
"Elsie will, I": Wallis, Violet Hunt to Ford Madox Ford, [c. 1910–11].
176
"I'm nibbling chocolate": Wallis, Violet Hunt to Ford Madox Ford, n.d.
176
"I am afraid": Ibid.
176
"Can it be": Ibid.
177
"I can feel": Ibid.
177
"I wonder if": Ibid.
177
"as well as": *The Bookman,* May 1911, p. 176.
177
"grim study in": *The Athenaeum,* April 15, 1911.
177
"absolutely alone all": Wallis, Violet Hunt to Ford Madox Ford [c. 1910–11].
178
"about two hundred": *The Flurried Years,* p. 147.
178
"When I write": Ibid., p. 148.
178
"glad to spend": Wallis, Violet Hunt to Ford Madox Ford [c. 1910–11].

179
"We are very": Stow Hill, Violet Hunt to Catherine Hueffer, n.d.
179
"the quietest place": *The Saddest Story,* p. 209.
179
"the snow hung": *The Flurried Years,* p. 154.
179
"cold, patient man": Ibid., p. 155.
179
"is every chance": Ibid., p. 165.
180
"Could you leave": Wallis, Violet Hunt to Ford Madox Ford, April 1911.
180
"It will be": *The Flurried Years,* p. 172.
180
"little tables bearing": Ibid., p. 173.
180
"their minds properly": Ibid., p. 177.
180
"Surely sky-larking": Ibid., p. 179.
180
"That set the": Ibid., p. 180.
181
"Isn't it jolly": Ibid., p. 182.
181
"It seemed to": Ibid., p. 185.
181
"I would rather": *The Saddest Story,* p. 216.
181
"I believe the": Stow Hill, Violet Hunt to Catherine Hueffer, n.d., from Fort-Mahon.
182
"both of us": *The Flurried Years,* p. 198.

12. MARRIAGE MIRAGE

184
"alleged to be": Cornell, "The Novelist's Two Wives," *London Opinion,* Oct. 14, 1911.
184
"Hang it all": *South Lodge,* p. 97.
185
"supposed wife for": Princeton, Violet Hunt to Edgar Jepson, n.d. [1920].
185
"never did become": *I Have This to Say,* p. vi.

_185_
"a final statement": _South Lodge,_ p. 129.
_185_
"Well, then, it": Author's telephone conversation with Janice Biala, Paris, April 3, 1987.
_186_
"The way to": _The Flurried Years,_ p. 202.
_186_
"She knew all": Ibid., p. 203.
_186_
"Do you know": Harry T. Moore, ed., _The Collected Letters of D. H. Lawrence,_ Vol. 1 (New York: Viking Press, 1962), p. 98.
_187_
"from the seventies": Mrs. Alfred Hunt and Violet Hunt, preface by Ford Madox Hueffer, _The Governess_ (London: Chatto & Windus, 1912), p. x.
_188_
"All through the": _The Flurried Years,_ p. 208.
_188_
"that nice new": Ibid., p. 211.
_189_
"a super-heated vorticist": Harold B. Segel, _Turn-of-the-Century Cabaret_ (New York: Columbia University Press, 1987), p. xxvi.
_189_
"I do not": Ford Madox Ford, _The Marsden Case_ (London: Duckworth, 1923), descriptions of the Cabaret Theatre Club and the shadow play staged by Ford are on pp. 38–44 and 88–97.
_189_
"Bismarckian images, severings": _I Have This to Say,_ p. 267.
_189_
"hideously but relevantly": Segel, _Turn-of-the-Century Cabaret,_ p. xxvii.
_190_
"buzz of hair": _I Have This to Say,_ p. 212.
_191_
"uncommon beauty, her": Brigit Patmore, _My Friends When Young,_ Derek Patmore, ed. (London: Heinemann, 1968), p. 50.
_191_
"very beautiful, with": _I Have This to Say,_ p. 217.
_191_
"people as if": Patmore, _My Friends When Young,_ p. 52.
_191_
"The young man": Ibid., p. 58.
_192_
"I confess I": _The Flurried Years,_ p. 217.
_192_
"You say you": Ibid., p. 216.
_193_
"My Poem turned": Ibid., pp. 216–219.

193
"a man who": *The Saddest Story,* p. 226.
193
"a whole column": *The Flurried Years,* p. 214.
193
"deals with aristocrats": *The Freewoman,* Sept. 26, 1912, p. 366.
194
"country-girlish straw": *The Flurried Years,* p. 214.
194
"stout, gangling, albinoish": Victoria Glendinning, *Rebecca West* (London: Weidenfeld and Nicolson, 1987), p. 38.
194
"a little ill": *The Flurried Years,* p. 219.
194
"My mother had": Ibid., p. 220.
195
"heads averted . . . the": Ibid., p. 222.
195
"setting little devil-kites": *South Lodge,* p. 92.
195
"could only be": Faith Compton Mackenzie, *As Much as I Dare* (London: Collins, 1938), p. 271.
196
"in a dingy": Brita Lindberg-Seyersted, ed., *Pound/Ford: The Story of a Literary Friendship* (New York: New Directions, 1982), p. 22.
196
"I was glad": *The Flurried Years,* p. 223.

13. THE TWO MRS. HUEFFERS

198
"no papers were": *The Times* of London, *Daily Mirror* and *Daily Mail,* Feb. 7, 1913.
198
"Think of the": *The Times* of London, Feb. 7, 1913.
199
"was supplied by": *The Times* of London, Feb. 8, 1913.
199
"When I was": Comyns Beaumont, *A Rebel in Fleet Steet* (London: Hutchinson, 1944), p. 75.
200
"dreadful things were": *The Flurried Years,* p. 227.
200
"I am instructed": *Daily Express,* Feb. 8, 1911.
200
"the English synthesis": *The Flurried Years,* p. 230.

200
"laws of libel": Comyns Beaumont, *A Rebel in Fleet Steet,* p. 75.
201
"He was not": Richard Aldington, *Life for Life's Sake* (London: Cassel, 1941), p. 140.
201
"It was a": *South Lodge,* p. 105.
201
"Buy them all": *The Flurried Years,* p. 233.
202
"always a sad": Thomas C. Moser, *The Life in the Fiction of Ford Madox Ford* (New York: Princeton University Press, 1908), p. 172.
202
"the great and": *The Flurried Years,* pp. 235–236.
202
"The only thing": Stow Hill, Violet Hunt to Catherine Hueffer, Feb. 16, 1913.
203
"I can't forget": Stow Hill, Violet Hunt to Catherine Hueffer, Feb. 19, 1913.
203
"a demure, white-haired": Violet Hunt, "The Corsican Sisters," *The Outlook,* April 10, 1915, p. 470.
203
"But I—morbid": *The Flurried Years,* p. 58.
204
"The whole island": Hunt, "The Corsican Sisters," p. 471.
204
"patch with purple": *The Flurried Years,* p. 240.
205
"*bona fides,* Ford": Princeton, Violet Hunt to Ethel Colburn Mayne [1925?].
205
"I hold very": *The Saddest Story,* p. 233.
205
"I'm sick of": Berg, May Sinclair to Ford Madox Ford [1910?].
205
"care two straws": *South Lodge,* p. 112.
205
"I don't think": Ibid., p. 108.
205
"I can't say": Ibid.
206
"I think it": Ibid., p. 109.
207
"Cabinet Ministers, by": *The Flurried Years,* p. 243.
207
"I am not": *South Lodge,* pp. 112–113.
208
"big, comfortably worn": *Providence Sunday Journal,* Sept. 20, 1944.

208

"on a level": Victoria Glendinning, *Rebecca West* (London: Weidenfeld and Nicolson, 1987), p. 84.

208

"I think it": Berg, Rebecca West to Violet Hunt, 1914.

209

"had never liked": *The Flurried Years,* p. 258.

209

"gossiping made many": Miriam J. Benkovitz, ed., *A Passionate Prodigality: Letters to Alan Bird from Richard Aldington, 1949–1962* (New York: Readex Books, 1975), May 15, 1955, p. 171.

210

"to contain something": *The Flurried Years,* p. 243.

210

"To see his": Cornell diaries, Feb. 3, 1914.

210

"probably the dirtiest": Richard Aldington, *Life for Life's Sake* (London: Cassell, 1941), p. 151.

211

"the incised narrow": *New York Times,* Nov. 15, 1987, p. 39.

211

"Mr. Peaound iz": Ezra Pound, *Gaudier-Brzeska: A Memoir* (New York: New Directions, 1960), p. 146.

212

"you turned into": Ford Madox Ford, *Return to Yesterday* (New York: Liveright, 1972), p. 410.

212

"Those young people": Ibid., p. 401.

212

"Lewis supplied the": Jeffrey Meyers, *The Enemy* (London: Routledge & Kegan Paul, 1980), p. 68.

212

"We will convert": Richard Cork, *Vorticism and Abstract Art in the First Machine Age* (New York: Davis & Long, 1977), p. 2.

213

"to blow away": Peter Ackroyd, *Ezra Pound and His World* (London: Thames & Hudson, 1980), p. 39.

213

"these young fellows": Ibid., p. 40.

213

"dying stag or": *The Flurried Years,* p. 215.

213

"very violent and": Meyers, *The Enemy,* p. 29.

213

"abstract panel over": Walter Michel, *Wyndham Lewis Paintings and Drawings* (London: Thames & Hudson, 1971), p. 56.

14. THE GOOD SOLDIER

217
"I never became": Ludwig, Ford to the Editor of *New York Herald Tribune Books,*
Feb. 15, 1927, p. 170.
218
"about the only": Wallis, Edward Heron Allen to Violet Hunt, Dec. 16, 1914.
218
"It seems to": Cornell, Brigit Patmore to Violet Hunt, Dec. 30, 1914.
219
"suddenly broke off": Richard Aldington, *Life for Life's Sake* (London: Cassell,
1941), pp. 141, 138.
219
"writes like a": Richard Aldington, *The Egoist,* Jan. 1, 1914.
219
"soft, kind grey": Richard Aldington, *Death of a Hero* (St. Clair Shores, Mich.:
Scholarly Press, 1979), p. 130.
220
"I have to": *I Have This to Say,* p. 203.
220
"Florence was a": Ford Madox Ford, *The Good Soldier* (New York: Vintage Books,
1960), p. 121.
220
"a sensitive piece": Wallis, Rebecca West to Violet Hunt, n.d.
220
"there is no": Ford, *The Good Soldier,* p. 115.
220
"somewhat repelled": Robert Secor and Marie Secor, "The Return of the Good
Soldier: Ford Madox Ford and Violet Hunt's 1917 Diary," *English Literary Studies*
(Victoria, B.C.: University of Victoria, 1983), p. 22; see also Thomas C. Moser,
The Life in the Fiction of Ford Madox Ford (Princeton, N.J.: Princeton University
Press, 1980), p. 314.
221
"It put an": Cornell, notes taken by Arthur Mizener during an interview with
Rebecca West, Dec. 17, 1965.
221
"supreme triumph of": *Daily News,* April 2, 1915.
221
"if one has": *The Saddest Story,* pp. 279–280.
221
"delightful in expression": Berg, Joseph Conrad to Violet Hunt, June 7, 1915.
(By permission of Cambridge University Press.)
221
"return from the": *The Outlook,* June 12, 1915.
222
"always seeking the": *The Times* of London, June 15, 1915.

222

"We have lost": Peter Ackroyd, *Ezra Pound and His World* (London: Thames & Hudson, 1980), p. 41.

222

"Violet's course seemed": Ludwig, Ford Madox Ford to C. F. G. Masterman, June 28, 1919, p. 95.

222

"I have never": *The Saddest Story,* p. 280.

223

"takes it rather": Ibid., p. 279.

223

"My dear Purple": *The Flurried Years,* p. 264.

223

"Perhaps you would": Violet Hunt, "The Last Days of Henry James," *Daily Mail,* March 1, 1916.

223

"Dirty Belgians! Who": *I Have This to Say,* p. 259.

224

"Why the devil": Edward Nehls, ed., *D. H. Lawrence: A Composite Biography,* Vol. 2 (Madison: University of Wisconsin Press, 1958), p. 412.

224

"The evening was": *South Lodge,* p. 118.

224

"When you are": *The Outlook,* Aug. 28, 1915, p. 271.

225

"himself into the": *The Outlook,* Sept. 11, 1915, p. 332.

225

"new dress or": Austin, Violet Hunt to Faith Compton Mackenzie, n.d.

225

"step out into": Anthony West, *H. G. Wells: Aspects of a Life* (New York: New American Library, 1984), p. 30.

226

"This is what": *South Lodge,* p. 119.

227

"I haven't the": Ludwig, Ford Madox Ford to H. G. Wells, March 22, 1916, pp. 63–64.

228

"I don't know": Ludwig, Ford Madox Ford to Lucy Masterman, July 28, 1916, p. 67.

228

"that horrible family": *Their Lives,* p. 4.

228

"V's novel . . . is": Ludwig, Ford Madox Ford to Lucy Masterman, July 11, 1916, p. 66.

228

"Their Lives is": Rebecca West, "The Art of Making Books," *Daily News,* March 7, 1917.

229
"There is nothing": Robert and Marie Secor, "Lives and Hearts in Pre-Raphaelite England: The Autobiographical Novels of Violet Hunt," *Pre-Raphaelite Review,* 2 (1979), p. 60.
229
"over the nerve": Ludwig, Ford Madox Ford to H. G. Wells, Oct. 14, 1923, p. 154.
229
"I rather suspect": Ludwig, Ford Madox Ford to Lucy Masterman, Aug. 25, 1916, p. 70.
229
"I am in": Ludwig, Ford Madox Ford to C. F. G. Masterman, Jan. 5, 1917, p. 82.
230
"Cheer up!": *I Have This to Say,* p. 110.
230
"not one single": Pattee diary, Feb. 26, 1917. See also Robert Secor and Marie Secor, "The Return of the Good Soldier: Ford Madox Ford and Violet Hunt's 1917 Diary."
231
"Then he became": Pattee diary, March 14–15, 1917.
231
"It was an": Ibid., March 22–23.
232
"was a most": Ibid., March 28.

15. Lying and Spying

233
"Shall I come": Pattee diary, March 28, 1917.
233
"a bed room": Ibid., March 29.
233
"Wait & see": Ibid., March 30.
233
"Oh what is": Ibid., April 5 and 7.
234
"be eternally grateful": Ibid., April 13.
234
"first 'non-calculated' ": Ibid., April 21.
234
"The idea of": Ibid., April 24.
234
"to find a": Ibid., May 9.
235
"He is growing": Ibid., June 1.

235
"If you were": Ibid., June 2.
235
"He will do": Ibid., June 8, 9 and 10.
236
"with a sublime": Iris Barry, "The Ezra Pound Era," *New York Bookman,* October 1931, p. 166.
236
"as absorbed in": Pattee diary, July 31, 1917.
236
"have been a": Robert Secor and Marie Secor, "The Return of the Good Soldier: Ford Madox Ford and Violet Hunt's 1917 Diary," *English Literary Studies* (Victoria, B.C.: University of Victoria, 1983), p. 71.
236
"my gold hat": Pattee diary, June 30, 1917.
237
"Possessed with a": Ibid., July 1.
237
"I felt as": Ibid., July 20.
237
"I want all": Ibid., Oct. 1.
237
"He asked for": Ibid., Sept. 6.
237
"He permits himself": Ibid., Aug. 4.
237
"Well, I'm tired": Ibid., Aug. 9.
238
"slug, or the": Ibid., Aug. 13.
238
"Aren't you going": Ibid., Aug. 14.
238
"It is absurd": Ibid., Aug. 21.
238
"Your goddaughter, Sir": Ibid.
239
"Ever since he": Ibid., Aug. 29.
239
"the literal sense": Ibid., Sept. 2.
239
"kinder than he": Ibid.
240
"there will be": Ibid., Oct. 2.
240
"Violet, with inspired": Grace Lovat Fraser, *In the Days of My Youth* (London: Cassell, 1970), pp. 239–240.

_240_
"I _could_ not": Pattee diary, Oct. 22–23, 1917.
_241_
"think of making": Ibid., Oct. 24.
_241_
"It is the": Ibid., Oct. 30.
_241_
"anaemic, selfish, thick-skinned": _The Times_ of London, March 6, 1919.
_241_
"the lump of": Pattee diary, Nov. 6–7, 1917.
_242_
"He left perfectly": Ibid., Jan. 24, 1918.
_242_
"the collection more": Ashmolean Museum, Oxford, C. F. Bell to Violet Hunt, June 20, 1918.
_243_
"of a type": Ashmolean Museum, Oxford, C. F. Bell to W. A. S. Benson, July 20, 1918.
_243_
"would sell anything": Ashmolean Museum, Oxford, W. A. S. Benson to C. F. Bell, Aug. 1, 1918.
_243_
"knowledge gathered from": Ashmolean Museum, Oxford, Violet Hunt to C. F. Bell, Aug. 11, 1918.
_243_
"in defiance of": Ashmolean Museum, Oxford, W. A. S. Benson to C. F. Bell, Aug. 23, 1918; Venice Benson to C. F. Bell, Aug. 24, 1918.
_244_
"most if not": Ashmolean Museum, Oxford, C. F. Bell to Violet Hunt, Aug. 31, 1918.
_244_
"quite the most": Stella Bowen, _Drawn from Life_ (London: Virago Press, 1984), pp. 62–63.
_244_
"I happened to": Ibid., p. 165.
_244_
"more reassurance than": Ibid., p. 80.
_244_
"Just a note": _The Saddest Story,_ p. 302.
_245_
"It is possible": Wallis diaries, March 4, 1934.
_245_
"As far as": Cornell, Stella Bowen to Violet Hunt, May 30, 1919.
_246_
"So I am": University of Illinois Library at Urbana-Champaign, Violet Hunt to H. G. Wells [c. 1920].

246

"to anyone outside": Ludwig, Ford Madox Ford to J. B. Pinker, June 5, 1919, p. 93.

246

"I have been": Stow Hill, Violet Hunt to Catherine Hueffer, n.d.

246

"I shan't appear": Ludwig, Ford Madox Ford to C. F. G. Masterman, June 28, 1919, p. 96.

247

"I did stick": *The Saddest Story,* p. 306.

247

"had planted herself": Ludwig, Ford Madox Ford to Ezra Pound, Aug. 30, 1920, p. 122.

247

"I am returning": Cornell (there are five letters from Mrs. R. Hunt to Violet, from August through December 1920).

248

"felt a great": Cornell, Violet Hunt to Elsie Hueffer, Aug. 10 [1920?].

248

"Your wonderful attitude . . . ,": Sketch in *Saturday Review,* Aug. 5, 1922. In this story, Violet refers to Elsie as Number One, herself as Number Two and Stella as Number Three. "She conceded to all three, including herself, fairly good looks. Number one, indeed, had been beautiful. There was a child at each end of the scale. She herself had money." At one point Number One, "in her blunt manner admitted to feeling compunction for the way she had persecuted Number Two— she would not have done it if she had realized how dreadfully Number Two had been exploited by him."

248

"I have come": Princeton, Violet Hunt to Edgar Jepson, Aug. 5, 1920.

248

"It sounds as": Ibid.

249

"If he was": Austin, Violet Hunt to R. A. Scott-James, n.d.

249

"more or less": Austin, R. A. Scott James to Ford Madox Ford, n.d.

16. Scoundrel Time

251

"the most abominably": Caesar R. Blake, *Dorothy Richardson* (Ann Arbor: University of Michigan Press, 1960), p. vii.

252

"The manly structure": Horace Gregory, *Dorothy Richardson: An Adventure in Self-Discovery* (New York: Holt, Rinehart & Winston, 1967), p. 68.

253

"Ford big, fair": Mrs. C. A. Dawson Scott, "As I Know Them: Some Women Writers of To-day," *Strand Magazine,* August 1923, pp. 158–160.

253
"her an amusing": Austin, Violet Hunt to Hermon Ould of PEN, n.d.
254
"Violet's passion for": _South Lodge,_ p. 127.
254
"a regular 'honey-pot' ": Ibid., p. 135.
254
"tenacious, possessive and": Ibid., p. 127.
254
"looks upon my": Cornell, Violet Hunt to Ford Madox Ford, n.d.
255
"If her subject": Rachel Ferguson, "The Art of Violet Hunt," _Sunday Chronicle,_ Nov. 2, 1919.
255
"peep into the": _Times Literary Supplement,_ Sept. 22, 1921, p. 614.
255
"sad stories. Some": _John O'London's Weekly,_ Nov. 11, 1922.
256
"sees something that": Wallis, J. L. Garvin to Violet Hunt [c. 1922].
256
"a _good_ title": Cornell, Violet Hunt to T. J. Wise, Nov. 20, 1934.
256
"about to burst": _The Saddest Story,_ p. 337.
256
"May I point": _Weekly Westminister,_ Jan. 19, 1924.
256
"for this sudden": Cornell, Ethel Colburn Mayne to Ford Madox Ford, May 5, 1924.
257
"At the time": _The Star,_ Feb. 9, 1925; articles also in _The Times_ of London, Feb. 10; _Daily Mail_ and _Daily Mirror,_ Feb. 9.
257
"The sinister brilliance": _More Tales of the Uneasy,_ Folcroft Library Editions, 1979 (reprint of 1925 London Heinemann edition), pp. i, xvi.
258
"a freak story": Ibid., p. xvii.
258
"the uneasy element": _The Times_ of London, Sept. 3, 1925.
258
"If they are": _The Saddest Story,_ p. 355.
258
"Rebecca, naturally, has": Ibid.
259
"The object of": _The Times_ of London, Feb. 18, 1926.
260
"comes from too": _The New York Times Book Review,_ Dec. 19, 1926.

17. ON BEING SYLVIA

262
"I have been": *I Have This to Say,* p. 203.
262
"If you wanted": Ford Madox Ford, *Parade's End* (New York: Vintage Books, 1979), p. 128.
262
"I do fancy": Princeton, Violet Hunt to Ethel Colburn Mayne, a typed draft, possibly never posted n.d. [c. 1925].
262
"talking: usually cleverly": Ford, *Parade's End,* p. 121.
263
"was no longer": Princeton, Violet Hunt to Ethel Colburn Mayne [c. 1925].
264
"For it is": Ford, *Parade's End,* p. 788.
264
"If . . . you had": Ibid., p. 172.
264
"rushing and roaring": Mrs. C. A. Dawson-Scott, "As I Know Them," *Strand Magazine,* August 1923, p. 160.
264
"She had that": *Sunday Telegraph,* May 7, 1972.
265
"You know I": *South Lodge,* p. 190.
265
"an eccentric old": Letter to author from Anthony West, July 5, 1986.
265
"Don't, for it": Lovat Dickson Papers, National Archives of Canada, Violet Hunt to Radclyffe Hall [c. 1927].
265
"I would rather": *The New York Times Book Review,* Sept. 5, 1985, p. 3.
267
"My life is": Violet Hunt, *The Wife of Rossetti* (New York: E. P. Dutton, 1931), p. 305.
267
"Dante Gabriel was": Wallis diaries, August 6, 1891.
268
"strong sense of": Godfrey Childe, "A Plea for Some Reprints," *The Bookman,* June 1932, p. 146.
268
"have a peculiar": Austin, Violet Hunt to T. J. Wise [c. 1929].
268
"one of the": *The New York Times Book Review,* Oct. 30, 1932.
269
"wonderful heaps of": Wallis, Virginia Woolf to Violet Hunt, Oct. 7, 1932.

269
"How happy the": Cornell, Hilda Doolittle to Violet Hunt, Sept. 30, 1932.
269
"not simply the": Cornell, Winifred Ellerman to Violet Hunt, Sept. 30, 1932.
269
"a manner unpleasant": Wallis, T. J. Wise to Violet Hunt [1930].
270
"It's only the": Wallis, autobiographical notes.
270
"I've got a": Austin, Violet Hunt to T. J. Wise [c. 1929].
270
"I always think": *South Lodge,* p. 186.
270
"You & your ": Wallis, Douglas Goldring to Violet Hunt, Sept. 24, 1931.
271
"The Gaudier head": Ezra Pound to Joseph Gorden MacLeod, March 28, 1936, in *Selected Letters, 1907–1941, Ezra Pound,* ed. D. D. Paige (London: Faber & Faber, 1950), p. 279.
271
"sexual organ in": Princeton, Violet Hunt to Nina Hammett, n.d.
271
"I wish he'd": Wallis, autobiographical notes.
272
"It is a": Cornell, Violet Hunt to Poppy Houston (Lady Lucy Byron), n.d.
272
"Violet Hunt long": Helen Rossetti Angeli, *The Story of Charles Augustus Howell* (London: Richard Press, 1954), p. 12.
272
"an arrant rascal": Ibid., p. 13.
272
"The lady with": Ibid., p. 145.
273
"What about your": Cornell, Violet Hunt's draft of Howell biography, p. 87.

18. LEFTOVER LIFE

276
"It is awful": Wallis diaries, Sept. 3, 1935.
276
"felt a skeleton": Ibid., Nov. 20.
276
"as near as": Ibid., Oct. 13, 1936.
276
"I can't *sort*"; Ibid., Dec. 25, 1935.

276
"loved me &": Cornell diaries, fragment, March 10, 1936.
276
"hardly mentioned Ford": Wallis diaries, March 4, 1936.
277
"This is the": Ibid., Nov. 28.
277
"an interesting writer": Letter to author from Graham Greene, Nov. 12, 1986.
277
"I can't bear": Cornell, Violet Hunt to Poppy Houston (Lady Lucy Byron), 1936.
277
"I can't think": Wallis diaries, March 10, 1936.
277
"published with the": Ibid., April 1.
277
"The effort required": *South Lodge*, p. xiv.
278
"she spoke plainly": Wallis diaries, Feb. 12, 1937.
278
"Papa wouldn't want": Ibid., Jan. 20, 1939.
278
"tried to do": Ibid.
278
"all the insouciance": Wallis, "Tor Villa" autobiographical notes.
278
"This year the": Wallis diaries, Jan. 2, 1938.
279
"Oh, my dears!": *South Lodge*, p. xi.
279
"You know, Douglas": Ibid., p. xiii.
280
"certain types—especially": *The Times* of London, Jan. 19, 1942.
280
"There can be": Douglas Goldring, *Life Interests* (London: MacDonald, 1948), p. 181.
281
"The house thus": *South Lodge*, pp. xix and xvi.
281
"For many years": Ibid., p. 200.
282
"Love seemed the": *Their Hearts*, p. 51.
282
"I seemed to": *The Flurried Years*, p. 96.

Index

abortion, illegal, 141
Adam's Breed (Hall), 265
Adelphi Terrace Club, 110
adultery:
    divorce and, 110, 157
    as novel theme, 117–18
Aesthetic Movement, 29, 43, 46–47
Affairs of the Heart (Hunt), 110, 111
Aiken, Conrad, 167
Albert, Prince, 27
Aldington, Richard, 191, 201, 209, 210, 218–19, 222
Alexandra, Tsarina of Russia, 172
Allen, Edward Heron, 107, 124, 192, 235
    Ford's quarrel with, 217–18, 247
Alston Rivers, 178–79
Ancient Lights (Ford), 174
Angeli, Helen Rossetti, 267, 272–74
Anti-Suffrage League, 135
"Antwerp" (Ford), 223
Aquarium, 78–79
Aria, Eliza, 185
Arlen, Michael, 265
Arnim, Elizabeth von, 208
Arnold, Matthew, 135, 279
art, artists, 21–25
    MacColl's role in, 70
    in Margaret Hunt's novels, 32, 33
    Post-Impressionist, 170
    Royal Academy's role in, 24–25, 42*n*

sculpture, 210–11, 222, 271
    Vorticist, 212–13
    World War I and, 222
    see also paintings; *specific galleries and museums*
Art Journal, 52
"Art of Violet Hunt, The" (Ferguson), 255
arts and crafts movement, 60
Artwork, 268
Ashmolean Museum, 242–44
Astarte Syriaca (Rossetti), 29
Athenaeum, 80, 102, 143, 177*n*
"Ave Imperatrix" (Wilde), 45
Avory, Justice, 198–200
Awakening Conscience, The (William Holman Hunt), 29, 122

Bagnold, Enid, 275
Baldwin, Louisa Macdonald, 23
Baldwin, Stanley, 23
Ballad of Reading Gaol (Wilde), 40
Barrington's Fate (Margaret Hunt), 34, 49
Barry, Iris, 236
Barton, Dr., 127
Bateman, May, 109
Batten, Mrs. Mabel (Ladye), 122–23, 230
Battersby, Provost, 124
"Beamer, The," 78–79
Beardsley, Aubrey, 29

333

Photo Credits

Carnegie Commission on Higher Education
Publications in Print

THE NEW DEPRESSION IN HIGHER
EDUCATION:
A STUDY OF FINANCIAL CONDITIONS AT
41 COLLEGES AND UNIVERSITIES
Earl F. Cheit

THE CAPITOL AND THE CAMPUS:
STATE RESPONSIBILITY FOR POSTSECONDARY
EDUCATION:
*a special report and recommendations by the
Commission*

FROM ISOLATION TO MAINSTREAM:
PROBLEMS OF THE COLLEGES FOUNDED
FOR NEGROES
*a special report and recommendations by the
Commission*

HIGHER EDUCATION IN NINE COUNTRIES:
A COMPARATIVE STUDY OF COLLEGES AND
UNIVERSITIES ABROAD
*Barbara B. Burn, Philip G. Altbach, Clark Kerr,
and James A. Perkins*

FINANCING MEDICAL EDUCATION:
AN ANALYSIS OF ALTERNATIVE POLICIES
AND MECHANISMS
Rashi Fein and Gerald I. Weber

LESS TIME, MORE OPTIONS:
EDUCATION BEYOND THE HIGH SCHOOL
*a special report and recommendations by the
Commission*

BRIDGES TO UNDERSTANDING:
INTERNATIONAL PROGRAMS OF AMERICAN
COLLEGES AND UNIVERSITIES
Irwin T. Sanders and Jennifer C. Ward

HIGHER EDUCATION AND THE NATION'S
HEALTH: POLICIES FOR MEDICAL AND
DENTAL EDUCATION
*a special report and recommendations by the
Commission*

GRADUATE AND PROFESSIONAL EDUCATION,
1980:
A SURVEY OF INSTITUTIONAL PLANS
Lewis B. Mayhew

THE AMERICAN COLLEGE AND AMERICAN
CULTURE:
SOCIALIZATION AS A FUNCTION OF HIGHER
EDUCATION
Oscar Handlin and Mary F. Handlin

RECENT ALUMNI AND HIGHER EDUCATION:
A SURVEY OF COLLEGE GRADUATES
Joe L. Spaeth and Andrew M. Greeley

CHANGE IN EDUCATIONAL POLICY:
SELF-STUDIES IN SELECTED COLLEGES AND
UNIVERSITIES
Dwight R. Ladd

THE OPEN-DOOR COLLEGES:
POLICIES FOR COMMUNITY COLLEGES
*a special report and recommendations by the
Commission*

QUALITY AND EQUALITY: REVISED
RECOMMENDATIONS
NEW LEVELS OF FEDERAL RESPONSIBILITY
FOR HIGHER EDUCATION
*a supplement to the 1968 special report by
the Commission*

STATE OFFICIALS AND HIGHER EDUCATION:
A SURVEY OF THE OPINIONS AND
EXPECTATIONS OF POLICY MAKERS IN NINE
STATES
Heinz Eulau and Harold Quinley

A CHANCE TO LEARN:
AN ACTION AGENDA FOR EQUAL
OPPORTUNITY IN HIGHER EDUCATION
*a special report and recommendations by the
Commission*

ACADEMIC DEGREE STRUCTURES:
INNOVATIVE APPROACHES
PRINCIPLES OF REFORM IN DEGREE
STRUCTURES IN THE UNITED STATES
Stephen H. Spurr

COLLEGES OF THE FORGOTTEN AMERICANS:
A PROFILE OF STATE COLLEGES AND
REGIONAL UNIVERSITIES
E. Alden Dunham

FROM BACKWATER TO MAINSTREAM:
A PROFILE OF CATHOLIC HIGHER
EDUCATION
Andrew M. Greeley

ALTERNATIVE METHODS OF FEDERAL
FUNDING FOR HIGHER EDUCATION
Ron Wolk

INVENTORY OF CURRENT RESEARCH ON
HIGHER EDUCATION 1968
Dale M. Heckman and Warren Bryan Martin

QUALITY AND EQUALITY:
NEW LEVELS OF FEDERAL RESPONSIBILITY
FOR HIGHER EDUCATION
*a special report and recommendations by the
Commission, with 1970 revisions*

*The following reprints are available from the Carnegie Commission on
Higher Education, 1947 Center Street, Berkeley, California 94704*

WHAT'S BUGGING THE STUDENTS?
Kenneth Keniston

THE POLITICS OF ACADEMIA
Seymour Martin Lipset

PRESIDENTIAL DISCONTENT
Clark Kerr

... AND WHAT PROFESSORS THINK
*Seymour Martin Lipset and Everett Carll
Ladd, Jr.*

*The New Depression
in Higher Education*

The New Depression in Higher Education

A STUDY OF FINANCIAL CONDITIONS AT 41 COLLEGES AND UNIVERSITIES

by *Earl F. Cheit*

Professor of Business Administration
University of California, Berkeley

A General Report for

*The Carnegie Commission on Higher Education
and the Ford Foundation*

MCGRAW-HILL BOOK COMPANY

New York   St. Louis   San Francisco   Düsseldorf
London   Sydney   Toronto   Mexico   Panama
Johannesburg   Kuala Lumpur   Montreal
New Delhi   Rio de Janeiro   Singapore

The Carnegie Commission on Higher Education,
1947 Center Street, Berkeley, California 94704,
has sponsored preparation of this report as a
part of a continuing effort to obtain and present
significant information for public discussion.
The views expressed are those of the author.

THE NEW DEPRESSION IN HIGHER EDUCATION
A Study of Financial Conditions at 41 Colleges and Universities

Library of Congress catalog card number 73-149300

123456789MAMM7987654321

07-010027-6

Foreword

The decade of the 1960s was characterized by the most rapid growth and development of institutions of higher education in American history. As the postwar babies reached college age, not only did the college-age population rise to unprecedented numbers, but the proportion of these young people seeking higher education also rose steadily. In the post-Sputnik era, moreover, there was a heightened appreciation of the contribution of higher education to national growth and scientific development, which encouraged rising state government appropriations, massive federal aid programs, expanded private gifts, and increased student fees. Thus institutions of higher education were equipped financially to absorb the swelling enrollment of students.

But toward the end of the 1960s, signs of financial stress began to be apparent in the world of higher education, and by 1970 increasing numbers of institutions were facing financial difficulties as the flow of funds from various sources ceased to rise at the rapid rate that had been experienced from the late 1950s to about 1967. There has been a clear connection between the extraordinary growth of the first seven years of the decade and the financial stringency that began to emerge toward the end of the decade. Not only had enrollment at both the undergraduate and graduate levels been mushrooming, but institutions had increased the quality and variety of their course offerings and had responded to the demand for greater equality of opportunity in higher education by increasing their expenditures on student aid and by developing special programs to facilitate participation in higher education of students with less than adequate preparation. Other highly significant factors in rising costs were the increase of graduate students as a proportion of the total enrollment and the rapid growth of expenditures.

All these factors, plus accentuated inflation in the economy, contributed to sharply increasing costs of education per student.

For 41 selected colleges and universities, educational and general expenditures per student rose at an annual average rate of 8 percent from 1959–60 to 1969–70. But when the rate of increase of total revenue available to these institutions from state, federal, and private sources began to decline, from about 1967–68 on, many institutions found themselves facing severe difficulties in meeting rising costs and sought ways of bringing the rate of increase in costs under more effective control. For, as Howard Bowen (1970, p. 81, reprinted with permission) has put it:

. . . the biggest factor determining cost per student is the income of the institutions. The basic principle of college finance is very simple. Institutions raise as much money as they can get and spend it all. Cost per student is therefore determined primarily by the amount of money that can be raised. If more money is raised, costs will go up; if less is raised, costs will go down.

The concern of presidents and other administrators about the general financial condition of higher education, and their desire to learn more about how individual institutions were adapting to the situation, inspired this report. Their concerns were brought to the attention of the Carnegie Commission on Higher Education and the Ford Foundation by representatives of the Association of American Universities. The Carnegie Commission agreed to coordinate the study, and the Ford Foundation provided generous financial support and valuable counsel. Earl F. Cheit, professor of business administration, and former executive vice-chancellor at the University of California, Berkeley, accepted responsibility for directing the study. The investigation involved 41 case studies, compiled from "on site" interview reports and appropriate financial records. The interview phase of the study could not have been completed in less than three months in the absence of the willingness of the 13 individuals named in the preface to undertake some of the interviews or without the excellent cooperation of the participating institutions. But the primary credit for the skillful completion of the study in record time goes to Cheit himself.

After analyzing the case studies, Professor Cheit found that 29 of the institutions (or 71 percent) were either headed for financial trouble or were already in financial difficulty. He considered an institution headed for financial trouble if, at the time of the study, it had been able to meet current responsibilities but either could not ensure that it could much longer sustain current program and quality standards or could not plan to support evolving program growth. Colleges and universities which were forced to reduce services or eliminate important educational programs were considered in financial difficulty.

The sample selected for the study was designed to include several types of institutions — public and private, universities, liberal arts colleges, comprehensive colleges and two-year institutions. But it was not precisely representative statistically of all colleges and universities of the country. For purposes of further analysis, therefore, the Carnegie Commission's staff weighted each group of institutions, by type and control, according to its representation among all institutions in the United States.[1] The same procedure was followed for enrollment. In 1968, excluding specialized institutions not included in the study, there were 2,340 institutions of higher education in the United States, enrolling about 7.3 million students.

On a weighted basis, the institutions that have been classified as not in financial trouble by Professor Cheit represented nearly two-fifths of all institutions and accounted for 22 percent of total enrollment (see Table I). This suggests that, on a nationwide basis, about 900 institutions, enrolling about 1.6 million students, were not in financial difficulty. The fact that the proportion of institutions that were not in financial trouble on a weighted basis was larger than on an unweighted basis is chiefly explained by the relative underrepresentation of comprehensive colleges (institutions with a liberal arts component plus additional specialized curricula) and two-year colleges in the sample. These two groups were less likely than universities and liberal arts colleges to be headed for financial trouble or in financial difficulty.

The substantially larger group of institutions that was found to be headed for financial trouble represented, on a weighted basis, 42 percent of the institutions and 54 percent of the students in the nation, again excluding the specialized institutions. This suggests that just about 1,000 institutions, enrolling nearly 4 million students, were headed for financial trouble.

On a weighted basis, slightly less than one-fifth, or 19 percent, of the institutions, accounting for 24 percent of the students, were

[1] It was also necessary to make assumptions, based on findings for similar groups of institutions, about the financial condition of certain relatively small groups of institutions, such as public liberal arts colleges, that were not included in the sample.

TABLE I *Estimated number, and enrollment, of institutions of higher education, by financial status, United States, spring 1970*

Institutions by control and type	All institutions	Not in financial trouble	Headed for financial trouble	In financial difficulty
*Total institutions**				
Number	2,340	905	1,000	435
Percent	100	39	42	19
Total enrollment				
Number (in thousands)	7,265	1,570	3,940	1,755
Percent	100	22	54	24
Public institutions				
Number	1,170	580	500	90
Percent	100	50	43	7
Enrollment — public				
Number (in thousands)	5,300	1,330	3,150	850
Percent	100	25	59	16
Private institutions				
Number	1,170	325	500	345
Percent	100	28	42	30
Enrollment — private				
Number (in thousands)	1,935	240	790	905
Percent	100	12	41	47
Universities				
Number	165	30	85	50
Percent	100	19	51	30
Enrollment — universities				
Number (in thousands)	2,380	450	1,470	460
Percent	100	19	62	19
Liberal arts colleges				
Number	730	210	310	210
Percent	100	29	43	28
Enrollment — liberal arts colleges				
Number (in thousands)	770	170	400	200
Percent	100	22	53	25

*Total includes comprehensive colleges and two-year colleges, but data for these types of institutions are not shown separately, since there were relatively few of these institutions in the study sample; total excludes specialized institutions of higher education, which were not included in the study. All numbers have been rounded, because precise numbers are not statistically significant.

SOURCE: Carnegie Commission on Higher Education staff.

in financial difficulty. This suggests that about 435 institutions, enrolling about 1.8 million students, would be in this category.

We found that private institutions were considerably more likely to be in financial difficulty in the spring of 1970 than were public institutions. We also found that universities, compared to other types of institutions, appeared to have the highest incidence of financial difficulty. Cutbacks in federal government research funds were, of course, affecting the universities considerably more than other types of institutions, as were reductions in foundation support in a number of instances. Private universities in large urban areas, where low-tuition public comprehensive colleges and community colleges were attracting increasing proportions of students, were especially likely to be in financial difficulty.

Next to the universities, it was the liberal arts colleges that included the largest proportion of institutions in financial difficulty. The great majority of liberal arts colleges (96 percent) in the United States are private, and all the liberal arts colleges in the study sample were private. They also are meeting increasingly severe competition from low-tuition public institutions.

Most of the comprehensive colleges and two-year colleges are public, and all the institutions in these two groups in the study sample were public. The results indicate that these groups of institutions were less likely to be in financial difficulty than either universities or the liberal arts colleges, but, in view of the limited numbers of these institutions in the study sample, the precise percentages deemed to be not in financial trouble, headed for financial trouble, or in financial difficulty may not be significant.

What are the implications of these findings for public policy and for the policies of private organizations that have provided support to institutions of higher education?

In the first place, it is clear that institutions of higher education will not be in a position to meet their responsibilities in the 1970s and subsequent decades if their financial status continues to deteriorate. Not only must they continue to provide education of high quality to increasing numbers of students, but they must also provide augmented student aid and special educational services to students from minority-group and low-income families if the rising aspirations of our society for equality of opportunity in higher education are to be fulfilled.

Secondly, the indications of a particularly high incidence of financial difficulty among private institutions, along with an acceleration of the decline in the proportion of enrollment in private institutions in the last few years, suggest that the survival of many of our private institutions of higher education is in jeopardy. The Carnegie Commission believes that it is extremely important to preserve and strengthen private institutions of higher education in the United States. It is in the private universities and liberal arts colleges that innovative amd imaginative approaches to higher education are most likely to be found. The greater freedom of private institutions from political interference helps to preserve academic freedom in the public institutions. And the competition of private institutions helps to improve the quality of education in the public institutions. I am convinced that the quality of education in many of our public institutions of higher education would be much lower than it is today if they were not seeking to model their programs after those in the best of the private institutions, and to attract and retain faculty members who would be loath to be associated with public institutions if their quality were distinctly inferior to that of the private institutions.

Thirdly, however, institutions of higher education will be able to meet their responsibilities in the 1970s without as sharp an increase in their revenues as was experienced during the greater part of the 1960s. Enrollments will continue to increase, but, largely for demographic reasons, not as rapidly as in the 1960s. And the shortages of qualified applicants for faculty positions that characterized the greater part of the 1960s will be replaced by a market for faculty members in which supply will be more than adequate to meet demand. In fact, signs of a deteriorating market for college and university faculty members were already plainly evident in the winter of 1969–70. For this reason, the unusually rapid advance of faculty salaries that characterized the 1960s is likely to be followed by a rate of increase in the 1970s more nearly commensurate with rates of increase of compensation to employees in the economy generally.

I do not believe that it is reasonable to expect an annual average rate of increase of as much as 8 percent in educational and general expenditures per student, as has happened in a number of institutions, to continue into the indefinite future.[2] It is true that higher education, along with some of the other service sectors of the economy, does not benefit from productivity increases, which have averaged about 3.3 percent a year for the total (private) economy in the years since World War II. Thus, increases in compensation to employees of institutions of higher education tend to be fully reflected in increased costs, whereas, in the economy as a whole,

[2] In fact, the average annual increase for *all* institutions of higher education was considerably less than 8 percent a year, reflecting lower rates of increase in groups of institutions, such as public four-year and two-year colleges, that were somewhat underrepresented in the Cheit sample.

wage increases are partially offset by productivity increases. And there is some tendency for costs of goods and services purchased by institutions of higher education to rise somewhat more rapidly than the average annual increase of about 2.2 percent in the consumer price index, because costly items such as computer services play a relatively important role in higher education. But, all things considered, an annual average increase in educational costs per student of 3 percent *more* than the general rise in the cost of living should be adequate to meet rising costs without a reduction in the quality of education, or in the comparative increase of faculty members. This would mean a total increase of 5 to 6 percent a year if the general cost of living rises 2 to 3 percent a year as it did over most of the past decade. A 3 percent rise in the costs per student, over and beyond the general increase in the level of prices, should, however, be looked upon as a "peril point" that institutions should not exceed, under current circumstances, without careful consideration. This would mean that some institutions would need to cut the excess of their rising costs over the general rise in prices by one-half—instead of a 6 percent "excess," they would need to seek a 3 percent figure. This might be viewed as a prudent course of action. I am convinced that, if cost increases can be held to that level, the nation can afford to provide the funds required for the future expansion of higher education.

The Carnegie Commission has made a number of recommendations which would, if implemented, enable institutions of higher education to overcome their current financial difficulties, at least in large part and in most cases.

1   In *Quality and Equality: Revised Recommendations, New Levels of Federal Responsibility for Higher Education,* we have recommended, for all of higher education, public and private, a substantial expansion of federal aid, including (a) grants for students from low-income and lower-middle-income families, (b) cost-of-education supplements to institutions enrolling students holding the grants, (c) an improved student loan program, (d) construction grants and loans, (e) start-up grants for new community colleges and urban institutions, and (f) continuation of federal government support of research at a constant percentage of the gross national product.

2   In *A Chance to Learn: An Action Agenda for Equal Opportunity in Higher Education,* we have made certain recommendations, including the establishment of recruiting and counseling pools among neighboring colleges and universities to coordinate resources

and staff efforts for admitting educationally disadvantaged candidates, which would enable institutions to meet their responsibilities in this area more efficiently.

3 In *The Open-Door Colleges: Policies for Community Colleges,* we have reviewed our recommendations for federal aid in the context of their implications for community colleges and have also recommended that states should expand their contributions to the financing of community colleges so that the state's share amounts, in general, to one-half or two-thirds of the total state and local financial burden, including operational and capital outlay costs.[3]

4 In *Higher Education and the Nation's Health,* we have recommended greatly expanded federal support for medical and dental education, as well as expanded state support in states that have lagged in providing financial aid for medical and dental education in the past. We have also recommended acceleration and reforms in medical and dental education which would make preprofessional and professional education in these fields less prolonged and less costly.

5 In *Less Time, More Options: Education Beyond the High School,* we have recommended changes in degree structure, including (a) a three-year bachelor of arts program for qualified students, (b) a one-year associate of arts program for qualified students, and (c) a reduction in the length of time required to obtain a Ph.D. or the new Doctor of Arts degree, which we believe should become the usual degree for college and university teachers. Substantial savings in costs could be achieved through the implementation of these recommendations.

6 In *From Isolation to Mainstream: Problems of the Colleges Founded for Negroes,*[4] we have recommended establishment of a special subdivision for the development of black colleges and universities within the National Foundation for Development of Higher Education, previously proposed in *Quality and Equality,* with an average annual allocation of $40 million in the 1970s for developmental programs in black colleges, as well as $1 million annually for planning funds to aid states and black colleges to plan for the growth and transition of these institutions. We have also pointed out that the federal aid recommended in *Quality and Equality* would be especially beneficial to the black colleges, with their large proportions of students from low-income families.

[3] In some cases, the state share currently meets, or exceeds, this criterion.
[4] To be published in February, 1971.

7 Finally, in *The Capitol and the Campus: State Responsibility for Postsecondary Education,*[5] we have recommended state government aid to private institutions, including (a) granting endowments to responsible groups to start new private institutions or making similar grants to existing private institutions to open branches in the granting state, (b) tuition grants for both public and private institutions to be awarded to students on the basis of financial need, (c) grants for specialized educational programs (e.g., medical education) in private institutions under appropriate circumstances, and (d) in a few states, particularly those relying heavily on private universities and colleges, cost-of-education supplements to private institutions.

The Commission also has in preparation several reports, including a report on the financing of higher education and a report on efficiency in higher education, which will include recommendations designed to enhance the capacity of institutions to meet their financial problems.

We hope that the findings of the Cheit study will be of assistance to institutions, associations in the field of higher education, and governmental bodies in developing policies to meet the problem of financial distress in higher education. Not only does it provide valuable insights into the factors responsible for the "new depression in higher education" and the types of institutions most affected, but it also provides a great deal of information on how institutions are seeking to overcome their financial problems. This information should be of assistance to all institutions facing similar difficulties.

Clark Kerr

Chairman
The Carnegie Commission
on Higher Education

December, 1970

[5] To be published in March, 1971.

Preface

Academic life — or at least much of academic life — has long fascinated writers and analysts. The fragile and sophisticated assumptions essential to collegial modes of government, the fond memories of alma mater, the innermost workings of radical student caucuses, the anguish and longings of the young instructor — all these command a literature. Thanks to the works of Edward Albee, Mary McCarthy, and Michelangelo Antonioni, no alcoholic professor of English, no ambitious coed, no clucking alumnus, no awkward student revolutionary need feel unrepresented in the chronicles of academe. They, their colleagues, and their ambitions are hallowed in novels, films, and essays.

Not so the president, the treasurer, or the chairman of the trustees' finance committee. Too much of their time is spent worrying about the dullest of all academic topics: money. Lacking the romance of revolution, the great moral issues of nuclear research, or the elevation of educational leadership, their search for funds commands little creative attention. When it does command attention, fund raising is usually seen as a necessary evil, an encroachment on the time the president should spend on important academic matters. Upton Sinclair (in 1923) put it bluntly: "The college President spends his time running back and forth between Mammon and God."

A statistical presentation to the state legislature, a compelling statement of need to a private donor, a careful husbanding of endowment funds — this is not the stuff that makes the academy fascinating. A skillful response to a budget crisis may succeed in maintaining academic programs, but it fails to excite popular interest. These are activities guided by foresight, prudence, and thrift, those curious virtues whose absence offends the public, but whose presence bores it.

Apart from the occasional story of the conflict between principle and the unscrupulous demands of a potential donor, public attention has not been gripped by the drama of how to finance colleges.

The situation is changing rapidly. Colleges and universities throughout the country are today struggling with a growing financial crisis. As its impact becomes directly felt on campuses and in communities around the nation, the money problem in the schools has begun to command attention. It may never be high drama, or become God's work, but it surely has become hard news. Accounts of the financial plight of the schools are now front-page stories and the subject of concerned editorials. The problem has also attracted the attention of the sports pages, where its impact on intercollegiate activities is lamented. A columnist in the *San Francisco Examiner* recently predicted that if present financial pressures on the colleges continue, collegiate football fans face the dismal prospect that the Rose Bowl game of 1980 may well be played between the Green Bay Packers and the Denver Broncos.

A bibliography prepared by the staff of the Carnegie Commission on Higher Education has some 70 entries for articles, reports, and studies, just for a three-year period, ending in February 1970, covering the growing financial problems of higher education. That number has probably doubled, for nearly every popular journal has by now recognized that higher education is in a financial depression and has published its "financial-crisis-on-the-campus" article.

This study of that depression was jointly sponsored by the Carnegie Commission on Higher Education and the Ford Foundation. They did so in response to the request of several college and university presidents who were alarmed by the crisis in school finance and eager to learn how general the problem was and what other institutions were doing in response to it.

The purpose of this study can be stated most clearly by identifying two things that it was *not* designed to do. First, the study was not designed as an exhaustive survey on the financial condition of all institutions of higher education. Such a work was done during the Great Depression (American Association of University Professors, 1937), and a similar work should be undertaken when, as seems almost certain, the financial situation of the schools continues to deteriorate. Secondly, this study was not intended to produce an aggregate statement of expenditures and financial need of higher education. Work in this important area is being done by June O'Neill of The Brookings Institution and will be published by the Carnegie Commission on Higher Education.

The purpose of this study is to make available to interested persons off and on campus a short, current, factual analysis of the nature of the financial problem as it affects institutions of various types. The emphasis here is on both the impact on the schools and on their responses. In addition, the study gathered the views of school administrators concerning what public policy should be toward financing higher education. The colleges and universities studied are illustrative of all the major types of institutions of higher education.

In every school selected for study except one, which declined to participate, campus administrators cooperated fully. This is no small matter, for the study required interviews at each campus lasting several hours (sometimes more than one day). Each campus was also asked for financial data, and this imposed an additional work burden. Moreover, the visits and interviews took place in May, June, and early July, 1970, a time of considerable upheaval on most campuses. Despite numerous competing demands for their attention, the administrators were generous with their time. I am most grateful to them, and I hope they will find that this analysis represents a correct understanding and fair interpretation of the facts about their campuses.

It was possible to schedule and conduct 41 campus visits in 21 states in a relatively short time period because several people aided in the interviewing process. For their help in conducting one or more campus visits and interviews for the study, I want to thank Frederick E. Balderston, vice-president, University of California; C. D. Bishop, vice-president, University of North Carolina, Chapel Hill; James V. Clark, associate director, relations with schools, University of California; Loren M. Furtado, vice-president, University of California; Lawrence Gladieux, assistant to the director, Council on Federal Relations of the Association of American Universities; John C. Honey, vice-president, Syracuse University; Joseph A. Kershaw, professor of economics, Williams College; Charles V. Kidd, director, Council on Federal Relations of the Association of American Universities; William W. Jellema, executive associate and research director, Association of American Colleges; Charles P. McCurdy, Jr., executive secretary, Association of American Universities; Dr. Alexander M. Mood, professor of administration, University of California, Irvine; Karl W. Payne, '71, School of Law, University of California, Berkeley, the project's research assistant; and Clarence Scheps, executive vice-president, Tulane University.

None of the volunteer interviewers studied his own campus, of course.

In addition to their help with campus visits, Fred Balderston, Joseph Kershaw, and Charles Kidd served the study in another capacity. Under the chairmanship of Clark Kerr, they constituted an advisory committee which helped to select the sample of institutions and to define the scope of the study. In addition, they read and criticized the manuscript. I am grateful to them, and for the advice and help of Margaret S. Gordon, associate director of the Carnegie Commission, who also read and criticized the manuscript.

The findings and interpretations presented here depend heavily on data gathered by the interviewers listed above. I emphasize this to acknowledge a debt, not to implicate them in possible problems of interpretation or judgment. Every interviewer provided a factual account of each campus visit as well as his interpretative comments. But none was asked to participate in the classification of institutions into the categories used for analysis in this study. Neither the interviewers nor the sponsors — the Carnegie Commission and the Ford Foundation — are responsible for interpretations or recommendations.

I owe special thanks to Karl W. Payne, my research assistant. He helped with the interviewing, participated in all stages of the analysis, and wrote the first draft of Chapter 2.

I wish to thank Mrs. Barbara Porter, who typed the manuscript, and my wife, who helped edit it and prepare it for publication. My colleague, Robert H. Cole, professor of law, School of Law, University of California, Berkeley, read the entire manuscript, and his comments helped it in many ways. I know of no one with a better understanding of the process of higher education, and I am pleased to acknowledge his contributions to this report.

Earl F. Cheit

Berkeley, California
November, 1970

Contents

1. The New Cost-Income Problem

No one can fix the exact date that marks the beginning of the depression now settling on American colleges and universities. Nor can anyone point to a major event, like the stock market crash of October 29, which in 1929 dramatized the hard times ahead. Chancellors, presidents, provosts, and deans generally trace the beginning of their financial difficulties to some time in the last three or four years of the 1960s, the time for most colleges and universities when the balance sheet began to show signs of trouble.

Some elements of the trouble have been present for a long time. Costs have been rising steadily since World War II. With the 1950s came a rapid acceleration in demands on the colleges and universities for public service, for costly new research efforts, and, above all, for new enrollment. The schools were forced to scramble for funds, but they managed to make ends meet.

But what seems to be a new fiscal phenomenon—a declining rate of income growth, and in some cases an absolute decline in income—appeared in the latter half of the 1960s. The effect of this reduced income flow was aggravated by the contemporaneous growth in the range of institutional activities and by a raising of academic standards, which in itself required more money. In short, due to inflation and growing demands on the schools for more service, for broader access, for academic innovation, and for higher quality, costs were rising rapidly. But income was not.

This cost-income squeeze is a phenomenon new to academic administrators, except perhaps for those whose service dates back to the depression of the 1930s. This new situation ". . . isn't just the old question of making ends meet," President Kingman Brewster recently told *The New York Times*. ". . . If the present shrinkage of funds were to continue for another year, we [at Yale] would have to either abandon the quality of what we're doing, abandon

1

great discernible areas of activity or abandon the effort to be accessible on the merits of talent, not of wealth or of race or of inheritance." On this matter, President Brewster's views are in full harmony with those of his presidential colleagues in public, as well as private, universities. On July 13, 1970, the *Times* published in two full pages a partial transcript and summary of the round-table discussion by 11 college presidents reviewing their major problems. The main theme which emerges from this report is that "an acute financial crisis is threatening the solvency or growth of many institutions of higher learning. . . ."

The major effect of this acute financial crisis is that our system of higher education is moving into an important period of readjustment. The eventual scope and significance of this readjustment cannot yet be determined. We can, however, identify its effects in individual institutions.

Like anyone reacting to adversity, academic administrators' first hope is that this new situation is temporary and that the painful cuts into operations, program, and quality can be postponed. They turn naturally to the adjustments that cause the least personal hardship and the least interference with essential academic activities. Thus, the first response is often to decline new obligations and to scale down or cancel plans for new activities. Next come reductions in services not central to the academic program. Finally, there come the cuts in the academic program itself. Along with these measures comes an increase in tuition and student charges, a trend strengthened by adversity. On the other hand, a school may, depending on economic and managerial factors, try to grow its way out of financial trouble rather than just cut its way out. Thus, some schools hope to avoid a serious impact by growing in enrollment and, thereby, in income.

Although cutting is not an inspiring academic task, several presidents in this position consider that they are among the relatively fortunate, for some state institutions have been required to continue expanding enrollment regardless of restrictive budgets. An increasing number of institutions, having made what painless adjustments they can, are now reducing or eliminating community service and cultural, athletic, and experimental programs; some are cutting back academic departments and professional schools and, in some instances, dropping them altogether. Neither cutting nor growing will be sufficient to remedy the financial squeeze very far into the future if present cost and income problems continue.

After a decade of building, expanding, and undertaking new responsibilities, the trend on campuses today is all in the other direction. The talk, the planning, and the decisions now center on reallocating, on adding only by substitution, on cutting, trimming, even struggling to hang on. Just a few years ago, the main assignment of a new college or university president was to develop plans for building the institution. Today's new president is more likely to find financial conditions dictate that his first priority is to scale down his school's plans and, perhaps, even its operation.

Speculation about what it will take to survive is intensified by an occasional rescue story. Washington University of St. Louis is the subject of such talk, for it was recently relieved from its financial crisis by the Danforth Foundation. On June 23, 1970, the foundation announced a gift of $15 million, for use in the general operations of the university and its medical school, with no strings attached. In announcing the grant, the Danforth Foundation stressed the "unusual financial difficulties" faced by universities. These difficulties include reports from a growing number of institutions that they are on the path of insolvency, unless within the next year or two they find ways to reduce costs and increase revenue.

In the medical schools, the financial problems have advanced from chronic to critical.[1] As of June 30, 1970, 43 of the nation's 107 medical schools were receiving from the National Institutes of Health what it called "disaster grants." These grants, now totaling $15 million a year, are being paid to keep the schools from closing or severely deteriorating in quality. Even with these payments, a large number of medical schools are reported to have life expectancies of three to five years, unless new funds are found. Among them are Tufts University, Boston; New York Medical College; Creighton University, Omaha; George Washington University and Georgetown University, Washington, D.C.; St. Louis University; and Loyola University.

For some institutions, the impact is just beginning to be felt.

---

[1] The medical schools are a complex, special case and not included in this study, except insofar as they are part of the problem of the parent institutions. Like their parent institutions, they face rapidly rising expenditures and declining rates of income growth. Some are being forced into deficits, cuts, expenditure of endowments, even bank loans and land sales. Several face closure, unless new funding can be found. For their part the parent institutions are trying to put their medical schools on an independent financial basis. This results in less burden on the parent institution but will not solve the problem of the medical schools. The serious problem they pose will require government funding.

In the academic year 1969-70, Princeton reported its first deficit. Some report no new effects. Administrators at Hamilton College report they have always been cost conscious and have not adopted new policies for decisions based on financial stringency. Some schools, such as the University of Texas, for a variety of reasons to be explored later, may remain largely unaffected. But despite any differences in their schools' situations, academic officers in all parts of the nation and in all types of institutions agree: Higher education has come upon hard times. The trouble is serious enough to be called a depression.

This study of that depression was conducted between April and September, 1970. Its aims were to determine for the 41 colleges and universities studied (1) whether they are in financial difficulty or headed for financial trouble; (2) what the reasons are for the financial difficulties; (3) how the schools are responding to their financial condition; and (4) what policies administrators of these institutions recommend for solving the financial problems of higher education.

The institutions selected for study were chosen, not as a representative sample of all 2,729 institutions of higher education in the nation, but as schools that are illustrative of the major types of educational institutions. A description of the institutions selected for study and of the selection procedure is presented in Chapter 2. Chapter 3 summarizes the classification system used in analyzing the data.

The study consisted first of gathering for each institution basic income and expenditure information for the decade of the 1960s. The second phase of the study involved visits to each of the campuses and extensive interviews with campus administrators— usually the president and his administrative colleagues most directly concerned with financing the institution and influencing its academic direction. The financial data form and the interview guide used in these two phases are reprinted in the Appendix. The findings from the analysis of financial data and the campus visits appear in Chapters 4 through 7. Chapter 8 presents the presidents' policy views and recommendations. Chapter 9 contains the author's views on some additional questions that follow from the study. This chapter summarizes the background and context of the financial problems which face academic administrators throughout the country and which led to the study.

The decade ending in the academic year 1967–68 was one of unprecedented growth for institutions of higher education. That growth did not protect the colleges and universities from a downturn. If anything, it probably made them more vulnerable. This may seem paradoxical. What the public, the faculty, and students see is the visible growth of the last 10 years. They see new buildings surrounded by clipped hedges; they hear about big research grants and affluent professors. These hardly qualify as symbols of financial hardship. Thus the president who pleads his case for financial help is likely to be told that the schools should be in a better position than most institutions to withstand a downturn. He is likely to be asked how, on the heels of the decade of their greatest growth, can the schools be in financial peril.

The late 1950s and most of the 1960s were, in fact, years of unprecedented growth for higher education. In the decade ending 1967–68 enrollments doubled, income and expenditures tripled. Expenditures for plant rose fourfold. According to estimates prepared by the Council for Financial Aid to Education, foundation support for education (at all levels) increased 500 percent between 1954–55 and 1964–65—from an annual rate of $70 million to a peak of $350 million. Alumni, business, and nonalumni support more than doubled during this same period.

Despite the growth, however, the fiscal structure of many institutions was not sound. There were problems of inadequate or neglected plant remaining from the Great Depression and World War II. Much of the library, laboratory, space, and equipment support needed for new programs and new students was either not funded or financed by heavy dependence on foundation and government assistance of an explicitly temporary nature. There was neither budget nor plan for permanent financing in the event of a downturn. Some institutions adopted new graduate programs without realizing how much it would cost to carry them on at their desired level of quality. Where plant expansion was financed, long-term maintenance and equipment replacement (sometimes only five years for scientific equipment) often was not. It was a time of competition for quality resources in the face of a generally rising price level. Many institutions were "trading up" in quality and getting caught by high expenses of transition. Some of the university administrators, who were aware during that time of the dangers of undercapitalization and overextension, either could not deflate the boom psychology on their campus or were willing (or forced) to gamble that subsequent income would be found to bail them out.

The bills still continue to come in, but now there isn't enough money to pay them. Suddenly the schools are aware that they have been vulnerable all along. Recent studies and reports make increasingly clear just how vulnerable some schools are. A *Study of Rising Costs at Ten Universities,* published in 1967 by Cornell University, [2] itself running a sizeable deficit, found for the highly regarded institutions that: "From 1961 to 1966 the group operated in the black with a constantly decreasing margin. About January 1, 1967, they crossed into deficit operation. Based on a cost and income projection the group show an increasing deficit for the next five years." This bleak prediction was accurate, and it applies to an ever increasing number of institutions.

A study underway by the Association of American Colleges is expected to show that one-quarter of all private colleges and universities are now drawing on endowment to meet operating expenses. In public institutions, the stringencies are much the same. They submit a proposed budget, and eventually receive an appropriation. This sum determines what their actual budget will be. They cannot draw on capital accounts or budget for operating expenditures beyond appropriations. When appropriations fall short of budget requests, they may force a reduction in quality. While public institutions can show no budgetary deficits, they do have quality deficits, and the consequences are no less severe for being hidden in diluted programs. As we shall see later in this report, there are in fact some specific differences in the problems facing public and private institutions, but there is no marked difference in the direction of their financial situation. It is deteriorating for both.

If doubts about the pervasiveness of the problem of the financial squeeze in higher education still existed, these doubts were dispelled when President Pusey released his report for Harvard for 1968–69. He reported that, in contrast to previous years, Harvard faced a serious financial situation. For the first time in many years, federal support had declined, and the Faculty of Arts and Sciences operated at a budgetary deficit. President Pusey reported that

---

[2] The 10 institutions are Brown, Columbia, Cornell, Dartmouth, Johns Hopkins, Pennsylvania, Princeton, Rochester, Stanford, and Yale.

Harvard is ". . . faced with a drastically altering situation, and it promises to be exceedingly difficult not only to effect further enrichment and development, but possibly even to sustain the level of operation recently achieved. It is hard at the moment to see how a measure of retrenchment can be avoided." It could not be. By the end of the year, the Harvard School of Education had reduced library expenditures, cut its spring term academic program, and planned an increase in the student-faculty ratio and a higher teaching load. Similar measures were taken in the School of Design.

EXPENDITURE-INCOME PATTERNS

Thus, the recent period of great enrollment, program, and plant growth of the colleges and universities failed to produce strength to ensure continued solvency. It left them more vulnerable than they were before in the event of a decline in their rate of income flow. Just how vulnerable they will prove to be is still uncertain, but this is clear: No one draws much comfort from the past. Educational institutions did prove highly durable in the Great Depression, but university and college presidents tend to be pessimistic about the likelihood that the schools will prove equally durable in the near future. They tend to believe that they are facing a problem more difficult than that posed just by inflation and a general economic downturn. In the campus interviews for this study, a few presidents spoke about the parallels with the Great Depression, but when the subject was pursued, the view of academic administrators was that the current economic crisis is unique and will become more difficult than the Great Depression. The reasons cited in support of this view concern both the expenditure and income accounts. Let us look at the expenditure side first, for that is where our attention was usually first directed in the interviews.

Costs

Unlike economic downturns that have affected higher education in the past, the present income squeeze is perverse. It is occurring while many economic indicators and all prices (but stock prices) are rising. Consider the effect on salaries—the major cost item in an academic budget. In the depression, salaries were cut (the estimated median cut was 15 percent) (American Association of University Professors, 1937), but the price level dropped faster than the decline in academic salaries. From the academic year 1928–29 to the low in 1932–33, the cost of living dropped from an index level[3] of 173 to 136. Therefore, a constant salary would have increased in real terms more than 20 percent during this period. After making adjustments for cuts in salaries and revised salary structures, the 1937 study estimated that the purchasing power of university salaries had increased about 20 percent by 1932–33, and at the lowest point (1934–35) before the upturn, the purchasing power of salaries was still 10 percent higher than in 1928–29.

In contrast, today salaries are barely keeping pace with price increases. In its study for 1968–69, the AAUP (American Association of University Professors) found that, in real terms, compensation levels grew less than 2 percent. In 57 percent of the institutions in the AAUP survey, real wages either remained at the price level or fell behind. Rising prices generate powerful pressures on the schools to increase their costs by increasing salaries.

Salaries of faculty and employees are not the only cost item affected. The wave of inflation engulfing the colleges and universities affects everything else. The rate is accelerated by the increasing costs of buildings, highly sophisticated research instruments and supply requirements, the knowledge explosion, and by the growing requirements for library and computer resources.

Student demand for enrollment in higher education is not depressed; it continues to rise. Growing enrollment can increase net income if costs are held down by increasing class size, but most institutions resist this move because of its assumed effect on quality. Therefore, greater numbers tend to impose additional costs on most institutions because they are accompanied by increasing demand for more graduate and professional training and intensify the problem of satisfying the students' rising expectations for their educational experience. Both in administrative relationships and in instructional modes, they want innovation and personal attention which add substantially to costs.

Campus disturbances—before, during, and after they occur—are an important new cost factor. They impose substantial security, insurance, property, and administrative costs on campuses. In addition, they divert staff attention from academic matters and fund raising.

[3] 1913–14 = 100. These estimates are from American Association of University Professors, 1937, p. 60.

The growing recognition of the plight of the cities, and concern about the poor who inhabit them, have brought new responsibilities to the campus. Virtually every campus in this study has some form of program that seeks to contribute to the solution of the problems of cities, poverty, and race. Newer programs aimed at environmental problems are being proposed and adopted. And these programs tend to be expensive, both in money and in staff time. In addition, there is new awareness of the need to extend opportunity for access. Schools are recruiting low-income students and are incurring heavy student financial-aid expenses.

In the spring of 1967, Provost William Bowen of Princeton made a skillful analysis of the expenditures and income of his own institution, Vanderbilt, and the University of Chicago. Bowen's study (1968) revealed that the marked upward trend in the budgeted expenditures for departmental instruction and research was not simply the product of inflation or increased enrollments. He found that for several decades expenditures for departmental instruction and research rose at the remarkably constant (compound) annual rate of 7½ percent, per student. Inflation accounted for only about one-fourth of this increase. In addition, the costs per student grew because of the growing responsibilities of the universities, their new research programs, broader community responsibilities, greater expenditure for research equipment, and the shift toward more graduate, and hence more expensive, instruction. In a labor-intensive activity such as education, there are virtually no savings through increased productivity. In a recent study for the Carnegie Commission, June O'Neill found that for colleges and universities there is "a more or less proportionate increase of inputs and outputs." In other words, there is no productivity increase, and higher labor costs cannot be offset by greater output. That was one important reason for Bowen's prediction that the educational and general expenditures would continue to rise at the compound average rate of 7½ percent a year per student, for the decade ending in the mid-1970s.

These elements in the cost side of the problem indicate why academic officials believe their situation is unique. Briefly summarized, there are three main points in their argument: (1) the schools are under more severe cost pressures than the surrounding and supporting economy; (2) there are no overall offsetting advantages, like the general price decline of the Great Depression which maintained salary purchasing power, nor is there reduction in demand for service or instructional forms which would give cost relief; and finally (3) there are many cost pressures over which institutions have little or no control.

The problems on the income side are also critical.

Income The colleges and universities are victims of inflation and of the policies used to fight it. At the federal level, the current policy is that the government must spend less money, and this consideration (with others) has resulted in decreasing rates of growth in federal support for higher education. The National Science Foundation (1969) reports that for 1964, federal funds obligated by all agencies to universities and colleges increased 15 percent over 1963. For 1965, they grew 41.9 percent over 1964. Starting in 1966, the rate of increase in federal funds began to decline. The rate of increase dropped to 30.6 percent in 1966, to 10 percent in 1967, to 2 percent in 1968. The 1969 estimate, the 1970 prediction, and the 1971 budget proposals all indicate a steady rate of growth of about 2 percent.[4] The increases in federal support in every year since 1967 are less than the increases in the price level. In other words, in real terms, federal support is declining. Ironically, one argument made on behalf of the decrease is the very inflationary spiral which places larger need on the campuses for more money.

Inflation has also affected government appropriations at the state level, and it has contributed to the taxpayers' revolt against bond issues. In June 1970, in California, a bond proposal for capital support of medical schools and health sciences was voted down in 55 of the state's 58 counties.

There is, of course, far greater competition for money than in the recent past. This affects public and private institutions. State legislatures must meet the needs of elementary and secondary education, which have their own economic problems, and also the needs of other claimants in an advancing welfare state. Private donors receive more requests for their benefactions. These requests are in behalf of urgent and long-neglected problems other than education. These same problems have attracted the interest of the large charitable foundations which, in comparison with the recent past, have shifted their emphasis away from education. Coming

[4] National Science Foundation 1969. Figures for 1969, 1970, and 1971 are estimates from published figures and budget proposals.

after a period of intensive support and successful fund raising by colleges and universities, this drop in foundation support is keenly felt in many institutions visited in this study. The demands of health and welfare expenditures and the war and defense obligations of course compete powerfully for federal funds, and they also contribute to the inflationary pressures that have led to the decline in federal expenditures for the schools.

The effects of campus disturbances on income are hard to measure precisely, but the estimates are that they are very substantial. Adverse reactions to campus disturbances have affected both private and legislative support, and they have affected the vote on bond issues. Moreover, these adverse effects extend to campuses which have not had disturbances.

High interest rates have not had the favorable effect on endowment income one might expect, for colleges and universities have been putting their money in the equity market. Moreover, trends in the stock market have not relieved the financial problems of the schools. Although most prices are rising, stock prices, overall, have been declining. Large, private gifts to educational institutions are frequently gifts of appreciated securities. The tax incentive for such giving is reduced when stock prices are declining. People who are losing money in the stock market are not eager to give large gifts to their alma mater. Not surprisingly, donors give less in a bear market.

For reasons such as these, private support has fallen below what the schools see as their needs. In one recent year, 1965–66, there was even an absolute decline in the dollar amount of voluntary giving for higher education. The forty-sixth annual survey of the John Price Jones Company, a firm of fund-raising counselors which samples 50 colleges and universities, found ". . . a decline in voluntary giving of 8.7 percent in 12 months." This finding was further corroborated by the Council for Financial Aid to Education. Using data from more than 1,000 institutions, it found that voluntary support for higher education in 1965–66 declined by some 1.2 percent from the previous year.

This downward trend in the voluntary support of higher education was reversed in 1966–67, and the rate of support has been rising since. Up about 3 percent in 1966–67, the rate of private support rose 8 percent the following year, and about 10 percent for the last year of the decade, according to the Council for Financial

Aid to Education. Although private support is once again increasing, its average rate for the last half of the 1960s is still below the average increase in budgeted educational and general costs (per student).[5]

In his study of the cost-and-income outlook for private institutions, Bowen predicted that a "typical" major private university, by 1975, would be faced with a deficit of $20 to $28 million, depending on the assumptions made. In other words, something between 28 and 39 percent of its budget for educational and general expenditures could not be met.

From his cost-and-income analysis, Bowen concluded in 1968 that "the economic squeeze already being felt by the major private universities is going to intensify greatly."

Unfortunately, Bowen's prediction that income would fail to keep pace with the rate of expenditures, and the Cornell finding that deficit operations would increase, have proved correct. And unless there are significant changes in attitudes toward investment in education, there are no immediate prospects that this serious income problem will improve. Many campus officials view this income situation as unique in their experience, due to the perverse effects of inflation on income, to the unusual stock market situation, and especially to the change in the attitudes of private donors and legislative bodies toward education and its support.

Tuition　One aspect of the income situation over which the schools have a measure of control is tuition and other charges to students. This is an income source of great concern to the colleges and universities because of its impact on access.

Before World War II, student fees accounted for about one-fourth of the income (and hence the expenditures) of colleges and universities. As we saw earlier, costs rose sharply after World War II, and although tuition rose too, it did not keep up with costs. By 1949–50, income from student fees accounted for only 17 percent of the income of colleges and universities.[6]

[5] The results of fund drives for the 1969–70 school year were mixed. A survey by the *National Observer* (August 17, 1970, p. 1) shows Yale up, Harvard down. The survey shows that several leading institutions are down (Stanford, Colorado, Pomona, Michigan), but others are up. Overall results continue to show an increase in private giving.

[6] For private institutions, fees represented an estimated 32 percent of income; for public institutions, it was approximately 11 percent.

In the 1950s this trend was reversed, and the rate of tuition increases began to catch up with the rate of cost increases. Bowen found that for Chicago, Vanderbilt, and Princeton, the rate of tuition increase overtook the rate of cost increase in 1958, by the slight margin of 8 percent to 7½ percent. The aggregated data for all institutions in the United States indicate that for the decade 1957–58 to 1967–68, the average rate of increase in tuition and required fees for private institutions was 7.5 percent, and for public institutions, 5.8 percent. The median charges in private coeducational institutions (tuition, fees, room and board) rose 9 percent in 1970–71 from the 1969–70 school year. This represents a median increase of $200 this year.

In the first half of the 1960s, Bowen (1968, p. 36) pointed out, student charges at private institutions rose more rapidly than at public institutions. The ratio of charges at the two rose, according to Bowen, from 3 to 2 in 1956 to over 2 to 1 in 1966. It now appears that the rate will be stabilized or the trend reversed slightly.

In recent years, public institutions have been shifting more of the burden of their cost increases to students. In 1970, the state of California broke its 101-year tradition and began charging tuition at its university. The previous year, the National Association of State Universities and Land-Grant Colleges had reported "staggering" increases in student charges in 113 public universities. In contrast to the academic year 1968–69 when tuition had gone up an average of 2.9 percent, for the year 1969–70, the raise was 16.5 percent. These are increases for resident students. For nonresident students, the charges had gone up 9.4 per cent and 13.6 percent in the two years. These higher student charges were the largest increases on record. The National Association of State Universities and Land-Grant Colleges reported for the academic year 1968–69 that various student charges were increased 14 percent by some 261 of its member institutions. These charges rose 38 percent since 1963–64.

Administrators at some private institutions believe that increases in student fees are reaching a "saturation point," that is, they are driving students from middle-income families away and creating conditions on some campuses such that only the very rich and very poor can afford to attend. These private schools share the concern of the public institutions that ever-increasing charges will bar access to students from low-income families. Concern about reaching the "saturation point" in tuition was expressed by many presidents in the study sample. It is as great a worry for Mesa College as for Harvard University.

THE DUBIOUS PUBLIC One of the overriding impressions gained from this study is that most college and university officials believe that their view of the financial troubles is generally not shared by others off campus or on.

When the presidents and vice-presidents of those institutions facing financial problems describe their condition, all but two report that their trustees have a good understanding of the situation. In only about half of them do the top administrators believe that the faculty has a good understanding of its financial problems. Somewhat fewer (about 40 percent) report that students have some awareness of the school's financial situation. Virtually none of the administrators believe that their view of the financial condition is shared by the general public.

A special study conducted in 1968 by the Council for Financial Aid to Education produced the discouraging finding that "82 per cent of persons in managerial positions or the professions do not consider American business to be an important source of gift support for colleges and universities; 59 percent of persons with incomes of $10,000 or over do not think higher education has financial problems;" and finally, the study found that "52 percent of college graduates apparently are not aware that their alma mater has financial problems." Nothing in the campus interviews contradicts this finding.

There are a number of reasons why the presidents' view of financial need is not shared by the public. The president with his hand out is an academic cliché, and it is to be expected that people think the present problems are not different from those of the past. Not only is the president closest to the financial center of the institution, but it is his responsibility to see that the money is there. As Clark Kerr (1970, p. 142) has pointed out, "The president, like the minister, pleads poverty—poverty with parents, alumni, legislators, foundation executives. He does not have a standardized product to sell at least price, but a specialized service to sell at the highest price he can get. His is an enterprise largely judged on its ability to maximize inputs, not outputs. Consequently, Alma Mater is always seen as being on the verge of bankruptcy as a method of raising inputs. The private goal is constant improvement; the public language is about constant deficits. Alma Mater is Pauline—constantly threatened, always saved."[7]

Confidence that alma mater will be saved this time, too, is supported by still another factor—academic administrators are often unwilling to take the actions which would give solid credibility to their plea that this is truly a different situation. In other words, there is an apparent need to keep up appearances and to continue even in the face of difficulty—to operate as if nothing has happened. The situation is like that of the Texas businessman who was in serious trouble with his creditors, but who could not risk hurting his income prospects by showing it. According to a *Wall Street Journal* story, he drove through a hot summer with his car windows tightly closed, to avoid revealing he could no longer afford an air-conditioned car.

Colleges and universities keep up appearances, too, although they have not had much success in using windows to do so. Presidential statements revealing a big deficit will usually be accompanied by a statement of confidence about the future. Layoffs of faculty members are damaging to morale and are considered an absolute last resort. Gloomy statements tend to become self-fulfilling prophesies—and a few presidents in this study, who saw financial difficulties ahead, asked that their institutions not be identified in this connection. Presidents believe that donors are not attracted to institutions in financial difficulty.

Appearances are kept up for other reasons. Most academic planning is done several years in advance; plans continue and obligated funds are spent, even if there is a current fund squeeze. Finally, there is the natural inclination to avoid unpleasant reality. In the 1937 study of the AAUP, this reluctance to accept hard realities is clearly identified. Despite the market crash in 1929 and the continuing downward spiral of the economy, institutions of higher education carried on for about two years without making expenditure adjustments which, in retrospect, it appears they could have made. The authors, perplexed that this should have occurred, say the only question is ". . . did administrators and faculties begin

---

[7] The minister, it should be noted, has as much reason as the president to plead poverty, for the churches are in financial trouble too. A survey in the *National Observer* (July 6, 1970, p. 1) says of the churches at local levels that there is financial pullback almost everywhere, and there is ". . . the most widespread retrenchment within national church bodies in decades."

making adjustments, both actual and psychological, as early as they might have done? There is some ground for arguing that perhaps they resisted what in retrospect appears to have been inevitable longer than was wise, thereby intensifying the difficulty of the adjustments that came in 1932–1933 and 1933–1934. By 1930–1931 it was evident that the economic disturbance was more than a mere market phenomenon. Yet in 1931–1932 the educational institutions apparently were not adapting themselves with any rapidity to the prevailing conditions. . . ."

Twenty-five years later, under somewhat similar circumstances, we found little evidence to indicate that this two-year lag has been reduced, and some indication that it may even be longer. In about 10 percent of the institutions in financial difficulty, interviewers for this study concluded that the school was probably in more serious financial trouble than its administrators thought or were willing to admit.

The net effect of the presidential stereotype and the effort to keep up appearances is that the public will conclude that alma mater is probably secure. She may be squeezed a bit, but that shouldn't hurt too much, because there is plenty of fat in her budget.

The "fat in the budget" argument is not easy to rebut. Given the lack of an obvious standard and the different goals and aspirations of academic institutions, what is called muscle at Tech may be called fat at State. Sometimes it seems that fat is interchangeable even with bone. In the four academic years between 1966–67 and 1969–70, University of California operating-budget requests were cut an average of 8½ percent a year from needs projected to support an enrollment increase of 20 percent. In 1970, the Governor proposed to cut the university's budget request 12 percent (and he succeeded), keeping its operating budget at the same level as the previous year, despite a 6 percent rise in the consumer price index and a 5 percent rise in expected enrollment. The *Sacramento Bee* headline for June 9, 1970, said "Budget Cuts for Welfare, Higher Education Loom." The *Sacramento Union* headed its story: "Reagan Pares Deficit, Eyes Fat in University Budget."

Those who are particularly zealous in instructing others in the performance of their duty seem to believe that if an academic institution survives a period of financial setback, this is proof that there was fat in the budget. The ability to survive a cut is evidence that the fat was there. In fact, a vice-president of one of the institutions in this study insisted that he wished ill to no school, but he confessed to harboring the secret hope that a large, high-prestige institution would be forced to close due to financial problems. "It's the Penn-Central phenomenon," he explained. "When small businesses go broke, no one notices. When something the size of Penn-Central can go bankrupt, people take notice and assume something must be wrong, and then support measures to make things right. That's how it will be with academic institutions in the 1970s."

Along with "fat in the budget," there is another argument that is revived from time to time when problems of financing higher education are considered. It ascribes virtue to poverty. If the views about budgetary fat have their origin in the lack of clear standards, the views about the relationship between poverty and virtue in the schools might come from the theological origins of the universities and colleges. In any case, the quaint proposition that the relatively low pay of teachers is important to maintaining moral virtue in the schools and in society—a view officially endorsed by President Eliot in his inaugural address at Harvard in 1869—is far from dead. The myth may be adapted to the times. Despite a 6 percent increase in the consumer price index during the academic year 1969–70, the California legislature specifically rejected paying the faculty of the California state colleges and university system the 5 percent cost-of-living salary adjustment it approved for all other state employees, including all nonacademic employees on each campus in the state. A legislative spokesman announced that the reason for the action was "disciplinary": The faculty had failed in its responsibilities to hold students to an approved path of conduct during the upheaval on campuses following the invasion of Cambodia in May, 1970. The legislative spokesman did not say that if the faculty were paid less they and the students would behave better, but the legislature apparently assumed that a good lesson in poverty amounts to a good lesson in morality.

A NEW CONCERN FOR FINANCES In the history of higher education for this century, perhaps even for its entire history in this country, the decade from the middle 1950s to the middle 1960s will stand as a golden age of college and university growth and current income. The flow of funds from public and private sources enabled growth of enrollment, function, and plant without precedent in higher education. Near the end of this great boom period for higher education, Clark Kerr observed that judging from the complaints and demands made on a university president, the most important things in the university were sex for the students, parking for the faculty, and athletics for the alumni. That agenda changed rather dramatically. In the last half of the 1960s the concern of the faculty was governance; of the students, relevance; of the alumni, dissidence.

Both of these lists retain importance in the continuing struggle in the university for diversity, freedom, and direction, but as the decade of the 1970s begins, apparently these concerns will be increasingly overshadowed by the new concern over who will pay the bills. In fact, information from 41 campuses in 21 states warrants the prediction that planning and decisions about reform, role, and direction of the academy will in the next decade be influenced more by its financial situation than any other. As the 1937 AAUP study of higher education points out, institutions of higher education expand and assume new activities when their flow of funds increases. And they face troubles when the flow of money is reduced. An old truth, stated as an axiom in the 1937 study, should be restated, for on campus it is being relearned: "Higher education in this country has its economic aspects no less than its academic, and the two are not separable."

The discovery of this relationship seems to be a recurring phenomenon in higher education. Yet major elements in the financial difficulty of higher education seem unprecedented. There are persuasive signs of this, and it is certainly the view of several university and college presidents interviewed in this study.

When college and university officials anticipate their future financing tasks, the rather traditional problems and attitudes are not their main worry. Answering charges about fat and frills is part of the job of raising funds from the public. So is dealing with myth. Every president realizes that where there is faith in education there will be support. Most of them would consider a reasonable measure of skepticism about school finance on the part of the public a good thing, for it creates an appropriate obligation and opportunity for the justification of education in the minds of those asked to support it.

As they look ahead to the problems of winning financial support for their institutions in the next decade, however, college and university officials are primarily worried about three new problem areas. The first concerns their ability to make the painful decisions required to make needed readjustments on campus given the new financial realities, a matter explored later in this report.

The second problem area concerns the ability of the schools to cope, not only with a new array of economic forces affecting educational finance, but also with new political and public attitudes about education. There are many persons off campus who are not pained by the financial distress on campus because they do not like what they see there, or what they think they see there. The *Journal of the House* of the state of Michigan (May 26, 1970, p. 1936) reports the Chairman of the House Appropriations Committee as saying: "If I had my way I'd cut the hell out of them (appropriations) until these kids decide they want to go to school." He promised he would "push for further cuts in state appropriations to universities unless 'student agitators' and 'gutless administrators' changed their attitudes."

He speaks for many others who have formed an unplanned alliance with those students and nonstudents who for romantic revolutionary reasons want a campus that cannot be governed, or can be destroyed. All parties to this alliance value a fiscally difficult situation on campus.

In addition, there are those members of the general public for whom higher education has lost its allure, and who have changed their priorities. Their view of financial hardship of universities and colleges may involve compassion and understanding of the financial problem on campus but little apparent motivation for active support to help ease it. As the new decade begins, there is little optimism on campus that this view will change for the better soon.

The third problem derives from the belief that the financial problems of the schools are not simply part of a general economic downturn but much more complicated, and will become more serious than what the schools have faced before.

As they reviewed the experience of their campus for this study, academic administrators and faculty members differed somewhat, depending on the location and circumstances of their schools, in their views as to the reasons for their financial difficulties and the extent to which they are due to the war in Vietnam and other claims on education funds. There is less disagreement on the extent to which the financial difficulties are due to inflation, to disturbances on campuses, to the political exploitation of these disturbances, and to the general and steady cost pressure all institutions feel. Most of all, at this point, these officials face their cost-income problem with a feeling of uncertainty. How general is our experience? Do other institutions have similar financial troubles? Are the reasons similar? Have other schools found a way to keep costs under control without reducing quality? What are the schools doing about efficiency? What are the program responses to reduced income growth?

These are some of the questions this study tried to answer. Let us look first at the institutions studied, and turn next to the findings.

2. The Colleges and Universities Studied

Forty-one institutions of higher education were selected for this study of the financial problems of colleges and universities. Alphabetically listed, they are:

Albion College, Albion, Michigan

Allegheny College, Meadville, Pennsylvania

Beloit College, Beloit, Wisconsin

Boston College, Chestnut Hill, Massachusetts

Carleton College, Northfield, Minnesota

Central Michigan University, Mount Pleasant, Michigan

City Colleges of Chicago, Chicago, Illinois

College of San Mateo, San Mateo, California

Cumberland College, Williamsburg, Kentucky

Fisk University, Nashville, Tennessee

Flint Community Junior College, Flint, Michigan

Gulf Coast Junior College, Panama City, Florida

Hamilton College, Clinton, New York

Harvard University, Cambridge, Massachusetts

Howard University, Washington, D.C.

Huston-Tillotson College, Austin, Texas

Knox College, Galesburg, Illinois

Meredith College, Raleigh, North Carolina

Mesa College, Grand Junction, Colorado

Mills College, Oakland, California

Morgan State College, Baltimore, Maryland

New York University, New York, New York

Ohio University, Athens, Ohio

Pomona College, Claremont, California

Portland State University, Portland, Oregon

Saint Cloud State College, St. Cloud, Minnesota

Saint Louis University, St. Louis, Missouri

San Diego State College, San Diego, California

Stanford University, Stanford, California

Syracuse University, Syracuse, New York

Tougaloo College, Tougaloo, Mississippi

Tulane University, New Orleans, Louisiana

University of California, Berkeley, Berkeley, California

University of Chicago, Chicago, Illinois

University of Michigan, Ann Arbor, Michigan

University of Minnesota, Minneapolis, Minneapolis, Minnesota

University of Missouri, Columbia, Columbia, Missouri

University of North Carolina, Chapel Hill, Chapel Hill, North Carolina

University of Oregon, Eugene, Oregon

University of Texas, Austin, Austin, Texas

Whitman College, Walla Walla, Washington

Twenty-three of these schools are private institutions, and eighteen are public. They are listed here with their 1968 opening fall enrollment as reported to the U.S. Office of Education, except for the following six institutions whose enrollment figures are those obtained in the interviews: Flint Community Junior College, Mesa College, New York University, Syracuse University, University of Chicago, and University of Minnesota.

Private

Albion College	1,801
Allegheny College	1,595
Beloit College	1,761
Boston College	9,972
Carleton College	1,451

Cumberland College	1,771
Fisk University	1,161
Hamilton College	853
Harvard University	15,198
Howard University	8,704
Huston-Tillotson College	832
Knox College	1,371
Meredith College	859
Mills College	792
New York University	33,562
Pomona College	1,313
Saint Louis University	9,768
Stanford University	12,045
Syracuse University	17,864
Tougaloo College	714
Tulane University	8,359
University of Chicago	8,286
Whitman College	1,103

Public

Central Michigan University	13,419
City Colleges of Chicago, 8 campuses	30,208
College of San Mateo	10,677
Flint Community Junior College	7,091
Gulf Coast Junior College	1,807
Mesa College	2,889
Morgan State College	4,391
Ohio University	22,067
Portland State University	10,206
Saint Cloud State College	9,267
San Diego State College	30,077
University of California, Berkeley	28,132
University of Michigan	38,021
University of Minnesota, Minneapolis	46,881

University of Missouri, Columbia	20,953
University of North Carolina, Chapel Hill	16,233
University of Oregon	14,761
University of Texas, Austin	33,797

As the map indicates, the 41 institutions are located in 21 states and the District of Columbia. Fourteen of the schools are in the Midwest, ten in the West, nine in the South, and eight in the East.

This sample of 41 institutions was not designed to be statistically representative of all American institutions of higher education. Nor is there any special significance in the number "41." That number resulted from an effort to include several examples of all major types of institutions and at the same time to keep the size of the sample within manageable limits. The schools selected were ones whose experience we thought would be *illustrative* of the major types of colleges and universities. No attempt was made to select any institution because of its financial situation, favorable or unfavorable. Financial situation was not considered in selecting the 41 schools.

The remaining sections of this chapter describe the method of selection of schools in the study. They also compare the schools selected with all United States institutions of similar type. These comparisons show: (1) that the liberal arts institutions in this study have an average enrollment similar to the average for all liberal arts institutions in the United States, (2) that the universities, comprehensive colleges, and two-year colleges in the study have average enrollments larger than the United States average for these types of institutions, and finally, (3) that the average expenditure per student for the 41 colleges in the study in the major expenditure categories is substantially similar to those for all United States institutions of comparable type.

Readers interested in the classification of institutions, the selection of the sample, and the data from which the above conclusions are drawn will find these matters discussed in the remaining sections of this chapter.

THE RATIONALE FOR SELECTION

The 41 schools in this study were individually selected by the author and the advisory committee named in the Preface. The schools selected are intended to illustrate the experience of six

Location of colleges and universities studied

1. Albion College
2. Allegheny College
3. Beloit College
4. Boston College
5. Carleton College
6. Central Michigan University
7. City Colleges of Chicago
8. College of San Mateo
9. Cumberland College

10. Fisk University
11. Flint Community Jr. College
12. Gulf Coast Jr. College
13. Hamilton College
14. Harvard University
15. Howard University
16. Huston-Tillotson College
17. Knox College
18. Meredith College

19. Mesa College
20. Mills College
21. Morgan State College
22. New York University
23. Ohio University
24. Pomona College
25. Portland State University
26. Saint Cloud State College

27. Saint Louis University
28. San Diego State College
29. Stanford University
30. Syracuse University
31. Tougaloo College
32. Tulane University
33. University of California, Berkeley
34. University of Chicago

35. University of Michigan
36. University of Minnesota
37. University of Missouri, Columbia
38. University of North Carolina, Chapel Hill
39. University of Oregon
40. University of Texas, Austin
41. Whitman College

major types of institutions. There are many more than six types, of course. In its classification of institutions of higher education by type, the Carnegie Commission on Higher Education lists a total of 18 separate types, including nine kinds of specialized institutions such as theological seminaries, medical schools, and schools of fine arts.[1] The specialized institutions were not included in this study. In this study we have divided educational institutions into the following six types: (1) *national research universities,* (2) *leading regional research universities,* (3) *state and comprehensive colleges,* (4) *liberal arts colleges,* (5) *primarily black colleges,* and (6) *two-year colleges.*

The last four categories—state and comprehensive colleges, liberal arts colleges, primarily black colleges, and two-year colleges —present no serious classification difficulties. Although there may be considerable variation in size, quality, and aspiration among schools *within* any of these four categories, each category itself presents distinctive institutional characteristics.

The first two categories—national research universities and leading regional research universities—do not represent distinctive differences in types of institution. The distinction is a matter of judgment, based on academic reputation. The author and the advisory committee made the judgments of how to categorize the schools.

Within the categories, the schools were chosen with a view to wide geographic distribution, representation of both private and public institutions, and inclusion of sectarian schools. Also to the extent that numbers permitted, an effort was made to include schools of different size, academic reputation (within a category), and role.

[1] The 18 types are:

1. Leading research universities (I)
2. Other research universities (II)
3. Other doctoral-granting institutions—A (I)
4. Other doctoral-granting institutions—B (II)
5. Comprehensive colleges (I)
6. Comprehensive colleges with relatively limited selection of programs (II)
7. Liberal arts colleges—highly selective (I)
8. Liberal arts colleges—other (II)
9. Theological seminaries, bible colleges
10. Medical schools and schools of osteopathic medicine
11. Other separate health professional schools
12. Schools of engineering and technology
13. Schools of business and management
14. Schools of art, music, design, and fine arts
15. Schools of law
16. Colleges of education
17. Other specialized institutions
18. Two-year colleges and institutes

Of the 41 schools selected for study, only one declined to participate. It is represented here by a substitute selection. The final sample produced a reasonably illustrative mix of institutions within each of our six major types.

National Research Universities

Harvard University

Stanford University

University of California, Berkeley

University of Chicago

University of Michigan

University of Minnesota, Minneapolis

University of Texas, Austin

Leading Regional Research Universities

New York University

Ohio University

Saint Louis University

Syracuse University

Tulane University

University of Missouri, Columbia

University of North Carolina, Chapel Hill

University of Oregon

State and Comprehensive Colleges

Boston College

Central Michigan University

Portland State University

Saint Cloud State College

San Diego State College

Liberal Arts Colleges

Albion College

Allegheny College

Beloit College

Carleton College

Cumberland College

Hamilton College

Knox College

Meredith College

Mills College

Pomona College

Whitman College

Primarily Black Colleges

Fisk University

Howard University

Huston-Tillotson College

Morgan State College

Tougaloo College

Two-Year Colleges

City Colleges of Chicago

College of San Mateo

Flint Community Junior College

Gulf Coast Junior College

Mesa College

CARNEGIE COMMISSION CLASSIFICATIONS The classification system employed in selecting the 41 institutions for study differs from the Carnegie Commission system referred to earlier in three respects. In order to gain information on the financial condition of institutions founded as Negro colleges, the study system includes an additional category for primarily black colleges, whereas the Carnegie classification system does not. Secondly, the Carnegie system divides liberal arts colleges into two groups, whereas the study plan included no separate analysis of different types of liberal arts colleges and therefore has only one category of these colleges. Finally, the Carnegie system divides universities into four groups—two for research universities and two for other doctoral-granting universities and institutions—on the basis of federal support of academic science and number of Ph.D.'s granted. We thought that the study could reveal more about the important regional institutions if we used slightly different categories, and therefore the study relied on overall academic reputation in classifying universities into the two groups—national research universities and leading regional research universities.

The differences in classification of institutions are important only in that they indicate how and why the study sample of institutions was selected. Both methods are used in several places in this study, as a means of determining whether important differences might be revealed.

For the purpose of determining the representativeness of the types of institutions selected for study, the Carnegie classification method is indispensable. The Carnegie Commission has organized the Higher Education General Information Survey (HEGIS) data —collected by the U.S. Office of Education in the Department of Health, Education, and Welfare—into its classification system by type of institution. These data permit us to compare the schools selected for study with all other institutions of each type.

Before we look at the data, let us first look at the main points in the Carnegie classification system. It divides American colleges and universities into these categories: *universities* (two groups); *comprehensive colleges* (two groups); *liberal arts colleges* (two groups); and *two-year colleges and institutes.* The universities category is divided into four subcategories: *research universities* (I and II) include the 150 leading universities as measured by federal financial support of academic science in 1967–68; and *other doctoral-granting universities and institutions* (I and II) include all other institutions that awarded at least ten Ph.D.'s in 1967–68. The comprehensive colleges (I and II) categories include institutions of higher education that offer a liberal arts program and at least one or two other programs such as engineering, business administration, or teacher education.

The category liberal arts colleges is also divided into two subcategories. One subcategory is the *liberal arts colleges* (I), which includes colleges that score 60 or above on Astin's (1965) selectivity index, *or* that were included in the list of 300 baccalaureate-granting institutions based on numbers of their graduates receiving Ph.D.'s at 40 leading doctoral-granting institutions, 1958–1966 (National Academy of Sciences, 1967). The second subcategory, *liberal arts colleges* (II), includes all other liberal arts colleges. Finally, the two-year colleges and institutes category includes all two-year institutions of higher education. When the 41 institutions in our sample are placed in the Carnegie Commission classification system, the following distribution results:

Research Universities (I and II)

Harvard University

New York University

Stanford University

Tulane University

University of California, Berkeley

University of Chicago

University of Michigan

University of Minnesota, Minneapolis

University of Missouri, Columbia

University of North Carolina, Chapel Hill

University of Oregon

University of Texas, Austin

Other Doctoral-Granting Universities and Institutions (I and II)

Boston College

Howard University

Ohio University

Saint Louis University

Syracuse University

Liberal Arts Colleges (I)

Albion College

Allegheny College

Beloit College

Carleton College

Hamilton College

Knox College

Mills College

Pomona College

Whitman College

Liberal Arts Colleges (II)

Cumberland College

Fisk University

Huston-Tillotson College

Meredith College

Tougaloo College

Comprehensive Colleges (I and II)

Central Michigan University

Morgan State College

Portland State University

Saint Cloud State College

San Diego State College

Two-Year Colleges and Institutes

City Colleges of Chicago

College of San Mateo

Flint Community Junior College

Gulf Coast Junior College

Mesa College

TABLE 1
*Enrollment
in the 41
schools
studied and
in all United
States
institutions
by category*

	Total number of institutions	
Category	*In U.S. in 1968*	*In study sample*
Research universities (I and II)	46	12
Other doctoral-granting universities (I and II)	119	5
Liberal arts colleges (I)	118	9
Liberal arts colleges (II)	576	5
Comprehensive colleges (I and II)	417	5
Two-year colleges	1,031	5

SOURCE: Data from Carnegie Commission on Higher Education. The total figures do not include 422 specialized institutions (such as theological seminaries, medical schools, etc.). In 1968, these institutions had a total enrollment of 248,595 students.

ENROLLMENT CHARACTER-ISTICS

With the 41 colleges and universities grouped into the Carnegie Commission's classification method, we can use the Commission's data to compare the schools we have selected for study with all United States institutions in each Carnegie class. The Carnegie Commission has enrollment data for 1968 and financial data for the academic year 1967–68 for all schools in its categories.

Table 1 compares the 41 institutions studied with all institutions in each category, by number of institutions and by enrollments. In addition to schools which fall within the six major Carnegie Commission categories, there are 422 small, specialized institutions, including theological seminaries, health professional schools, independent schools of law, schools of art and music, and so forth. These 422 specialized institutions had a 1968 total enrollment of 248,595 and are not included in the analysis.[2] Excluding these specialized institutions, there were, in 1968, a total of 2,307 institutions of higher education with a total enrollment of 6,633, 358.

While research universities constitute only 2 percent of the total number of institutions of higher education, they enroll 13 percent of the students. The 12 research universities in the study constitute one-fourth of all such institutions in the country. Other doctoral-granting universities constitute only 5 percent of all

---

[2] As Chapter 1 explained, we have also sought to exclude medical schools that are part of the parent institutions in the study. That was not always possible. The exceptions are noted in the text.

Total enrollment in 1968	Average enrollment in 1968		Percent of all institutions of higher learning, 1968	Percent of all students enrolled in colleges and universities, 1968
	All institutions	In study sample		
930,434	20,249	24,537	2	13
,411,782	10,334	14,902	5	20
179,593	1,522	1,338	5	3
533,906	963	1,067	25	7
,188,426	5,248	13,472	18	31
,904,800	1,848	4,375	45	26

institutions, and they enroll 20 percent of the students. Thirty-one percent of American college students attend the comprehensive colleges, which account for 18 percent of all schools. In contrast, liberal arts colleges (II) make up 25 percent of all institutions, but they enroll only 7 percent of the students. The two-year colleges make up 45 percent of all schools. They enroll 26 percent of all college students. Similarly, while constituting 5 percent of the schools, liberal arts colleges (I) educate only 3 percent of the students.

The average 1968 enrollment of the 12 research universities (I and II) in our sample was 24, 537, as compared to the average of 20,249 for all American research universities. Our five other doctoral-granting universities had an average enrollment of 14,902, while all American other doctoral-granting schools had an average of 10,334. The average enrollment of our five comprehensive colleges was 13,472, as compared to an average of 5,248 for all comprehensive colleges in the United States. Our nine liberal arts colleges (I) had an average enrollment of 1,338, compared to an average of 1,522 for all schools in that category. The average enrollment of our five liberal arts colleges (II) was 1,067, while the average for all such schools was 963. The five sample two-year colleges had an average enrollment of 4,375, compared to an average of 1,848 for all two-year colleges.

In sum, the table shows that in the two liberal arts categories, the schools in the study have average enrollments similar to those of all United States institutions of this type. The universities in

TABLE 2
*Dollar
expenditures
per student,
1967–68*

Category of institution	Educational and general	
	Study sample	*All schools*
Research universities (I and II)		
Public	$3,338	$3,286
Private	8,440	8,538
Other doctoral-granting universities (I and II)		
Public	1,700	2,023
Private	2,349	3,043
Comprehensive colleges (I and II)		
Public	1,117	1,073
Liberal arts colleges (I)		
Private	2,611	2,426
Liberal arts colleges (II)		
Private	1,736	1,454
Two-year institutions		
Public	727	739

SOURCE: Data from the Carnegie Commission on Higher Education and from individual institutions' financial information. The figures for "study sample" include all 41 institutions, while the figures for "all schools" include about 80 percent of the nation's institutions of higher education. Data from the Rockefeller Institute and California Institute of Technology are excluded from the figures for private institutions in this table.

the study and the comprehensive and two-year colleges have larger average enrollments than the United States averages in those categories.

EXPENDITURES BY FUNCTION

From data gathered by the Carnegie Commission, it is also possible to compare the expenditures by function of the 41 schools studied here with all United States institutions in each category. Approximately 80 percent of all institutions of higher education report their financial data in the Higher Education General Information Survey. The Carnegie Commission has these data for the academic year 1967–68—the latest year such data were available.

We have calculated for the six expenditure categories listed in Table 2 the average dollar expenditure per enrolled student for each of the schools in the study and made a similar average per student calculation for all United States institutions that responded to the HEGIS survey for the year 1967–68. The results are summarized in Table 2.

				Expenditure category					
struction and partmental search			*Library*	*Organized research*		*Student aid*		*Total current fund*	
dy ple	*All schools*	*Study sample*	*All schools*	*Study sample*	*All schools*	*Study sample*	*All schools*	*Study sample*	*All schools*
297	$1,146	$119	$ 95	$ 859	$ 824	$235	$142	$ 4,165	$4,000
379	1,890	288	265	4,576	4,073	632	627	10,030	9,964
935	821	62	74	45	410	82	85	2,301	2,573
002	1,076	87	119	435	659	174	301	2,972	3,902
537	601	72	64	22	16	50	51	1,432	1,467
214	1,113	126	127	34	57	336	287	4,048	3,675
755	651	88	82	21	8	234	146	2,424	2,188
426	432	39	37	0	0	15	15	918	877

Table 2 shows that the average expenditure per student by the 41 schools in our survey is comparable to those for all American institutions of higher education. As the table shows, the public research universities (I) in our study had a slightly higher average expenditure figure in all six expenditure categories than did the average public research university. Similarly, the average expenditure per student in the liberal arts colleges in our survey was somewhat higher in all six expenditure categories than that of the average liberal arts college. On the other hand, the other doctoral-granting universities in the survey had lower average expenditures per student other than all other institutions except in one category. The four other types of schools in our survey, the private research universities, the comprehensive colleges, the liberal arts colleges, and the two-year colleges, had average expenditure-per-student figures very similar to those of all institutions in their respective categories.

Thus, considered overall, the average expenditures of the 41 schools in the survey are quite similar to the average American institution of higher education in each Carnegie Commission category. Although several of the schools in the study are larger than the average in their type across the nation, the similarity of average expenditure suggests that the cost-income situation is probably similar to all schools.

3. Criteria for Determining Financial Trouble

Colleges and universities in a healthy financial state, although not rare, are clearly in the minority, and, in fact, their situation is so much at variance with the daily experience of most presidents that some find it hard to believe that such campuses truly exist.

"From my recent observations of college and university campuses," President Paul C. Reinert told the interviewer who visited Saint Louis University, "I conclude that institutions of higher education can be divided into three categories: First, there are those in serious financial trouble, but who don't know it; next, there are those that are in serious financial trouble, but have not yet faced up to it; and finally, there are the institutions that are in serious financial trouble, who know it, and who are working on it."

There is no ambiguity about the position of his own university. Having just dropped its schools of dentistry and engineering for financial reasons, it is now in the midst of a reevaluation of its entire academic program and its supporting financial structure. It is solidly in Father Reinert's category three.

As for his categories one and two, there are apt examples of each among the campuses visited in this study, but they do not exhaust the list. A highly respected president now in his twenty-first year in office, Reinert is often called upon as consultant for institutions in financial difficulty, and he is, therefore, less likely to have on his itinerary a fourth category of institutions, such as the University of North Carolina or Gulf Coast Junior College, schools not in financial trouble and apparently not headed for it. They are well represented in this study — 12 of the 41 schools visited are in this category — and Chapter 4 analyzes their characteristics. First, however, it will be helpful to examine what is meant when we discuss financial health and financial difficulty, and to establish the definitions used to classify the colleges and universities in this study.

In making judgments of the financial condition of an academic institution, one must begin by stating the criteria of financial health and financial difficulty. The standard we use here defines difficulty in terms of the institution's ability to carry out its self-determined mission at the level of quality it sets for itself. We believe such a standard is objective although it is contingent on any particular institution's academic goals. For purposes of this study, an institution is judged *in financial difficulty* if its current financial condition results in a loss of services that are regarded as a part of its program *or* a loss of quality. An institution is classified as *headed for financial trouble* if, at the time of the study, it has been able to meet current responsibilities but either cannot ensure that it can much longer meet current program standards or cannot plan support for evolving program growth. Those colleges and universities which can meet their current program standards, and can with some assurance plan program growth, are classified *not in financial trouble.* These definitions are elaborated in the next section of this chapter, but it should be emphasized at the very outset that our financial classifications *not in financial trouble, headed for financial trouble,* and *in financial difficulty* are not based on, and do not themselves reflect, any judgments of the academic and educational excellence of the institutions studied. Moreover, because our definition of *in financial difficulty* depends on whether the institution is cutting programs, there is no necessary connection between the quality of a school's administration and its financial classification here. In any given case a school could be in financial difficulty precisely because it has good management which is making the changes necessary to remedy financial problems.

Our definitions of financial health and difficulty are quite different from ones based on the criteria of success in business, such as profits or rates of return on investment — criteria which are generalized in the business community and do not specifically take account of the organization's mission. It does not seem useful to try to apply criteria of financial health derived from business analogies.

There is no academic criterion comparable to price-earnings ratios or profit-and-loss statements, but persons often invite comparisons with business organizations by saying that the methods of business make for institutional success. It may be that schools would benefit financially from more businesslike methods, but even if there were a reliable standard characterization of methods as those "of business"—and business practices vary widely—it is most unlikely that the quality of an enterprise's methods would be an adequate guide to its financial health.

More importantly, it is essential to distinguish methods from goals. Financial condition is itself the goal of business organizations, but it is only the enabling condition of academic organizations. This difference is worth emphasizing for it reminds us that an assessment of a university's financial condition is a statement of the relationship between its objectives and its ability to carry them out.

There is another tempting parallel between business organizations and academic organizations. It goes something like this: If we can say that a business' health is improved when it makes more money, can we not also say that a college's health is improved when it can spend more money? Robert M. Hutchins offered such a formulation in 1933, in an article entitled "Hard Times and Higher Learning." "The excellence of a commercial corporation depends on the amount of money it can make. The excellence of an educational corporation depends roughly—very roughly, I admit —on the amount of money it can spend."

It is true that colleges and universities tend to spend all the money they raise. Their "costs" therefore are determined in large part by their income. It is reasonable to assume that increasing expenditures for things like library facilities, better faculty, and research support does improve the quality of the institution's teaching and research programs. Nevertheless, the "more is better" argument, which makes the ability to spend the criterion of quality, is unsound. For one thing, it is primarily adapted to one kind of institution—the large university oriented toward graduate and research work. It provides no basis for evaluating the circumstances of a large university in comparison with those of a small liberal arts college; indeed, on the spending criterion alone, a small college could probably never be said to be excellent or free of financial difficulty. In fact, there is a variety of types of institutions of higher learning—as is shown in Chapter 2—with different objectives and serving different educational and social needs. The criteria for evaluating institutions of different types must take account of the institution's type of objectives and social role.

Thus, the "more is better" argument is unsatisfactory for the same reasons that the "fat in the budget" argument in Chapter 1 was unsatisfactory. Both are right in proposing an objective standard, but both are wrong in making the criterion of health external to the institution's characteristics. The "fat in the budget" argument meant that, if an institution can spend less and survive, it is healthy to spend less, for the higher expenditures must be fat. Just as the "fat in the budget" argument is unsatisfactory for university presidents, the "more is better" argument will not satisfy those who must supply funds to higher education. Individual donors, legislators, and foundations want an independent criterion, one which judges the adequacy of income for the program and aspirations of an individual institution.

There is another difference between business and academic organizations that is worth noting. When one has a question about the financial health of a business corporation, he consults the fundamental reference volumes, such as Standard & Poor's *Corporation Records,* or Moody's *Manuals,* where he will find a brief history of each company and the data which measure financial success: assets, income, earnings, dividends, and stock prices. There are prompt revisions when new corporate reports are issued or when other important developments occur which affect the outlook for a company; there are daily supplements and biweekly supplements which summarize news bulletins about matters likely to affect the financial health and outlook of individual companies. And there are analyses of conditions, industry by industry. There are no comparable sources to which one can turn for information about the financial health of colleges and universities. The absence of uniform data adapted to a uniform process of evaluation tends to confirm the need to use criteria of financial condition that relate to the institution's individual characteristics.

Information about program, quality, and growth can probably be obtained only by visits to individual campuses. That is often true of a school's financial data also. In assessing an individual institution's financial condition, therefore, this study relied primarily on the information obtained from the president and his administrative colleagues during the personal interviews conducted at the school. The information concerned program growth and prospect as well as financial condition. In addition, all available financial data for the academic years 1959–60 through 1970–71 were obtained from each institution. These data consist of itemized current fund expenditures and income, and enrollment figures. From this one can calculate annual rates of change in expenditure for instruction and departmental research per student, educational and general expenditures per student, educational and general less sponsored-research expenditures per student, and student aid expenditures per student. The trend in these expenditure calculations, especially during the last few years, is an additional factor used in assessing the financial situation of each school.[1]

We see, therefore, that the standard for evaluating the financial condition of an academic institution cannot be derived from business standards but rather should relate resources to program and mission. It is difficult to imagine a useful standard that does not do that. Such a standard answers the questions the potential

---

[1] The data used here warrant the conclusions drawn from them, but, since they have limitations, it is important to note them. Several problems are involved in attempting to make itemized income and expenditure data from an institution of higher education internally consistent over an extended period of time, and in attempting to make these data consistent with figures from other institutions. We attempted to locate and correct internal problems due to changes within an individual institution's classification (for example, making consistent what has been included in the accounting category *student aid,* or *general administration* expenditures). However, there may be a number of relatively minor accounting changes from year to year which would have been identified if we had made a complete examination of past books and records. Given the objectives of this study, we did not believe it necessary to do so. Insofar as we can tell by sampling such past records, no trends or classification used here would be changed, although some magnitudes might be. The interested reader may wish to consult Jenny and Wynn (1969, pp. 261–294), a careful statistical analysis of the economics of 31 private liberal arts colleges. In that important work, the authors gathered highly detailed financial data and adjusted them so as to be as consistent as possible both within each institution and among the various institutions.

Another limitation on the usefulness of the financial calculations made here is caused by certain gaps in the data. Although we attempted to gather itemized income and expenditures from each institution for each year of the last decade, in a number of institutions there are gaps in some series. The reasons for these gaps are varied—a complete overhaul of the accounting system, the fact that the data for the most recent year(s) were not yet available, the lack of confidence by the institution in some of its earlier data, even the fact that the institution did not compile financial data until very recently.

In addition, while we attempted to exclude from the data the expenditures and income for medical schools, in a few schools the figures could not be separated.

In sum, the study does not have expenditure and income figures for all 41 institutions for each year since 1959–60. Nor can we always be confident that all the data are internally consistent. We are confident, however, that the financial data are sufficient to support the conclusions we draw about trends and changes in income and expenditure.

donor, or the faculty member considering offers from rival competing schools, or the student deciding where to enroll must ask. One can disagree with an institution's program plans and aspirations, but in this study we accept the institution's definition of its mission and impose no judgment of our own on what it ought to be doing, except perhaps to assume that the institution has quality and growth aspirations which are, in some objective sense, appropriate to it.

Clearly, our approach of deferring to the institution's definition of its mission can be troublesome. At the extreme, one can do nothing at zero cost, and hence not be in trouble. Thus there is the problem that, by relying on an institution's own goals, the study will consider more favorably those institutions with lower aspirations, for they will have fewer financial obligations and be in a better position to meet them. Our approach therefore requires that the reader make an independent judgment about the aspirations and quality of the institutions in each of the three categories in this study.

APPLYING THE CRITERIA
The authors of the 1937 AAUP study point out that the first test faced by colleges and universities was how to economize without loss of quality or abandonment of services it regarded as essential and integral parts of its program. As we indicated in the preceding section, this is a good formulation of the minimum conditions of a secure financial position, and we use it with some modification. Once our interview and financial data were gathered, each institution was put to the test as to whether its financial situation has changed to the extent that it must abandon services (other than those which are obviously peripheral or trivial), or cannot reliably plan for normal program growth and continuity. Out of our analysis of the application of this standard, we derived what we take to be a reasonably fair and descriptive financial classification of institutions into those *not in financial trouble,* those *headed for financial trouble,* and those *in financial difficulty.* These are explained immediately below. Although the standard may appear to be authoritative and the categories definitive, there are a number of qualifications to be made in the exhaustiveness of the standard and in its application. These are discussed in the next section of this chapter.

To repeat from our statement in the preceding section, an institution is judged in financial difficulty if its current financial condition results in a loss of services that are regarded as parts of its program *or* a loss of quality.

There are, of course, complicated degrees of severity of financial difficulty. In some instances, the difficulty is clear. For other schools it is not easy to make judgments as to whether the proper classification is *in financial difficulty* or *headed for financial trouble*. The issue arises because of the process of response to financial adversity by colleges and universities. They first take steps that do not hurt (such as leaving vacant positions not yet the subject of active recruitment); they decline new obligations; and they make revisions in plans. Next comes a deterioration in the standards applied to current program. Usually, after that, come the program cuts, held for last because they are the most painful. Whether an institution is judged in financial difficulty or headed for financial trouble depends on the evidence as to how far it has moved in this process.

There is a paradox here: The more a school is doing to adjust its expenditures to its income, the more likely it is to be considered in financial difficulty. A school that takes few steps will be considered headed for financial trouble as long as its financing permits it to postpone serious readjustment. There is at least one such case in this study. On the other hand, a school which aggressively faces up to the need to make hard decisions cutting "dead wood" and reallocating priorities may for those reasons be classified here as in financial difficulty. Moreover, as indicated above, there is no necessary connection between academic quality and financial trouble; in fact, in some cases financially induced program changes may result in qualitative improvement.

To repeat again, an institution is classified as headed for financial trouble if, at the time of the study, it has been able to meet current responsibilities but either cannot ensure that it can much longer meet current program standards or cannot plan support for evolving program growth. As with the classification *in financial difficulty*, there are complicated degrees of the problem.

Where there is a period of financial stringency, as Bowen (1968) points out, there is a ". . . relatively unspectacular decline in effectiveness, a decline whose onset is marked to the discerning observer only by the things that the institution is not doing which it ought to be doing." When a decline in effectiveness could be detected, the institution was judged to be in financial difficulty. When the decline was not a present reality, but a likely prospect in that the institution either could not plan essential program growth or ensure that it could very long meet quality requirements, it was classified as headed for financial trouble.

Finally, those colleges and universities which can meet current quality and program standards, and can with some assurance plan program growth, are classified not in financial trouble. These institutions are easiest to identify, but even this category is subject to problems of interpretation.

JUDGING FINANCIAL HEALTH Our campus visits convinced us that the findings from this study would be most useful if they made a clear statement about the financial condition of individual institutions. We have done so, and in the process had to make several difficult judgments. There are at least six kinds of problems one encounters in making such judgments. The first is that in some instances judgments of financial condition made important assumptions about the future. For example, we have assumed for one institution that particular donors will make substantial contributions, that election results will be favorable (College of San Mateo), or that a certain budget bill will pass (University of Michigan). All of these were pending at the time of the campus visit.

Second, the ability to finance programs is a reliable long-term indicator of financial health, but it can be misleading for short periods. By borrowing, selling assets, or drawing on endowment or reserve funds, an institution can maintain quality, program, and even growth standards which current income alone cannot maintain. This may be a relatively short-term situation depending upon an institution's resources and willingness to gamble. The University of Chicago and Boston College are examples of institutions that have been drawing on endowment to avoid quality or program cuts in the short run but that cannot expect to escape serious readjustments through continued deficit financing.

The financial condition of schools doing deficit financing must be classified in the light of their prospects for finding new income. From a program standpoint alone, Harvard could be classified as in financial difficulty, but its endowment is so large and its long-term income prospects good enough that it is judged here as neither in financial difficulty nor out of financial difficulty. It is a unique case which is best characterized as headed for financial trouble.

Third, there are institutions which, during the last decade, expanded enrollment and graduate and professional programs very rapidly but could not build the necessary underlying financial support (for library, laboratory, and related facilities). Judged by annual increments in budgeted expenditures for instruction and research alone, institutions in this situation might appear free of financial difficulty. But without new financial resources to build the necessary facilities, they will be in qualitative trouble. Portland State is an example of this situation.

Fourth, we have assumed that increasing the student-faculty ratio is a quality cut. That judgment is open to challenge on empirical grounds.

A fifth problem is posed by the marginal cases. Meredith College, for example, is classified here as not in financial trouble. That represents our best judgment, but a case can be made for putting it in the group headed for financial trouble. Pomona College is classified as headed for financial trouble, but it, too, is a close case; it has much in common with schools not in financial trouble. The University of Minnesota is a similar case. NYU is classified as in financial difficulty, but that, too, is a marginal judgment, and it could be in the category headed for financial trouble. The University of Missouri is a similar example, except the categories are reversed. Its situation was judged, on balance, to be one best described as headed for financial trouble. Yet it is in an advanced stage of that category, and it could be argued that the school belongs in the group in financial difficulty.

Finally, the rate of depression in academic finance appears to be accelerating. Those schools in financial difficulty and headed for financial trouble reported that the adversity of their situation was mounting rapidly. In no case is there basis for assuming that the situation would be better than this study found it. Even schools not in financial trouble show signs of the depression in school finance. Not all members of this group will remain immune if the problem continues for long.

4. *Institutions Not in Financial Trouble*

Of the 41 institutions examined in this study, 12 (29 percent) were not in financial trouble at the time of the campus visit. Nor, according to the definition used here, were they headed for financial trouble, although as we shall see shortly, income and expenditures for this group are showing a downturn. Their relative health depends on continued support. None is permanently shielded from a prolonged downturn. But as of the time of this study, these schools were in a significantly better position than the other 29 institutions examined.

Listed by our method of classification, the 12 schools "not in financial trouble" are:

National research university
  University of Texas, Austin

Leading regional research university
  University of North Carolina, Chapel Hill

State and comprehensive college
  Saint Cloud State College

Liberal arts colleges
  Hamilton College
  Meredith College
  Mills College
  Whitman College

Primarily black colleges
  Howard University
  Morgan State College

Two-year colleges
  College of San Mateo
  Flint Community Junior College
  Gulf Coast Junior College

These schools are considered not in financial trouble primarily on the basis of the campus interviews. In the interviews the administrators reported they were able to meet their current self-determined quality and program standards and could, with some assurance, plan new program growth. The interviews also show that these schools have not had to make program cuts, nor abandon existing plans for future programs because of financial difficulty. These schools are not immune from the cost-income problem that gave rise to this study. Like most of the institutions in the study, they worry about money and have been cost conscious. But, unlike the other schools, as a group they are more confident about their financial prospects. The interviewer found one school not in financial trouble but noted that the administrators "wouldn't agree." There may be others in this situation. The administrators at each of these schools did report at the time of the interview that their school's financial outlook was such that it will be able to maintain its quality standards and program growth. Those assessments tend to be confirmed by the expenditure data for these schools which, when compared with the data for all others, show a similar rate of growth and a smaller rate of decline in expenditures due to the financial problems now facing all schools. We shall examine these financial data later in this chapter.

It would be well at this point to repeat a caution about the sample noted earlier in Chapter 2. The 41 institutions selected for study here are not intended as a representative sample of all 2,729 institutions of higher education. The process of choosing them was not random, but was selective in a conscious effort to study institutions that are illustrative of the major types of institutions of higher education. This means that the above finding of 29 percent of the study sample as not in financial trouble does *not* warrant general inferences about the percentage of institutions in financial difficulty, or not in financial trouble. We can, however, draw certain conclusions from the institutions studied, first by comparing them with other schools in the sample, and next by looking at the factors common to those colleges and universities not in financial trouble.

COMPARISON WITH OTHER SCHOOLS The following comparison of the institutions not in financial trouble with the entire sample of institutions in the study is designed to see whether the schools not in financial trouble have common characteristics that distinguish them as a group from the other schools. The presence of common characteristics may be instructive in explaining the financial situation of the group not in financial trouble. In comparing the distribution over certain variables of the group not in financial trouble with that of the whole group, we have picked variables that lend themselves to quantitative comparison and for which figures could be readily obtained. Our intent was to pick relatively reliable ingredients in a kind of common-sense overall profile of the institutions. Thus, we have asked whether the schools not in financial trouble are distinguishable by their breakdown into public and private schools, by types of educational role, by geographic and urban characteristics, and by size of student body.[1]

First, the breakdown between public and private institutions. In the sample, 18 colleges and universities (44 percent) were public institutions, and 23 (56 percent) were private.[2] Of the schools classified as not in financial trouble, seven (58 percent) are public institutions and five (42 percent) are private. The numbers are small, but two generalizations seem justified (and are supported by other observations): Although both types of institutions are facing economic adversity, there are also both private and public institutions still spared from its effects. Secondly, public institutions have thus far had somewhat more success in avoiding economic difficulty than have private institutions, especially the large private institutions. There are private colleges in each of the three classifications used in this study *(not in financial trouble, headed for financial trouble, in financial difficulty),* but the large private institutions are heavily disproportionately in financial difficulty. Of the nine large private institutions in this study, only Howard University appears in the category not in financial trouble.[3]

[1] Similar comparisons are also made in Chapters 5 and 6. Some quantifiable data —such as student-faculty ratios, student attrition rates, number of degrees granted, educational quality ratings—were not used here because they are either unreliable, difficult to obtain, or have little potential in accounting for financial situation.

[2] As is often pointed out, patterns of financing raise fundamental questions about the meaning of the distinction between public and private institutions. For this study we have simply accepted an institution's statement of its ownership, public or private.

[3] There are no private two-year institutions in this study, and one might therefore want to exclude two-year institutions—there are five altogether, with three not in financial trouble—from consideration when computing the distribution of public and private institutions not in financial trouble. The figures then become less striking: 44 percent of the schools not in financial trouble are public (4 out of 9) as compared with the 36 percent of all schools in the reduced sample that are public (13 out of 36); 56 percent of the schools not in financial trouble are private (5 out of 9); but 64 percent of the entire sample (23 out of 36) are private. Our study indicates that, in recent years, the specialized public service mission of the public two-year colleges has had the greatest protection against the cost-income squeeze; the mission of the large private research university has received the least.

When the institutions are grouped by type according to the method used in selecting the sample for this study (see Chapter 2), two types of schools seem underrepresented in the category not in financial trouble. These are the national research universities and the leading regional research universities. The ratios for the liberal arts colleges, state and comprehensive colleges, and primarily black institutions seem too close to permit any inference of difference; and the two-year colleges are more heavily represented in the category not in financial trouble.

	National research universities	Leading regional research universities	State and comprehensive colleges	Liberal arts colleges	Primarily black institutions	Two-year colleges
Schools not in financial trouble	8%	8%	8%	33%	17%	25%
All institutions studied	17%	20%	12%	27%	12%	12%

The rough overall trend of these findings is about the same when the schools are regrouped according to the classification method used by the Carnegie Commission on Higher Education.

	Research universities (I and II)	Doctoral-granting universities (I and II)	Comprehensive colleges (I and II)	Liberal arts colleges (I)	Liberal arts colleges (II)	Two-year colleges
Schools not in financial trouble	17%	8%	17%	25%	8%	25%
All institutions studied	29%	12%	12%	22%	12%	12%

There are some regional differences between the entire sample of institutions studied and those found not in financial trouble, as the following figures suggest:

	South	Midwest	East	West
Schools not in financial trouble	33%	17%	25%	25%
All institutions studied	22%	34%	20%	24%

The East and West Coast regions are represented by approximately the same relative number of institutions in the total sample and in the institutions found not in financial trouble. The South is more heavily represented in the category not in financial trouble, whereas the Midwest has less than its proportionate share of schools classified not in financial trouble.

About one-half of the schools in the sample (22 out of 41) are located in large metropolitan areas. Although that ratio is also true of the schools classified not in financial trouble, a large urban location does tend to be associated with our category *in financial difficulty,* as we shall see in Chapter 6.

Finally, when the schools not in financial trouble are compared with the other institutions by size of the student body (using fall, 1968, figures), one finds that, overall, the former schools are slightly smaller than the latter, and there are two differences by type of institution that seem more interesting. The two primarily black institutions not in financial trouble have an average enrollment of 6,547 as against 902 for the other three, all of which are judged in financial difficulty. Among the liberal arts colleges, average enrollment for those not in financial trouble is 901, and for the others it is 1,605. Since the size comparisons must be made among similar types of institutions (i.e., two-year colleges not in financial trouble as against all two-year colleges, etc.), the number of schools involved in each comparison is very small, and these observations should be treated with caution.

In sum, compared to all institutions studied, those classified as not in financial trouble include relatively more public than private institutions; among the private schools, the classification includes relatively more smaller institutions; schools from the South are more heavily represented in this category, as are the two-year colleges; among the primarily black schools in this study, those not in financial trouble are the large ones, and among the liberal arts colleges in this study, those not in financial trouble are the small ones. To some extent this profile of the characteristic tendencies of the schools not in financial trouble is helpful, along with other factors, in explaining their situation, and we will consider it in the "salutary factors" section of this chapter. First, we should ask whether there is a single hypothesis that accounts for the exceptional financial condition of the 12 schools classified not in financial trouble.

EXPENDITURE PATTERNS

Although it is natural to try to find one unifying explanation that accounts for any school's being not in financial trouble, there is almost certainly not a single theory that will do so for the schools in this study. It seems reasonable to say "almost" because the total number of institutions studied is not large and does not warrant analysis under tests for statistical significance. But, it is doubtful that a larger number of cases would produce a single explanation that accounts for why this category of institutions differs from the others.

The essence of the financial crisis is a cost-income squeeze, and one might expect that there is some cost or income characteristic unique to the most healthy schools that accounts for their avoidance of the squeeze. This does not seem to be the case. It is easier to detect the causes of impaired financial health than it is to determine the cause of continued good health. On the basis of an examination of the income and expenditure records of all institutions for the entire decade of the 1960s, and analysis of the information obtained by interviews with campus officials, we cannot find a sole financial factor to account for the success of these schools. Rather, when these records and the interview information are compared with those from the other institutions, a variety of factors stand out as members of a set that probably accounts for the more secure financial condition. These factors are easier to identify than they are to weigh; they are discussed later in this chapter.

Changes in the major expenditure categories of the institutions not in financial trouble do not reveal a hypothesis that might singly explain their significantly better financial condition. An analysis of these patterns is presented in Table 3 showing average annual rates of increase in important categories of expenditures per student. We use average annual percentage increase in cost per student as the best summary of expenditure experience. It permits reliable comparisons between different institutions and is not distorted by enrollment growth.[4] We examine four major expenditure categories; the footnotes to the table explain the expenditure items included in each of these categories.

Both groups of schools had a similar average annual rate of increase in their educational and general expenditures, and for their educational and general expenditures less sponsored research. The overall rate of expenditure growth for these areas (and for the sponsored research) was virtually the same. For schools not in fi-

[4] Presenting the data in this form also permits us to compare it with Bowen's finding, referred to in Chapter 1, that budgeted instruction and departmental research, per student, rose at an annual rate of 7.5 percent over the period 1949–1966.

TABLE 3 *Average annual rate of expenditure increase per student, 1959–60 to 1969–70*

	Educational and general*	Educational and general less sponsored research†	Instruction and departmental research‡	Student aid§
Schools not in financial trouble	8.0%	7.7%	7.3%	12.0%
All other institutions studied	7.9%	7.6%	7.8%	19.4%

*The total current fund expenditures, including sponsored research and excluding expenditures on auxiliary enterprises and student aid. This category of expenditure thus includes instruction, research, departmental and campus administration, maintenance, extension, and public service.

† The total current fund expenditures, excluding research sponsored from nonuniversity sources as well as expenditures on auxiliary enterprises and student aid.

‡ Expenditures on instruction, consisting of expenditures on faculty salaries for teaching and research and departmental administration. This expenditure item constitutes a portion of educational and general expenditures.

§ Total expenditures on financial aid for students, including grants, scholarships, and fellowships, but excluding loans. This expenditure item is not included in the category of educational and general expenditures.

nancial trouble, the rate of increase in expenditure for instruction and departmental research is slightly smaller than for the other institutions studied. It could be argued from this that the schools not in financial trouble place slightly more emphasis on increasing supporting activities than academic program or faculty, although the differences are small.

There was, as the table shows, a sizable difference in the rate of increase in expenditures for student aid. Schools that were not in financial trouble had an average annual increase for the period (per student) of 12.0 percent, whereas for all other schools in the study, the comparable figure was 19.4 percent. This constitutes an important difference in the expenditure burden between the two groups of schools, although this fact in itself would not account for the entire difference in their financial position. Student aid amounts to 5.9 percent of total current fund expenditures (except for auxiliary enterprises) at the schools not in financial trouble and 8.6 percent at the others.

In summary, the expenditure data show that compared to the other schools studied, the schools not in financial trouble spend less for student aid, spend slightly less for instruction and research, and spend slightly more for program and institutional support. Since the study gathered only aggregate expenditure data for major expenditure categories (as listed in the foregoing table), we cannot determine what changes have occurred within any of these categories over the decade. The interviews at the schools not in financial trouble indicate that these institutions do have different expenditure patterns within the categories which may be related to their financial condition, as we shall see later in this chapter. Since we have no accounting data for the items that make up the aggregate expenditure categories, we shall report these differences when we consider the interview findings.

From the foregoing discussion, we conclude there is no simple explanation from expenditure data alone for the relatively more secure financial condition of the schools not in financial trouble.

INCOME FACTORS The same is true of the income data. They provide no single explanation, but they provide clues. During the decade of the 1960s, income of schools not in financial trouble grew at approximately the same rate as total expenditures until the year 1967–68. In that year, expenditure growth exceeded income growth and has continued to do so each year since. As the table below shows, for the period 1959–60 to 1969–70, the average annual rate of expenditures was 7.5 percent per student for these institutions. Income increased at an average over those years of 7.1 percent per student per year.

Average annual rate of increase in current income and current expenditures per student, schools not in financial trouble (1959–60 to 1969–70)

Rate of income growth	7.1%
Rate of expenditure growth	7.5%

The income figures reported in the above table are based on all current fund income. They include income from auxiliary enterprises and all other sources. The income data available to us make it necessary to present them this way. Therefore, in order to make the expenditure data comparable, they, too, are calculated on the basis of all expenditures, including student aid and auxiliary enterprises, which were treated separately and excluded in the previous section. For that reason the rate of expenditure increase here differs slightly from the one reported earlier in this chapter. The difference is apparently due to the fact that the expenditures for auxiliary enterprises did not increase as rapidly as those for the rest of current fund.

As the table indicates, the average annual difference in the rates of expenditure and income growth was less than one-half of one percentage point throughout the decade—an amount which could be a "normal" variance, or in any event might be absorbed for a limited time without abnormal drain on reserves. The fact that the difference occurred mostly in the latest years confirms that these institutions are not immune from the cost-income squeeze. Like all other schools, their income growth rate is declining, although as we note later in this chapter, administrators of these institutions are relatively more confident about future income prospects than are their colleagues at the other institutions. With one exception, they have not had to resort to deficit financing. Thus 1 of the 5 private institutions not in financial trouble is deficit spending, whereas 13 of the 18 other private institutions in the study are deficit spending.[5] For most of those 13, this is a relatively recent phenomenon. Over most of the decade their income growth was the same as that of the schools not in financial trouble. The cost-income squeeze has forced the deficits in the last few years.

The factors that constitute the income decline apply to all schools, not in financial trouble and otherwise. These factors were discussed in general in Chapter 1. Thus, for the schools not in financial trouble, the rate of growth of income from private gifts and grants is declining. Second, the rate of growth of income from endowment is declining. Finally, the rate of growth of income from federal sources is declining. These three trends all appear in the experience of the other schools in this study, but their effects are more serious for those institutions. These three trends in income growth are discussed in some detail in connection with the institutions headed for financial trouble and in financial difficulty in Chapters 5 and 6 and are analyzed in Chapter 7 along with expenditure trends.

SALUTARY FACTORS The preceding review of expenditure and income data reveals no obvious, single basis for certain schools being not in financial trouble. However, we can identify in the data several differences between the schools not in financial trouble and others which provide clues to an explanation for some being not in financial trouble.

---

[5] Mills College had a deficit of $185,000 in 1969–70, but administrators consider it a one-time occurrence. It was eliminated in the next budget year by an increase in tuition and fees, and the institution does not face a basic situation which threatens to generate continuing deficits.

We found on the expenditure side, first, that schools not in financial trouble did not spend as much on student aid and, second, that in their allocation of education and general expenditures they spent relatively less on faculty salaries and academic departments and relatively more on supporting activities. On the income side, the differences in the decline in the rate of growth can be seen in several factors. First, although the rates of growth of income from private gifts and grants, from federal sources, and from endowment are declining, they are declining less at the schools not in financial trouble; second, reliance on income from the federal government as a share of income grew less rapidly in the 1960s at these schools; third, endowment income is a relatively larger share of total income at these schools. Correlatively, there was less rise in tuition as an income source at the schools not in financial trouble.

Together, these differences add up to a not-in-financial-trouble balance sheet. But they are not self-explanatory. They are obviously the result of other conditions. We will try in this section to describe what the conditions are that have, overall, given rise to the better financial position of the institutions not in financial trouble. We derive our description of these underlying conditions primarily from the detailed interview data. When the interviews are combined with the financial data, some 10 factors of importance stand out. These factors seem to apply favorably to all, or virtually all, schools not in financial trouble, and by and large apply unfavorably to the other institutions studied. Taken together, these factors, in our judgment, generally account for the relatively favored financial condition and outlook of the schools not in financial trouble.

Not each of the factors is equally important for each school, and some of these factors explain or give rise to other factors in the set. In some degree, some of these conditions may be the result of financial stability as well as its basis. We state these factors at an intermediate level of depth; that is, they do not purport to be an irreducible set of causes of the academic economic depression or to exceed the study's competence. They are stated at about as basic a level as the study permits in order to maximize what condition they may make to an understanding of the record. They are also basic enough to begin to be useful, to be considered in the behavior of institutions and their members who are concerned with the economic situation. Some may commend themselves, others of course may not; and some are fixed circumstances that cannot be directly controlled. In any event, we have not considered competing values or disadvantages which some of these conditions may entail as bases for action. In short, we are not suggesting what any schools ought to be doing, in finance or in program. We are saying what, on the basis of our financial study, has been happening at the schools not in financial trouble that relates specifically to their financial condition.

We think these are the important conditions:

1 *Less affected by campus disturbances.* Freedom from the adverse income and expenditure effects of serious campus disturbances is a condition common to all institutions classified not in financial trouble.

Of the 12 schools in this category, 7 reported that they have had no campus disturbances. Several reported that freedom from campus disturbances had helped in obtaining private gifts; in keeping legislative funds coming for reasonable budget requests; and in avoiding high security, insurance, and related costs. President Martin Jenkins told the interviewer who visited Morgan State that "there have been no serious campus disruptions," and in consequence there is "no public sentiment against this college." That best summarizes the views stated by the others in the group. In one way or another, all seven say the same thing: Income is not hurt because we have had no disturbances. This is true of income in the form of both private gifts and legislative appropriations.

Three of the institutions—Mills, Flint, and College of San Mateo—have each had a single campus disturbance, but all ended relatively quickly and, as of the time of the interview, had had no discernible effect on income. Texas and Howard report they have had disturbances, but, for reasons which were not explained, these have not *yet* (emphasis theirs) had an effect on income.

To the extent that the effects of campus peace are measured by private gifts and grants, there is some corroborating evidence in the current fund accounts of the schools studied. In all institutions, the percentage of current fund income received from private gifts and grants remained fairly stable until just after the middle of the decade. Since that time, there has been a small decline in the relative share of overall income coming from gifts at the schools not in financial trouble as well as all other institutions studied; but the decline in that relative share for schools not in financial trouble is smaller than for the other schools. Several administrators attribute these differences to the presence or absence of disturbances on campus.

Complementing the income side, these institutions were also saved from much of the increased expenditure burden that comes with campus disturbances, particularly violent ones. They have not escaped altogether, for some insurance premium increases have affected all institutions whether or not they have, in fact, had damage claims. But the costs of increased security, property replacement and repair, and increased staff have not been a factor with this group. Those schools that have not had a disturbance have not incurred significant new expenses. Even those institutions not in financial trouble that have had disturbances, such as the University of Texas, have not yet been significantly affected. The dollar amounts spent on security can be quite large. One middle-sized university, which we classify as headed for financial trouble, at one point indicated that the cost of its security forces has increased by $1 million a year and had doubled over the past two years. "The total amount spent for security would run two small good departments," this university reported.

The president of the nationwide University Insurance Managers Association recently reported that campuses around the country face "astronomical insurance rates." Speaking in San Francisco, he provided two local examples of what he called a national situation, involving universities that have had major disturbances. When the University of California recently renewed its property insurance, the cost rose from a premium of $200,000 for three years to a premium of $344,000 for just one year. At the same time, the self-insured deductible amount rose from $250,000 to $1,000,000. Another example of rising costs cited in his report was the experience of Stanford University. It was forced to renegotiate its insurance before its current policy expired. The university was able to keep its insurance at the existing premium only by agreeing to change its $25,000 deductible per year to a new deductible limit of $500,000 per occurrence.[6] The consequence of these insurance changes is not only that premiums will rise, of course, but also that with continued destruction of property, the schools' direct outlays for repairs within the deductible limits will increase dramatically.

[6] *San Francisco Examiner* (May 20, 1970, p. 3). If a new proposal by the Wisconsin State Insurance Laws Revision Committee is adopted, that state will shift these insurance costs to students via a $100 a semester anti-riot insurance fee. It provides for pooling of funds over the state and reimbursement to students for semesters in which there are no losses.

Security, property, and insurance costs can be absorbed by cutting other expenditures as well as by increasing total outlays. There is another form of opportunity costs for disturbances as well: These are the forced reallocations of staff time and of administrators' time and energies away from activities and initiatives that in the long run make for a better economic situation, as well as a better educational one, and toward attempts to solve short-run crisis situations.

This study did not try to determine how these institutions have avoided serious campus disturbances. There is a large, rapidly growing, and rather conflicting literature on this question. Fortunately, this study was not intended to provide answers to it. But one aspect of the relative absence of serious campus disturbances is suggested by the next condition common to these institutions, the fit between program and expectations.

2 *Good fit between aspiration and program.* The interview guide, used for the campus visits, asked of each president, "How good is the fit between aspiration and actual program? For your students? For your faculty?" Most administrators felt able to answer this question. About one-fourth of the responses were too general to be used here. Among the rest, however, there is a marked contrast between the responses from institutions not in financial trouble and others. In the latter group, only one-quarter of the institutions said that their program was in good fit with their students' expectations; 40 percent said the fit between faculty aspiration and program could be described as good. By contrast, in the schools not in financial trouble, two-thirds said that their program constituted a good fit with student aspiration. In the case of faculty, the reported correspondence was 100 percent: All of these schools said the fit was good.

We should note that these are secondhand judgments. The study made no independent check on these administrative descriptions of the attitudes of faculty and students. Administrators are in a good, although not entirely neutral, position to make these judgments. Moreover, the fact of their confidence, their belief that there is a good fit between aspiration and program achievement, is itself a significant finding about the schools not in financial trouble. The study also did not attempt to take into account how these attitudes might be affected by the mission of the institution; as noted in Chapter 3, the study accepts the institution's definition of its mission and aspirations as given. These qualifications apply to the following condition and also to the other conditions that are listed below.

3 *High community regard for what the institution is doing.* There was no specific question on the interview guide asking how good the fit is between community aspiration and program. Yet, the statements on this subject volunteered at the schools not in financial trouble are noteworthy. Nine of the twelve institutions specifically reported that there was strong public confidence in what the institution was doing. Some of the institutions in the remainder of the study sample also reported that their programs have public approval, but neither in frequency, nor in quality of response, are the administrators' perceptions comparable for the two groups of schools. The two-year and comprehensive colleges in this group not in financial trouble are naturally close to their communities, and they provide a service the community wants and tends to admire. One hears statements like this one from Gulf Coast Junior College: "People in the community feel the institution really belongs to them." One finds similar statements from other types of schools in this group. For instance, the University of North Carolina: "There is public affection and pride in the institution," and Whitman College: "Graduates like the college, like what it is doing." The essential ingredients are community understanding and support, even affection, based on knowledge of what the institution is doing and agreement that what it is doing is of value. It is probably reflected in the more favorable gifts and grants experience of these schools discussed earlier.

These first three conditions seem interrelated, reflecting as they do elements of morale in the institution and its environment. The next condition — student aid expenditures — is also probably related to such matters, for it bears on the extent to which society's problems are to be dealt with on the campus.

4 *Smaller student aid expenditures.* In the decade of the 1960s expenditures for student aid represented an increasing portion of the operating budget for virtually all institutions in this study. There is a clear difference, however, in the rate of increase between the schools not in financial trouble and all others. For those not in financial trouble, student aid expenditures have not risen as rapidly, relative to operating budget, as for other schools. It is hard to say precisely how much difference there is between the two groups of

schools because of gaps in the data and some differences in accounting conventions. Also there are differences between the distribution of the types of institutions in the group not in financial trouble and all others in the study that make it difficult to make a precise comparison of the percent of the operating budget spent on student aid.

Given these qualifications, there is nonetheless a difference, and it is important to get some estimate of its magnitude. Our data indicate that in the academic year 1959–60 the schools not in financial trouble were spending about 3.9 percent of their operating budget for student aid. The other institutions were spending about 5.0 percent. In the decade 1959–60 to 1969–70, student aid expenditures for the schools not in financial trouble rose about two percentage points to approximately 5.9 percent of the operating budget. For the other schools, the portion of the operating budget devoted to student aid rose more than 3½ percentage points to approximately 8.6 percent of operations.

The magnitude of this difference is shown more clearly by the fact that, for the period 1959–60 through 1969–70, the increase in student aid expenditures per student rose at an average rate of 12.0 percent per year in schools not in financial trouble. The comparable figure for all other schools in the study is 19.4 percent.

The significance of this difference is partly the extra budgetary burden — approximately 2½ percentage points of operating expense borne by the institutions headed for financial trouble or in financial difficulty. This extra burden cumulates with other apparently extra burdens, such as the security and related costs discussed earlier. These cumulative burdens relate to our definition of being headed for financial trouble or in financial difficulty in that they represent costs that may be borne by cuts in present program or future program growth. One could argue that expenditure for student aid is not competitive with quality growth, or even that it promotes quality, although it clearly does in some degree compete with expenditures for faculty recruitment, academic fellowships, library resources, and the like.

5 *Program defined, growth controlled.* Schools not in financial trouble tend to differ from the other institutions in the study sample in the extent to which they have limited program goals and a more controlled rate of program growth over the last decade. This is due partly to the fact that two-year institutions are heavily represented in this category. Yet the characteristic goes beyond

that, and indeed, all but one of the institutions not in financial trouble referred in the interviews to policies designed, whether or not deliberately, to achieve the ends of careful program definition and measured growth. Several institutions emphasized that it was their policy to do a limited number of things but do them well; others, including the large state institutions, emphasized stability in program growth. Most stated that program growth must be justified by filling a specific need. St. Cloud State reported a rapid rate of program growth and now is in the midst of detailed self-analysis designed to reduce programs, relate them to need, and trim their rate of growth.

Does this controlled rate of program growth and tighter program definition mean that these institutions have not had to deal with rapid enrollment growth? No. The 12 schools rated not in financial trouble have as a whole grown at a faster rate than the other institutions in the study sample. For the period starting with the academic year 1959–60 and ending 1969–70, all institutions in the study grew in enrollment by an average of 85 percent. The enrollment increase for the 12 schools rated not in financial trouble was 110 percent. One institution in the latter group grew 400 percent (and twice as much as any other): Gulf Coast increased during this decade from 400 to 2,000 students. If it were removed from the figures, the average rate of growth of the schools not in financial trouble would be approximately the same as all the others, an average of 82 percent for the decade.

What this program definition and controlled program growth do reveal is that many of these institutions are what they want to be. Their expansion has not, apparently, been undercapitalized. One of the questions in the interview guide asked officials at each campus to list the unmet needs of their campus. For schools not in financial trouble the needs tend to be noncapital needs (more so than the other institutions), and the capital needs tend not to be those needed to shore up academic programs (for instance, office space rather than libraries). Thus, the most significant item in the statement of unmet noncapital needs is money for academic salaries. The reason seems clear: The average compensation of full-time faculty for schools in this category is lower than that of the other schools in the study.

6 *Lower average compensation.* For each of the 41 institutions in this study, the current (1969–70) average compensation of full-time faculty was obtained. To have meaning, this information must be related to type of institution. The average compensation figures for those of the schools classified not in financial trouble in each of the six categories in the Carnegie Commission classification system were compared with the average for the other institutions studied in each of those categories. The result, as the table below shows, is that in every category but one, schools not in financial trouble have a lower average compensation figure.

	Research univer- sities (I and II)	Doctoral- granting univer- sities (I and II)	Compre- hensive colleges (I and II)	Liberal arts colleges (I)	Liberal arts colleges (II)	Two-year colleges
Schools not in financial trouble	$15,758	$13,770	$12,369	$13,519	$ 9,787	$11,990
All other institutions studied	$16,942	$14,397	$13,652	$13,988	$11,007	$11,943
Percentage difference	7.5%	4.6%	10.4%	2.7%	12.5%	—.4%

These differences may in part be accounted for by differences in distribution of faculty by rank. But the concern expressed by presidents of schools not in financial trouble over the need for additional salary money suggests that the difference is due primarily to differences in salary scales. This is borne out by the published AAUP report grading average compensation.[7] According to the 1969–70 gradings, the schools not in financial trouble are approximately one-half a grade below those in the other institutions in the study. The difference in salary scales has apparently not had an effect on retention of faculty and has had only a limited effect on recruitment. Each school visited was asked whether it was having difficulty recruiting and holding faculty. Of the 12 schools not in financial trouble, 7 responded that they were not. The other 5 reported no difficulty retaining faculty, but varying degrees of trouble in recruitment.

At first glance, the consistency of these differences in salary seems significant, but it is difficult to describe just what the significance is. It is not clear from the data gathered in the study whether lower salaries are causally related to the condition not

[7] See American Association of University Professors, 1970, pp. 60–105. These gradings do not include the two-year institutions in this study, due to the fact that those institutions did not have professorial ranks.

in financial trouble, and, if they are, it is not clear how lower salaries help avoid the cuts in program or growth which define financial "trouble." There are several possibilities. For one thing, the level of faculty salaries may be related to the level of quality and aspiration of the institution, which may, in turn, influence whether there are costly campus disturbances or needs for costly research activities. A second possibility relates to our earlier finding that, while the schools not in financial trouble had a lower rate of growth in faculty salaries, they had a higher rate of growth in other components of their education and general expenditures account— libraries, campus administration, maintenance, extension—than did other institutions. By thus spending money in a period of growth on more support of program rather than on more program, and thereby not having programs for which support must be found if cuts are to be avoided, the institutions not in financial trouble may have been better able to avoid the adverse effects of a downturn in income. Finally, the different pattern of allocation in the rate of growth may mean relatively greater expenditure on administration and staff support, which would provide the schools not in financial trouble with more management resources to deal with the cost-income squeeze and to operate more efficiently.

7 *Efficiency.* In response to the question, "How would you rate your institution's efficiency?" (see Appendix, interview questions 20–22), administrators of the schools not in financial trouble gave their schools a better rating than administrators of the other schools gave to their institutions. For schools not in financial trouble, the ratio of "good" to "poor" responses is 6 to 1. For other institutions, that ratio is 2 to 1.

This finding is similar to some of the conditions discussed earlier in that we have no dependent check on these administrators' assessments, but at the very least, we believe that their responses are themselves significant. Certainly, these administrators have more confidence in the efficiency of their institutions than other administrators have in their own schools. This finding might corroborate the possibility we have just examined, namely, that a relatively greater expenditure on administrative and staff support enables these institutions to operate more efficiently.

8 *Less affected by reduced federal support of higher education.* During the early and middle 1960s, the percentage of current fund

income[8] from the federal government[9] rose steadily. However, since 1967–68 the percentage has begun to decline. These trends are evident in both the schools not in financial trouble and the other schools. However, the trends are of less magnitude in the schools not in financial trouble than in the others. For the schools not in financial trouble the percentage of current fund income from the federal government has remained fairly stable over the last few years, whereas in the other schools the relative share of income from the government has declined. These observations derive from both interviews with college officials and a comparison of the available financial data.

9 *Room for financial growth.* An important element in the financial situation of the schools rated not in financial trouble is their confidence about additional sources of income—from both tuition and gifts. Room for financial growth is important because we define "trouble," in part, in terms of cutbacks in future program growth plans. Although the possibility that tuition is reaching the "saturation point" tends to be a common view among college and university presidents, it is not as serious a concern in these institutions. One reason for this difference is revealed when the current fund income figures of schools not in financial trouble are compared with those of the other institutions in the study. For the latter group, the percentage of current fund income received from tuition and fees rose fairly steadily through the period 1959–60 to 1969–70 (from 35 percent to 38 percent). In contrast, for the schools not in financial trouble, the percentage of current fund income received from tuition and fees rose during the early 1960s, but then (1965) a small, gradual decline began. Not surprisingly, four of the schools not in financial trouble indicated that they had room for tuition growth. In addition, one which does not now have tuition indicated that it ought to have it.

Every school in this group indicated that it had resources, especially private gifts, it had not yet fully tapped. Five of the schools have only now opened development and fund-raising offices, and four more are just starting new fund-raising campaigns. All expressed confidence about their ability to raise additional funds from this source.

[8] Excluding income from auxiliary enterprises.

[9] The institutions' financial data were reported by income source alone and do not identify the specific uses of federal money, except for sponsored research.

10 *Luck and circumstance.* It is not unfair to the administrators of the schools rated not in financial trouble to point out that several benefit from luck and circumstances. The University of Texas, for example, has a growing endowment from its oil lands (in 1968–69 the income was $14 million); this is an unusual income source from what was once considered worthless land. None of the other examples is quite so dramatic, or involves so much money, yet each is important and comes under no other factor cited above. Thus, Howard University is relatively better off than other primarily black institutions because, in part, of its congressional charter and its congressional financial support. Meredith College cites its strategic location, "at the corner of the research triangle," and benefits from the cooperative relations with North Carolina, Shaw, and Duke.

The only two women's institutions in the study sample, Meredith and Mills, are both in the category not in financial trouble. They have been spared some of the major expenditure and income jolts of the past several years, primarily, it appears, because of their relative lack of emphasis on expensive science courses and their freedom from campus disturbances.

Income figures indicate that endowment income did not decline as rapidly for the schools not in financial trouble as it did for the other institutions in the study. We do not have a basis for explaining that fact and, therefore, include it, not unfairly we hope, in this "luck and circumstance" category.

Although our data and small sample of institutions permit only the barest beginnings of a generalization here, it should be noticed that 9 of the 12 schools not in financial trouble are located in the South or nonmetropolitan North, where they may be shielded from some of the current pressures of social conflict, pressures that may, over time, have adverse effects on a school's income and costs. Mills is in the metropolitan North but is relatively isolated physically from the surrounding urban area. Howard and Morgan State are in Washington, D.C., and Baltimore, respectively, but both are primarily black institutions, in neighborhoods where they are respected and perhaps especially well symbolize the community's aspirations, which in turn may shield them from some of the costs of social conflict.

OMENS OF DIFFICULTY In the campus interviews each president was asked to characterize the prospects for the financial condition of his campus in the decade of the 1970s. Among the 12 schools rated not in financial trouble, there is general optimism. This is in sharp contrast to the general view of the presidents of the other schools in the study. Three of the schools in the group not in financial trouble expect the seventies to be better than the sixties.

The major worry expressed by this group concerns the need for new money and the problems that could arise from a reduced rate of income growth in the next decade. An analysis of the interview and financial data strongly suggests there is good reason for caution in making predictions about the future. The relatively good position of these institutions is due to several factors, and not all of them are within the control of the schools themselves. Moreover, there are some early signs of trouble. To be sure, it is still more a matter of trouble appearing on the books than in operations, yet it is revealing to see what the figures show. They show that the effects of the depression in higher education are beginning to be felt in this group, although it is too early to say how serious the impact will be.

Consider these four indicators:

1 *Expenditures for budgeted department instruction and research.* These are the funds budgeted for faculty teaching and research through academic departments, and they constitute the best single indicator of instructional cost. They include departmental administration but not sponsored research. These funds represent what in academic budgeting is often called "hard money." For the years 1959–60 through 1968–69, the institutions not in financial trouble had an average increase in this expenditure item per student of 7.4 percent per year. In contrast for 1969–70 to 1970–71, the average increase was 4.2 percent, probably less than the increase in the cost of living and, since schools tend to spend what they receive, an indicator that income as well as program growth is faltering.

2 *Educational and general expenditures, less sponsored research.* This represents total current fund expenditures, excluding auxiliary enterprises, student aid, and sponsored research. For the decade 1959–60 through 1968–69, the average increase, per student, was 7.7 percent per year. The comparable figure for 1969–70 to 1970–71 is 4.4 percent.

3 *Education and general.* This is the total current expense budget and excludes only funds spent for auxiliary enterprises and student

aid. The average increase per student per year for the decade was 8 percent. The increase in the last year was 4.1 percent.

4 *Student aid.* Funds spent (not loaned) by the schools not in financial trouble for student aid in the decade 1959–60 through 1968–69 increased an average of 12.4 percent per student, per year. Between 1969–70 and 1970–71 the increase was .7 percent.

These data must be qualified in two ways. First, the decade figures are for all 12 schools, but the most recent figure is based on the experience of only one-half of the group. Data from the others were not yet available when this study was done. This means the average figure could rise (or fall) when the data are complete, although there is no reason not to expect the trend to continue. A second qualification should be made. In the decade of the 1960s there was some year for each institution for which the average expenditure increase in each of the four items above was as low as the most recent year's increase. Therefore, the latest year's experience may or may not signal an extended downward trend.

As one looks at the figures for these schools, he is tempted to find a parallel between them and the other schools in this study as they were in the middle of the 1960s. Will the schools not in financial trouble follow a similar course? It will take at least another year or two to find out. If the present direction continues for long, the category not in financial trouble might be retired, for it may well not be needed.

5. *Institutions Headed for Financial Trouble*

At the time of the campus visits, 18 schools (44 percent of the 41 institutions in this study) were considered to be headed for financial trouble. This means that at the time of the campus visit, these 18 colleges and universities were able to meet their current, self-defined responsibilities without reducing quality. They are carrying on their academic program and related educational services, research activities, public service, and extracurricular programs. In fact, they have all made some cuts, but they assess these to be cuts that do not adversely affect what would be regarded in light of the institution's role as quality or essential activities. In some cases, administrators did not attempt to characterize cuts as nonessential but, on the basis of the interview, we believe they should be so regarded. Of course, there is no clear line determining when cuts individually or cumulatively begin to affect quality or essential program, and we have had to impose our judgment of the academic significance of an institution's response to the cost-income squeeze.

The basis of our categorization of these schools as headed for financial trouble is that they cannot expect to continue to meet current standards and maintain program or they cannot ensure support for existing planned program growth. Their income and expenditure prospects are such that they can now confidently predict a time in the near future when they will have to increase income substantially or cut expenditures so much that program or quality will be revised downward. These schools may have concrete plans and a definite timetable for the introduction of new programs, but they do not have a timetable for producing the money necessary to introduce them; it is now known that the plans or something else will therefore have to give.

There are problems in the application of this criterion, as we discussed in Chapter 3. One of these problems is the marginal case. Several of the institutions classified as headed for financial trouble came close to meeting the criteria for classification in one of the other two categories. The University of Minnesota is a case in point. It is judged as headed for financial trouble, but its financial and interview data are close to meeting the criteria of the group not in financial trouble. The University of Missouri required a close choice between the category headed for financial trouble and the category in financial difficulty. As we noted in Chapter 3, these judgmental questions were resolved in an effort to make a clear statement about the financial condition of each institution at the time of the campus visit. The results appear definitive, but they rest in part on the qualifications discussed in Chapter 3.

Listed by our method of classification, the 18 colleges and universities considered headed for financial trouble are:

National research universities
   Harvard University
   University of Chicago
   University of Michigan
   University of Minnesota

Leading regional research universities
   Ohio University
   Syracuse University
   University of Missouri
   University of Oregon

State and comprehensive colleges
   Central Michigan University
   Portland State University

Liberal arts colleges
   Albion College
   Allegheny College
   Carleton College
   Cumberland College
   Knox College
   Pomona College

Primarily black colleges
   None

Two-year colleges
   City Colleges of Chicago
   Mesa College

As one reviews this list, a first impression is that these 18 colleges and universities are fairly representative of the entire list of 41 institutions in the study. A closer examination bears out that impression, with one important exception. None of the five primarily black institutions in the study is considered headed for financial trouble. Two of them, as we have already seen, are considered not in financial trouble, and the remaining three appear in the group of schools considered in financial difficulty.

When the group headed for financial trouble is compared to the entire study group by the classification method used in this study, the similarity of the distribution of the two groups by type of school (save for primarily black institutions) is apparent.[1]

	National research univer-sities	Leading regional research univer-sities	State and compre-hensive colleges	Liberal arts colleges	Primarily black institu-tions	Two-year colleges
Schools headed for financial trouble	22%	22%	11%	33%	0	11%
All institutions studied	17%	20%	12%	27%	12%	12%

When the schools headed for financial trouble are grouped by the classification system used by the Carnegie Commission, the finding is the same: The distribution by type of school headed for financial trouble is quite similar to the entire list.[2]

	Research univer-sities (I and II)	Doctoral-granting univer-sities (I and II)	Compre-hensive colleges (I and II)	Liberal arts colleges (I)	Liberal arts colleges (II)	Two-year colleges
Schools headed for financial trouble	33%	11%	11%	28%	6%	12%
All institutions studied	29%	12%	12%	22%	12%	12%

Forty-four percent of the colleges and universities in the study group are public institutions, the remaining 56 percent are private. As we saw in Chapter 4, there were proportionately more public

---

[1] See Chapter 2 for a discussion of the classification method used in this study.

[2] Again, see Chapter 2 for a discussion of the classification system used by the Carnegie Commission on Higher Education.

institutions among those not in financial trouble than in the entire study group, although the difference was not large. The same is true of the category headed for financial trouble. Private institutions are underrepresented in this category also, although the margin is a small one. As we shall see in Chapter 6, they are overrepresented in the group classified as in financial difficulty.

	Public institutions	*Private institutions*
Schools headed for financial trouble	50%	50%
All institutions studied	44%	56%

When the schools classified headed for financial trouble are compared by location with the entire group studied, we find that relatively more of the schools headed for financial trouble are in the Midwest and relatively fewer in the South.

	Midwest	*West*	*South*	*East*
Schools headed for financial trouble	56%	22%	6%	17%
All institutions studied	34%	24%	22%	20%

When we compare the schools rated headed for financial trouble with the entire study group on two other criteria, metropolitan v. nonmetropolitan location and enrollment, we see that the locations of schools headed for financial trouble are similar to those of the entire group studied, but that the schools headed for financial trouble tend to be larger (except the comprehensive colleges). Of the 41 institutions in the entire study, 22, or 54 percent, are from metropolitan areas; 46 percent are not. Among the institutions headed for financial trouble, 44 percent are in metropolitan locations, 56 percent are not.

	Enrollment, 1968–69					
	Leading research univer- sities (I and II)	*Other doctoral- granting univer- sities (I and II)*	*Compre- hensive colleges (I and II)*	*Liberal arts colleges (I)*	*Liberal arts colleges (II)*	*Two-year colleges*
Schools headed for financial trouble	27,053	23,034	11,813	1,397	1,771	16,075
All institutions studied	22,021	9,481	14,578	1,219	892	5,385

SOURCE: Carnegie Commission on Higher Education.

Finally, when we compare faculty salaries, we find that the average compensation paid for all ranks of instructors in the schools headed for financial trouble is higher than the average for the other institutions in the study. The latest salary data available (1969–70) indicate the following:

	Leading research universities (I and II)	Doctoral-granting universities (I and II)	Compre-hensive colleges (I and II)	Liberal arts colleges (I)	Liberal arts colleges (II)	Two-year colleges
Schools headed for financial trouble	$17,155	$14,571	$14,109	$13,540	None	$12,591
All other institutions studied	$16,505	$14,071	$13,322	$13,522	$10,600	$11,990
Percentage difference	+3.9	+3.6	+5.9	+.1		+5.8

As the table shows, the average compensation of schools headed for financial trouble is higher in every category (for which there are cases). The average difference for all groups is $510. This difference in average compensation is corroborated by the differences in average compensation rank shown in reports of the AAUP. The latest AAUP gradings show the schools headed for financial trouble to be more than one-half rank higher than the other institutions in this study.

In summary, the 18 colleges and universities considered headed for financial trouble are distributed representatively over each of the categories of academic institutions developed by the Carnegie Commission on Higher Education. Institutions of all types are in this stage of financial trouble. When this group of 18 schools is compared on other criteria to the others in this study, one finds some differences in location (there are fewer schools headed for financial trouble in the South, more in the Midwest), relatively more public institutions in the category headed for financial trouble, and relatively more private institutions in financial difficulty, indicating that although both public and private institutions are feeling financial stringency, it is affecting private institutions more severely. In addition, the schools headed for financial trouble are generally larger than the other institutions in the study, and their average compensation is higher. Thus, this rough statistical profile of the schools headed for financial trouble indicates some differences from a random distribution, but none marked or systematic enough to suggest a hypothesis that explains why schools are headed for financial trouble. If anything, these differences seem slight enough to suggest that perhaps the category headed for financial trouble is typical of higher education. That conclusion is more strongly suggested by the high proportion of schools in this study found to be headed for financial trouble.

The schools headed for financial trouble constitute almost half the schools in this study. We have stressed that the 41 institutions in this study were not intended to be representative of all institutions of higher education but were selected as schools illustrative of the different types of academic institutions. Given that qualification, it would still seem fair to say that the financial situation of the 18 schools headed for financial trouble is representative of institutions of higher education. This is not a finding, but a judgment. It is based on (1) the large number of schools in this degree of financial difficulty, (2) the "representativeness" of their distribution by type of institution when compared to the entire group studied, and (3) the surmise that, compared to a random sample, our sample underrepresents the institutions likely to be in this category, a surmise confirmed by published information about the financial condition on college and university campuses.

These are not the institutions one reads about in stories of an impending closing or a drastic cutback. These are the schools that are feeling the effects of financial stringency, but whose serious problems are still somewhere in the future. They may still have time, if they can do what must be done.

EXPENDITURE FACTORS

Schools headed for financial trouble are meeting their current program commitments. But the rate of growth of their income is declining. Necessarily, therefore, they have started to postpone, trim, and, in some instances, cut activities in order to cut costs. Their actions in response to the decline in income are reflected in the basic expenditure data summarized in Table 4.

Column 3 shows us that the average annual rate of increase (per student) in budgeted departmental instruction and research expenditures for the schools headed for financial trouble was 7.7 percent for the period 1959–60 to 1969–70. The schools headed for financial trouble have reduced these expenses by 1½ percentage points in the last year. The average rate of increase for the most recent year is 6.2 percent. A similar drop in expenditures appears

TABLE 4 *Average annual rate of increase in expenditure per student, schools headed for financial trouble*

Period	Education and general*	Education and general less sponsored research†	Instruction and departmental research‡	Student aid§
1959–60 to 1969–70	7.0%	6.8%	7.7%	18.1%
1969–70 to 1970–71	5.9%	6.8%	6.2%	3.6%

NOTES: Data for this table were obtained from individual campuses. Figures for the change from 1969–70 to 1970–71 cover only eight institutions—the ones which could supply this late information at the time of the study. There is no indication that the sharp drop in expenditures from 1969–70 to 1970–71 is overstated, however.

*The total current fund expenditures, including sponsored research but excluding expenditures on auxiliary enterprises and student aid.

† The total current fund expenditures; excluding expenditures on auxiliary enterprises, student aid, *and* research sponsored from nonuniversity sources.

‡ Expenditures on instruction, consisting of expenditures for faculty salaries and departmental administration. This expenditure item constitutes a portion of educational and general expenditures.

§ Total expenditures on financial aid for students, including grants, scholarships, and fellowships, but excluding loans. This expenditure item is not included in the category of educational and general expenditures.

in column 1, showing the education and general expenditures for schools headed for financial trouble. From an average annual rate of increase per student of 7.0 percent for the period 1959–60 to 1969–70, the most recent year shows an average rate of increase of 5.9 percent.

Much of this cut in educational and general expenditures seems to be a cut in sponsored research (in addition to cuts in instruction and departmental research), although that influence could be partly a result of our method of averaging varying annual expenses over a decade. Thus, the average rate of increase for education and general *less* sponsored research of 6.8 percent is the same for the entire period 1959–60 to 1969–70 and for the latest year. From that fact it also appears that some current fund expenditure items grew recently to offset the decline in instruction and departmental expenditures.

The dramatic drop in the rate of increase in student aid expenditures is shown by the last column of the table. After an average annual rate of increase of 18.1 percent for the entire period 1959–60 to 1969–70, the rate of increase for the year 1970–71 was but 3.6 percent.

Although Table 4 compares the rate of increase in expenditure for the most recent year (1970–71) with the annual average over the previous decade, in fact the rate of increase in expenditures for most of these schools began to decline in 1967–68. The rate of decline since that time has been relatively constant rather than accelerating.

Expenditures have had to be cut because in the past few years income growth has been declining. As we noted earlier in this chapter, schools are rated headed for financial trouble on the basis of our judgment about the necessary program effects of their income situation. Their serious adjustments lie ahead of them, and, therefore, their past relationship of income to expenditure is similar to the schools not in financial trouble. The table below shows that to be the case.

	1959–60 to 1969–70
Rate of income growth	6.6%
Rate of expenditure growth	7.3%

*These income figures are based on all current fund income. They include income from auxiliary enterprises and all other sources. The income data available to us makes it necessary to present them this way. The expenditure data are calculated on a similar basis. In consequence the figures differ slightly from the expenditure data shown elsewhere in this chapter, which exclude auxiliary enterprises and student aid.

These data do not show the full divergence of income growth from expenditure growth, however, for the income figures available to us unavoidably include as "income" some items that are more accurately "capital" or "reserves." Whereas only one of the five private schools rated not in financial trouble had a deficit, four of the nine private schools in the category headed for financial trouble are in deficit spending. Therefore, the differences in rates of expenditure and income are greater than appear in the above table.

The factors that constitute the declining rate of income growth are the same as those discussed in connection with the changing income situation of the schools not in financial trouble. These are the declining rate of growth of income from the federal government, from gifts, and from endowment. Unlike the schools not in financial trouble, the schools headed for financial trouble have placed increasing reliance on tuition as an income source.

In Chapter 7 we shall attempt to estimate the importance of these income components to the overall financial condition of the schools in this study. For now, however, let us look at some of the effects they have had on the schools' income accounts.

For the public schools headed for financial trouble, in 1959–60 private gifts and grants accounted for about 2 percent of current fund income (exclusive of auxiliary enterprises). By 1967–68 this figure had risen to almost 7 percent. However, at the end of the decade it had fallen to just over 5 percent. Tuition accounted for about 17 percent of current fund income in 1959–60. By 1965–66 tuition had risen in importance as an income source, providing 23 percent of current fund income, but by the end of the decade this figure had fallen to 21 percent. Income from state governments fell from 51 percent in 1959–60 to 45 percent in 1964–65. Since that time, it has risen somewhat in importance as an income source, accounting for over 48 percent of current fund income by the end of the decade. Income from the federal government rose sharply in importance between the years 1959–60, when it accounted for 19 percent of current fund, and 1966–67, when it accounted for 31 percent. Since 1966–67, this income source has declined in importance, accounting for 28 percent of current fund at the end of the decade. Income from endowment declined slowly in importance throughout the decade, accounting for about 2 percent at the start of the decade and 1.5 percent at the end.

The trends in income sources for the private schools headed for financial trouble were very similar to those for the public institutions, with the exception of the trends regarding tuition. By 1965–66 private gifts and grants had risen from 11 percent to 13 percent of current fund income, but by the end of the decade they had fallen to 12 percent. Tuition provided about 52 percent of the current fund income in 1959–60. By 1964–65 this figure had fallen to 50 percent, but by the end of the decade tuition had increased substantially in importance and accounted for 56 percent of current income. In 1959–60 the federal government provided about 17 percent of the income for these schools. By 1964–65 this figure had risen to over 22 percent but, by the end of the decade, had fallen to under 18 percent. Endowment income declined gradually in importance throughout the decade, falling from about 18 percent in 1959–60 to 15 percent at the decade's end.

What do these figures mean about the last three or four years? In those years, schools headed for financial trouble have been feeling the increasing pinch of declining rates of increase in federal government expenditures and private gifts and grants. They have also been affected by a longer-term decline in the rate of increase in endowment income. Private institutions have relied more heavily on tuition increases than have public institutions, which have relied more on state funds. Finally, income from federal sources apparently declined less rapidly in public than in private institutions. At the same time that the relative inputs in income have changed, the rate of increase in income is declining. As a result, these schools have also had to trim expenses in research, operations, and program areas. If these schools are to reverse these trends and increase their rates of growth in income and expenditures, it seems likely that they will have to increase the relative share of nontuition sources of income; there is considerable doubt that tuition can bear an increasingly larger proportion of growing university budgets.

THE ADMINIS-TRATORS' ASSESSMENTS

Before we examine what the schools are doing in response to the cost-income problem, here are excerpts from interviewers' notes on the situation on these 18 campuses as their administrators struggled with an increasingly troublesome financial situation. They convey a sense of what the problem looks like to the campus.

Two-Year Colleges

City Colleges of Chicago. Administrators believe that the colleges will not be voted additional tax-levy authority. Most administrators are certain that they could not win a referendum. At present, Chicago has a very small rate of increase in assessed valuation. The colleges have taken on a number of partially funded, low-priority programs. There have been some campus disturbances, and security costs have risen (from $100,000 to $250,000 in one year). Some legislators don't like the name "Malcolm X College" given to one of its units. Inflation, and the great pressure for new programs, particularly in community service and black studies, have pushed costs up sharply. Some new administrators were inexperienced. The faculty union has become militant in resisting administrative efforts to cut costs by reducing the number of faculty members (not by firing, but rather by not filling as many vacancies).

Mesa College. Income is becoming fixed as costs continue to rise. Administrators see no chance of an increase in the mill-levy authority or in the state formula for allocating faculty salary support. Any further raises in fees would place Mesa in a noncompetitive position, and it would have to borrow heavily because of lack of reserves. The only chance for flexibility is to increase enrollment, a difficult task given the fact that Colorado has opened seven new junior colleges in the last three years. Minor campus disturbances have had some effect on private gifts. The number of bids for insurance dropped from 15 to 2 in one year. The computer has become a large financial factor which may grow. The need for salary increases is a major cause of the seriousness of the situation. Federal student aid funds have been cut. A $100,000 federal reimbursement for vocational programs was allocated by the state to the *state* system. The federal work-study program has been cut.

Liberal Arts Colleges

Albion College. Ford program funds ran out in 1970, and by 1971 college reserves will be gone. Student aid costs are massive (the college is currently spending $900,000 annually). Enrollment may not hold. Inflation is affecting gift receipts. College officials are unsure that people are going to continue to be willing to pay for private higher education. Other important cost factors are: rising costs and inflation, a higher level of expectation on the part of the faculty, and decreasing respect of students for property (resulting in higher maintenance costs). Officials are worried about the unknown cost consequences of the knowledge explosion.

Allegheny College. Campus unrest has caused a great deal of antagonism in the locality. The climate for higher tuition and larger giving has deteriorated. The endowment is growing at a slower rate. Administrators believe that continued tuition increases will result in changing the composition of the student body. Pressures to enroll more disadvantaged and foreign students are rising, and increasing commitments to minority students are very costly. The Pennsylvania Scholarship Fund is in difficulty. Security and insurance costs will rise substantially. Because of a strong possibility of collective bargaining, costs might become even more fixed. There are no funds for an urgently needed library building. The college is in a bad financial squeeze. It had to put all available funds into an arts and music building, a project too far advanced to stop, despite fund shortages.

Carleton College. Expenses are rising more rapidly than income. Foundation grants are running out. Student aid is in serious trouble because costs for financial aid and student services are increasing so rapidly. Federal aid is falling off. Gifts are not increasing as fast as expected, partly due to the decline in the stock market. Although there have been few campus disturbances, they may have affected giving.

Cumberland College.   The only realistic possibility of increasing income is to increase fees. To do this, the college would have to recruit heavily from outside the area, because Appalachian families would no longer be able to afford the costs. Therefore, the purpose for which the school was intended would not be served. Already, the financial aid budget is inadequate. During the recent period of federal aid to higher education, the Kentucky Baptists did not allow Cumberland to obtain federal building money. Enrollment may decline because of out-migration from mountain counties and the proximity of two public junior colleges. Tightness in federal student aid funds is beginning to hurt. College officials want to expand in the area of community service, but foundations are not favoring this type of institution.

Knox College.   Reserves are down from $1,200,000 to $250,000. The growing quality of the University of Illinois is being felt. College officials believe that, even though there have been no major disturbances on campus, Knox has nevertheless been hurt in the eyes of private donors. They fear that the parents of this generation may become still more unwilling to underwrite an expensive education. Insurance and security costs have increased, but the most important additional cost is the staff time and energy spent attending to or anticipating campus disturbance problems. The knowledge explosion has created problems in financing computers and the library. Since the rate of inflation exceeded predictions, Knox is spending more on student aid than it had expected.

Pomona College.   Rising costs are the primary concern. Administrators report increased expenditures now and in the future for student aid and minority programs, computer and library resources. Last year reserves were used for student aid. Next year they will have to start using general college funds. Student aid and counseling funds are not adequate to allow Pomona to admit significantly more minority students, although there is pressure to do so. Pomona has a substantial deficit. Until recently the college has been able to afford relaxed management. Administrators do not agree on whether, if the situation worsens, the president has the power to move the students-to-faculty ratio significantly upward.

State and Comprehensive Colleges

Central Michigan University. Administrators are concerned whether the university is well regarded in the public mind. Legislative budget cuts reflect a growing hostility to higher education. Past surpluses are used up. The tax base is inadequate. The only flexibility possible is that which would come from enrollment growth. The decline in the auto industry at the time of the interviews was having an important effect on state schools. Campus disturbances have affected the conditions for raising income and probably were a significant factor in this year's budget cuts. Rising increased-cost factors include: police (up 100 percent in two years); a sharp increase in the number of separate departments caused by the knowledge explosion; student pressure to diversify faculty and courses; and reduction of federal spending for student aid.

Portland State University. The present political climate in Oregon reflects substantial resistance to additional taxes and changes in the tax structure. Administrators believe student unrest is the most significant depressant factor in Oregon. The university is seriously understaffed and lagging behind in library books and equipment. The administration has been starved for support. Inflation-impact problems are serious with respect to equipment, books, supplies, utilities, maintenance, computers, and salaries. Student aid costs and tutoring costs have increased. Generally, programs expanded at a great rate, but support, including salaries, was neglected.

Research Universities

Harvard University. Costs are increasingly relentless. During the 1960s operating costs rose at the average of $12 million a year, due much to inflation. Federal support is declining. Arts and Sciences is operating at a deficit. Cutbacks have severely weakened the School of Education, School of Design, and Divinity School. Other parts of the university—Public Health, Medical School, the Division of Engineering and Applied Physics, and several other departments—are being threatened. Federal fellowship and traineeship cutbacks are serious. Much more student aid will be needed. Computer and library costs are rising rapidly. Student and faculty aspirations are increasing, and unless the funding situation changes, they cannot be met.

Ohio University. The climate for obtaining additional funds is very poor in Ohio. Administrators report that the legislature disapproves of campus protest activities and appears to have lost confidence in education as the solution for society's problems. Rapid growth in the 1960s was not accompanied by adequate planning: The library has been seriously undersupported; insurance rates have increased greatly; the university has a heavy load of deferred maintenance. The nonacademic employees' union is pressing hard for wage increases. Federal support has fallen off. Fees are as high as they can go. Enrollment cannot be raised. Campus disturbances will have a strong legislative impact which has not yet been felt because, at the time of the interview, the university was in the two-year budget.

Syracuse University. The university has been deferring maintenance, but it is no longer able to do so. It is rapidly approaching an upper limit on tuition. Improvements are needed in library, computer, and research facilities. The university has suffered from cutbacks in foundation and federal support, and administrators fear cutbacks in state support as well. Endowment, which is small, is being used to meet deficits. Changes in tax regulations, the stock market decline, and campus disturbances have had significant effects on private giving. Campus budget reallocations will become more necessary as "catch up" expenditures are made for items that were deferred in the past.

University of Chicago. The budget has been balanced recently only by using the Ford Challenge grant, which will probably be used up this year. Government funds have leveled off. Because of a heavy shift toward reliance on federal money in the 1960s, the university is extremely sensitive to changes in federal spending. It is heavily committed to graduate instruction and, therefore, prospects for cutting costs are dim. A large deficit is expected again in 1970–71, which will this time necessitate using endowment principal. At that point the school would have reached what its administrators describe as "a critical financial situation." Student fees are nearing the ceiling. One prospect administrators see for meeting increased costs is substantially increased private giving—and this has been affected by inflation and campus disturbances. The university is under great pressure to finance day-care centers. It has recently moved heavily and expensively into community service. Campus concern with pollution resulted in conversion from coal to gas at a cost of $2 million per year. The cost of security is significant and has doubled over the past two years. The student aid budget will probably decrease. Computer costs have risen rapidly. The new library will be extremely expensive to operate.

University of Michigan. Inflation and a poor outlook in the auto industry will be reflected in state support of the university. Administrators say the outlook is dismal. Next year, it will no longer be possible to keep budgetary savings. The university is suffering from a critical lack of capital funds and, simultaneously, is subject to new demands in areas such as ecology. The problem of how to support students from low-income families is becoming acute, both because of increased commitment and because charging higher fees is the only major possibility of increasing income. Federal support for hard sciences has dropped. Administrators foresee federal cuts in research, fellowships, and student aid. Although at the time of the interview campus disturbances had not yet had direct effects on appropriations, administrators believed there would be an effect.

University of Minnesota. Federal cutbacks have begun to affect the university severely in several areas, and because of the decline in the economy, administrators see little chance of improving gifts and endowments. Accelerated development of other types of educational institutions has increased competition for state monies (junior colleges, in particular, are growing in favor). Withdrawal of federal funds for local projects aggravates the local need for state tax resources. Federal traineeships have been reduced. The Medical School, underfunded by the state, has become overly dependent on federal funds. Costly efforts have been undertaken to reduce environmental pollution. Computer costs have skyrocketed. Student aid funds are inadequate to meet the growing need caused by a greater university commitment to the disadvantaged. Campus disturbances thus far have had no apparent effect on appropriations, but backlash in the state is real and may be felt in the next legislative session. The public is losing confidence in higher education. Reapportionment may hurt the university since it has traditionally counted for support by the rural legislators, whereas punitive bills have come from the urban legislators.

University of Missouri.   Because the public voted down an income
tax increase and the governor and the legislature are stalemated,
the school will receive the same amount from the state in 1970–71
as it did in 1969–70 (with a student enrollment increase of 1,700).
Recent necessary fee increases have made fees higher than average.
The legislature appropriated no university construction funds in
1969 or 1970 (except for an urgently needed power plant addition).
Already there is a serious space shortage. In addition, the university
has been required to build and operate a medical school in Kansas
City. The outlook for legislative support is bleak at least until
1973–74. This economic deterioration is attributed to inflation,
decline in the national economy, federal budget cutbacks, taxpayer
backlash, and the general loss of confidence in higher education.
There have been some student disturbances, and the university
has been affected by a public mood of retaliation against students
and universities. According to administrators, Missouri is forty-
third among the states in per capita taxes paid to the state government. Missouri higher education finds itself in growing competition
with other public service needs (public schools, conservation,
mental health), and the university is experiencing growing competition from state colleges. The effects of federal cutbacks in research,
construction, and student aid funds are beginning to be felt. Enrollment pressure continues. In the years ahead, the university will
be very hard pressed in plant maintenance and improvement.
There is virtually no chance of raising the needed money to meet
increased minimum needs resulting from projected increases in
enrollment. Salaries need to be improved (but this could only be
done this year by raising tuition). There are also many unmet
library needs which must compete with very high computer and
data processing costs.

University of Oregon.   The university is facing cuts, recommended
by a consulting firm, which the firm assumes can be easily made
by trimming off "fat" and improving efficiency. Administrators
anticipate a decline in federal research funding. The 1960s expansion was not accompanied by sufficient growth in support, especially for library and administration. The state has not changed
its tax base significantly. Administrators report that campus
disturbances have been damaging to the university's ability to
obtain budgetary and other significant support. The legislature
may be favorably impressed with California's recent denial of

requested faculty salary increases. Administrators believe that the current nationwide economic situation has caused Oregon to suffer a somewhat steeper drop than the economy as a whole, particularly because of the decline in residential building, which adversely affects Oregon's large lumber industry.

THE INSTITUTIONS' RESPONSE

How are the schools headed for financial trouble responding to their increasingly difficult financial situation? This was one of the main questions that gave rise to this study. The campus interviews gave considerable attention to gathering information on the kinds of administrative actions being taken and plans being made (see Appendix, interview questions 8–25). There is no indication from the interviews that modern technology as applied to instruction and libraries is an important source of savings. The responses indicate that administrators on these campuses are doing a variety of things. We have already seen that several of these institutions are unavoidably spending reserves or endowment funds. The active responses designed to control the financial situation can best be summarized for this report under five main categories of activities: postponing, general belt-tightening, cutting and reallocating within existing structure, scrambling for funds, planning and worrying.

Postponing

One of the first casualties of a difficult financial situation is new program growth. It is easy to understand why. To finance new programs, "new" money is required, but there is no "new" money. To go ahead with plans would mean transferring "old" money away from an existing program commitment to a new one. Put more specifically, this means canceling existing courses, trimming back schools, colleges, and departments, laying off faculty, or increasing student-faculty ratios so that new courses can be added, new faculty can be hired, and new centers, schools, colleges, and departments can be opened. These are painful cuts, and to make them in the interests of new programs requires commitment to a plan, criteria for performance and output, and administrative authority beyond what is found on campuses headed for financial trouble, whether in this study or not. Campuses in financial difficulty may be more ready to make such painful cuts, both because they are reconciled to unpleasantness and because they may view certain new programs as essential for improvement.

Therefore, the initial impact of declining income growth is likely to be absorbed by cutting back planned program growth. In fact, there is an earlier cutback, represented by the policy of declining new obligations which are not already in the planning stage. On campuses today there is very little enthusiasm for projects which mainly receive high priorities off campus, and there is little support even for new projects generated from within. Institutions, rated here as headed for financial trouble, are declining new obligations (a typical statement reported by a interviewer is, "There are things we'd like to do but can't even consider"). Programs which are dismissed without serious consideration are not easy to identify or measure precisely. The interviewers did not even attempt to record these. In seeking information about plans cut back or postponed, the interviewers specifically asked about actual plans, plans which had gone through campus agencies and were approved for implementation by the necessary authority. In short, we were seeking information about decisions already made about new programs, and not about abstract hopes.

The interview results show that almost every college and university in the group of schools rated headed for financial trouble is postponing academic program plans. The things being postponed or cut back cover a wide range of subjects. Examples are: graduate and professional programs, interdepartmental programs, oriental languages, engineering and agricultural technology, religious studies, geology, graphic arts, public affairs, black studies, urban studies, and Asian studies.

Another kind of postponed commitment concerns capital outlay for programs which are only partially funded by government or other outside sources. Several schools in the group headed for financial trouble have already adopted, and others are considering, the policy of making no capital expenditure unless it is fully funded and accepting no new program that is only partially funded.

Some program and building plans already started cannot be economically stopped. These go forward amid a general cutback and raise doubts about the credibility of an administration that claims financial trouble. This is part of the two-year lag problem discussed in Chapter 1.

There are, in addition, examples from most of the institutions of postponements in maintenance, landscaping, minor capital improvements, purchase of needed land, and much-hoped-for administrative staff.

General Belt-Tightening A second response of schools headed for financial trouble is to trim expenditures in a way that is best described as general belt-tightening. This means cuts in the expenditure amounts, but not large or central enough to change academic structure or format. General belt-tightening is done to preserve funds for instruction by reducing such expenses as supplies and equipment.

A wide variety of belt-tightening measures were identified in the interviews. Some schools have been doing it for a long time; other institutions are just getting started. Some say that they have been making these kinds of economies for such a long time that there is nothing more to do. Belt-tightening responses can be divided into several types; we list them here in a sequence that seems rather likely.

1 *Cut maintenance.* When financial troubles arise, the first budget item cut is maintenance. This is apparently true historically, for the 1937 AAUP study found that it was the activity most frequently turned to in an effort to cut expenses. Administrators will confess that these savings often turn out to be illusory, for costs of needed work are frequently higher in the end. But maintenance is vulnerable. It is seen as an impersonal and relatively painless cut. When an interviewer told one vice-president that at his home institution the windows were being washed only once a year, the vice-president replied, "We have long ago stopped washing windows." He couldn't remember when his windows were last washed.

2 *Trim expenditures for supplies, equipment, and travel.* This category comes next. Like maintenance, the subject is seen as impersonal and is turned to early for savings. This area of economy also includes laboratory equipment. The theory would seem to be that old equipment can be made to do longer, and since supplies are budgeted at the beginning of the year, an upward adjustment can always be made over the year. The same is true of travel funds.

3 *Cut funds for experimental programs.* Most of the institutions in the category headed for financial trouble have recently introduced experimental programs. In almost every case they reported to interviewers that these programs are being cut back, "starved" as one president reported, or "merely spinning wheels." It is clear that innovation suffers, and suffers early in the process of adjusting to more difficult financial circumstances.

4 *Reduce extracurricular activities and events.* Many institutions have cut funds for these programs and activities. But since some

are funded by earmarked "student" funds (collected by the school or by the students), reallocation is often more difficult than simply cutting an extracurricular activity. Moreover, several institutions continue some of these activities because they are income-producing and support other things. This is especially true of intercollegiate football, where ideas for cost cutting run to things like returning to the one-platoon system or washing football uniforms on campus. A consulting firm hired by Harvard to study ways to be more efficient in expenditures for intercollegiate athletics produced the recommendation that the school spend more money. The function was understaffed.

5 *Cut student aid and special admissions.* Because of the great expense in this area, and its rapid growth in recent years, student aid is made an item for belt-tightening, however reluctantly. As we saw earlier in this chapter, the rate of growth of student aid is declining sharply. Some campuses are cutting the growth of special admissions. In some cases there are cuts in funds available to out-of-state students. Two other schools are imposing new financial limits on eligibility. There is simply less money for this purpose made available by most schools.

6 *Eliminate selected communications, cultural, and student services.* General belt-tightening in most institutions reaches one or more of these areas: publications budget, lectures and concerts, public information services, health services, and certain library services (such as hours of service).

7 *Freeze on hiring nonacademic employees.* Several of the schools in this group have stopped hiring nonacademic employees, using turnover and vacancies to relieve financial pressure.

8 *Cut salaries.* In one institution in this study, the top administrators have taken a voluntary salary cut of 10 percent. The information was reported as confidential, and the institution cannot be identified. If this is being done elsewhere, it was not reported in the interviews. Most salary pressures are so strong the other way that many schools may consider offering a small increase, which in the face of rapid price increases does not avoid the effect of a cut in real income.

Cutting and Reallocating within Existing Structure

A third type of response to an increasingly difficult financial situation is to cut some academic costs to permit reallocation to other academic activities within the existing structure. These are not painless cuts, but they are marginal rather than major moves, for they do not alter the school, departmental, or basic program structure. From the interview responses, it is possible to identify three kinds of such actions.

1 *Move money between academic departments by attrition, increasing enrollment where students are an asset, reducing enrollment where they are a liability.* The pattern emerging is quite clear. Institutions put a freeze on replacements for staff vacancies. This produces a short-run saving, but, more important, it allows reevaluation of the use of these resources in the department concerned. The school can bring about modest fund shifts to other departments. The same effect is sought by holding the faculty constant, but increasing enrollment in those areas where the result is to increase net income. Some institutions, for the same reason, are cutting graduate enrollments. They are too costly.

2 *Cut academic programs whose priority ranking comes primarily from outside the university.* Not all schools have this option, but where they do, several have exercised it. Some instances are minor cuts in centers or institutes, but the schools headed for financial trouble include two important instances which reveal difficulties in making this type of cut. Central Michigan University dropped its laboratory schools and incurred the ill will of many townspeople. Ohio University tried to drop its flight instruction program but was admonished by the legislature and therefore continued it, though in reduced status.

3 *Cuts in academic departments for reallocation.* Not many actions are being taken, but several schools have started in this direction. An early target tends to be summer instruction, if it is not profit-making. Next come selected courses and nontenured faculty positions. Essentially, however, schools headed for financial trouble have not made serious cuts in academic activities other than experimental programs. Harvard is an exception. True to its "every tub on its own bottom" policy of decentralization, it has permitted sharp cuts to occur in individual schools, but these do not involve significant reallocation of money to other departments.

Scrambling for Funds

A fourth response of schools headed for financial trouble is to try to increase income. Almost every one of the 18 colleges and universities considered headed for financial trouble is in the process of increasing efforts to raise private funds. Several have revised their investment policies and anticipate improved returns. Most are considering tuition increases, and many are working on a variety of extramural funding sources, ranging from lobbying for new state revenues to engaging in private business ventures which will produce added income.

Planning and Worrying

Finally, the schools headed for financial trouble are planning and worrying. The institutions are sufficiently diverse so that their experience in planning is not easy to generalize about. In the past, some of them have undergone major changes without consciously planning at all. One generalization that does seem warranted from the interview responses is that planning with the shortage of funds as a constant is relatively new to many administrators. The kind of planning that several administrators, at a variety of schools, talked about is for growth by substitution, adding only by reallocation. Some schools have established institutionalized devices for doing this. "Money," said one, "determines all our planning now." At Ohio University a "Program Implementation System" requires that all new program proposals are brought together for centralized evaluation. None is approved unless the availability of "hard money" is certain. The interviews indicate that whatever planning was done in the past was not nearly so conscious of funding problems. Administrators are worrying because the prospect for "new" money is bleak, and that means the schools face an external struggle just to keep the flow of funds continuing and an internal struggle in reallocating money to keep program growth alive.

One important aspect of planning concerns the methods by which decisions about university resources are made. Financial stringency brings with it more centralized decision making. There is need for more control, for reference to overall priorities, and for the ability to make decisions promptly. At the same time there is much greater interest in obtaining as much review and advice as possible about the decisions that must be made. Hence, the creation on many campuses of budget review or resource committees. In response to interview guide questions (Appendix, questions 8 and 18) about the effect of the financial situation on campus decision making and academic plans, about 40 percent of the schools indicated that they were establishing broadly based committees to provide input on the impact of finance upon the academic life of the institution. The charge to these committees varies from institution to institution. They tend to be review committees, assessing the plans of the institution given its new financial situation. Their members typically include administrators and faculty members, students, and, in some cases, trustees.

In general, these five strategies — postponing, belt-tightening, marginal reallocations, scrambling for funds, and planning and worrying — are efforts toward a more controlled and sophisticated management. They are designed to prevent the acceleration of financial difficulty from headed for financial trouble to in financial difficulty. Although many administrators recognize the real possibility of severe crises ahead, it seems fair to say that these strategies do not yet reflect a response to either the underlying causes of the financial depression in higher education or a reexamination of the schools' missions or long-run prospects, nor do they purport to work major changes in the schools' structures or characters. Not surprisingly, they are an intermediate level of response to financial situations that are still at an intermediate level of severity.

We cannot quantify the effects of these strategies. It is too soon for their effects to have shown up in operation, and the recondite data on which one might reliably estimate their effects were not gathered in this study. We can offer some general observations, however.

This combination of responses is clearly slowing down the rate of expenditure growth at the institutions headed for financial trouble. The reduced rate of expenditure growth will relieve some of the pressure of the cost-income squeeze, but administrators do not believe these measures will solve their financial problem. Some administrators believe they can stabilize their financial situation for a time, but they have little faith that the situation can affirmatively improve unless there is a change in major external conditions — the state of the economy and policies of the federal government. In short, the administrators believe things are likely to get worse at their schools for the next several years or even the next decade.

Why, then, are the schools not taking more fundamental steps to cut their expenditure growth? There is no single answer for all the schools in the group headed for financial trouble. Some may be avoiding the disagreeable task of making deep cuts; some may be developing fundamental solutions, but have not yet taken steps to implement them, and so did not report them in the interview. Others may be preparing to take more drastic measures, but do not think they can do so yet, believing that a year or so of increased financial pressure may make it possible to take actions that are not now acceptable on campus. There is also some optimism that the state of the economy or public policies toward higher education will improve. Schools are thus willing to gamble, believing that it would be a mistake to compromise heavily with the present downturn. They believe a better strategy is to avoid major concessions until they are necessary, for the ground thereby lost would be hard to recover.

6. *Institutions in Financial Difficulty: A Description*

Eleven colleges and universities in this study (27 percent of the 41 institutions) are considered in financial difficulty, based on information gathered at the time of the campus visits. For most of these schools the cost-cutting devices discussed in Chapter 5 have been a fact of life for some time. They have gone well beyond postponing and general belt-tightening measures. "We can't save any more money that way," the interviewer at Tulane was told. "We have been postponing maintenance for almost 10 years. This year we eliminated six graduate programs." Very few of the 11 schools in this category have been in the cost-income squeeze for that long, and most have not had to make such dramatic program cuts. Yet despite the differences in the duration or severity of their financial problems, these 11 colleges and universities have been (or, at the time of the interview, were about to be) moved by financial considerations to make cuts which, fairly judged, affect essential program *or* quality. For that reason they are rated in financial difficulty.

In all cases the cuts are due to financial considerations, but not all situations are alike. Some schools—such as Stanford University—are working on a plan which over a period of four years is designed to bring the school's income and expenditures into balance and produce funds for program flexibility and growth. A somewhat similar plan is being followed at New York University. It adopted the recommendation of a faculty committee on effective use of faculty resources—appointed as part of an administration plan to deal with the school's financial difficulty—that, to keep faculty salaries competitive with the market, modest increases in teaching loads and other economies be put into effect. Unlike many comparable institutions, Beloit College anticipated the current depression in higher education and has made extensive program revision to maintain its distinctive educational position. Other institutions—such as the University of California, Berkeley—have little control over their financial situation.

We doubt that any president or administrator of the institutions studied will want to have his school considered in financial difficulty. Not only may such a characterization create a need for explanations in fund raising, but also it is susceptible to mistaken inferences. As we have just indicated, being in financial difficulty may often be the consequences of factors entirely beyond the control of administrative management. Yet an alumnus, legislator, or potential donor reading that his institution is considered in financial difficulty may somehow assume it is there because of the school's administration. It bears repeating that a conclusion about the adequacy of administration of schools classified as headed for financial trouble or in financial difficulty is simply not warranted on the basis of this study, and the special problems of our criterion of financial difficulty bear remembering. Certainly, in some cases it would rather have to be said that administrators of schools in financial difficulty have taken more basic steps to remedy their situation. There may be schools in our category headed for financial trouble which, under some different objective standard, say, size of deficit and income prospects, are in worse shape than some of our schools in financial difficulty; they have been able to postpone being in financial difficulty by not having dealt fundamentally with their problem.

The 11 colleges and universities considered in financial difficulty, listed by our method of classification, are:

National research universities
  Stanford University
  University of California, Berkeley

Leading regional research universities
  New York University
  Saint Louis University
  Tulane University

State and comprehensive colleges
  Boston College
  San Diego State College

Liberal arts colleges
  Beloit College

Primarily black colleges
  Fisk University
  Huston-Tillotson College
  Tougaloo College
Two-Year Colleges
  None

Unlike the group of schools rated headed for financial trouble, which included a distribution of types of schools quite similar to the mix of all schools in the study, the group of schools in financial difficulty differs from the total list in several ways. First, 3 of the 11 schools in financial difficulty are small primarily black institutions (Huston-Tillotson College, Tougaloo College, and Fisk University). In contrast to the larger institutions founded for Negroes—Howard University and Morgan State, both of which were found not in financial difficulty—each of these schools is in a serious financial situation. At Fisk, the interviewer was told that the school was now operating at a $1 million per year deficit and that it could hope to continue at most for four years. Administrators at Tougaloo College said that although their school is currently running a cumulative deficit of between $300,000 and $400,000, it is continuing to function, but only with difficulty in meeting its current obligations. Huston-Tillotson College is in a precarious position. With virtually no endowment, in 1969 it raised its tuition sharply to balance its budget but faced a sudden drop in enrollment (from 832 to 710). Its current deficit is $95,000.

A second distinguishing characteristic of this list is that it includes a heavily disproportionate number of private institutions in financial difficulty and only two state institutions, both in California (San Diego State College and the University of California, Berkeley). In the total list of 41 schools in this study, 44 percent are public institutions. In contrast, these two public institutions represent only 18 percent of the schools in financial difficulty. Thus, private institutions, which constitute 56 percent of the overall list studied, constitute 82 percent of the schools in financial difficulty. By and large, the private institutions are in a more difficult financial condition than the public ones because they have been in the cost-income squeeze for a longer time. The California public institutions in this study appear to share that condition with the private institutions. They have had a growing cost-income problem over a period of three years.

A third distinguishing characteristic of the list of schools in financial difficulty is that no two-year institution is on it. Also, relative to their number in the entire list, there are fewer comprehensive colleges and liberal arts colleges. Universities appear on the list of schools in financial difficulty in the same proportion as they do on the entire study sample, but there are relatively more regional ones in financial difficulty and relatively fewer national ones.

Schools in financial difficulty tend to be in urban locations, and, as we shall see later in this chapter, they have high student aid costs. Of the 11 schools in the group in financial difficulty, only two, Beloit College and Tougaloo College, are not in an urban location. In the entire sample, 54 percent of the schools were classified as being located in metropolitan areas. In the group in financial difficulty, 82 percent are in metropolitan areas.

There are no apparent important regional differences between the group of schools in financial difficulty and the entire list studied. There are, relatively, somewhat fewer schools in financial difficulty in the Midwest, and more in the South, when the group is compared to the entire sample. In general, these schools in financial difficulty tend to be paying faculty salaries that are higher than the schools not in financial difficulty and lower than the schools headed for financial trouble.

COMMON CHARACTER-ISTICS We saw in Chapter 3, in the discussion of the criteria used to determine financial health and financial difficulty, that the category *in financial difficulty* used here is based on judgments and includes institutions in varying degrees of financial difficulty, even though it may appear definite and clear. This is true of all three of our categories, but especially so in the case of the category *in financial difficulty*. A school was considered properly in this group if its current financial condition forced on it cuts which, fairly judged, offset essential programs or quality. The situations range from the elimination of schools and departments, as at St. Louis University; or cutting back faculty positions, as at Stanford; to those at New York University and Boston College, whose cuts have been relatively small compared to the others in the group but where the financial condition is serious enough to expect significant cuts shortly.

One would expect variations, given the great variety in size, type, and aspiration of the 11 schools in financial difficulty. But whatever the other differences, these schools have certain characteristics in common that mark their financial condition and their necessary responses to it. Based on the interviews, this group of campuses is distinguished by the following six characteristics:

1   All nine private institutions are deficit financing. Both of the public institutions are on what administrators describe as "stand still" budgets.

2   These institutions are reducing the number of faculty positions either by cutbacks, or by a freeze on further faculty hiring without centralized approval, or by both. Where there is graduate work, the number of teaching and research assistants is being reduced.

3   These schools are holding enrollment stable, or growing. Either way, they are increasing their student-faculty ratios.

4   Each of these institutions is making cuts in programs. These cuts range widely and include such things as reduction in the number of courses, reductions in graduate programs, and (in the case of St. Louis University) elimination of two professional schools— dentistry and engineering—and an affiliate college.

5   Each of these institutions is either reducing the number of administrative positions or not adding ones that are needed.

6   Finally, research institutions are reducing the budgets of research centers, institutes, and related activities which they consider important parts of their academic programs. Other institutions, and some research institutions, are reducing programs that are considered important parts of campus intellectual life.

COST AND INCOME FACTORS   The general reasons for schools being in financial difficulty are similar to those we examined earlier in discussing the schools headed for financial trouble. These schools are feeling the consequences of rapidly rising costs, growing demand, and a declining rate of income growth. Their overall cost and income figures tell the story.

Consider costs first. Administrators of schools in financial difficulty told campus interviewers of the great cost pressures constantly on them. The combined expenditure figures of these institutions are summarized in the table below. For the period 1959–60 to 1969–70, schools in financial difficulty had been increasing their educational and general expenditures at the compound average annual rate of 9.5 percent per student.

Average annual rate of expenditure increase per student,* schools in financial difficulty		Educational and general	Educational and general less sponsored research	Instruction and departmental research	Student aid
	1959–60 to 1969–70	9.5%	9.0%	8.0%	21.5%
	1969–70 to 1970–71†	—.7%	3.6%	3.0%	—.9%

*See chapter 4 for definitions of the expenditure categories involved.

† Figures for 1969–70 to 1970–71 based on data from four institutions, the total number of schools in financial difficulty with figures available at the time of the study.

As the table demonstrates, the schools in financial difficulty were able, during the decade of the 1960s, to increase their expenditures at a rapid rate. However, for the schools reporting data for the year 1969–70 to 1970–71, the average rate of change in expenditures per student is much less than the yearly average of the preceding decade. The educational and general and student aid expenditures per student for 1970–71 were, on the average, lower than those for 1969–70. The difference in the 1969–70 to 1970–71 figures between expenditures for educational and general less sponsored research and those for educational and general (which includes sponsored research) reflects the seriousness of the cutbacks in organized research.

The expenditures for educational and general less sponsored research increased over the decade at the average annual per student rate of 9.0 percent. Sponsored research expenditures increased at an average rate somewhat higher than that, for, when it is included, educational and general increases at the higher rate of 9.5 percent. Budgeted departmental instruction and research increased at an average annual rate, per student, of 8.0 percent for the decade.

Finally, we noted earlier that schools in financial difficulty are overwhelmingly urban schools. That fact seems reflected in the rate of student aid expenditures of these colleges and universities. For the period 1959–60 to 1969–70, student aid expenditures rose at the average annual per student rate of 21.5 percent. The table also shows the rate of change in expenditures for the most recent year, 1969–70 to 1970–71, in which there was a decline in the absolute amount of student aid expenditures from the preceding year.

Although costs for educational and general expenditures have been rising at an annual per student rate of 9.5 percent, the institutions rated in financial difficulty have not been able to get the income to meet those costs in the most recent years. The cost-income squeeze has forced them to cut expenditures. This is already shown in the table, which indicates that, in contrast to the 10-year rate of increase per student in expenditures of 9.5 percent, the rate of change was —.7 percent in 1970–71. Not only did the average rate of growth decline, but there was no growth at the schools for which there is data: The average expenditures actually dropped. They dropped —.9 percent for student aid. Expenditures rose at somewhat less than half of their average rate of growth for the preceding decade for educational and general less sponsored research—3.6 percent as compared to 9.0 percent. Expenditures for instruction and departmental research also rose at only a fraction of their previous growth rate—3.0 percent as compared to 8.0 percent.

The overall figures for income tell the other half of the story. The reason for the sharply declining rate of expenditure growth is that these institutions have been taking in less money than they had been spending, and now they are trying to close the deficit gap. The average annual rate of income growth per student, for the period 1959–60 to 1969–70, was just over one percentage point lower than the average annual rate of expenditure growth. These figures are summarized in the table below.

These are the income figures for all current fund income, including auxiliary enterprises. Our income data require our reporting income in this fashion. Expenditures are calculated on the same basis and therefore are slightly higher than those shown in the earlier table, where auxiliary enterprises are excluded and student aid is shown as a separate expenditure category.

The table below shows that total income grew during the 1959–60 to 1969–70 period at an annual rate of 1.1 percent per student less than expenditures. Moreover, this difference is understated in our table in several ways. For one thing, our figures show annual averages over the decade, but in fact the disparity between

Average annual rate of income and expenditure growth, per student, schools in financial difficulty, 1959–60 to 1969–70

Rate of income growth	9.2%
Rate of expenditure growth	10.3%

income and costs has almost all occurred in the last few years. Furthermore, the rate of income growth is declining faster than the rate of expenditure growth. Finally, the difference is understated in some cases because the income figures available to us unavoidably included as "income" items that are more accurately "capital" or "reserves."

This disparity between income and expenses means that the private institutions must be deficit financing. In fact, every one of the nine private institutions in this group in financial difficulty is deficit spending. Their deficits for the latest year reported at the time of the campus interviews, along with the percentage those deficits constitute of current fund expenditures less auxiliary enterprises, are: Beloit College—$200,000 (3.8 percent); Boston College—$3,500,000 (12.5 percent); Fisk University—$1,000,000 (20.5 percent); Huston-Tillotson College—$95,000 (6.1 percent); New York University—$5,000,000 (5.0 percent); St. Louis University—$1,200,000 (3.3 percent); Stanford University—$1,400,000 (1.6 percent); Tougaloo College—$239,000 (10.6 percent); Tulane University—$1,500,000 (4.2 percent). These deficits become the more serious when one notes that several of these schools have carried deficits for more than one or two years and have not managed to reduce them.

THE ADMINISTRATORS' ASSESSMENTS In general terms, then, the overall problem is the excess of costs over income. A visitor to these campuses is quickly made aware of the financial situation and its operating effects. A synopsis of the interviewers' notes for each campus follows.

Beloit College. Administrators say that the college faculty is 12 positions below what it should be. The number of nonacademic employees has been reduced. For 1970–71, $100,000 has been cut from the total spent on student aid in 1969–70. The planned library budget allocation has been reduced. A planned American studies program was postponed as well as an undergraduate tutorial program. Student research has been cut back. Performing arts programs and cultural affairs have been reduced.

Boston College. A badly needed library building has been postponed, and plans for dormitories have been cut back. Special admissions have been reduced. The percentate of graduate students has been frozen at the present level. Administrators are stopping the growth of faculty, despite the reservations of faculty and deans. The college carried a deficit in 1969–70 of $3.5 million and expects a deficit of $830,000 in 1970–71.

Fisk University. In 1970, Fisk carried a $1 million deficit. The endowment is being used up and will be gone in three to four years. This year the Afro-American Institute will be phased out. Several departments would have been eliminated were it not for deficit spending. Drastic across-the-board cuts have been made wherever possible. Construction has been cut back, and the number of faculty has been frozen at 90 for the last three years.

Huston-Tillotson College. Research has been cut back and the athletic program greatly reduced. Several faculty positions were eliminated. Further reductions have been made in intercollegiate athletic competition, music, and the number of course offerings. Insufficient income has necessitated cutting into the budget base. Despite cuts, the deficit of $55,000 for 1969–70 will grow to $95,000 in 1970–71. The number of course offerings has been reduced, and needed library expansion has been delayed. Efforts to pay competitive salaries have been stymied.

New York University. In 1970–71 the university will carry a deficit of over $5 million and will need to borrow to cover it. The university has partially offset its difficult financial situation by the sale of noneducational business assets. The number of faculty has been frozen and the number of teaching assistants reduced. Research has been cut back, and a moderate reduction has been made in the number of administrative posts. The student-faculty ratio will rise in 1970–71.

Saint Louis University. The School of Dentistry, the four engineering departments, and Parks College—a small affiliate specializing in aeronautical science—have been closed. Forty-five faculty positions were eliminated, and 40 permanent faculty members were consequently given two years' notice of severance from employment. The current allocation of the Medical School is one-third what it was three years ago. Library acquisitions and research programs were trimmed. Faculty salaries were raised only 3 percent—it is feared that some faculty may leave as a result. Many courses were postponed, and the student-faculty ratio has risen. The debate program has been eliminated for next year.

San Diego State College. Class size has risen. This year it was necessary to let 48 faculty positions go unfilled and to eliminate certain research positions. Sabbatical leaves have been cut in half. The equipment budget was cut by $20,000. According to school administrators, faculty and staff morale is low.

Stanford University. The university has cut $1,000,000 from its original budget for 1970–71 but will still have a deficit of $1,427,-000. Its budget planning requires that $2.5 million be eliminated in the next four years. Deficits are being financed from reserves. All unfilled faculty posts are frozen. A total of 21 faculty positions have been eliminated, although no tenured faculty members have been severed. Library acquisition growth has been cut. General funds have been withdrawn from the Hoover Institution and the Medical School. New programs in urban and environment studies are not being funded for the time being. Plans for library and law school building are on the shelf awaiting funding. The drama program was drastically reduced.

Tougaloo College. The college, with an enrollment of about 700, is running a deficit between $300,000 and $400,000 with an endowment of only $500,000 and, at the time of the interview, was in arrears on current bills. Financial stringencies make it increasingly difficult to recruit qualified black faculty. Membership in various intercollegiate organizations has been eliminated.

Tulane University. The number of faculty has been frozen. That and increased enrollment have resulted in a higher student-faculty ratio. Cutbacks have been made in teaching assistants and research activities. Ph.D. programs were eliminated in the fields of classics, Italian, geology, music, theater, and social work. Maintenance has been deferred for many years, and the library budget starved. A cut of $100,000 was made from the speech and theater budgets. The laundry and printing press were eliminated.

University of California, Berkeley. The student-faculty ratio is rising. One research institute in the social sciences has been eliminated. Seven other research units (including earthquake engineering and urban social problems) are forced to operate without a regular support budget. Others, such as an institute on race and community relations, are only partially funded. Administrators report that an "indeterminate number" of proposed new courses have been postponed, as have plans for development of a medical school. Some courses, such as freshman seminars, have been cut. The summer quarter was eliminated to save expenses; as a result, the state withdrew funding for 208 new faculty positions, most of them unfilled, that would have been required for year-round campus operation. Summer instruction will now have to be on a self-supporting basis. The number of graduate students and teaching assistants is being reduced. There are no capital funds. Plans for administrative growth were shelved, and the number of administrative posts was reduced. Cuts have been made in community service and various research programs. Administrators believe that the fact that faculty received no salary increase in 1970–71 has had an adverse effect.

Although these 11 colleges and universities differ in size (from Tougaloo College with about 700 students to the University of California with about 28,000) and in resources and mission, their combined experience does illustrate clearly the cost-income problem facing all institutions of higher education. What it does not reveal is the extent to which they are doing something about it. How many of these schools would Father Reinert put in his third category (the institutions in financial trouble, who know it and are working on it)? Most, perhaps all. This group of schools also includes the institutions that are making the most creative response to the new cost-income problem. For this group of schools his classification has an advantage over the one we have used, in that his explicitly gives credit for a serious effort at solving the problem. In so doing, he raises the important question, how much can an individual institution do to solve its financial problem? To get an answer to that question, we must first analyze in greater depth the nature of the cost-income squeeze. In the next chapter, therefore, we shall attempt to make such an analysis and to estimate how much of the financial problem is within the control of individual institutions.

7. Financial Difficulty: The Dimensions of the Problem and of the Solution

If we are to analyze in greater depth the nature of the financial difficulty facing the schools, we must know more specifically what the rising components of their costs are and what their income requirements are. It is remarkable how difficult it is for colleges and universities to provide precise amounts for the components of expense and income.[1] In this study we have had to rely on incomplete income data, on interview assessments by administrators, on methods of estimating cost and income components that vary for different components, and on categories of components that are general.

At each campus in this study, the administrators were asked to identify and weight the main components in their institution's cost situation (see Appendix, interview questions 4 and 5). This request sometimes produced a ranking of factors and a few efforts to weight them. Administrators are clearly aware of the factors that constitute their cost rise, but they are not in a position to offer a quantitative causal assessment of these factors.

The interview responses can be summarized in a list of five main components of the cost side of the problem. These are: (1) the effects of inflation; (2) rising faculty salaries; (3) rising student aid; (4) campus disturbances, theft, and destruction of property; and (5) growth in responsibilities, activities, and aspirations. Two points should be stressed about these factors. First, they are not mutually exclusive. The first factor—inflation—influences the others in a variety of ways. Second, the last one—growth in responsibilities, activities, and aspirations—is, in part, a residual

---

[1] Most schools are now preparing more complete and uniform income and expense data than they have before. In due course, it might be possible to do detailed individual case studies for a number of institutions, which could provide a firm analytical basis for overall estimates.

factor. It is intended to cover several types of costs cited in the interviews. These include those costs often associated with the "knowledge explosion," with its increase in demand for more sophisticated equipment, such as computers. It also includes the costs associated with new academic and community activities of campuses, increased operating costs of new buildings put into service,[2] any increases in per student costs attributable to enrollment growth,[3] and new legal responsibilities under social legislation for unemployment benefits, minimum wages, etc.

Although the factors would not apply equally at each school, these five factors can be said, on the basis of the interviews, to account for the historic rise in costs, the impact of which was most keenly felt in the three-year period 1966–67 to 1969–70. In order to estimate the contribution of each component, we must first state what that rise in costs has been.

From Chapters 4, 5, and 6, we know that total current fund expenditures per student (including student aid and auxiliary enterprises) rose between 1959–60 and 1969–70 at the average rate of 7.5 percent per year for schools not in financial trouble, 7.3 percent for schools headed for financial trouble, and 10.3 percent for those considered in financial difficulty. The average for all schools in the study was 8.1 percent per student per year. Thus the range between the high and low decade average annual cost increase for different categories of institutions is approximately 3.0 percentage points. During the last three years of the decade, the average expenditures per student rose at a slightly higher rate than the average for the decade. The difference for all schools in the study is about .6 percent per student per year.[4] Although we emphasize the last three years of the decade in this chapter, we shall use the decade figures for our estimates of the significance of the various factors in cost increases. The range between high

---

[2] Capital outlay itself, however, is not included in this study.

[3] We have not taken separate account of cost increases attributable to the rate of enrollment growth, but have dealt with the cost on a per student basis. The study by Jenny and Wynn (1969) found that there is a positive relationship between the rate of enrollment growth and the rate of growth of aggregate educational and general expenditures.

[4] Thus, for all schools in the study, our data indicate that total current fund expenditures per student rose during the decade at the average rate of 8.2 percent, and during the last three years they rose at the average rate of 8.8 percent per student per year.

and low expenditures is the same in both cases, and the decade figures are based on more complete data.

At the high end of the range, we would put our schools in financial difficulty where costs have increased 10.3 percent per student per year. An attempt to make an estimate of the contribution of each of the five components of the cost side of the problem thus requires an estimate of how much each contributed to this 10.3 percent per student annual rise in costs. At the low end of the range, we would place the average of the schools not in financial trouble and headed for financial trouble, which is slightly below 7.4 percent per student increase in costs annually. Again, one could estimate how much each of the five cost factors contributed to this 7.4 percent total rise in costs.[5]

An accurate determination of their contribution could be made only by detailed examination of the data for individual institutions. We have not made such a determination, and, as we indicated above, neither have most institutions themselves. We do not have the data for such analysis, and, therefore, we shall have to make aggregate estimates of the contributions of each of the five factors to the rise in costs. Although this is not precise, it will permit us to indicate the dimensions of the problem and of its solution. Finally, we shall estimate how much of the solution is within the control of the institutions.

FIVE COST COMPONENTS With those objectives in mind, let us look at each of the five factors we have cited and attempt to estimate the contribution of each to the cost side of the problem.

Our estimates emphasize the years 1966–67 to 1969–70—the three years in which the problem has been most serious.

---

[5] Still another low figure for cost increases could be posited by using schools outside this study sample. Thus, from the American Council on Education *Fact Book on Higher Education,* we can calculate roughly that, for all institutions in the United States, current fund expenditures (less auxiliary enterprises) rose at the average per student rate of 5.8 percent per year in the decade ending 1966, the latest year for which there are published data. If the national expenditure figure changed in the same degree as the expenditures for the schools in our study, it should have risen in the neighborhood of .8 of a percentage point, or 6.5 percent per student per year. Probably the reasons why this national figure is lower than those for our sample are that the sample over-represents research universities and liberal arts colleges and underrepresents the two-year colleges and, to a lesser extent, the comprehensive colleges and other liberal arts colleges.

Inflation The average annual rate of inflation (as measured by the average increase in the national consumer price index) for the three-year period was 4.2 percent. For simplicity, let us exclude faculty salaries and the other two components dealt with as separate items below. Faculty salaries (by our calculation from the HEGIS data for all schools for the academic year 1967–68) constitute 33 percent of the total current fund expenditures. Student aid in that year accounted for an average of 6.4 percent of current fund expenditures. From estimates in this section, we shall assume that the figure for campus disturbances is 3.0. Therefore, an average increase of 4.2 percent in the residual 57.6 percent of the inputs of the schools—those that remain after excluding the components itemized—would result in an overall cost increase of 2.4 percent. By this estimate, therefore, inflation accounts for about one-fourth of cost pressures on the schools.[6]

It can be argued, with considerable justice, that for purposes of cost projection the figure 4.2 percent per year used for the inflation factor is too high. Historically, that would be true. If we were to assume that, in the years immediately ahead, the average rate of price increase were to return to its long-term average, the 4.2 figure would be closer to 2 percent. If we say, therefore, that an optimistic estimate on the future course of prices is that they will go up at one-half the rate of the last three years, the inflation factor would annually require 1.2 percentage points of future cost increases.

Faculty Salaries Considered over long-term periods, faculty salaries tend to rise at approximately the same rate as wages in other sectors of the economy. June O'Neill has shown that for the full period 1930–1967, the average annual percentage rate of change for faculty salaries is 3.4; for earnings in all industries it is 4.1. In the 1950s, however, the average rates of increase were the same for both, and during the last decade faculty salaries rose more rapidly than did wages in other sectors of the economy. According to O'Neill's figures, the comparative annual percentage rates of increase for the period 1960–1967 are 5.8 for faculty, and 4.0 in all industries.

In those industries where productivity increases equal or exceed wage increases, rising wages need produce no cost effects. But

---

[6] This comp res with Bowen's estimate of 25 percent, based on cost data and price index, for the period 1955–56 to 1965–66. See Bowen (1968).

education is like other service industries where productivity increases are at best very small, if there are any at all. The consequence is that rising salaries push up educational costs.[7] Of course, an important reason for rising faculty salaries is rising prices, and this is reflected in our treatment of the inflation component above.

To estimate the amount of the cost push due to faculty salaries (including inflation), using as a base the period 1966–67 to 1969–70, we use an annual rate of salary change of 6.1 percent, the amount which the American Association of University Professors reports as average faculty salary increases nationally for that period. Faculty salaries constitute 33 percent of the total current fund expenditures (by our calculation from HEGIS data for the year 1967–68). The product of these two figures is about 2.0 percent. This would mean that about one-fifth of the 10.3 point annual cost increase for the schools in financial difficulty was attributable to cost increases of faculty salaries.

It seems rather unlikely that faculty salaries will rise in the 1970s at the same rate as in the 1960s, for the demand is not increasing as rapidly as the supply of academic labor. This would mean that for several years in the 1970s, until the market changes, average faculty salaries are likely to rise at a rate closer to the long-term trend in wages in the rest of the economy, probably between 4 and 5 percent per year. Let us assume 4 percent as our low estimate.

Under the estimate of 6.1 percent average annual increase in faculty salaries, the combination of faculty salaries and the other effects of inflation account for slightly less than one-half of the recent annual cost push on the schools in financial difficulty. Three components, derived from interviews with the administrators of these schools, remain to be estimated.

Student Aid We have seen earlier in this study that student aid has been increasing very rapidly. For the years 1966–67 to 1969–70, student aid expenditures grew at an average per student rate of 31 percent per year at those schools in financial difficulty for which there are data. Student aid (again by our calculation for the year 1967–68) constituted 7.7 percent of current fund expenditures for schools

---

[7] See Bowen (1968), pp. 12–16) for an excellent brief discussion of this problem of the technology of higher education. See also his volume with co-author William J. Baumol (1966).

in financial difficulty. This would mean that the rise in student aid costs added 2.4 percentage points to their total rising costs. This remarkable increase is partly the product of dramatic responses in a given year to the problems of minority students. A more reliable guide to the future probably is the figure for the decade: From 1959–60 to 1969–70, expenditures at schools in financial difficulty grew at the annual rate of 21.5 percent per student, which would account for 1.7 percentage points of growth in their expenditures.

For the other schools in the study, student aid (by calculation for 1967–68) constituted 5.6 percent of total current expenses. For the three-year period, 1966–67 to 1969–70, their student aid expenditures grew at the average annual rate of 12.5 percent per student, adding .7 of a percentage point to costs. The average increase in student aid costs for the decade for these schools was 15.5 percent per student per year, which would add .9 percentage points to growth of costs.

Since the decade figure for the schools in financial difficulty seems safer to rely on than the figure for 1966–67 to 1969–70, we shall use the decade figure for the other schools also. Thus, our high estimate for student aid costs is 1.7 and the low is .9 percentage points.

Campus Disturbances This leaves the effects of campus disturbances and growth in responsibility, activities, and aspiration. So far as we know, none of the schools visited has specific cost estimates of these factors.

The staff at one institution prepared for us an estimate of the costs of campus disturbances as a percentage of all expenditures for education and general purposes for 1969–70. The result of that calculation is presented in Table 5. The table shows that the estimated costs of preventing, and recovering from, campus disturbances was for that institution 4.7 percent of its total expenses for educational and general purposes for the academic year 1969–70. That was not a particularly good year for that school, but even so, its expenditures do not seem to us inordinately higher than what one would expect at several schools whose experience was related in the interviews for this study. This expenditure is, however, clearly more than some of the other institutions have spent. We concluded, therefore, that our estimate of this cost factor should be reduced, and we chose a factor of about one-third as a reasonable guess. This estimate produces the following result. The figure of 4.746, when converted from a percent of educational and

Security	.890
Insurance	.275
Property replacement and repair	.414
Additions to staff	.192
Diversion of existing staff time (includes loss of time due to closing buildings)	2.953
Costs of disciplinary hearings, administration of regulations, not otherwise accounted for above	.022
TOTAL	4.746

*TABLE 5
Estimated costs of campus disturbances as a percent of all expenditures for educational and general purposes, one institution, 1969–70*

NOTE: The above figures are based on actual cost estimates prepared by the staff of an institution for this study. The figures provided us were dollar amounts in each case. We have converted them to percentage of educational and general expenditures.

general expenses to a percent of total current fund expenditures, becomes 4.2. Two-thirds of 4.2 is 2.8. We believe, therefore, that for many of the schools in this study, total expenditures related to campus disturbances for the 1969–70 academic year realistically constituted something in the neighborhood of 3 percent of total fund expenditures.

This figure must now be converted to an average amount of increase in the last three years, the period of the most acute cost-income squeeze, and, also, the period of greatest cost due to student disturbances. Since the interviews indicate that these costs have skyrocketed in the last three years, we have assumed that this cost factor of 3.0 was very low at the beginning of the period, 1966–67 to 1969–70, say, .5 percent of current costs. From this assumption we can determine the average annual change to the current figure of 3.0 percent for the three years. It is just under 1 percent, which we shall round to 1.0 percent. This estimate, therefore, is that, during each of the last three years, 1 percentage point of the total cost push has been the rise in costs related to campus disturbances. As we saw in Chapter 4, some schools have largely escaped these costs. For others, this figure will be low. We have added a low estimate for each of the other components; therefore, let us assume a low estimate for this factor is one-third of the 1 percentage point, or .3.

Although we have been calling this factor "campus disturbances," it also reflects another cost factor, the increasing incidence of theft, destruction, and defacement of campus property. This is a growing problem according to the campus interviews, and is a somewhat different phenomenon from campus disturbances.

The first four factors, therefore, account by our estimates for an annual cost push of 7. 1 percentage points per student, by the higher estimates, and 5.6 percentage points, by the lower estimates.[8] If we subtract these figures from the high and low estimates of the recent cost increase, namely 10.3 percent and 7.4 percent per student per year, the residual—the component that includes growth in responsibility, activities, and aspiration— would conceivably range anywhere from 4.7 percentage points (subtracting only the low estimates of the other components from the high rate of cost growth) to .3 (subtracting all the high estimates for the other components from the low rate of cost growth). It is unlikely that either of these extremes is empirically accurate, and the residual component for either schools in financial difficulty or the average of schools not in financial trouble and headed for financial trouble presumably lies somewhere in between.

Growth in Responsibilities, Activities, and Aspirations

The rate of growth in costs represented by this item reflects growing costs of graduate study and increasing library and computer costs. At almost every school these and related items were cited. The movement of campuses into new fields of responsibility—especially community service, programs concerning the cities, and related research—all come under this general heading. So do the rising quality standards that have marked education since World War II. Included also are costs due to new legal responsibilities under legislation.

These new activities appear in some degree in all institutions. Yet they vary so widely that it is difficult to deal with them except through detailed studies of individual institutions. On the basis of our observations of the 41 schools in the sample, we think it fair to say that no significant segment of schools has entirely stopped growing in responsibilities, program, and quality. Within the theoretical range of .3 to 4.7 percentage points of cost growth, 1.5 percentage points is our best guess as a reasonable minimum;

[8] The high estimates are: inflation, 2.4 percentage points of cost growth per year; faculty salaries, 2.0; student aid, 1.7; and disturbances, 1.0, for a total of 7.1 percentage points. Our low estimates *for the future* for inflation and faculty salaries are, respectively, 1.2 percent and 1.3 percent. However, for purposes of calculating the residual component in the *historical* growth in costs for 1966–67 to 1969–70, obviously we cannot use low figures which are simply projected for the future. Rather, we must use the historic figures for inflation and faculty salaries. Thus, our low estimates for this purpose are: inflation, 2.4 percent; faculty salaries, 2.0 percent; student aid, .9 percent; and disturbance, .3 percent, for a total of 5.6 percentage points of annual cost growth.

we will use it as our low figure. On the other hand, colleges and universities cannot be expected to expand their operating activities rapidly in the next few years. It seems doubtful that any significant number would reach 4 percent per student per year for this component; we take as our high figure for this component in the near future 3.5 percentage points of cost.

EXTENT OF INSTITU- TIONAL CONTROL

The question raised by these estimates of cost is, of course, how much can they be reduced? The estimates indicate that the postponing, belt-tightening, and adding by substitution measures that we described in discussing the schools headed for financial trouble are dealing with the largest single area of cost, namely, the residual assigned to growth in responsibilities, activities, and aspirations. But how much control does the campus have?

Inflation is outside the control of the campuses. If the government gets better control of the price level, the schools would get relief from the next major item of their costs. This, too, might bring some relief from salary needs of faculty. Faculty salaries are affected by inflation and competition and are, therefore, also partly outside the campus's control. Even schools in grave economic difficulty have recently granted salary increases in response to market conditions.[9]

If campus disturbances and the defacement of property cease to be the fashion, and these costs can be reduced, another important saving could be effected. Or, once adequate security measures exist, these costs need no longer increase significantly. (These alternatives still seem somewhat in the future.) It is more difficult to argue that all increases in student aid could be eliminated, given the present rate of inflation, the demand for access to higher education and the student aid costs it imposes. Growth in responsibilities, activities, and aspirations could be cut sharply. Adding by substitution can effect cost reductions, but it is difficult to see how academic institutions, and especially research institutions, can totally ignore innovation and technology, which will surely entail new expenses.

In short, the schools have no control over inflation, have only

---

[9] The market forces responsible for rising faculty salaries are felt by all types of institutions. A special illustration of the effects of the market occurs at the primarily black institutions: It appears from our interviews that in recent years they have had, for the first time, to compete for faculty in a national labor market and therefore have had to raise salaries more rapidly than local conditions alone would require.

partial control over faculty salaries and disturbances, and could if necessary have greater control over student aid and the residual amount assigned to growth in program, activities, and aspirations. We have estimated the contribution of each of these cost factors to the recent high rate of increase of 10.3 percent per student per year in expenditures. If our assumptions about lower rates of increase in prices and salaries are correct, what would be the importance of these cost factors in the early 1970s under conditions of prudence, assuming minimal growth and costs? What would their importance be under the most stringent "rock bottom" conditions? Table 6 attempts to estimate cost factors of these two possible situations.

By assuming the lower figure for prices and salaries and by using the "low rate" of overall increase derived earlier in this chapter, we find that a prudent budget would still require an increase in the rate of expenditure of 5.2 percent per student per year. And that this would be 6.4 percent if the estimate about inflation is wrong and prices continue to rise at their recent rate. Under the most stringent assumptions, with virtually no expenditure growth except that assumed for low level of inflation and salary increases as one-half the prudent "low," expenditures will still grow at the annual per student rate of 2.2 percent, or if infla-

TABLE 6 *Estimates of annual percentage increase in current fund expenditures per student needed for operations*

Cost factor	Extent of campus control	Projection from 1966–67 to 1969–70 levels, assuming actual or high costs	Early 1970s policy of minimum growth, assuming low costs	Early 1970s rock bottom policy, assuming maximum control and low costs
Inflation	None	2.4	1.2	1.2
Faculty salaries	Partial	2.0	1.3	.7
Disturbances and security	Partial	1.0	.3	.1
Student aid	Substantial	1.7	.9	.1
Responsibility, activities, and aspiration	Substantial	3.5	1.5	.1
TOTAL		10.6	5.2*	2.2†

*6.4 minimum if inflation continues at 1966–67 to 1969–70 rates.

† 3.4 minimum if inflation continues at 1966–67 to 1969–70 rates.

tion continues at its recent rate, at the rock bottom amount of 3.4 percent per year.

This means, in sum, that given no change in the rate of inflation, costs under a determined policy of prudence will rise at the rate of between 6 and 7 percent per student per year. This comports with the 7.5 percent figure Bowen found for the increase in direct costs over much of United States history. If inflation is controlled, a policy of prudence would require an annual increase of just over 5 percent. Our stringent, rock bottom, and improbable figure (except for short periods of time) is 2.2 percent increase in expenditures per student per year.

INCOME FACTORS Whatever a rock bottom figure for expenditure growth might be, income growth will have to match it if these schools are to be solvent. As we know, the rate of growth of income has not kept pace with actual expenditure growth. In this section we discuss what the components of income are, how their growth rates have declined, and how those declines have contributed to the decline in the growth of overall income.

It is more difficult to analyze the income accounts of the schools than it is their expenditure accounts. Income sources, as between schools, vary more widely than do expenditure patterns. In addition, expenditure data are easier to obtain and tend to be more reliable. We have complete income data for only about one-half of the schools in the entire study. From the Carnegie Commission data (which record and classify the federal government's 1967–68 HEGIS figures), we can determine with some precision the important sources of income. We shall do this for the schools in financial difficulty, for their situation poses the clear test of the dimensions of the cost-income squeeze and of what it will take to get out of it. We will look first at the private schools.

About 96 percent of the income of private colleges and universities comes from four sources: (1) tuition and fees; (2) federal government; (3) private gifts and grants; and (4) endowment income. When the income of the schools in financial difficulty is averaged for the year 1967–68, the above four sources provide the following percentages of total income:[10]

---

[10] Exclusive of auxiliary enterprises. We assume this income source will grow at the average rate of the other components.

Source	Percent
Tuition and fees	39
Federal government	33
Gifts and grants	18
Endowment income	6
Other	4

Although this summarizes the average income for the private institutions, the average conceals great variations in the relative importance of income from these sources. Thus, the federal government provided only 4.6 percent of the income for Beloit College, but it provided 64.7 percent of the income for Stanford University. Endowment brings 13.5 percent of Fisk's income, but only .8 percent of Tougaloo's.

The income data simply do not permit us to make a precise measurement of the amount of change in several of these components. The trends are clear, as we have noted in earlier chapters. In recent years the rate of growth of government funding has declined, as has income from gifts and grants, and from endowment. The private schools in financial difficulty have placed increasing reliance on tuition as an income source.

These same trends apply to the income components of the public institutions, which of course include an additional major account for state funds. Average income of the two public institutions in financial difficulty comes from the following sources:

Source	Percent
State funds	55
Federal government	28
Fees	10
Endowment income	1
Private gifts and grants	1
Other	4

The differences between these two public institutions in the percentage of income from each source are not as great as some of the divergencies among the private schools cited above. Thus, California received 45 percent of its income from the state and 34 percent from the United States, whereas San Diego received 64 percent from the state and 22 percent from the United States.

We have identified trends in these components of income, both for public and private institutions, over the period 1966–67 to

1969–70. However, our income data are not good enough to permit us to project the future growth trends of the individual components of income for the schools in financial difficulty. Using a variety of income data from varying sources for varying types of schools, we can attempt to project income by component for a hypothetical —or, perhaps more accurately, a hybrid—institution. We shall assume that the components of income for our hybrid institution are the same as the components shown above for the schools in financial difficulty. Such a projection for a hypothetical school provides a basis for predicting what the possibilities for income are; the prediction can be adjusted for different, actual institutions, depending on how their income components differ from those hypothesized.

Our projection indicates that our hybrid institution cannot expect income to grow even as much as 5 percent per student per year over the next few years. Conversations with administrators at two schools in financial difficulty, and what specific data we have about the actual experience of four other schools in financial difficulty, indicate a more reliable figure may be closer to 2 percent. These income predictions fall considerably short of the expected increases in cost for a prudent institution—from 5.2 percent to 6.4 percent per student per year—shown in the preceding section. They are even below our rock bottom estimate of 3.4 percent, for recent price levels.

Our estimate for the tuition component of income for a hybrid private institution is as follows. Tuition has been increasing at the average rate of about 7.5 percent during the past few years. Let us assume, optimistically for the schools, that this is a usable figure. Since tuition accounts for 39 percent of the average income of the schools in financial difficulty, the increase in tuition of 7.5 percent means an annual per student increase of 2.6 percent in the income of our hypothetical private institution.

The federal government component for income for our hybrid institution should be projected as increasing at the rate of 2 percent per year. As we noted in Chapter 1, obligated federal funds grew from 1967 to 1968 by 2 percent, and the 1969 estimate, the 1970 prediction, and the 1971 budget proposals all indicate a steady rate of about 2 percent.[11] Since federal funds account for

---

[11] Obligated funds are not necessarily spent in the year in which they are obligated, but since the rate of obligation seems to have been steady for several years, it is likely that the rate of actual spending—and hence of the schools' incomes from federal sources—is the same.

33 percent of our hybrid private institution's income, the 2 percent growth rate would mean an actual increase in income of .66 percent per year. This is the overall rate of income growth, not the rate of income growth per student. Since enrollment at these institutions grew approximately 13 percent during this three-year period, the overall rate overstates income by that amount, per student, and should be adjusted to .6, which is a per student estimate.

The gift component accounts for 18 percent of the income of our private hybrid school. Our figures from Chapter 1 indicate that the national average rate of increase is approximately 8 percent annually for the past three years. Since 18 percent of income grew 8 percent per year, total income would grow 1.4 percent per year. Again we should adjust this for enrollment growth to make it a per student estimate. Thus, we calculate the rate of increase in income from gifts to be 1.2 percent per student per year.

Finally, the endowment income component represented an average of 6 percent of income at our private hybrid school. Our data indicate that during the three-year period, 1966–67 to 1969–70, income increased annually at approximately 7.5 percent per student for all institutions in this study and that endowment income decreased as a portion of total income by .5 percent per year. Assuming endowment accounts for about 10 percent of the total income of all the schools in the study and that it is losing ground as a percentage of total income, we calculate that it grew for our hybrid school at the rate of 2.5 percent per student during the past three years. If 6 percent of our hybrid school's income thus grew at that rate, it accounted for .15 percent of income per student per year, which we round to .2.

What do these figures show, in sum?

Projected rate of income growth per student per year, hybrid private institution

Source	Percent
Tuition	2.6
Federal government	.6
Private gifts and grants	1.2
Endowment income	.2
Other	.2
TOTAL	4.8

Thus this method of measuring the relative contribution of the components of income indicates that income for the hybrid institution currently would be increasing at the rate of about 4.8 percent per student per year.

Our projection of income growth by component for a hybrid public institution results in expected income growth of 4.4 percent per student per year over the next few years. Again, this falls somewhat below a prudent, minimum level of operation of 5.2 percent per year growth—which assumes the current rate of inflation will promptly be cut in half. Our income projection by component for a hybrid public institution applies the same growth factors that we applied to the hybrid private institution. Thus, we project 2.0 percent growth rate in federal funding; when adjusted to a per student figure for a 27.6 percent component of income, equals a .5 percent per student new contribution to overall income. A 7.5 percent increase in tuition and fees, applied to a 10.3 percent component, produces .8 percent growth in income per student. Gifts constitute 2.3 percent of the total income of the hybrid public institution; an increase in 8.0 percent adjusted for per student growth produces an estimated .2 percent per student income growth. Endowment income increases at the estimated per student rate of 2.5 percent per year; when applied to the 1.2 percent of income produced by endowment at the hybrid public institution, it would produce less than .1 percent of income growth per student. We round it up to .1 percent per student per year.

Our hybrid public institution receives 54.7 percent of its income from state funding. To that income component we have applied a growth factor of 4.8 percent per student per year, based on the experience of the University of California, Berkeley, one of our two public institutions in financial difficulty. This results in 2.6 percent per student annual growth in total income. The total of these figures is shown below:

Projected rate of income growth per student per year, hybrid public institution

Source	Percent
State government	2.6
Federal government	.5
Tuition and fees	.8
Private gifts and grants	.2
Endowment income	.1
Other	.2
TOTAL	4.4

To conclude, from immediate past experience, we have projected income growth as being between 4.4 and 4.8 percent per student per year. We have projected minimum expenditure growth at the current rates of inflation as 6.4 percent per student per year. This would leave a range of minimum deficit between 1.6 and 2.0 percent of total operating funds per student per year. This means that the schools would have to operate closer to the rock bottom basis we indicated above if they are to begin to break even again.

What data we have for 1970–71 indicate that, in fact, income is beginning to force operations toward rock bottom. Several schools predicted for us that next year their income growth will be between 2 and 3 percent per student, or less. Thus, the immediate future for many schools is one of operating on a survival budget or increasing the gap between income and expenditures, an increasing aggravation of the cost-income problem. Over the decade that gap ranges from an annual average of .4 percentage points of current fund income for schools not in financial trouble to 1.1 for the schools in financial difficulty. Given the limited scope of the study and of our data, we have not sought to relate those schools with high costs in one or another cost component to their total costs or income. We have confined our estimates to aggregate estimates of the problem and of the solution. These show that projected cost growth will outstrip projected income growth by an annual margin of several percentage points of current fund income. The schools must find more new money, or make cuts, or do both. These are the financial facts facing most college and university administrators.

Administrators of the schools in financial difficulty said, in response to our inquiry, that their financial prospects for the decade ahead are "glum" (New York University), "grim" (Beloit, Stanford), "potentially a disaster" (San Diego State), "bad" (University of California, Berkeley), and so on. Although our hybrid institutions follow the income patterns of schools in financial difficulty, there is every reason to believe that a similar range of minimum deficit applies to the schools headed for financial trouble, and even to the schools not in financial trouble, if present trends continue for long. Although the schools in financial difficulty have been suffering the gap between expense and income for a longer time than other schools, for most the difficult financial situation has only occurred during the last few years.

8. Administrators' Policy Views about Solutions

In each of the 41 campus interviews in this study, the president and his administrative colleagues were asked: "What policy measures do you recommend to improve the financial situation of your institution and all institutions of higher education?" (See Appendix, interview question 29.) All their responses are summarized in this chapter. No effort was made in the interviews to channel the recommendations toward any particular issues or to obtain evaluations of any specific policy measures or legislative proposals. The question was not intended to structure the response, and the result is a wide-ranging collection of policy views. These include suggestions relating to private fund raising and internal academic administration, as well as public policy at the federal, state, and local level. The interviewers asked the presidents and their colleagues to talk about money, for money is the presidents' problem. The policy views given in response reflect the knowledge that money alone will not solve all their problems, but of course it is outside the scope of this study to discuss other issues of educational policy. To some extent the larger policy views of the administrators interviewed are reported in other chapters of this study as they are reflected in remedial actions taken on the 41 campuses.

The responses of the academic administrators do not for the most part elaborate in detail how their policy views would be effectuated nor predict the extent to which these measures would produce financial recovery for the colleges and universities. This is not surprising, for the interviews did not emphasize the development of policy solutions; they emphasized the existence of financial problems and their program consequences. As a result, we have expanded some of their points and occasionally commented on them.

No attempt is made to connect specific policy views or recommendations with individual presidents. At most of the 41 colleges and universities, several administrative officers participated in the interviews. A single staff view did not always emerge from these extended interview sessions, and it is not possible to ascribe particular views fairly to individuals. Moreover, many of the presidents are publicly on record in articles, speeches, and testimony before legislative committees; specific attribution of views in the summary that follows might not adequately represent the details and differences in their views. Finally, the policy views are presented here in a composite summary; not every administrator would agree with them or agree that they say all that needs to be said about the issues.

TWO-YEAR COLLEGES

The two-year institutions in this study are all public. We consider three of them to be not in financial trouble and two to be headed for financial trouble. From the interviews with the administrators of these five schools, several main policy themes emerge:

1 *Change the methods of federal financing.* The federal government provides about 6 percent of the operating support[1] of these institutions. There is little enthusiasm for the methods of federal financing, and none of the administrators volunteered an endorsement of them. Federal financing includes grants for operating costs of certain specialized educational programs and capital grants for facilities.[2] Many projects are only partially financed by the government, either because it provides only planning and starting-up costs of the project or because it finances only a stated share of the total cost. Institutions have initiated projects to take advantage of this partial financing, although the projects might not otherwise rate as high priority. When the time comes for the school to take over the project entirely or contribute its share, it sometimes realizes that the drain on its resources is disproportionate to the project's value. It finds itself in this position not simply because administrators cannot resist temptation, but also because many partially funded programs are generated at the faculty level and are approved, apparently, without adequate recognition of the school's

---

[1] Excluding auxiliary enterprises.

[2] Although capital budget problems are referred to in these responses, this study does not deal with capital outlay but is directed toward operations. Capital budgets raise an important series of related problems but were beyond the scope of this study.

overall priorities. Since overcommitment has been a factor in the current depression and since federal financing may well increase, there should be careful review of the effect of the form of federal financing on the setting of institutional priorities.

Some financing by state governments is also on a funds-matching basis, and presumably the administrators who made the foregoing points believe that school decisions would more carefully reflect priorities if the state's grants were made outright. We might add that the logic of this view would also argue for annual state appropriations in the form of unrestricted grants and for unrestricted private giving.

Changing the form of federal financing to outright, unrestricted grants would also meet another complaint which some administrators made, namely, that federal financing entails unjustifiably costly bureaucratic and accounting controls.

Although several of the administrators said they hope federal aid will increase, they apparently would prefer that federal aid go to the states and then be distributed locally rather than come directly from the federal government. Apart from complaints about bureaucracy, the main reason for this view probably is that these schools have strong local ties, and they can influence decisions concerning how to use the money more intelligently and effectively on the local level than on the national level. Presumably this policy would help relieve the financial situation of the two-year institutions because of a greater willingness of the states to use federal money to support them in competition with other types of state colleges.

In the area of student aid, academic administrators prefer that grants be made directly to students, rather than to institutions.

2 *Revise the equities in the allocation of funds.* Presidents of the two-year institutions in this study are generally concerned about the equities in financing higher education. Although none tended to separate their overall financial fate from that of their sister institutions in their state, three of the five presidents specifically raised the issue. In each instance, their point was the same: They believe that their type of institution should have a higher funding priority relative to others. To gain this shift in funding priority, they believe two-year institutions will have to acquire an improved educational image and improve the quality of their programs. These administrators believe that the importance of the two-year institutions has not been adequately recognized.

3 *Increase efficiency.* The two-year institutions appear to have fewer problems of inefficiency than other types of schools. Most of them are smaller, simpler, more manageable. Yet they, too, believe they can improve their financial condition by more efficient operation. The views emphasized here ranged over a variety of topics. It was suggested that systems analysis and unit-cost analysis be used in planning and evaluation and that savings would result from elimination of dormitories and from increased use of the large lecture format. Savings would also result from enabling students to go through school on time without costly periods of dropping out and without having to take less than a full load because of the pressures of outside jobs. To achieve this savings in efficiency would require increased student aid.

4 *Find new money sources.* The two-year institutions in this study have made relatively little effort to raise funds from their alumni, but they are all interested in doing so and give the impression that they will be increasing their efforts in the near future. Less than 1 percent of operating income of these institutions comes from private gifts. Some two-year institutions charge tuition. For those that do not, one of the presidents interviewed expressed support for tuition, both as a revenue source and as a means of gaining more commitment from students to their work and of improving efficiency. Most believe that there are important revenue sources, both local and state, such as sales taxes, excises on mining or manufacturing, and so on, which their particular communities and states have not yet used or have not yet used adequately for higher education. While these officers are concerned about tax burdens, they believe that there are adequate funds for growth and quality if government officials are willing to tap these revenue sources.

In summary, these are not the views of academic administrators in panic. None of the two-year institutions studied is classified as in financial difficulty. Their presidents want more influence in the allocation of federal money, especially since it is likely to become a more important funding source; they want to hold their own or improve their position vis-à-vis state institutions with more academic prestige, and they believe that, to do this, they must improve their image and demonstrate their efficiency; and they want to start raising money from their alumni.

LIBERAL ARTS COLLEGES Altogether there are 14 liberal arts colleges in the study, including 3 primarily black colleges. All of them are private. We consider 4 of them to be not in financial trouble, 6 to be headed for financial trouble, and 4 to be in financial difficulty.

An analysis of their administrators' responses to the interview questionnaire shows these main needs for policy:

1 *Close the gap between what students pay and what it costs to educate them.* Students have never borne the full cost of their education. Through institutional income, someone has in effect been subsidizing them (or subsidizing the schools, if one prefers). Academic administrators clearly do not disagree with the theory of subsidizing students. What concerns them is where the incidence of the subsidies should fall and how the costs of the subsidies should be allocated. Several factors are now making this question crucial. It was the main concern stressed by liberal arts administrators in the interviews. The financing of private education is in a crisis because of rising costs, fears that tuition has reached a "saturation point," desire to extend access to those who cannot afford it, decline in growth in the income which made up subsidies, and, finally, increased competition from state institutions. The threat is that an institution's endowment income, other than that dedicated to student aid, and the corpus of the endowment itself, will have to become the source of student subsidies.

We measure the subsidies by the institution's current fund expenditures, less expenditures for auxiliary enterprises, less the amount of tuition; the remainder are the subsidies for student education, which of course may be calculated on a per student basis.

When this method is applied to the data from the 14 liberal arts colleges in this study, we find that in the academic year 1959–60 these colleges spent an average of $1,476 per student. Student fees paid for 62 percent, or $915. The student subsidy (or, as one institution in the study calls it, "the hidden scholarship") was $561. By 1967–68, the expenditure per student was $2,677. Student fees paid for 61.1 percent, or $1,636. The subsidy had climbed to $1,041. The data for the years since 1967–68 are not complete for all 14 colleges in the study, but from the data available, it is clear why the "saturation point" concern is raised about tuition. It has been rising rapidly, and by 1969–70 it accounted for 67 percent of the general fund expenditures of $2,867 per student, for those institutions for which we have data. In the last few years fees have been rising slightly more rapidly than expenditures, but, measured over the past few years, the subsidy is approximately

$1,000 per student per year for these institutions. That is the gap between what students pay and what it costs to educate them.

One type of proposal was regularly made in the interviews as to how this gap between what students pay and what it costs to educate them privately could be closed: namely, government grants to students. Although some costs of the liberal arts colleges might not be directly related to educating students, the great bulk of their costs is. Traditionally, these schools have been largely financed by students—at present some two-thirds of their income for nonauxiliary activities comes from tuition. It is natural for officials at these schools to conceptualize financial issues in terms of per student subsidies and to characterize solutions in ways that are not inconsistent with a private status. Thus, the overwhelming view of the administrators was that the subsidies to their schools should be made in the form of per student grants rather than figured on some other basis, for instance, relating to the school's performance. The subsidies would be paid by the United States or by the student's or institution's state, presumably to be financed out of general revenues; that is, they advocate government scholarships for students at private colleges. All agreed that the subsidies should be paid directly to the student (who presumably would pay it over to the school in the form of increased tuition) rather than to the institution. Most of the officials seem to favor a government scholarship to be paid regardless of the student's need or academic achievement—a kind of "civilian GI Bill," as some called it. Most of the administrators favor some flat sum per student (which might or might not vary with the institution). Only one president suggested a specific sum, $1,000 per student per year.

Among those who favor subsidies from the state instead of the United States, there are some variations on the theory of the subsidies; that is, some believe that, instead of paying scholarships, the state should pay the institution for its public service by making a grant to it on the basis of the number of people it graduates annually, as New York State presently does.

Obviously, these proposals could result in a relatively simple and clear-cut resolution of the institutions' needs for more income and would do so indefinitely if the amounts were adjusted from time to time. They also raise important questions of policy, including how exclusively the presidents would rely on the government subsidies rather than on other new sources of income; to what extent subsidies would justifiably entail governmental interest in college policy; what the resulting relationships would be between public and private institutions; and what the equities, the incidence of taxation, and the other public and private expenditures foregone could be that justify this level of government support of higher education.

Although the primary emphasis of the administrators is on government support, not all the emphasis is there. Officers of several of the institutions believe increased support from private fund raising is possible. The main concern here seems to be giving by business corporations. Not only in this group of institutions, but in others in this study as well, the view was expressed that among private fund sources, business corporations are, on the whole, giving less than they should be asked to give and less than they ought to give. We can only speculate to what extent increased business giving would resolve the financial problems of private schools; currently, about 17 percent of the current income of these 14 institutions comes from all forms of private giving and grants.

2 *Support pluralistic approaches to higher education.* A comprehensive study of change in higher education just completed for the Carnegie Commission on Higher Education (Hodgkinson, 1970, pp. 8, 9) reveals that amid the noticeable changes affecting higher education there is considerable stability. The relative percentage of institutions in public and private control, for example, has changed almost not at all since 1941, when 33 percent of all institutions were public and 67 percent were private. In 1966 (the latest year for which there are comprehensive data), the figures were 36 percent public and 64 percent private. Never in the 25-year span, the study shows, did the relative forms of ownership vary more than four percentage points.[3] In the same 25-year period, the sectarian schools also held their own, in fact, more than held their own. The total number of all institutions rose 28 percent; the number of sectarian institutions grew 34 percent, from 679 to 910.

[3] Although the proportion of institutions in public and private control has remained stable over the years, the proportion of students in the public and private sectors has not. In 1947, 49 percent of all students were enrolled in public institutions. By 1966, 67 percent of all students were enrolled in public institutions. The growth in enrollment in public institutions has not come from the number of institutions, but by a doubling of the average number enrolled on the public campuses.

Against this background it might seem unnecessary for the academic administrators of liberal arts colleges to stress as one of their policy views the need to support pluralistic approaches to higher education. Yet that is what they did in the campus interviews, and they appear to believe that the experience of the past is not a reliable guide to what is about to happen. Some small institutions, including some primarily black institutions, are concerned that they are being marked for eventual extinction, on someone else's criteria of size, efficiency, or quality, even though the number of such institutions has steadily grown over the last 50 years. Other schools, including some church-related institutions, fear they will find it increasingly difficult to compete with public institutions unless they are permitted to remain in operation through public policies explicitly designed for that purpose.

In one way or another, this subject came up in almost all the interviews at the liberal arts colleges. Some administrators believe that this is the key issue in their financial difficulties. One president puts it this way: The reason for the financial problem of the liberal arts college is "not that the independent liberal arts college is becoming an anachronism as an undergraduate institution because of educational deficiency, as is implied, but rather that public policy leading to the creation of state monopolies of higher education makes it impossible for them to compete effectively in attracting students and thereby threatens their financial security." His point is that, in this competitive situation, the liberal arts colleges cannot charge an appropriate level of tuition and still retain students. He advocates that government at all levels, through loans or grants, subsidize students' educations and let them choose their own schools. In short, he advocates a market situation in which students can pick their schools on educational rather than economic grounds, a marketplace that will determine whether the liberal arts colleges can survive. Not every academic administrator views this problem as one of immediate survival. Most emphasize that they would like to see federal and state educational planning that incorporates their colleges as part of a larger pattern designed to promote a pluralistic system of higher education.

Several policy proposals were suggested by the administrators in the study to promote pluralism, and all have in common the idea of increasing government support but keeping the private status of the institution. One approach is that referred to above:

subsidizing the student and creating a market condition that would permit the liberal arts colleges to compete on more even economic terms with other institutions—including large private research institutions, which are also heavily financed by the federal government. Some administrators favor outright grants to institutions, if they can retain their private, independent character. One administrator contends that pluralism could be partially secured if the National Science Foundation had programs for development and support of instruction as well as of research.

Perhaps almost as important as these recommendations for support are some of the "negative" approaches mentioned by administrators in the study. Pluralism can be promoted by forward planning which would require that when states develop new institutions, strenuous effort be made to avoid duplication of functions filled by existing private schools. The aspirations of former teachers' colleges, said one academic administrator, "must be checked." Apparently, administrators fear new academic institutions are spawned less for educational-planning reasons than for political ones, which results in uneconomic duplication of functions to the serious disadvantage of the liberal arts college.

It can be seen that this theme of protecting pluralism is another way of formulating the administrators' first theme of subsidizing the cost of students' educations: The liberal arts college, with its unique dependence on tuition, is peculiarly threatened by the growth of the competition from the public sector in higher education. These colleges, their contributions, and pluralism may disappear without government subsidies.

Certainly, policies such as those described above are designed to equalize the cost differences to students choosing between public and private institutions and are likely to help ensure the continued existence of many schools. There is much appeal to the argument that student choice should not be made on narrow economic grounds. But this, in turn, raises other questions: Can these institutions obtain needed government assistance and yet retain their "private" and independent character? Why should they have a degree of independence different from that of the public institutions, if both are heavily subsidized by the public? And, more fundamentally, what are the special characteristics and unique contributions of the liberal arts college? Does it have special claim for support? Is pluralism—meaning the existence of vigorous liberal arts colleges—an important value?

3 *Redefine the role of the liberal arts college.* More than the administrators of any other type of institution in this study, officers of the liberal arts colleges feel the need to modify the role and image of their institutions. This need may have relatively little to do with the schools' financial situation; still, a few suggestions for institutional change were offered in response to the study's questions about financing policies and recommendations. First, there is the desire to make the liberal arts colleges more immediately part of the greater society. Some administrators believe that the environment of their college is too isolated, that curricula should include more coverage of socially current subjects, or that greater community input in decisions about program is desirable. It is not certain how such change would affect a school's income, but there is a fashion in education, as in other things, and perhaps an image that is too traditional in a time of social change impedes fund raising and recruiting. The idea of making the college part of the larger society was volunteered by a few of the colleges in the study; at the same time, several of the colleges reported that their traditional environment is their main asset.

Secondly, as with all institutions, liberal arts colleges are concerned about attracting students from low-income families, and there is a common recommendation for grant and loan programs to that end.

Finally, there is general interest in reducing the number of course requirements (illustrations range from foreign language to physical education) and reducing the number of departments. The apparent strategy, insofar as it can be inferred, is to maintain appropriate student-faculty ratios and teaching loads by trimming program offerings. (As one president put it, student-faculty ratios should be about 13 or 14 to 1 and the teaching load nine hours.) Interest was expressed in developing better criteria for determining allocations and what can be eliminated. These are reactions, presumably, to the widespread trend toward academic specialization, proliferation of courses, and experimentation. We mention it here, although it probably is more a matter of improving institutional efficiency than of changing image and role.

In brief, administrators of the liberal arts colleges are struggling with the cost-income squeeze in a context that raises a larger issue. Their institutions offer an educational program that was once unique. Today, however, state institutions offer much the same program, often just as good qualitatively, and at much lower cost to the student. Not only does this pose a problem of financial competition, but it also raises the larger question of the role of the liberal arts college. Administrators of these institutions argue persuasively the case for diversity, for pluralism, and see the solution to their problem in gaining access to more federal and state funding while retaining their independence. They believe this should be done and can be done. For them the issue is when. The current financial squeeze adds urgency to this longer-range problem, for many of these institutions are getting into financial difficulty.

STATE AND COMPREHENSIVE COLLEGES All five institutions in this study classified under the Carnegie method as comprehensive colleges are public institutions. Two of these schools we considered not in financial trouble, two we classified as headed for financial trouble, and one we rated in financial difficulty. The interviews at these institutions show administrators concerned about two main points: improved state coordination and administration of finance, and student aid.

1 *Improve state coordination and the administration of finance.* Comprehensive colleges rely for their income primarily on state appropriations. Sixty percent of the operating income of the five colleges in this study comes from state sources. By contrast, the seven state universities in this study receive only 43.5 percent of their operating income from state sources. Given this heavy reliance on state support, it is not surprising that the main emphasis in the interviews was on allocation and coordination of state funds. Administrators from several institutions stressed the importance of better methods of determining need, allocating resources, and—through planning—avoiding waste. The desire for improved resource allocation and coordination reflects frustration with excessive budgetary controls, red tape, and lack of flexibility, as well as the hope for more income.

One official, who had obviously given this matter much thought, strongly urged that each institution of its kind in the state be put on a lump-sum budget tied to its enrollment on a formula basis. This would accord the institution the freedom to carry out its mission. Fiscal responsibility would move to lower levels in the state system, producing more responsible fiscal management, and would enable student influence to be applied at the level where it could be effective. This official also advocated that a similar method be adopted for federal finance. There is no reason to believe that this method of allocating funds is about to be tried. In fact, Michigan, which heretofore provided greater flexibility to its state institutions than many other states, recently passed legislation specifying teaching loads and introducing other new controls.[4]

Those administrators who recommended improved methods of allocating and coordinating income believe that such improvements would eliminate waste due to the repetition of high-cost programs; in the end that would make more income available to all institutions. Proposals for better coordination have in mind both technical programs and advanced-degree programs carried out in some of the comprehensive colleges. There is pressure from the faculties of comprehensive colleges, whose early enthusiasm for state master educational plans has waned, to generate more advanced-degree work and provide more research opportunities following the university model. Quite naturally, administrators working under these conditions would prefer strong direction from the state concerning the different missions of the state institutions and, with it, assured financial support for the role of the comprehensive college.

2   *Increase student aid.*   The need for increased funds for student aid was stressed at every campus of every type in this study, except some of the comprehensive colleges and some of the two-year institutions, where it is not yet a general problem. The average expenditure on student aid in the two-year institutions in this study is $15 per enrolled student. For the comprehensive colleges student aid is now beginning to pose a general problem. It is not as pressing as that facing the liberal arts colleges or the universities, but it is growing. Last year, the five comprehensive colleges in this study spent an average of $52 per student for student aid (as contrasted with $170 per enrolled student for the public universities in this study). Since the enrollment of comprehensive colleges is growing very rapidly and they face the cost problems of all institutions, their student aid needs are for the first time emerging as a problem. The proposals for aid made in the interviews were similar to those discussed earlier in connection with the liberal arts colleges, centering on government scholarships. It is noteworthy that, on two of

[4] This experience suggests the kind of difficulty private institutions might expect to attend the state financing that many of them seek. Perhaps this explains the popularity of the idea that additional government funding for private institutions should come through the student and not the institution.

five campuses in this group of institutions, the subject of the need for more student aid did not come up at all.

To summarize, comprehensive colleges occupy a somewhat ambiguous position between the universities on the one hand and the liberal arts colleges on the other. They emphasize undergraduate and technical work, but also are expanding into graduate and even doctoral programs. They are growing rapidly, but are still primarily oriented toward state financing. For them the main problem seems to be one of working out their role within the state's educational plan. These interviews reveal financial pressure, but not a sense of crisis. The impression gained from administrators is that once the mission for these institutions is firmly defined, the financing problems can be solved.

UNIVERSITIES AND OTHER DOCTORAL-GRANTING INSTITUTIONS Of the 41 institutions in this study, 17 are in this group. Eight of the universities are public institutions, nine are private. Under the criteria for determining financial trouble used in the study, three of the universities are not in financial trouble, eight are headed for financial trouble, and the remaining six are in financial difficulty.

1 *Increase federal aid.* Owing to their scientific and research commitments, these large universities rely heavily on federal financial aid. In the views of administrators from these schools, policies about the federal government loomed largest. For the private institutions in this group, federal funds represent the largest single source of operating income. In 1968–69 these private universities received 33 percent of their operating income from the United States. Tuition was second at 31.5 percent. The state institutions got 27 percent of their operating income from the federal government, with state sources providing an average of 43.5 percent. The significance of federal financing policies is based, in part, on the importance of the federal share of operating income and, in part, on the fact that in recent years it has been declining.

On the campuses visited in this study, there is strong support for federal assistance in the form of unrestricted institutional grants. The rationale is that the funds would be better used than they are under restrictive provisions. The problem is not fear of federal control of education, but rather that money is not being used as effectively as it could be with more campus freedom to allocate it. Officials do not want the evolution of program to be dictated by opportunity money that might distort the order of campus priorities. Earlier in this chapter, we discussed this problem in detail in connection with the two-year institutions. It is a much more serious problem in the research universities. Since planning initiative is still largely decentralized and isolated faculty members may effectively initiate research programs, funds in the form of grants can lead the institution in directions that prove costly later and compete with higher priority projects for funds. Administrators admit that the problem is, in all fairness, one for the campus more than for the government; but given the universities' rather limited control and planning systems, administrators seem to be saying that their job of managing resources would be easier and the public's money better used, in fact, if the government had a policy of unrestricted grants to institutions.

A second policy view is that if federal aid is tied to programs, it should be used for construction or support, probably on a regional basis, of the kind of specialized centers or activities that are very expensive. Examples of such activities cited by administrators in the interviews are regional computer centers, regional libraries, international studies centers, and medical schools.

2 *Increase student aid.* Almost every institution in this category has difficulty meeting the demand for student aid, and each stresses the urgent need for increased aid funds from federal, state, and private sources. In the academic year 1968–69, the public research universities in this study were spending an average of $170 per enrolled student for student aid. For all the private universities in the study, the figure was an average of $428; for the subgroup of private research universities that we characterize as "national," the figure was an average per enrolled student of $632. For the period 1959–60 to 1969–70, student aid expenditures by the research universities in the study for which there are data rose at an average annual rate, per enrolled student, of 16.3 percent. Given this rate of growth, there is good reason for the administrators of these institutions to be worried about their ability to meet these needs.

The administrators' proposed solutions are similar to those already mentioned in this chapter: increased state scholarships and tuition-equalization programs. The officials believe that continued expansion of opportunity for access to education depends heavily on the federal government's participation through its several student aid programs.

The president of one private university proposed that the federal student aid program be designed to provide 75 percent of the difference between the cost of educating the student and a minimum amount of student aid, which all institutions would be required to provide. He would require all private institutions to pay from private funds (presumably their restricted endowment) a minimum amount for student aid, perhaps about one-third of the needs of each student receiving aid. Under this proposal, therefore, if fees amounted to $3,000 the student who received aid would receive $1,000 from the school and $1,500 from the federal program and would be required to pay the other $500 from his own sources.

3 *Broaden the revenue base for state support.* As we noted earlier, the state is the largest single source of financial support for the state research universities. For the year 1968–69, 43.5 percent of their operating income came from state sources. Understandably, then, the administrators of several state institutions said that the state could broaden its revenue base for educational support, and that it should do so. These proposals raise local legislative issues and, often, politically sensitive ones. We do not report them here in detail, but simply note that it is a common view among academic administrators that the states have revenue sources, not now adequately exploited, which could help ease the fiscal problems of higher education. Suggested revenue sources include income and sales taxes, increased levies on mineral extraction, and taxes on business profits.

The private institutions in this sample received in 1968–69 an average of only 1.1 percent of their operating income directly from state sources. They are interested in the states as a source of increased revenue. Administrators of several of the private institutions stressed the dangers that they will one day have to become public institutions if the state does not come to their aid. The ironies in this situation are lost on no one. As the administrators of these schools see it, the issue is how they can obtain state aid without giving up their independence from the control and fiscal intervention that seems to go with state support of state institutions. The answers offered are either: outright, unrestricted grants (what John Gardner once called the "leave it on the stump" approach); payment for service, based, for instance, on the number of graduates, as in the New York state program; or, finally, payment for major service programs, such as hospital services. In connection with this latter proposal, there are preliminary, and apparently highly fragile, discussions underway between state and city officials and some of the institutions we visited, looking toward state, and perhaps city, payment to private institutions for hospital services and even certain kinds of community programs. Until now these have been wholly supported by the universities or financed by private or federal grants. Several administrators told the interviewers that they believe that service program payments will become the most important state source of income for their schools, although it will be another two years or so before the state will be ready to make such payments.

The alternative to unrestricted state grants or state service or program payments, of course, may be state support tied to substantial budget and operating control. In fact, in the course of the interviews for this study, we learned of at least three private institutions (not all in the category of research universities) for which the prospect of state control through merger into the state system was under current confidential discussion.

4 *Find additional private funds.* Like all other institutions in this study, the research universities are making greater efforts, or preparing to make them, to raise private funds. Private gifts and grants account for 14 percent of the operating income (in 1968–69) of the private institutions in this category and about 3.5 percent of the operating income of the public institutions. Administrators in most of these institutions are convinced that they must rely on diversified sources for income, and they believe they can obtain additional funds from private sources, especially their alumni and business corporations. On the basis of the most recent fund-raising reports from individual institutions and from the Council for Financial Aid to Education, it appears that this income will not soon become a major factor in solving the financial problems of the universities. Preliminary indications are that private giving in 1969–70 is declining and that, at the best, these institutions can expect to hold their own, or make modest gains, in generating income through gifts.[5]

5 *Improve internal operations.* Concern about internal operations and their relationship to finance was strongest in this category

[5] The trends in private fund raising and some of the difficulties in fund raising are treated in somewhat more detail in Chapter 1.

of institutions. Some, such as St. Louis University, are making a complete review of all programs in relation to financial base, looking toward major revisions in the school's operations. Others feel the need for review of how priorities are set and of how quality can be evaluated for purposes of allocating resources; administrators at Harvard, for instance, anticipate that this will become one of the first duties of the new president. Several institutions have created new broadly based budget committees and assigned them the overall task of helping to reduce costs. At substantially every campus there is at least some form of partial or pilot review of operations, or plans for review of operations, designed to improve efficiency through new means of internal approval of expenditures; new methods of measuring output; control over course proliferation; and devices for internal reallocation of funds. Most schools in this category suffer from a shortage of administrative staff, and they lack management and analytical capability to develop performance standards, measure performance, and allocate funds accordingly.

A final suggestion for improved efficiency was made in the context of administrators' recommendations for federal financing of projects on regional bases. This was the idea that neighboring institutions should coordinate activities to avoid expensive duplication. To the extent that such coordination would envision cutting back of an existing academic program at one school, in view of a neighbor's strength in that field, these suggestions appear to be still mostly in the envisioning stage. Federal funding of regional projects might well encourage and complement university initiative in coordinating activities.

In summary, the universities are the most immediate victims of the cost-income squeeze. They have undertaken heavy research responsibilities and are now sharply affected by the cutbacks in federal finance. Most have become engaged in problems of the cities and have incurred heavy responsibilities there, but they have gained only moderate financial support for this added responsibility. They urgently seek federal help, both for their institutions and special programs and for student aid. Given the slowdown in federal financing, these institutions have been looking seriously to state support. There will be growing interest in selling services to the state. Finally, the financial stringency has convinced administrators of these institutions that their financial base must be diverse—hence the increased efforts at private fund raising—and that they must gain better internal control over costs and fund allocations and, in the end, over program and its growth.

9. Summary and Some Concluding Observations

At the outset, we described how this study was initially sponsored by the Carnegie Commission on Higher Education and the Ford Foundation in response to the urging of several college and university presidents. The presidents were alarmed by the growing money crisis on their campuses and were eager to learn how general the problem was and to find out more about what other institutions were doing in response to it. Thus the main effort of this study was directed toward answering these three questions: (1) What are the characteristics of the financial problem facing higher education? (2) How general is the problem among institutions of different types? (3) How are the colleges and universities responding to their financial problems—with programs, cost reduction, and income production?

We summarize briefly the main overall findings responsive to the above three questions here, and we add a fourth question concerning the effects of medical schools on university costs. The final section of this chapter will present the author's views about several additional questions that naturally evolve from a study like this.

1 *What are the characteristics of the financial problem facing higher education?*

The essence of the problem is that costs and income are both rising, but costs are rising at a steady or a slowly growing rate, depending on the period and the measure used, whereas income is growing at a declining rate. The rate of growth of expenditures may decline in any given year—as it has at some schools for 1970–71—but the longer-range trend has been toward a growing rate of costs. For most colleges and universities, the main consequences of the resulting divergence of cost and income began to appear in the academic year 1967–68 or 1968–69. This financial problem arose immediately after a decade of unprecedented growth in higher education. But, contrary to what might be expected, that growth had not protected the schools but may well have made them more vulnerable to a downturn. Many were undercapitalized, overextended, moving into enlarged areas of responsibility without permanent financing, or still raising quality standards. Because the increasing demands on the schools (both from without and from within) for research, for services, for access, and for socially current programs are an important part of the reason for cost increases, the cost-income problem is far more than the consequence of inflation, overextension, and an external economic downturn.

The experience of 41 schools is examined in this study. Total current fund expenditures have been rising during the 1960s at the rate of 8.1 percent per student per year. For the schools in financial difficulty it has been 10.3 percent. Campus interviews identified five important components of expenditure. Their percentage point shares of the cost growth during the last three years of the decade are estimated in this study as (1) general inflation, 2.4; (2) faculty salaries, 2.0; (3) student aid, .9 to 1.7; (4) cost of campus disturbances, .3 to 1.0; and (5) growth in responsibility, activities, and aspiration, 1.5 to 3.5. Almost all institutions in the study are cutting expenditures, and most private schools are being forced into deficits. For most, the expenditure rate has dropped sharply in the last year or two. But they appear still to be running behind.

Income has been growing, but the rate of growth has been declining in recent years. The components of this declining rate of income growth are declining growth rates in federal government support, gifts and grants, and endowment income. State appropriations have, in most instances, continued their past rate of increase. However, some schools have already felt, and many more are anticipating, the effects of legislative backlash.

Colleges and universities are increasing tuition rapidly—the current annual increase is about 7.5 percent. Many fear however, that they cannot for long continue to raise tuition at this rate, for it will deny access to some, and put some private schools in a poor competitive position. Moreover, the overall situation is getting worse. The rate of income growth reported for the academic year 1970–71 is substantially smaller than for the year 1969–70.

Our estimate is that income will have to grow at the rate of 6.5

percent per student per year for many schools to break even at the present level of inflation—assuming that they cut growth in costs, and presumably some absolute amounts of costs, significantly below the average of the last decade. Our projections, however, are that income cannot be expected to grow as much as 5 percent per student per year, and this is supported by what little hard evidence is now available. If this proves true, the schools will have to live on budgets approaching "rock bottom" which allow for substantially no growth at all in several major cost components.

2 *How general is the problem among institutions of different types?* On the criteria used in the study, 29 of the 41 colleges and universities in this study (71 percent) were, at the time of the campus visit, headed for financial trouble or were in financial difficulty. The remaining 29 percent, 12 schools, were considered not in financial trouble at the time of the campus visit.

For purposes of this study, an institution was judged in financial difficulty if its current financial condition forced upon it a loss of program or services that are regarded as part of the program. An institution was classified as headed for financial trouble if, at the time of the study, it had been able to meet current responsibilities without reducing quality, but either could not ensure that it could much longer meet current program and quality standards or could not plan support for evolving program growth. Those colleges and universities which could meet current quality and program standards and could, with some assurance, plan the program growth they wanted, were classified not in financial trouble.

Since the 41 institutions selected for study were not chosen as a random sample of all 2,729 insitutions of higher education in the country, this finding does not mean that 71 percent of all schools in the United States are in financial trouble or headed for it, or that 29 percent are not. The finding means, precisely, that these are the figures for the 41 schools at the time of the campus interview. (Even the figures for these 41 schools have changed since the interviews.)

Although this finding alone does not warrant a general conclusion about all United States colleges and universities, the study does permit certain generalizations about how common the problem is. First, it is clear that all types of institutions are affected. The study included a sample of national research universities, leading regional research universities, state and comprehensive colleges, liberal arts colleges, primarily black colleges, and two-year colleges, and, of course, both public and private institutions. No class of institution is exempt from the problem or free from financial difficulty. This is illustrated by the following list of schools, grouped by our study classification and categories:

NATIONAL RESEARCH UNIVERSITIES

Not in financial trouble	*Headed for financial trouble*	*In financial difficulty*
University of Texas, Austin	Harvard University University of Chicago University of Michigan University of Minnesota	Stanford University University of California, Berkeley

LEADING REGIONAL RESEARCH UNIVERSITIES

Not in financial trouble	*Headed for financial trouble*	*In financial difficulty*
University of North Carolina, Chapel Hill	Ohio University Syracuse University University of Missouri, Columbia University of Oregon	New York University Saint Louis University Tulane University

STATE AND COMPREHENSIVE COLLEGES

Not in financial trouble	*Headed for financial trouble*	*In financial difficulty*
Saint Cloud State College	Central Michigan University Portland State University	Boston College San Diego State College

LIBERAL ARTS COLLEGES

Not in financial trouble	*Headed for financial trouble*	*In financial difficulty*
Hamilton College Meredith College Mills College Whitman College	Albion College Allegheny College Carleton College Cumberland College Knox College Pomona College	Beloit College

PRIMARILY BLACK COLLEGES

Not in financial trouble	*Headed for financial trouble*	*In financial difficulty*
Howard University Morgan State College		Fisk University Huston-Tillotson College Tougaloo College

TWO-YEAR COLLEGES

Not in financial trouble	*Headed for financial trouble*	*In financial difficulty*
College of San Mateo	City Colleges of Chicago	
Flint Community Junior College	Mesa College	
Gulf Coast Junior College		

Of the 18 public institutions in the study, 7 were classified not in financial trouble at the time of the campus visit, 9 were classified headed for financial trouble, and 2 were classified in financial difficulty. Of the 23 private institutions, 5 were considered to be not in financial trouble, 8 were considered to be headed for financial trouble, and 9 were considered to be in financial difficulty. Two of the primarily black institutions were classified not in financial trouble, and the other three were classified in financial difficulty. The two Catholic institutions in the study, Boston College and St. Louis University, were both considered to be in financial difficulty. Both of the two women's colleges studied— Meredith College and Mills College—were not in financial trouble.

The cost-income problem has most severely affected institutions in urban areas. It would appear that private institutions and schools in the North are most severely affected. As a group, the private research universities are the hardest hit, but there are other types of institutions that are seriously affected.

Based on their large number in the study, the group of schools headed for financial trouble would seem to be the most representative. In addition to the category headed for financial trouble listing the most schools, this group invites that judgment because of their representative distribution by type of institution in the study. None of the primarily black institutions in this study, however, falls within this category.

Whatever the precise number of schools in financial difficulty or in crisis, it is most significant that, even among schools not in financial trouble at the time of the interview, the effects of the cost-income problem were being felt. Expenditures for these schools are declining, and it is clear that they will not be immune if the gap between expenditure and income continues. In this sense, the financial problem is universal among the schools studied here.

3 *How are the colleges and universities responding to their financial problems?*

The schools not in financial trouble were classified as such because they are making no cuts in program or in planned program growth based on financial condition. The other schools are making such program responses.

The schools headed for financial trouble are engaging in a variety of program cuts and changes in plans, which can be summarized as postponing planned program growth. This is one of the first methods of absorbing the impact of declining income. Almost every school headed for financial trouble has postponed and is postponing academic program plans. Taking those schools as a group, the courses and programs postponed cover most disciplines and include undergraduate and graduate work. At the time of the campus interviews, there were limited efforts at cutting academic costs to permit reallocations from one academic activity to another. This is being done by not filling staff vacancies and by cutting marginal academic programs. There is very little evidence that the schools headed for financial trouble are cutting out academic programs, other than summer schools, or making important reallocations that, in effect, change academic structure.

Schools rated in financial difficulty have, by and large, gone more deeply into that phase of cost cutting, and some have begun to drop departments and graduate majors. But these changes in structure still occur only at a minority of schools. The responses, other than these program responses, are generally of the belt-tightening variety. They may cut some costs below current levels as well as cut the growth rate of costs. These responses follow the likely sequence of cuts in maintenance first, with the next cuts being in expenditures for supplies, equipment, and travel. Funds are dropped for experimental programs and extracurricular activities and events. The pressure of the cost-income squeeze is strong enough that schools have begun to reduce funds made available for student aid and special admissions. There are reductions in campus communications budgets, cultural activities, and certain kinds of student services. Also, there typically are cuts in the number of nonacademic employees.

The almost universal response of all categories of schools is to seek more funds, especially from private sources. Almost all schools in the study are intensifying efforts in this direction, or are starting a development office if they have not had one before.

There is more planning, with money as the key variable, than ever before in all institutions. Finally, there is a universal response of worrying. The trends, for most schools, are not good.

4 *Are medical schools an important factor in the financial trouble of universities?*

We know from other sources that medical schools are in financial difficulty. A special report on medical education by the Carnegie Commission (1970) indicates that medical and dental education is critically underfunded and recommends policies for increased financial support.

We discussed the medical schools' financial problems briefly in Chapter 1 and noted that their problems are special and that they were excluded from this study. In order to identify whether the financing of a medical school might be a significant variable in analyzing the parent institutions studied here, our interview guide did, however, include one question (number 4), namely, "Is the medical school a significant factor" among the major factors influencing the financial situation? The responses to this question would seem to show that medical schools are not invariably an important factor. They may or may not be a factor at any given university.

Of the 41 institutions in this study, 13 have medical schools. Among the schools not in financial trouble, there are three with medical schools. At two of them—Texas and North Carolina—administrators reported that the medical school was not a significant cost factor to the campus. Texas gets a separate appropriation for its medical school. At North Carolina, income from clinics assists in financing expansion. Howard University reported that its medical school is the most expensive unit on campus and is a cost factor of some concern.

Among the schools headed for financial trouble, there are six universities with medical schools. Two of them—Michigan and Minnesota—clearly believe the medical school is a significant cost factor to the campus. Administrators at the University of Michigan reported that medical school salaries represent 12.1 percent of the university's total instruction and departmental research expenditure. Similarly, administrators at the University of Minnesota reported that the medical school was seriously underfunded and was a major financial problem to the campus. Only 24 percent of its support comes from state funds, and recent cutbacks in federal funds for medicine have hurt the university greatly.[1] The

[1] Medical school data for these and all other schools studied, except the universities of Missouri and Chicago, St. Louis, and Tulane, are excluded from the financial data used in this study.

University of Missouri has a medical school at Columbia which does not present a serious financial problem. Administrators are concerned about a prospective drain from a new medical school being built at Kansas City. There were no reports that medical schools at Chicago, Harvard, or Oregon posed special financial burdens on these universities. If they are especial burdens, the interviews did not identify them.

Finally, there are four universities in financial difficulty that have medical schools. Each of these, according to the university administrators, is a significant financial factor. Tulane administrators report that the medical school is a major financial drain. New York University administrators report the same thing. At Stanford University and St. Louis University, administrators report that the medical school is a significant element in the overall financial difficulty of the university, and they are in the process of cutting back support as much as possible.

Further examination of the interview responses shows that where the medical school is an important factor, the parent institution is often working to make the medical school financially independent. Partly, of course, this is a defensive measure—a precaution against the medical school becoming a very serious drain on the parent institution. Partly, it is an effort to maximize income from the medical school. Finally, it is also an effort to clarify the cost and income relationships of these important facilities and improve the case for additional public support. To the extent that these efforts to put medical schools on their own isolate their financial problems, it might be argued that medical schools are no longer a factor in the parent institution's financial condition. But it would seem more realistic to consider medical schools as part of the parent institution.

RELATED QUESTIONS The study and summary of the new cost-income problem and its effects lead naturally to other questions, questions which are not the main focus of the study but grow out of such an inquiry. Some of the data gathered speak to these questions, and they will be referred to here, but this concluding section consists primarily of the views of the author. There are two introductory points to make.

First, this study makes clear that the money crisis in higher education is indeed real. Almost no school is immune from its effects. For most schools, it will mean serious problems of retrenchment and readjustment. As this study has shown, the extent to which colleges and universities of all types are in economic trouble is great, and they are genuinely working at reducing their financial difficulties. But the schools cannot solve the problem alone. Public policy must help.

Secondly, the previous chapters about the financial problems of higher education reported and analyzed the views of academic administrators. These are not the responses of disinterested observers. They all have a stake in the outcome. We have seen that there is no single "academic establishment" line. Yet it seems useful to add to the previous chapters the views of an outsider.

These comments are directed to four main questions: (1) Is the money crisis on campus having beneficial effects? (2) Are the schools doing enough to gain control of their financial situation? (3) How serious is the financial problem likely to become if present trends continue? (4) What broader issues must colleges and universities face as a result of their financial problems?

1 *Is the money crisis on campus having beneficial effects?*

Adversity is not always without benefits, and in this study we attempted to find out the extent to which the colleges and universities found (or made) it an opportunity as well as a burden. At each campus the administrators were asked in the interview (see Appendix, question 19), "Has your financial condition produced desirable results (i.e., chance to get rid of 'dead wood,' a needed impetus toward reorganization and reduction of inefficiency, more attention to cost, productivity, program goals, etc.)?" The question was applicable at 29 of the 41 colleges and universities studied, those considered headed for financial trouble or in financial difficulty. We have rather probing responses from 25 of these 29 institutions. Some of the answers are confidential. We present all the information in summary form and do not identify it with particular institutions.

First, it is noteworthy that administrators at only three schools responded with an unequivocal "no" to the question, "Has your financial condition produced desirable results?" At two of these schools, the administrators said their money crisis was an unrelieved burden, and, at the third, the president and his staff said the crisis could also produce some advantages, but the administrators did not have enough control of the internal situation for that purpose.

The second noteworthy finding is that administrators at only four of the schools said that their money situation has afforded an opportunity to "get rid of 'dead wood.'" They included in "dead wood" certain functions performed by their schools, as well as individuals in academic, nonacademic, and administrative posts.

Given the degree of financial difficulty on the campuses, 4 out of 29 seems like a rather small number of campuses energized to use their financial situation to eliminate nonproductive or non-essential functions or positions. It is hard to believe that there is not a greater need and opportunity to reorganize. An analysis of the interview responses from the campuses indicates there are several reasons why administrators at only four schools say they are "eliminating 'dead wood.'" First, some have (in the words of one president) "been poor too long" to have any "dead wood" left. Several of the schools in this study have been in financial difficulty long enough to have taken whatever organizational advantages there are in financial adversity.

A second reason why adversity has not been of greater importance in reorganization is that most institutions are still in the process of deciding what "wood" is, in fact, "dead." As we have seen, cuts tend to be of future program commitments or general rather than selective reallocations dictated by a system of priorities.

Not only are the schools mostly still deciding, but even when there is a good administrative position on what should be cut, there is a third reason why the cut may not yet have taken place: There is still not enough support for it on campus. This, in turn, indicates the fourth reason for less pruning than one might expect (and, as administrators might like to do): They do not either have or use the organizational authority to make the kinds of reallocations they would like. In one school the administrators reported that the financial crisis had improved their bargaining position with the faculty and would be helpful in making needed changes.

The main beneficial impact of the money crisis on campus has been to make administrators, faculty, and students more cost conscious. On 15 campuses, administrators said there was much more husbandry as a result of their problems. The major impact has been to create impetus for cost analysis, for installing or talking about installing program budgeting, and for attempting to work out a system of priorities.

We are not able from the interviews to evaluate the effectiveness of the measures being adopted as a result of this new cost consciousness. Two measures seem to have promise beyond that usual for cost cutting and efficiency measures taken in adversity. One is the plan for program growth by resource reallocation, being seriously tried on some campuses, and the other is the interinstitutional cooperation in certain high-cost fields being developed in some areas of the country.

The consequences of this new cost consciousness range from general willingness of faculty to accept higher enrollment (or abandon efforts for lighter teaching loads) as an economic necessity, to greater student and faculty participation in the budget process, to the prevention of undisciplined growth. At one institution the senior faculty have offered to accept a pay cut if that proves necessary.

At an institution which grew rapidly in the past decade, the president is facing a serious financial problem. Members of his staff told the campus interviewer that the cost-income problem had one good effect for schools like theirs, for it was for the first time in many years forcing the school to determine what is really important. Most schools in this study are just beginning to face this job in a serious way. That is the main by-product of a deteriorating financial situation.

There is another by-product of the cost-income squeeze—although it is not one that is characterized as beneficial in the short run—and it is that college and university finance is being brought to a more realistic basis by the declining rate of growth of government research funds. That decline imposed serious hardship on individuals affected and seems to be having more impact on institutions than one would suppose given the basic terms and intent of such federal aid. This is occurring because the reduction in federal support reveals that in some institutions federal money found its way into the operating budget, through overhead funds, through split appointments, and even through tenure appointments supported by "soft" (government research) funds. This means that some of our colleges and universities have been operating on funds not intended for operations and that the actual costs of colleges and universities have been understated. The public should have a better understanding of the cost of operating their colleges and universities. A good system costs more than most think, and the current squeeze will help make that clear.

2 *Are the schools doing enough to gain control of their financial situation?*

Certainly, those institutions we have classified headed for financial trouble, and especially those in financial difficulty, are doing much to relieve their financial problems. Even the schools not in financial trouble are cost conscious, and, as we saw in Chapter 4, are reducing their rate of expenditure growth. Given the magnitude of the financing problem, one cannot insist that, if these measures do not ensure solvency, they are inadequate. We have seen that cost cutting alone cannot be expected to solve the cost-income problem. Nor is it likely that any other policies of the schools alone will suffice.

If we ask, instead, whether the schools are doing enough to reduce expenditures and increase income in order to maximize their ability to resist the cost-income squeeze, then the answer one fairly derives from this study is "not yet." The colleges and universities are making efforts to increase income and to reduce expenditure through methods such as those described in Chapter 5. They are making increased efforts to secure their campuses against disturbances, and they are directing attention to more efficient operations. Our interviews reveal an increasing interest in measuring productivity and in increasing efficiency of operations. On some campuses today there is talk about the possibility of increasing teaching loads. We have not emphasized these developments in the effort to reduce costs because it is still too early to determine what their effect will be.

What does not come through to the visitor to the campuses is a sense that the institutions are deeply involved in establishing a set of priorities or that they have the administrative direction or authority to reallocate money promptly in accordance with their priorities. If our judgment of the severity and duration of the financial problem is sound, then this capacity to get beyond the usual fund-raising and cost-cutting measures, to get promptly into the establishment of priorities and use of effective administrative machinery, is central. It seems a necessary condition for the maintenance of quality under financial stress.

If the schools are "not yet" doing enough, we are entitled to ask why they are not doing more. Are administrators looking everywhere but at themselves? How can a private school run a deficit and not simply cut down on expenditures? Why should a public institution have to cut quality? Can't it simply reorganize its academic program? The answers are that the schools headed for financial trouble and in financial difficulty are making adjustments to their new financial situation. That is the main fact of their situation. But as they consider the kinds of adjustments they might make, administrators of public and private institutions face certain problems which prevent them from taking the kind of prompt, decisive acts which the above questions seek.

Any planned adjustment of funds between academic fields must take account of faculty tenure as a bar to flexibility and the academic tradition that precludes laying off faculty. There is a difference in expectations between campus and industry. It may be due to the higher pay and better perquisites that go with market hazards, but whatever the cause, college presidents have a harder time effecting a reduction in force than do executives in private industry or government officials.

Proposed changes in campus structure that significantly reallocate resources face several barriers. There is little general credibility on campuses for sharp cuts. This may change soon, but as of the time of this study, administrators in many institutions report they do not have support for major decisions requiring sharp cuts or reallocations of funds. Partly this reflects history. Schools tend to change primarily by growing, not by cutting or rearranging. Schools, therefore, do not have the decision-making apparatus needed to make and effectuate important new priority decisions. Therefore substantial reductions or changes that involve basic assumptions about the institution and its major programs are not made until they can no longer be avoided. The issue of teaching loads will not come up until forced by very serious economic circumstances.

There are other reasons why institutions are not making more decisive moves now. Some administrators believe that the new depression in higher education will end by the middle of this decade. They believe that a combination of price, labor market, and funding policy changes will improve their situation. They are planning for a period of several years of difficulty and believe they should avoid retrenchments designed for a longer run. Those administrators who are less optimistic about the length of time of this depression may be reluctant to move quickly; they believe that ground lost this way is difficult to recover.

Finally, to ask for prompt decisive acts to balance the books may in fact be shortsighted. It has often been the case in higher education that an insitution built quality by taking risks, by expansion, even by what, at the time, seemed overextension. This is true of public and private institutions, and true of their capital programs as well as their academic programs. In short, what might look like a failure to adjust to depressing conditions might with hindsight be visionary.

As public and private institutions ponder their moves, each faces some special problems. Private institutions have somewhat more fluctuating sources of support. Their growth has been undersupported. Given their greater expenditure per student, they have probably been forced more than have public institutions to use federal government funds to support their operating budgets. If so, they are being especially hurt by the cutback in government funds. These institutions worry about the competition for students with public institutions. They have maintained high standards and, despite the above barriers, have more flexibility than the public institutions. Their strategic problem in making adjustments is to redefine their purpose while getting needed new financing. More of it will have to come from public sources.

The public institutions have not yet been hurt as much as the private ones. Given the growth burdens they have been assigned, they have done remarkably well, with relatively low expenditures per student. Their problem is to avoid being leveled by the new depression. Administrators fear that good public institutions may be denied the resources to compete on quality terms with the best private schools. They seek more private money and a public commitment to quality.

In addition to the problems discussed above, the adjustment problems of public institutions are more complex than those of private institutions. An administrator at one public institution in this study gave us a compelling account of the rigidities that a public institution faces in making definitive readjustments in the allocation of resources. We quote here from the memorandum he generously sent us:

We are locked into an income pattern that is far more rigid than is generally understood, and from my experience, I believe what is true of us is in some degree true of all public institutions. Our income comes to us essentially in the form of some 20 separate appropriations, the great majority of which are earmarked for particular purposes. State funds are restricted to a legislated set of program heads, fee income to another, and federal funds to another. We have more freedom in regard to gifts and endowment fund income, but even here State policy constrains their use within certain territorial preserves.

Within the State fund appropriation there are 16 separate control appropriations. Constitutionally the governing board has the power to shift funds between these 16 heads. But experience has made it clear that the State (a) views funds foregone in one appropriation as returnable to it, and (b) has the power to (and will) take steps to veto what it considers to be unauthorized permanent augmentations of any individual appropriation. Thus de facto we are precluded under the present structure from making the kind of large-scale horizontal adjustments which, given complete administrative freedom, might be the means of amalgamating the available resources to sustain central program priorities (*e.g.,* eliminating student health service or cutting back severely on plant services to maintain the student-faculty ratio). Of course, realistic planning would contemplate getting some of these rigidities alleviated. One of the unfortunate by-products of disruption and the consequent disaffection is that more budgeting flexibility has become less likely.

There are other policy-type restrictions which impede public institutions from making the kind of adjustments within program heads and appropriations which might at least enable us to ease the financial squeeze on the programs we consider the most important educationally. For example, we have considered the possibility of eliminating completely one or more schools or colleges or departments and diverting the released resources to other programs. But we are required by the State Higher Education Plan to accommodate the large number of students assigned to us. Hence eliminating one unit means in essence transferring the students. And while one might generate some savings by transferring students in this fashion, the simple fact is that (excepting some areas of Engineering) the annual cost per student of our departments generally falls in a range from $200 a year to $1,000 a year. Thus, short of educationally dysfunctional shifts which would transfer large numbers of students from high cost to low cost areas, no massive savings can be made by this route. The situation is complicated by the fact that the more "efficient" areas tend to be the most expensive (*e.g.,* a Ph.D. in Chemistry, Physics and Electrical Engineering—where most who start finish, and do so on schedule—costs about $\frac{2}{3}$ of the Ph.D. in Sociology—where attrition is high—but the annual cost per enrollment in the former fields is at least 5 times that of the latter). And since we can't budget on a multi-year basis, "efficient" reallocations don't help the income-cost squeeze.

The situation is further complicated by the fact that the academic departments represent tenure and other types of academic personnel commitments which cannot readily be undone in the short-run. In large measure they are fixed costs.

You ask what are the controls on a public institution's freedom to make program adjustments that would bring its cost and income curves together without seriously impairing the quality of its essential programs. I have cited our rigid income pattern and the problems of trying to effect internal economies. I shall add one more, the attitudes which surround the budget-making process. On the one hand, the faculty and students expect that the institution's budget requests will continue to express the real needs of the educational program as they see them (*i.e.,* that they will seek to restore established standards of support, to sustain existing commitments, and to provide for incremental changes). On the other hand, the external budget review agencies automatically start from the position that an institution's financial plan establishes the ceiling within which the annual budget review takes place. Thus a public institution aiming to solve its income-cost problem by a long-range budget plan based on a realistic prediction of future State appropriations, in effect is enunciating a self-fulfilling prophecy. This is a course of action, moreover, which not only eliminates its chance (however small) to sustain the quality of its programs by eventually convincing the review agencies that it is in the State's interest to preserve educational standards; it also hazards appreciable internal disaffection and misunderstanding.

The situation is greatly complicated for institutions whose State legislatures appear to be hell-bent as a matter of policy on securing an overall increase in faculty "productivity" (*i.e.,* input) irrespective of financial considerations. For such institutions, the development of budget plans based on what might seem to them to be realistic prognostications of future income are unlikely to head-off this policy thrust thereby. Consequently, they invite a kind of double jeopardy.

It is no surprise that the proposals of private institutions for public funding are careful to avoid this kind of state control. And it is no surprise, in view of these rigidities in making adjustments in expenditures, that academic administrators prefer solutions based on increasing income.

3 *How serious is the financial problem likely to become if present trends continue?*

Throughout this study we have shown income and expenditure trends for schools in different conditions of financial health. One thing all schools have in common is that they are likely to be in financial difficulty if the present trends continue. This conclusion from our data is confirmed by other important indications that the situation is deteriorating further. Even in the brief time since our campus interviews, the prospect of schools in this study is changing. At two of them, College of San Mateo and University of Michigan, certain financial issues were pending at the time of the interview; we checked back later and both schools are worse off.

The college of San Mateo was considered not in financial trouble. Today, it would have to be classified as in financial difficulty. A local tax measure to continue its current level of finance, and increase it slightly, was defeated by the electorate, automatically returning the college to its pre-World War II level of tax support. The school is now planning to reduce its staff by a full 40 percent, and it will reduce enrollment accordingly. Its president believes that school, which has been highly regarded in the community, lost its tax support for four reasons: (1) general revolt against high taxes; (2) a reduced regard for higher education generally; (3) a reaction of older people against the current styles of younger people; (4) a lingering resentment against some campus activities following the May, 1970, invasion of Cambodia.[2]

The Michigan legislature reduced appropriations for the University of Michigan much below what the school had anticipated. According to our subsequent conversations with the campus, a visit today might bring it close to the in financial difficulty category.

All other evidence points in the same direction. Seven of the eight Ivy League schools had to operate through deficit financing in 1969–70. Harvard, as we saw in Chapter 5, did not, but it, too, may be forced into deficit financing for 1970–71.

At the October, 1970, meeting of the Association of American Universities, the presidents of those institutions were asked to rate their schools, using the criteria from this study. Of the 35 presidents in attendance, 21[3] rated their institutions, including 4 of the 11 AAU institutions already in the study. As of the fall term, 1970, four (19 percent) of the presidents said their institutions were not in financial trouble. Twelve (57 percent) said their

[2] It may be that the "good fit" we noted in Chapter 4 between community colleges and their communities is harder to judge or more fragile than we suspect.

[3] The 21 schools are: Case Western Reserve University, Clark University, Cornell University, Duke University, Harvard University, Iowa State University, University of Iowa, Johns Hopkins University, University of Kansas, Massachusetts Institute of Technology, McGill University, Michigan State University, Ohio State University, University of Oregon, Purdue University, University of Rochester, Stanford University, Syracuse University, University of Virginia, University of Washington, and Yale University.

schools were headed for financial trouble; and five (24 percent) said their schools were in financial difficulty.

The presidents were asked to rate their schools for the fall of 1971, given present income and expense projections. Three (14 percent) said their schools would be not in financial trouble. Nine (43 percent) said their schools would be headed for financial trouble, and nine (43 percent) said their schools would be in financial difficulty.

Eight of the presidents felt able to predict their school's current fund income for the next academic year, 1971–72. The average for the eight is a predicted growth in current fund income of 3 percent per student, which is below our "rock bottom" figure of 3.4 percent at recent price levels.

4   *What broader issues must colleges and universities face as a result of their financial problems?*

College presidents invariably respond with a statement about the need to restore public confidence in higher education. Virtually every interview in this study made the point that the public is no longer highly motivated to support increased investment in higher education. But what will it take to restore confidence and make higher education a more attractive investment to parents, tax-payers, foundations, donors, and legislators?

We would emphasize three aspects of the task of restoring confidence. First, the colleges and universities must have campuses that reveal themselves as being reasonably governable. The interviews in this study suggest this does not mean a placid campus, but it does mean a stable one, with discernable evidence of administrative direction.

A second requirement for confidence is that the colleges and universities demonstrate that they are reasonably efficient in their internal operations. Again, many campus interviews referred to legislative study groups, proposed studies by the campus, and other means of developing criteria to measure the effectiveness of educational expenditures. There is some concern on campuses that such criteria of performance will turn out to be crude, mechanistic, or anti-intellectual, ignoring quality as a central component in performance. One cannot discount that concern. At the same time, interest in efficiency and productivity can be well motivated.

For many years, budget requests by state institutions and financing requests by private institutions often commanded an authority simply by virtue of the fact that an academic institution needed funds. Somehow in spite of the "myth of the virtue of poverty," there was often a willingness to support requests because there was a general belief in the value of higher education. What seems to have happened in the last few years is that the burden of proof of the value of educational financing has shifted. The fact of a request is not enough. It must also be demonstrated that the money will be put to efficient use. In a society devoted to human betterment in a world of scarcity, requiring that resources are productively used need not contradict the premises and values of higher education. Colleges and universities ought to know what their functions cost, what their purposes are, and whether by some reasonable standard they are spending their money efficiently. Our interviews show that many campuses are working to develop that knowledge.

Thirdly, in our judgment, restored confidence will require convincing evidence that the activities of colleges and universities have a unifying set of purposes—purposes that the supporting public can understand and defer to. In the period since World War II, college and university finance has been related to important purposes that commanded public support. For instance, in 1946 the colleges and universities, especially through the GI Bill, made education and upward occupational mobility available to hundreds of thousands of young Americans. Ten years later, spurred on in part by competitive responses to the Soviet Union's space program, the nation bestowed important scientific purposes on the colleges and universities and was willing to finance work toward those purposes and, directly and indirectly, much else, too. Ten years later, in the late 1960s, the campuses, under challenge from students, have not convincingly demonstrated what their mission is. When many students and faculty find little sense of purpose on a campus engaged in a web of service, research, instructional, and specialized community roles, it is not surprising that the supporting public begins to doubt the schools' sense of priorities or mission. It is an unhappy irony that the expansion in higher education that inevitably followed a great expansion in public support and public involvement has helped to undermine higher education. It demonstrated the delicacy of the interaction between educational leadership and the public's support.

On campus today there is growing interest in purpose and in priorities. It is too early to tell where the quest for purpose will lead, but there are some interesting early signs. One is the effort to create a market situation in which federal student aid would enable students to choose between different types of institutions. There is an increasing, related interest in decentralizing the responsibility for financing within a campus, so that the different units on the campus must raise their own money; this creates a market condition among the schools and colleges on the one campus. Even in the secondary and elementary schools, there is growing interest in a voucher system, which would permit parents of children to choose among schools. It may be that purposes will thus evolve under the pressure of the market. On the other hand, there are some encouraging signs that purpose may develop from different pressures, from the concerted good judgment and forthright projection of academic programs and academic values by faculties and administrators. In any event, until there is more agreement about purpose there will be less interest in financing.

Finally, it must be recognized that these three interrelated courses of action will not alone restore financial stability. That will take major new public policies directed toward the cost-income squeeze and reflecting the varying missions and utilities of the different types of institutions we have studied.

Among persons who are aware of the financial problems of higher education, it is often assumed that an end to the war in Vietnam and improvement in the stock market would lead to quick recovery on the campuses. We doubt that even those highly welcome events would ensure some reasonable degree of financial stability. The gap between income and expenditure prospects can be closed only by a conscious, positive effort to restore school finance. Recovery will not be the by-product of other events and other policies. It requires the deliberate application of major policies by the schools and the public, directed to the future of higher education.

References

American Association of University Professors: *Annual Report on the Economic Status of the Profession, 1969–70,* Washington, D.C., 1970, pp. 60–105.

American Association of University Professors: *Depression, Recovery and Higher Education,* McGraw-Hill Book Company, New York, 1937.

Astin, Alexander W.: *Who Goes Where to College?* Science Research Associates, Chicago, 1965.

Bowen, Howard R.: "Financial Needs of the Campus," in *The Corporation and the Campus: Corporate Support of Higher Education in the 1970's,* Academy of Political Science, New York, 1970.

Bowen, William G.: *The Economics of the Major Private Universities,* Carnegie Commission on Higher Education, Berkeley, 1968.

Bowen, William G., and William J. Baumol: *Performing Arts: The Economic Dilemma,* Twentieth Century Fund, Washington, D.C., 1966.

Carnegie Commission on Higher Education: *Higher Education and the Nation's Health: Policies for Medical and Dental Education,* McGraw-Hill Book Company, New York, 1970.

Hodgkinson, Harold L.: *Institutions in Transition,* Carnegie Commission on Higher Education, Berkeley, 1970.

Hutchins, Robert M.: "Hard Times and Higher Learning," *Yale Review,* vol. 22, pp. 714–730, 1933.

Jenny, Hans H., and G. Richard Wynn: "Short-Run Cost Variations in Institutions of Higher Learning", in Joint Economic Committee, U.S. Congress, *The Economics and Financing of Higher Education in the United States—A Compendium of Papers,* Washington, D.C., 1969.

Kerr, Clark: "Presidential Discontent," in David C. Nichols (ed.), *Perspectives on Campus Tensions,* papers prepared for the Special Committee on Campus Tensions, American Council on Education, Washington, D.C., 1970.

National Academy of Sciences: *Doctorate Recipients from United States Universities, 1958–66,* Washington, D.C., 1967.

National Observer, July 6, 1970, p. 1; August 17, 1970, p. 1.

National Science Foundation: *Federal Support to Universities and Colleges,* NSF 69-32, Washington, D.C., September 1969.

O'Neill, June O.: *Resource Use in Higher Education: Trends in Output and Inputs of American Colleges and Universities, 1930–67* (manuscript).

San Francisco Examiner, May 20, 1970, p. 3.

Study of Rising Costs at Ten Universities, Cornell University, New York, September 1967.

Appendix: Interview Guide

Be Specific. Where possible get numbers, dollars, concrete illustrations, dates, etc. Note clearly any entry that is confidential.

I. OVERALL FINANCIAL CONDITION (Q. 1-3)

1 How would you characterize the present financial condition of your institution? (In trouble? Scope? Problem area?) Is this view shared by faculty? Students? Trustees? Public?

2 What are the prospects for the decade ahead? (Demands of new projects. Prospects for "new"—flexible—money.)

3 How does the current and prospective financial picture compare with the decade of the 1960s?

II. FACTORS INFLUENCING FINANCIAL CONDITION (Q. 4-5)

4 What are the major factors influencing the financial situation of your institution? (Rank factors, weight, if possible.)

a Income side (effect of campus disturbances)

b Expenditure side

   (1) Academic (Is medical school a significant factor? Get details.)

   (2) Nonacademic (effect of campus disturbances)

5 Has the "knowledge explosion" been a significant financial factor?

III. PROGRAM GROWTH (Q. 6–7)

6 Looking over the last decade, how would you describe the rate of program growth at your institution? (New schools, colleges, departments, programs, etc.—get details.)

7 Will this rate continue in the 1970s?

IV. IMPACT OF FINANCIAL CONDITION (Q. 8-19)

8 What is the main impact of your current financial condition on the academic plan for your institution?

9 Have actual *plans* for any of the following been eliminated, *postponed,* or cut back?

   a New colleges

   b New departments or institutes

   c New courses

   d Undergraduate seminars or tutorials

   e Library

   f Special admission of "underqualified" students

   g Community service programs

   h Capital expansion—land acquisition

   i Research programs

   j Other programs

Note effect of financial situation on planned (or normal) rate of increase in:

a Faculty salaries

b Teaching assistant salaries

c The number of T/A's

d The number of regular faculty

e The number of administrative posts

f The number of nonacademic employees

g Nonacademic salaries

h Undergraduate seminars or tutorials

i Experimental programs

j Admission of "underqualified" students

k Funds for student aid

l Percentage of graduate students

m Overall enrollment targets

n Funds for athletics or similar activities

o Research activities

p Community service programs

q Other

10 Has your financial situation forced you to eliminate any of the following?

a Colleges

b Departments

c Faculty positions

d Courses

e Enrollments

f Summer instruction

g Intercollegiate athletic competition

h Debate, music, or similar activities

i Community service programs

j Undergraduate seminars, or tutorials

k Research activities

l Experimental programs

m Other

11 What are your most important unmet needs? (Rank if possible.) (How affected by financial situation?)

12 Has your financial situation had a significant effect on your ability to attract and hold qualified faculty? Has the "mix" of the faculty changed? What percent have tenure?

13 Has there been an increase in class size? (Overall student-faculty ratio)

14 How good is the fit between aspiration and actual program (or situation)?

a Your faculty

b Your students

15 Has there been a significant reallocation of resources among the various departments or functions? (From more expensive to less expensive areas? More productive? What criterion?)

16 Are you being forced to cut into your budget base?

17 What percentage of student aid is financed by restricted private gifts and endowments? How much from general funds? (Get past detail.)

18 Has your financial situation affected campus decision-making processes (priority setting, reallocation)? (Get details.)

19 Has your financial condition produced desirable results (i.e., chance to get rid of "dead wood," a needed impetus toward reorganization and reduction of inefficiency, more attention to cost, productivity, program goals, etc.)? (Increased faculty, student understanding of financial problems?)

V. EFFICIENCY AND PRODUCTIVITY (Q. 20–22)

20 How would you rate your institution's efficiency? (Identify problems.)

21 How should productivity be measured?

22 What efforts have been (are being) made to raise productivity, increase efficiency?

    a Cut attrition rate   What is attrition rate?

    b Night and Saturday classes

    c Change in terms (semesters/quarters)

    d Program budget procedures

    e Relating expenditure to output

    f Departmental (school, college) efficiency

    g Eliminate course overlap

h   Reorganization of administration

i   More effective space utilization

j   Use of new technology in instruction

k   Modernization of library

l   Increase in the teaching load

m   Studies of operations

n   Other (in detail)

VI.   INCREASING INCOME (Q. 23-24)

23   What are the prospects for increasing income in the decade of the 70s?

24   Are there current increased efforts to raise income?

a   New areas for procuring income?

b   New approaches to procure income from existing areas?

c   Change in investment policy regarding the stock portfolio?

d   Increased tuition or fees?

e   Increased efforts at obtaining gifts and grants?

f   An information campaign aimed at the public and governmental bodies for the purpose of increasing the amount of government support?

g   Which area(s) are the most successful in increasing income?

VII.   REDUCING EXPENDITURE (Q. 25)

25   In addition to factors already mentioned, are you taking specific measures to reduce expenses? (Scope of measures, overall impact)

VIII. POLICY VIEWS AND RECOMMENDATIONS (Q. 26–30)

26 Have you made any public statements regarding financial condition (get copy)?

27 What reallocations of resources would you make if you had the power?

28 What policy measures do you recommend to improve the financial situation of your institution and all institutions of higher education? (Role of federal and state government — get details, priorities.)

29 Other comments on financial condition and its impact? (Things the public, alumni, legislators, should know)

30 Are there additional questions you would like this study to deal with?

INTERVIEWER SECTION (Note to interviewer: Rate and support in detail.)

1 Increasing Base Growth (enrollment rising, income rising, as fast as related student load expenditures)

2 Steady State Base Growth (enrollment stable)

Phase I (income rising enough to permit general program flexibility and growth)

Phase II (income rise inadequate for program growth)

3 Reduced Growth or Cutback (enrollment stable, or rising, but income shortage requires cut in base)

Phase I (general belt-tightening)

Phase II (small reallocations within existing structure)

Phase III (major reallocations or elimination of programs)

Current fund expenditures, 1959–60 to 1970–71 (medical schools not included)

	1959–60	1960–61	1961–62	1962–63
Educational and general				
Instruction and departmental research				
Sponsored research				
General administration				
Library				
Other				
Student aid				
Auxiliary enterprises				
TOTAL				

Current fund income, 1959–60 to 1970–71* (medical schools not included)

	1959–60	1960–61	1961–62	1962–63
Federal government				
State government				
Local government				
Student fees				
Private gifts and grants				
Auxiliary enterprises				
Endowment				
Other				
TOTAL				

*By dollar amounts or percentages.

Enrollment, 1959–60 to 1970–71* (medical schools not included)

	1959–60	1960–61	1961–62	1962–63
Undergraduate				
Graduate				
TOTAL				

*Specify if head count or full-time equivalent.

	Professor
AAUP average compensation ranking, 1968–69	
Average compensation of full-time faculty, 1969–70	

1963–64	1964–65	1965–66	1966–67	1967–68	1968–69	1969–70	1970–71

1963–64	1964–65	1965–66	1966–67	1967–68	1968–69	1969–70	1970–71

1963–64	1964–65	1965–66	1966–67	1967–68	1968–69	1969–70	1970–71

Associate professor	Assistant professor	Instructor

Current fund expenditures as percentage of total

	1959–60	*1960–61*	*1961–62*	*1962–63*	
Educational and general					
Instruction and departmental research					
Organized research					
Libraries					
General administration					
Other					
Student aid					
Auxiliary enterprises					

Current fund income by source as percentage of total

	1959–60	*1960–61*	*1961–62*	*1962–63*	
Federal government					
State government					
Local government					
Tuition and fees					
Private gifts and grants					
Auxiliary enterprises					
Endowment					
Other					

1963–64	1964–65	1965–66	1966–67	1967–68	1968–69	1969–70	1970–71

1963–64	1964–65	1965–66	1966–67	1967–68	1968–69	1969–70	1970–71

This book was set in Vladimir by University Graphics, Inc. It was printed on Vellum Offset and bound by The Maple Press Company. The designer was Elliot Epstein. The editors were Herbert Waentig and Laura Givner for McGraw-Hill Book Company and Verne A. Stadtman and Margaret Cheney for the Carnegie Commission on Higher Education. Frank Matonti supervised the production.